THE FIFTH ARMY IN MARCH, 1918

THE FIFTH ARMY IN MARCH 1918.

BY W. SHAW SPARROW. WITH AN INTRODUCTION BY GENERAL SIR HUBERT GOUGH AND TWENTY-ONE MAPS BY THE AUTHOR

The Naval & Military Press Ltd

Published by

The Naval & Military Press Ltd
Unit 10 Ridgewood Industrial Park,
Uckfield, East Sussex,
TN22 5QE England

Tel: +44 (0) 1825 749494
Fax: +44 (0) 1825 765701

www.naval-military-press.com
www.military-genealogy.com
www.militarymaproom.com

In reprinting in facsimile from the original, any imperfections are inevitably reproduced and the quality may fall short of modern type and cartographic standards.

AUTHOR'S NOTE TO THE SECOND EDITION

THERE are persons who circulate the opinion that in March, 1918, the total Allied force on the Western Front was equal in numbers to the German power. Believers in the Versailles Council keep this opinion in circulation, but they never try to support it with evidence. They tell us that the French had 97 divisions; and we know that Haig had 58, nearly all in great need of drafts. Here are 155 divisions. Ludendorff had either 192 (the figures given by Haig), or 195 (the French figures as given by Général Mangin). How do the Versailles folk fill in the difference between 155 and 192 divisions? They do not say. On March 11, 1918, the American rifle strength in France was 49,000 men, and many of them were not yet sufficiently trained to be sent into a tremendous battle. Even if we count the whole of them, 49,000 rifles form only five divisions with ten battalions in each, and with a thousand men in each battalion.

Général Mangin—a very notable Fochite—has declared (*La Revue des Deux Mondes*, June 1, 1920) that Ludendorff had a superiority of 33 divisions, but without a reserve for their maintenance. Ludendorff was certain that he had enough superiority in both numbers and training to justify a tremendous effort. I believe that the Allies had in all not more than 162 divisions.

Since this book was published I have received the lamentable news that Brigadier-General Dawson, D.S.O., who commanded the South Africans, died of enteric fever last October, while big game shooting in East Africa. There was not a nobler actor in the great drama of March, 1918.

Some reviewers have accused me of "attacking" Byng because I try to show in focus certain events which belong essentially to my subject, and which hitherto have been either hidden or heavily veiled. Let me remind these critics that the Third Army has been used as a weapon with which to slay the reputation of the Fifth. Apart from this, what

vi AUTHOR'S NOTE TO THE SECOND EDITION

right have they to desire that history should be perverted? A writer is certain to make mistakes when his subject is vastly complicated. Four errors of detail are corrected in this new edition. But to ask a writer to pass from unavoidable mistakes into falsehood is a grave indiscretion.

W. S. S.

8th February, 1921.

INTRODUCTION

BY GENERAL SIR HUBERT DE LA P. GOUGH,
G.C.M.G., K.C.B., K.C.V.O.

WHEN Mr. Shaw Sparrow first asked me to write an Introduction to his book, I refused, because I felt the subject was too personal to myself. Then I saw the following in the *Morning Post*:—

"IN MEMORIAM.
"To the glorious and undying memory of the Heroes of the Fifth Army who gave their lives for Britain, March 21st-22nd, 1918.
"We thank God upon every remembrance of you.
"Lest we forget."

After reading this remembrance I felt that my personal inclinations did not count, and that I owed it "to the glorious and undying memory" of my Comrades of the Fifth Army, living as well as dead, to help to throw on their heroism the light which has been so long withheld.

I write this Introduction, then, in a full regard of their Memories and in no sense of my own capacity.

On the shoulders of the officers and men of the Fifth Army was thrown practically the whole burden of holding up Ludendorff's powerful attack, one which was as carefully and ably organized in all its details as it was weighty in its physical and material resources. As Mr. Shaw Sparrow shows by his figures of the divisions engaged, the great and main blow was directed against the Fifth Army, two of Ludendorff's armies being employed on this task.

Thus, the fate of France, of Great Britain, of Europe, rested with those few men who composed the Fifth Army, and who, perforce scattered and unsupported, were worn and exhausted by strain and fatigue for nights and days in succession, yet still fought on against the numbers which tried to overwhelm their defence.

There may have been men who showed weakness, indeed there were, and some others made mistakes; but it must not be overlooked that though they might be British soldiers they were also human beings. For no one to fail would have been beyond the power of human effort. And when we look at the picture in its broad lines and see the numbers of divisions engaged by all parties in the drama, then with no more than justice we can assert that no soldiers of any nation ever displayed so richly the military virtues of courage, endurance, and staunchness under a strain so long and so terrible.

We have been brought up to admire and praise "the thin Red Line" which so often stayed the foe. Never was the Red Line so thin as the Khaki Line which manned the long front of forty-two miles for which the Fifth Army was responsible on March 21, 1918. Mr. Shaw Sparrow discusses the reason for the thinness of our line here—a thinness known to Ludendorff—and makes some valuable and interesting observations.

The people of Great Britain, not to say those of all the Allies, owe the officers and men of the Fifth Army a debt of gratitude which neither words nor deeds can sufficiently repay.

Unfortunately, owing to a variety of causes, to some of which Mr. Shaw Sparrow refers, my countrymen, with few exceptions (confined principally to those bereaved ones who lost their dearest and best), have not shown an appreciation of the splendid deeds of these men.

This book throws some clear and true light on what they were called upon to do, and how they did it, and it is my sincere hope that my countrymen will realize from reading its pages the splendour and the achievement of the soldiers of the Fifth Army.

Mr. Shaw Sparrow has written a clear and powerful narrative. His book gives proof of much research, and he is in possession of valuable information which, I believe, will be mainly new to the general public. From the point of view of history, he writes clearly and lucidly of the broad outlines of the story, and of the several absorbing questions of military policy and strategy which centre round this tremendous battle. But he does not confine himself to the mere recital of the main events and their causes. He adds

INTRODUCTION

drama and reality to the tale by many personal anecdotes which vivify the story and give it life, enabling the reader to judge what manner of men these were who were called on to face the storm. The one would not be complete without the other.

Plans, organization of preparation, and the orders of the higher Commanders and Staffs of all forces engaged in a great battle, have undoubtedly an enormous influence, often a decisive one; but in this world we can never escape, least of all in a battle, from the human element. It is these touches which Mr. Shaw Sparrow has introduced into his book which make his whole picture so real and gives it such value. Whatever the plans may be, and whatever the preparations and orders, it is inevitable that the conduct of the officers and men actually engaged in a great struggle should be of the utmost importance. It was so in this case, and to a greater degree than is usual, for as a mere military problem on paper, the battle was prodigious. The troops of the Fifth Army were exposed in such scanty numbers to an attack so well organized and so formidable that, without exaggeration it can be said, they seemed to have no chance whatever of saving the situation.

Yet they did save it, and that they succeeded is due entirely to the truly wonderful and magnificent manner in which they fought and fought on. Courage to face terrific dangers for a few hours would not have sufficed. Their claim to honour rests on a much greater foundation than this, since they supported fatigue and exhaustion through days and nights, and yet maintained throughout their courage and their " will to act."

We wonder how they did it. I can only surmise that it came from the great and gallant spirit that animated the Fifth Army, super-imposed on the virtues of honour and self-sacrifice which are the heritage of all our race.

Mr. Shaw Sparrow enables us in his pages to see glimpses of the magnificent human element on which depended in the last resort the safety of the Cause. It was this element that imposed strategical failure on Ludendorff. It maintained intact an ever thinning line, a line that perished, yet remained cheerful; kept it intact in front of the German masses which strove to surge forward and to submerge rapidly all the country beyond. These masses hoped to take Amiens and Abbeville, in order to pin us against the sea; they wished to take Paris also, and (perhaps the most potent influence of all) they yearned to end the war, in a victorious peace.

Let me say, too, that the Commander-in-Chief has added a footnote to his republished account of the battle, in which the fine temper of the Fifth Army is summed up truly and vividly:—

"A marked feature of almost all reports sent in by liaison officers during the battle was the good spirit of the men in the fighting line, and their confidence that they had given a good account of themselves. The following passage from the report of an officer who visited the front south of the Somme on the 28th of March is worth quoting, as giving a first-hand impression of the spirit prevailing at that time:— 'From what I saw and from the people with whom I talked, there seems little doubt that although our men are dog-tired they have not lost heart, and I was told that they are all convinced that we are winning. During the earlier stages of the battle they fought exceedingly well, and killed large numbers of the enemy. Even now portions of the line are putting up a very good fight, and even at times counter-attacking with success. Divisions are very much disorganized, and have with them men of all sorts of divisions, and all Divisional Commanders with whom I have spoken have said that once they are able to reorganize they think they will find their divisions much stronger than they expect. . . . I have not heard any grousing from anybody.'" *

Why my country failed to realize or to appreciate the splendid valour and great results achieved by the men of the Fifth Army is a difficult and perhaps a delicate matter for me to touch upon.

The fact certainly was that London Clubs and Drawing-rooms, and the columns of our Press, were filled with the most extraordinary stories. It is of no public interest to repeat those tales now, or to attempt to refute them; truth is slowly emerging, and with the truth we can rely on the people's innate sense of justice and fair judgment.

Can we wonder that the country failed to estimate the truth when a Minister of the Crown, who was in a position to winnow facts from foolish rumours, could repeat, even to me, that "the troops left their positions on many occasions without sufficient reason"? If such was the case, it was certainly not true of the troops of the Fifth Army, as is sufficiently proved by the numbers who remained "in their

* "Sir Douglas Haig's Dispatches," p. 213, footnote.

positions" and are buried there. But fear does not make men either just or generous; it is only the greatest and the noblest characters who can maintain these qualities under such conditions, and there is no doubt that our Ministers and others were torn with fear during those fateful weeks.

The Prime Minister is responsible probably more than most others for the slurs that were cast on the Fifth Army, for in his speech in the House of Commons on April 9 he made some peculiar comments. Though he declared that he did not wish to say anything unjust, and though he paid a tribute to the gallantry of the whole British Army, yet by implication, if not also by directly inaccurate statements, he made various charges against the Fifth Army. Not one of them can be supported by facts, yet none of them has yet been withdrawn. Among our representatives in the House of Commons is there not a single man who will rise and tell the whole truth while challenging the implications (to use no severer term) put into circulation by the Prime Minister?

The impressions created by the Prime Minister's speech were these: (1) that the enemy broke through the resistance of the Fifth Army; (2) that the organization of all and every means to stem the torrent was neglected by the Staff of the Fifth Army, and that it was left to the fortunate initiative of General Carey to save at least one critical situation; (3) that the line of the Somme was abandoned before the Germans brought up their guns; (4) that the bridges were not adequately destroyed; (5) that the Third Army held, "never giving way 100 yards, and that their retirement took place in order to conform to a retreat on their right flank."

Readers of Mr. Shaw Sparrow's book will find the true answers to all these "tales." Of special interest will be the fact which he brings out that the Third Army retired because it was obliged to by the position and losses of its own troops; and that if it could only have held its ground, threatening the German right flank along the boundary uniting the Fifth and Third Armies, such action would have been pregnant of most advantageous results, relieving greatly the strain on the hard-pressed Fifth Army, whose urgent need of more men should have been stated by the Prime Minister. It will also appear from these pages that the Fifth Army did not withdraw from the Somme in the Péronne sector till the Third Army was some six miles behind its left. This fact is equally clear in the large coloured map of the retreat given by Lord Haig in the second volume of his "Dispatches." Between March 24 and 27 the Third Army's right was constantly west of the Fifth's left.

Mr. Shaw Sparrow discusses in an interesting manner some grave questions of generalship. I do not say I agree with all his deductions, but he has at least placed before the reader all the facts, including the numbers of the divisions on all sides, so the reader should be able to arrive at correct conclusions for himself.

As regards the positions and movement of reserves, he presents both to civilians and to military students a problem of intense interest and importance.

I do not propose to discuss this question at length. Both British G.H.Q. and French G.Q.G. had a difficult task. They had many diverging interests to protect, and the arrangements for co-ordinating their efforts, which were in the hands of an Executive Committee of Allied Generals speaking different languages and responsible to different Governments, were not such as to commend themselves to students of war. It was easy for Ludendorff to play upon their fears, and in fact he seems to have been rather too successful in doing so. This will be realized when it is seen that the French Reserves were grouped behind (*a*) Reims, (*b*) Verdun, (*c*) Belfort, to meet an attack through Switzerland! The British Reserves were grouped behind Ypres and Arras.

The one part of the line behind which there were *no* general reserves was behind the long forty-two-mile front of the Fifth Army. It was quite apparent to the Fifth Army that they were going to be the object of a great attack, and fortunately they were as ready as their small resources would permit. The general situation, however, made it necessary that we should run no risks in the north, where we had little room to spare between the German lines and the Channel ports.

Therefore, until he knew definitely that the attack on the Fifth Army was to be the main attack, Sir Douglas Haig felt compelled to keep reserves in the north. To the Fifth Army, therefore, fell the rôle of sacrificing itself for the common good in order to gain time for the transfer of the distant reserves to the battlefield. This is an operation of war which has often been carried out before, and is often one of the most brilliant combinations of strategy.

It is always a very difficult task, and entails heavy loss on the force to which it is entrusted. "La manœuvre en

INTRODUCTION xiii

retraite" is usually the only correct course to adopt on these occasions, for the essential thing is to gain time, to delay the enemy, and not to secure territory. It is essential also to preserve the containing force from overwhelming defeat, as of course, if it is once overwhelmed, the enemy becomes free of all his movements, and he can gain ground rapidly.

In this case, the task set the officers and men of the Fifth Army was particularly hard by reason of the great disproportion in numbers which existed between the opposing forces.

A study of Mr. Shaw Sparrow's pages and his maps will show that the task imposed on the Fifth Army was fulfilled, in spite of its immense difficulties, and in fact it is difficult to recall from history a case in which a force has better fulfilled that extremely difficult and dangerous rôle.

It was bitter, therefore, to the officers and men of the Fifth Army, but more particularly to the families of those who gave their lives in these dark days of struggle, to hear the misconceptions which were so freely bandied about of their action and their conduct, and the hard judgments passed upon them.

For various reasons my troops had taken over a part of the line held by the French Army. It may have been understood by the British G.H.Q. that the French would be solely responsible on my front for all supports and reserves; but certainly it was not my impression that all my supports and reserves should come from French sources, though a plan of gradual relief by French troops had been worked out, commencing from the South. When I relieved the Third French Army under Général Humbert, it was withdrawn and posted round Clermont. There I thought it remained. In reality all the divisions of the French Army were ordered away and posted elsewhere, Général Humbert and his Staff alone remaining.

During the battle, when Général Humbert arrived at my Headquarters to support the line, and eventually to take it over as previously arranged, I said I was very glad to see him, as my men were struggling against terrific odds. He replied, however, "Mais je n'ai que mon fanion," referring to the small flag on his motor-car. This was not exactly the amount of support that the moment seemed to require.

The difficulties and disorganization caused by the hurried return of French divisions from distant parts of the theatre are referred to by Mr. Shaw Sparrow.

INTRODUCTION

One French Corps Staff arrived with a few candles for a dozen Staff Officers simultaneously to study maps and write orders. Verily we all had to improvise much.

Whatever the cause, the actual result anyhow was that by Sunday, March 24, I believe I am correct in saying, three British divisions had reached the Third Army,* while the fourth to arrive was sent to me, and was able to get hurriedly into action that morning, but without previous reconnaissance. This was the 8th Division, coming from the vicinity of Ypres, viz. the left of the British line, whereas the danger which the Fifth Army was struggling to meet as best it could with its most inadequate resources was on the extreme right of our line.

Mr. Shaw Sparrow justly criticizes the distance which the 50th and 20th Divisions were from the front when the battle opened. They were my local supports, though still retained under the orders of G.H.Q., for reasons previously given by the C.G.S. to myself.

Mr. Shaw Sparrow's book is a serious and valuable contribution to History, and the British public owe him a debt of gratitude for a task of considerable research and ability which does justice to British soldiers, and elucidates and discusses in a clear and interesting manner the different causes which influenced the battle, showing a real appreciation of strategical principles, worthy of the consideration of all military students.

H. P. GOUGH.

* The 42nd, in support east of Adinfer on March 23; the 62nd, in support west of Arras on the 24th; the 35th, which on the fifth day fought under General Byng; and the 12th in the Fricourt neighbourhood on the evening of the 25th.

CONTENTS

INTRODUCTION. By GENERAL SIR HUBERT DE LA POER GOUGH, G.C.M.G., K.C.B., K.C.V.O. vii

PART I

THE PRE-BATTLE: DIFFICULTIES AND PREPARATIONS, BRITISH AND GERMAN

CHAPTER
I. How to Begin 3
II. On a New Front: Defence and its Limits 10
III. Foresight, and Gough's Manifestoes 25
IV. Haig and Ludendorff: their Contests in Pre-Battle Affairs 33
V. Other Pre-Battle Contests of Mind, with some of their Effects 40
VI. Was the Fog a Hindrance to the Fifth Army's Defence? . 56

PART II

THE BATTLE IN ITS MAIN ASPECTS

I. German Shells and British Redoubts: the First Day of Oskar von Hutier's Attack 63
II. Hutier's Attack moves on to be Baffled 82
III. The Centre Fighting North and South of the Vermand-Amiens Road 100
IV. The Centre Fighting, *continued*: Framerville, Cérisy, Harbonnières, and other Combats 121
V. The Northern Attacks: Preliminary Points and Questions 136
VI. The Joint Attack by Marwitz and Otto von Below: the First Day's Battle 146
VII. Marwitz and Below continue their Joint Attacks . . 159

CONTENTS

CHAPTER		PAGE
VIII.	SOME POINTS AND CROSS-QUESTIONS RAISED BY THE FOREGOING CHAPTERS	168
IX.	SATURDAY AND SUNDAY IN THE NORTHERN FIGHTING	174
X.	LAST DAYS OF THE NORTHERN FIGHTING	186

PART III

THE BATTLE IN SOME CHOSEN INCIDENTS AND EPISODES

I.	A FEW SCATTERED IMPRESSIONS	201
II.	DAWSON'S FIVE HUNDRED. HOW THE SOUTH AFRICANS WERE OVERWHELMED: SUNDAY, MARCH 24, 1918	222
III.	A FEW LETTERS WRITTEN BY OFFICERS OF THE *Sixty-first* DIVISION	232

PART IV

AFTERMATH, INCLUDING CONTROVERSIES, SIDE ISSUES, AND POLITICAL EFFECTS

I.	ON THE LOSS OF PERONNE AND BAPAUME	245
II.	THE TRANSFER OF FIFTH ARMY TROOPS TO THE THIRD ARMY	258
III.	ORIGIN OF THE CÉBISY EPISODE	266
IV.	HOW OUR MEN WERE RELIEVED IN THEIR GRAPPLE AGAINST HUTIER	275
V.	UNITY OF COMMAND	289
VI.	THE TROUBLES OF MINISTERS	293
VII.	SOME SIDE ISSUES AND POLITICAL EFFECTS	304
VIII.	WIDESPREAD INJUSTICE AND THE PEOPLE'S EQUITY	312
	INDEX	319

SKETCH MAPS

INSET PLATES

1. March 21, 1918: Approximate Order of Battle, British and German
   Between pages 40–41
2. Maxse's Corps, with its Forward and Battle Zones, its Brigades and Battalions, and the German Corps and Divisions
   Between pages 72–73
3. Attack on the *Fourteenth* DIVISION, March 21. Hutier breaks through the Battle Zone, but fails in his effort to cross the Crozat Canal . . . . . . *Between pages* 80–81
4. The Cérisy Drama and the very important Combat of Harbonnières
   Between pages 128–129
5. The Boundary uniting Byng and Gough . *Between pages* 136–137
6. Front of the *Ninth* DIVISION and the Entrenched Land north and south of it . . . . . . *Between pages* 144–145
7. March 21 and 22: German advance to the Péronne Bridgehead, north and south of the Vermand-Amiens Road
   Between pages 168–169
8. Four Days of the Retreat . . . . *Between pages* 184–185
9. The Pressure on Byng's Right and Centre on the Evening of March 25 . . . . *Between pages* 192–193
10. Map to show how Divisions from the FIFTH ARMY on March 26 formed the THIRD ARMY's Right Wing . *Between pages* 272–273

IN THE TEXT

		PAGE
1.	Sketch Map on which the German Plans can be followed . .	49
2.	Brigades of the *Sixty-first* DIVISION, with the Forward Zone and its Redoubts	71
3.	Front of the *Eighteenth* DIVISION at 6 p.m. of March 21 . .	77
4.	Malcolm's Front after Colonel Little's arrival, March 26, 1918, evening	125
5.	Flesquières Salient, March 21, 1918, with the German Divisions, and the Land lost by our THIRD ARMY north-west of the Salient	149
6.	Zone Map, Northern Fighting	151
7.	South African Front, March 21, 1918, and the Land held below it by the *Twenty-first* DIVISION	155
8.	Cavalry Fight at Collezy, March 24, 1918	219
9.	Last Stand of the South African Brigade	223
10.	The Nesle Sector	233
11.	The Crisis north-west of the Ancre, March 26, 1918 . .	269

THE FIFTH ARMY'S ORDER OF BATTLE FROM NORTH TO SOUTH:
MARCH 21, 1918

1. 7th Corps, Sir W. N. Congreve, V.C., K.C.B., M.V.O. Its front —14,000 yards wide—went southward from a point about half a mile north of Gouzeaucourt, at the top of a hill about 400 yards west of Gonnelieu, through Gauche Wood to Vaucellette farm, then south-eastward to Epéhy and Ronssoy. A few hundred yards south of Ronssoy the *Sixteenth* (South Irish) DIVISION, 7th Corps, joined the *Sixty-sixth* DIVISION, 19th Corps. Congreve had three divisions in line:

Ninth, at first under H. H. Tudor, who commanded finely through four days of battle until Blacklock returned from leave in England.
Twenty-first, D. G. M. Campbell.
Sixteenth, South Irish, Sir Amyatt Hull.
Reserves: *Thirty-ninth* DIVISION, E. Feetham; he was killed in action while visiting his troops in the front line.

2. 19th Corps, Sir H. E. Watts, K.C.B., C.M.G. Its frontage of nearly 13,000 yards went southward from its union with Congreve to about 1500 yards south of Pontruet, across the river Omignon. Two divisions in line, both below strength:

Sixty-sixth, Lancashire troops, Neill Malcolm, who was wounded; and
Twenty-fourth, A. C. Daly.
Reserves: *First* CAVALRY DIVISION, R. L. Mullens, and *Fiftieth* (North English) DIVISION, at first under Brigadier A. F. U. Stockley, R.A.*

3. 18th Corps, Sir F. Ivor Maxse, K.C.B., C.V.O., D.S.O. Its frontage clasped upon St. Quentin and was 18,000 yards wide, extending from its union with Watts, near Gricourt, southward to St. Quentin-Vendeuil road, west of Itancourt. Three divisions in line:

Sixty-first, Sir Colin Mackenzie;
Thirtieth, W. de L. Williams; and
Thirty-sixth, Ulster, O. S. W. Nugent.
Reserves: *Twentieth* DIVISION, W. Douglas Smith.
It reached the battlefield on the evening of March 21, detained too long by G.H.Q.

* A few days before the battle, greatly to the regret of our FIFTH ARMY, the able Commander of this Division, Pine-Coffin, V.C., was removed to another post by G.H.Q. The new Commander, H. Jackson, D.S.O., of the Bedfords, had not arrived when the *Fiftieth* DIVISION, early on the second day, entered the battle, almost too late. It was nearly kept too long by G.H.Q.

ORDER OF BATTLE

4. 3rd Corps, Sir R. H. K. Butler, K.C.M.G., C.B. Its frontage to the south of Barisis was 30,000 yards, protected somewhat along 14,000 yards by the River Oise. In a wet season this protection would have been great; but very little rain fell between January 1 and March 21. Marshes dried up, and the water channels narrowed and became shallow and fordable; so the river had little defensive value. Only three divisions were in line on this exceedingly wide and perilous front:

Fourteenth, Sir Victor Couper;
Eighteenth, R. Lee; and
Fifty-eighth, A. B. E. Cator.

Reserves: *Second* and *Third* CAVALRY DIVISIONS, Robert Greenly and A. E. W. Harman.

PART I
THE PRE-BATTLE
DIFFICULTIES AND PREPARATIONS
BRITISH AND GERMAN

THE FIFTH ARMY IN MARCH, 1918

CHAPTER I

HOW TO BEGIN

§ I

THE second battle of the Somme may be called also the second battle of St. Quentin. It began on March 21, 1918. Its main phases lasted through eight days, and rolled over so many square miles of land that details gathered around them into limitless confusion. Is it possible to resolve this anarchy of items into a truthful whole? Perhaps this labour may be impossible, but yet it is one which many a writer might well attack with unstinted patience.

Too much detail is always a lie to those gifts of the mind that reduce a chaos into harmony, map out for us the accumulations of research, and reveal how their collective worth may be brought to bear on the same object.

An immense battle has four united parts, into each of which details throng and jostle:

I. *The pre-Battle Period of Difficulties and Preparations*, when incessant contests of mind and will go on between those who have decided to attack and those who are obliged to settle down on a defensive policy. The whole fighting may be determined by these pre-battle affairs; so they should be summed up and weighed with impartial carefulness.

II. *The Battle in its Main Aspects.*—This part is beset with so many difficulties that no writer can hope to beat them all. He can do no more than offer his own epitome to that open and keen debate out of which, perhaps, as the generations pass, a complete one may come. The last word on all big subjects may be left to the last man—or maybe the last woman.

III. *The Battle in some Chosen Incidents and Episodes.*—

Every writer will make a different selection, following his own bent; but the general effect is likely to be the same, just as honest samples represent the mass.

IV. *The Battle's Aftermath, including Controversies, Side Issues, and Political Effects.*—As often as possible controversy should be separated from narration; it inflames the party temper, and warm discussion and narrative should not be mingled together unless we wish to destroy the value of both. For all that, facts around which disputes are rife must be stated in their proper places, and sometimes repeated, since huge battles have many events that overlap from the same causes; it is the disputes themselves which, as often as possible, should be placed among the aftermath of armed strife.

I have used this division into four parts, and have tried earnestly to see the whole subject under the form of visual conception, in pictures clear to the mind, this being the only method of work that is worth while.

Part IV. has been a very distressing one to study, and for two reasons. Haig was deplorably short of men. During 1917 he had not received even the minimum levies he had asked for, and afterwards his increasing needs were unsupported by proportionate reinforcements. So he was obliged to keep his best divisions far too long in the line of trench routine, and his combatant strength had in it far too many men who were imperfectly trained. These distressing facts were hidden from the people, and the public temper became one of over-confidence. Then Ludendorff struck, and at once the British people passed into reaction. Over-confidence vanished, and slander and injustice poured over our FIFTH ARMY both during and after its ordeal against huge odds. There are times when the political party temper becomes as eager to find scapegoats as big game hunters are to shoot lions and tigers. And in war too many persons like to regard truth as a mere candle, a smoking, feeble thing long displaced by more brilliant lights, and fit to be put out by Dora's extinguisher.

Sir F. Maurice has declared that in March, 1918, Haig's rifle and sabre strength—namely, the number of troops available for duty in the trenches—was inferior by 180,000 men to the power that it possessed in March, 1917, when the British front was much narrower. Could a graver charge than this be brought against a British War Cabinet? Sir F. Maurice's figures will be found in his epitome of " The Last Four Months." They remain unchallenged, and help to complete the information which Earl Haig himself has published in his Dispatch

HOW TO BEGIN

on the battle. Yet the War Cabinet, while practising unfairness to the FIFTH ARMY, strove to hide the tragic need of more men. For three months, or thereabouts, to take an example, the official dispatch from G.H.Q. was withheld from publication; and when at last it appeared as a Supplement to the *London Gazette*, October 21, 1918, some passages were cut, and the British people were occupied with Germany's approaching downfall.

When scapegoat-seeking was in its first freshness, a war correspondent at the front, Mr. Hamilton Fyfe, after watching many phases of the retreat, wanted to tell in print what he knew to be true. He tried, and was forbidden. Authority would not let him.*

"It was not thought desirable then to show up the falseness of the view taken by many English reviews and newspapers, that upon the FIFTH ARMY lay the responsibility for the loss of so much ground to the enemy; that this Army was badly handled and therefore unable to put up a stout resistance; and that it 'let down' the THIRD ARMY, which, but for the collapse of the FIFTH, would have been able to hold its ground. This view in my opinion is grotesquely at odds with the truth. . . ." †

It was indeed; and a slander grotesquely unfair to Gough and his men was unfair also to Byng and his troops, against whom a reaction would set in when suppressed facts found their way at last into print. Who can explain why two British armies were not kept on the same level towards the nation's patriotism and truthfulness? To slander the FIFTH ARMY, while magnifying hugely what the THIRD had achieved, is one of those follies which are worse than crimes. Both did their best in the most fateful battle of the whole war; together they spoilt Ludendorff's ample strategy, as Ludendorff himself admits; but we owe much greater gratitude to the FIFTH ARMY, because the odds against it everywhere on March 21 certainly exceeded three to one, while Byng along his narrower front had seventeen divisions with which to oppose twenty-four. On the right, along a stretch of 30,000 yards, Gough had an average of only one bayonet to the yard, while the German average was four; and the odds against his right were as high in guns, machine guns, and mortars.

On the first day, it is true, Byng was attacked on only two portions of his front: directly and formidably from Sensée

* In this case, I regret to say, authority was G.H.Q.
† *Contemporary Review*, January, 1919.

River down to the Bapaume-Cambrai road; indirectly, but menacingly, across Flesquières salient. Along this total frontage the foe had fourteen divisions in line, including one just north of the river, and nine in support, while Byng had eight in line and seven in support; but during the first day's grapple Byng reinforced his fighting line with three divisions from his reserves.

§ II

Troubles caused by injustice are not the only painful difficulties that students of this battle have to encounter. Among other troubles there is the profusion of names, military and geographical, by which most readers of the war's battles are irritated. Very often they give a sort of dropsy to a printed page. Can anything be done to set limits to this annoyance? Now and then a name can be deleted without harm to history; but there are no means of saving readers from close attention. Maps must be studied if a battle is to be seen by the mind; and many corps, divisions, brigades, battalions, must be named, with many villages, towns, rivers, and other essential elements in a battle. Personal names can be shortened in one way only—by omitting titles. If we speak bluntly of Haig, as we do of Nelson and Wellington, we are briefly admirative, not curtly rude. In this book, then, titles will be given only here and there; and some other brevity can be got by linking leaders with their positions. The surname Ludendorff, for example, applies not only to the General himself, but also to the German Higher Command, just as the surname Haig sums up the whole policy of his G.H.Q. Similarly, the surnames Gough and Byng mean the BRITISH FIFTH and THIRD ARMIES, just as Otto von Below, briefly Below, represents the SEVENTEENTH GERMAN ARMY, and Oskar von Hutier, briefly Hutier, the EIGHTEENTH GERMAN ARMY. Or suppose we say that Maxse, Congreve, and Watts are hard pressed along their battle fronts. Surely this phrasing is briefer and better than to say: "The 18th, 7th, and 19th Corps are hard pressed along their battle fronts, under command respectively of Lieut.-Generals Sir F. Ivor Maxse, K.C.B., C.V.O., D.S.O., Sir W. N. Congreve, V.C., K.C.B., M.V.O., and Sir H. E. Watts, K.C.B., C.M.G." When official dispatches are written with this excessive courtesy the movement of battle stories cannot be rapid; it is impeded by high and higher titles.

Then there is the word Division, which appears far more often in military writing than is good for narration. Sometimes it cannot be deleted, but often it can, happily, and in two ways:
1. *When a numeral begins with a capital letter and is printed in italics, it means that it is the number of a Division, and that the word " division " is omitted.* Example: " After a night journey with a march of seven miles through fog, the *Fiftieth* came up, bringing necessary help to the *Twenty-fourth* and *Sixty-sixth.*"
2. The names of Divisional Commanders can be used to denote their commands. Examples: Stockley represents the *Fiftieth*, Daly the *Twenty-fourth*, and Neill Malcolm the *Sixty-sixth*.

So it is necessary to show Gough's order of battle, with its corps, divisions, and principal officers. *For this reason, in the Table of Contents, after the List of Maps, I have shown the four corps on their fronts.* If readers will consult this Order of Battle when a new surname is mentioned in the text, they will help greatly in the hard task of simplifying a scientific battle teeming with difficulties.

§ III

It is a belief among many persons that the only writers who should treat of the War are those who witnessed the battles with their own eyes. For two reasons this belief might well be put aside. First, if the War is to be remembered by a whole nation as the most painful and useful admonition in history, its ups and downs of awful waywardness should take hold of and shake scores and scores of lay authors, as in past times British battles put a spell over Southey, Carlyle, Macaulay, Kinglake, and a great many other authors, major and minor. There are laymen who, like myself, would sooner read good books on great battles than most novels.

Military writing addressed to professional soldiers may be limited to the technical anatomy of war; but other military writing must pay honour to that very important democrat who is forgotten by most specialists—the general reader who *does* generally read, as often as not in odd half-hours after his day's work. Besides, few real soldiers are dry-as-dusts. Wellington was as charmed as were schoolboys by chapter xiv. of *Charles O'Malley,* where Lever relates the battle on th

Douro, in a style not often equalled by military writing. The Great Duke wondered how Lever knew certain facts that he tells. Let many try to emulate this right passion for great deeds that Lever here reveals!

Next, anyone who fights *inside* the swirl and fever of a modern battle sees only the small span of ground over which he advances or retreats; and frequently he misjudges events on his flank only a few hundreds of yards off. Indeed, only a soldier here and there admits that his battalion was compelled to fall back; most soldiers complain that their flank was left in the air by a neighbouring unit, whose troops have precisely the same tale to tell. At first I was worried by this general complaint.

Only from officers who are *not* always inside the fever of a battle—only from commanders over brigades, divisions, and corps, and armies—do we get more or less in focus extending views of large and larger fronts. The lesser Generals sift and collect evidence for the Army Commander, who alone knows what is passing all along his front; knows all this roughly, since events may change all at once; and here and there in widespread fighting, a gap of silence irritates the Commander's mind, for it adds guesses to that dread uncertainty which rules over all armed strife till a battle ends.

An Army Commander, then, is a *mind*-witness, not an *eye*-witness; a new sort of historian who receives reports from expert sifters, and whose intellect must have vision as well as coolness and candour. Soldiers inside a great battle are like persons in a sand storm, while the vision of an Army Commander is like a spectator who from a favourable distance sees a grand stretch of groyne-protected shore and a storm tide flooding or ebbing.

As for lay students of the War's immensity, they should practise the craft of map-drawing. More than anything else in the study of war it compels the mind to keep at close quarters with very troublesome points and problems. For this reason I have given more than twelve weeks to map-drawing alone; and soon I began to feel that modern trench warfare has a certain kindredship with fundamental problems of architecture and engineering; problems of jolts, thrusts, repercussions, recoils; of action and reaction, and poise and equipoise.

To overwhelm equipoise on Gough's wide front was the nut which Ludendorff wanted to crack, aided by lessons gathered from past failures in attack, both German and Allied. To keep a sort of devious or vagrant stability, after vast odds had crumbled a very thin defence, was the duty which Gough and his officers and men had to fulfil, and just managed to fulfil, in spite of indescribable sufferings. As Sir F. Maurice says, "our men showed coolness, courage, determination, and endurance in adversity which pass all understanding and are beyond all praise, but they should never, and need never have been called upon for such sacrifices as they made without stint and without complaint." *

Since August, 1918, this battle has occupied my days, very often till midnight; authentic materials of many sorts have turned me into their pupil; and I hope never to forget their best lessons—lessons of gratitude, and also of reverence. Once more, in this grapple against enormous odds, British statesmanship asked Providence to let our country perish; and once more this request was nearly granted. As Clemenceau has stated, " we were playing a hand on which hung the fate of the Fatherland."

* "The Last Four Months," p. 54.

CHAPTER II

ON A NEW FRONT: DEFENCE AND ITS LIMITS

§ I

AT the close of 1917 a Tommy said of the FIFTH ARMY: "It's always bein' moved abart to tackle nasty jobs," but nasty jobs by dozens came to all troops after deep dugouts and elaborate trench systems were introduced by German caution and thoroughness. Gough and his officers and men may have had more than a fair share of the nastiest jobs, though their ordeal in the horrific Ypres salient seems to have been less abominable than was that of Plumer's troops when they plodded through mud and blood and captured Passchendaele.

After the Ypres salient campaign had ended, the FIFTH ARMY rested for a brief time in General Reserve. Then, on December 18, 1917, it was put on a new front, replacing a portion of Byng's forces on a twelve-mile line from a point about half a mile north of Gouzeaucourt to the Omignon River. The 7th Corps came under its command, and the Cavalry Corps also.

Nearly a month later, between January 10 and 12, 1918, a one-corps front was taken over by Gough from the FRENCH THIRD ARMY; it ran southward from the Omignon to a point south-east of St. Quentin and north-east of Urvillers. And one more change was to come, between January 26 and February 3, when the FRENCH THIRD ARMY was relieved on another one-corps front as far south as Barisis, a village south of the Oise between two forests, Coucy and St Gobain.*

Much controversy has eddied around this transfer of land from French to British troops,† but at present we pass away from it in order to keep at close quarters with the main sequence of events. From February 3, 1918, Gough had

---

* Pray keep these dates before your mind; their bearing on the preparation work to be done is very important.
† Part I., p. 25, and Part IV., p. 300.

A NEW FRONT: DEFENCE AND ITS LIMITS 11

forty-two miles of front to safeguard across the heart of France, and the work to be done was enormous. Every mile had to be remodelled and combined in accordance with a series of rules issued by G.H.Q. on December 14, 1917. When compared with these rules, even the land taken over from Byng was unfit for the most recent phases of defence; and as for the French fronts, they had a forward area well dug and supplied with shelters; but the main battle positions had nothing but a belt of wire, and neither roads nor railways were yet good enough for the lessons which had been learnt from recent bitter experience.

Only a cable here and there had been buried below the reach of shells, and no area of defence was organized in depth. Stretches of the front had been ravaged by a German retreat in the spring of 1917,* and along the Oise and Somme sectors, dry weather was having a very bad effect, drying marshes, narrowing water channels, and making rivers gradually fordable between the usual points of passage. So new problems of defence were thrust by unusual dry weather on Haig and Gough, problems too extensive to be solved in about seven weeks, but not too extensive to be considered in this book from several standpoints.

Battle Zone.—Planned for defence to a great depth, varying from 2000 to 3000 yards, with good successive lines carefully sited and combined. Diagonal switch trenches gave support to strong points and wired strategical places. It was hoped that they would stop the foe from spreading outwards and rolling up our position, if he managed to penetrate at dangerous spots in our defences.† The most important localities were always garrisoned. Plans and preparations for the best use of troops both in defensive battle and in counter-attack were worked out with skill, partly for the service of those men who were chosen to guard the various sectors, and partly for the proper handling of reinforcements arriving from elsewhere.

Forward Zone.—Its defensive scheme was ordered also in depth, and, of course, its garrison was always on guard against surprise, to break up the foe's attacks, and to force him to waste large quantities of ammunition and to

---

* The great "Alberich Movement," between Arras and Soissons, by which Ludendorff withdrew his troops to the Siegfried Line, and put out of joint the Allied plans of combined attack. This retreat began on March 16, and was carried through without a break in a few big stages.

† The branch trenches called switches, forming protective flanks to put the foe into pockets if he gets through at dangerous points, turn stretches of country into blind alleys, so to speak.

bleed an increasing number of his brigades. The backbone of defence in this zone was a combination of wire entanglements with machine guns very well hidden in dugouts.

Rear Zone.—Ludendorff struck when the rear lines were very imperfect, ranging in depth from a foot to thirty-six inches. A foot deep seems to have been about the average in most places. These lines were placed from four to eight miles behind the battle zone, and G.H.Q. did all that could be done in a few weeks, always in conjunction with our armies, to choose the best positions, and to spit-lock their projected defences. They formed very good halting places for stern rearguard actions, but not for a decisive stand by weak numbers against superior forces constantly renewed. Yet they were valued greatly, even far too much, by G.H.Q., as the official dispatch proves.

The whole defensive scheme, very ample and cautious, was copied from German principles and precedents; and if Ludendorff had not struck before it was brought to completion, G.H.Q. and its armies would have had reason to be surprised and very glad. The work to be done being enormous, priority had to be given as follows to certain essentials:—

1. Wire.
2. Shell-proof accommodation, including machine-gun emplacements, observation posts, and battle headquarters.
3. Communications, including roads, tracks, railways, and communication trenches.
4. Earthworks.

On March 21, the battle zone in most sectors was finished—that is to say, a decisive grapple could have been fought in it by a defence reasonably manned. Its weaker parts, as a rule, were those taken over from the French. Had there been time, Watts would have added further strength to his battle zone; and this applies also to Butler's 30,000 yards of front. For the rest, the battle zone lay at varying distances behind the outpost area, sometimes touching it, and within 1500 yards of forward sentry posts, as on Gough's extreme left. Sometimes, as in Maxse's Corps, a stretch of unfortified country, in places 2000 yards wide or more, connected the outpost zone with our battle zone, and gave natural cover for manœuvring.

I have drawn a detailed map of Maxse's Corps, which faced St. Quentin, and have shown which battalions defended the zones, and which German divisions assailed them. The grapple was one of thin British brigades against German divisions at full battle strength.

As for the lightly-held outpost screen covering our main positions, it had many excellent redoubts or strongpoints, which were held to the last with the utmost courage, as we shall see. Into his forward or outpost zone, Gough put a third part of his men, reserving two-thirds for his battle zone. Or, counting reserve troops, the proportion was two-ninths in the outpost area and seven-ninths in the battle zone. Each defensive belt or zone had a front line, with a support line 300 yards behind; next, a certain number of strongpoints or redoubts; and last, a reserve line. Trenches were not continuous in the outpost screen, where men in detached groups had to attack the foe with a criss-cross of machine-gun fire; while in the battle zone and rear defence continuous lines were used as often as possible.

Here and there men were employed in sections, in "blobs," as by our *Eighteenth*.* Military opinion was moving away from continuous lines, with communication trenches—obvious and steady targets for artillery fire. Australians and New Zealanders liked to place their men in "blobs," well dug in and supporting one another by machine-gun barrage; and it was found that men placed underground in dispersed "slits" suffered fewer casualties than men in trenches. A "slit" was two feet broad, six feet long, and six feet deep: just room enough for two men. At one end was a step on which the men stood to fire. When slits were dug in ploughed land, they were very hard to see, and only direct hits made them unsafe.

Still, an Australian said to me, "Oh yes, one felt all right in a slit till a flight of Hun planes flew low overhead; and then, somehow, a slit seemed to be a good acre square—and certain to be bombed in."

When defences are formed into deep systems, and when they have to be manned by young troops rapidly trained, it seems a hazardous venture to use thin and scattered garrisons, as human impulses are never so gregarious as in times of peril, and too much nerve strain should not be thrust on very brave boy troops who were recently civilians. One extensive redoubt, for example, held by a tiny force, had a dozen scattered posts, and from six or seven the lads fell back through sheer loneliness, when an attack followed hard upon the German creeping barrage. They came together, forming a company; then they were as cool as a board meeting, and held their foes at bay in a very fine spirit.

* A numeral beginning with a capital and printed in italics means the number of a division.

Now and then G.H.Q. gives me the impression that its attitude towards youthfulness was too bureaucratic; that it was colder and less human than were Wellington and Napoleon when lads had to be set to do the work of veterans. Its remarks on Economy of Force really imply that British armies in 1918 had received the complete training described by Napier as necessary to the education of a British soldier— a training of three stern years. Though G.H.Q. knew that the FIFTH ARMY was very weak in numbers, and also composed of youthful troops, recently civilians, it issued these instructions :—

"*Economy of Force.*—Economy of troops must be studied in preparing positions and allotting troops to defences, in order that the strength of reserves, both tactical and strategical, may be as great as possible. *At the same time, defences designed to secure valuable tactical features must be continuously and adequately garrisoned.* The stronger and better sited the defences are, and the more impassable the obstacles, the fewer men will be required to hold them, and consequently the larger the reserves to be held in hand. As the work on these defences progresses it should be possible gradually to reduce the numbers allotted to the defence of the forward zone, and thus increase the numbers available as reserves."

Thus to gain reserves from a grave weakness in rifle strength already overstretched across forty-two miles of vital front is an adventure which I am unable to understand, because I think of similar risks in bridge building. No engineer would say: "We can't afford more material and we've got enough to carry our bridge safely halfway across this confounded wide river. Never mind. We'll take risks. By building everything lighter than it ought to be we'll reach the other bank all right, and perhaps luck won't be too devilish when goods trains pass across during a gale." Still, G.H.Q. was obliged to eke out with risks its insufficient man-power; but whether it chose the best way is another question, over which historians cannot fail to debate keenly.

"Defence in depth," says an English Colonel, "means forces more scattered and greater difficulty in keeping up communication." Yes, no doubt; and a dire fact in the battle suggests another criticism hitherto unnoticed by writers; namely, that *two* forward zones, and a battle area well placed behind them, might have been much better than the three deep systems chosen by G.H.Q., as on several occasions the

A NEW FRONT: DEFENCE AND ITS LIMITS 15

battle zone of one division was outflanked by the foe's rapid advance beyond the single forward zone of a neighbouring division. On the first day this happened both north and south of Maxse's Corps, whose positions were uncommonly strong.

Ludendorff learnt from events to fear a single forward zone, as men retreating from it after a bad grapple brought disorder with them into the main battle area. But the FIFTH ARMY'S forward defence was accepted by every one as a great position of trust where all must fight as in forlorn hopes. Only a few men returned from it, and these few, almost without exceptions, returned honourably, under orders, after many a noble combat like those which are told in this book, Chapter I., Part II.

§ II

In several maps I have shown portions of the defensive systems, sometimes with their battalions, but as my drawings would have to be reduced by a block-maker to about a third of their size, I could not give the trenches in elaborate ground plans.

Though the finished work in these zones was all that could be brought to completion, many complaints have been printed. According to some ideal critics, wonderful trenches were dug but not held; according to others, no trenches could be held because none had been made; and on August 7, 1918, Mr. Lloyd George told the House of Commons that "Practically the whole British front was new ground which had been won from the enemy where there had been no time to set up defences, and these tired troops, instead of enjoying rest, or instead of having time for training, had to make defences." The exaggeration in this quotation is evident. There is no reference to the huge labour squads, or to the vast amount of work which was done with the utmost care. And why did the Prime Minister speak of our tired troops without deploring the main cause of their fatigue—that falling off in the supply of enough men for which his Government was responsible? He said that " Our troops were tired by a prolonged offensive, by the most exhausting conditions under which any troops ever fought." Why, then, were they not reinforced adequately and in time for Ludendorff's offensive?

Here, too, is another criticism. It is written by a war correspondent who witnessed for himself many phases of the retreat, after seeing beforehand the positions in which our troops awaited the attack, and the preparations made in the rear of those positions for defensive action in the event of the front lines being overrun :—

"My own opinion is that the positions prepared for the troops to fall back upon, one after another, in the event of their being hard pressed, might have been more effectively wired. But this criticism applies with equal force to the THIRD ARMY front. . . . I have a note in my diary of a conversation I had with Gough as early as January 30. He said then: 'The Germans might very likely attack his army front, and would probably gain some ground if they did. The best line of defence would be the line of the Somme. Until they got across that there would be no tragedy. It might be a tragedy if they did!' This view had been discussed with G.H.Q., and G.H.Q. knew the strength of the Somme and other defences quite as well as Gough. Yet very little was done to improve our positions anywhere. I recollect thinking, some weeks after the enemy had been brought to a standstill before Amiens, when trenches were being dug and wired in every direction and to a great depth even behind Amiens, that if the British Army had done half this amount of work before the 21st of March, there would have been no retreat. . . . British G.H.Q. knew, thanks to the activity of the Intelligence Department under General Cox (whose accidental death deprived the Army of a painstaking and vigorous officer,) where the blow would fall. Most Generals of Division refused to believe that there would be any blow. A fortnight before the offensive opened I heard from the Staff of one of the FIFTH ARMY divisions that they could not see why G.H.Q. had warned them to be prepared.* But neither at FIFTH ARMY Headquarters nor at Montreuil did any illusion prevail. Since he knew that the FIFTH ARMY would be attacked with vast numbers, and knew also its weakness, Haig must be blamed no less than Gough if the preparations were inadequate."— Hamilton Fyfe, *Contemporary Review*, January, 1919.

These views from an article otherwise right in aim are misleading for several reasons. First of all, they produce a false impression, though their writer hates injustice and wants to be entirely true. When writing about modernized war, with its enormous complexity and its millions and millions of

---

* Several divisional commanders, wishing to rest and train their men, complained to General Gough against the incessant defence labour; but they were told, of course, to drive on and on with defensive preparation.

A NEW FRONT: DEFENCE AND ITS LIMITS 17

detached facts, correct impression is all-important; the complexity and innumerable facts cannot be given, and if they could be, most civilian readers would fail to understand them. Even Haig's dispatch is too difficult for most lay readers, who find it a mere confusion for a lecturer to explain with much aid from lantern slides and large G.H.Q. maps. Now correct impression depends partly on a right suppression of most minor items, and partly on what may be called an axiomatic epitome of major facts. Hence it is absurd to dwell on those rear defences which could not be finished unless other systems of defence nearer the coming attack were neglected. Maxse was satisfied with his forward and battle positions, which were excellent; Congreve regarded his own lines as the best he had seen in France; and Butler and Watts did all that could be achieved in the time.

On Gough's front, the Labour Commandant, in thirteen weeks—December 22 to March 16—found that his men increased from 26,567 to 67,967, these last figures including 12,255 Italians, 5185 Chinese, 10,272 prisoners of war, 4446 Indians, and 35,809 British—a Labour League of Nations. These men had a day's rest in the week, not all at the same time, of course, but in daily batches of fifteen per cent.; and men were needed every day for area employments, escorts for prisoners of war, Labour Group Staff, and some were sick; but, after all these deductions were made, *the men daily at work increased in thirteen weeks from* 13,468 *to* 40,212, though Haig had 125 miles of front all threatened by German preparations, and thus all in need of Labour Commandants and their enterprise. . . . Haig himself says that there was not labour enough for all his pressing needs.

General Smuts visited the British front—in February, I think—to inspect defences for the War Cabinet; he reported that FIFTH ARMY work, well ordered and organized, was being pushed on with energy; and here and there in this book we shall see how alert and wide awake were the preparations. A very great strain had to be borne by the Signal Service, for example, and also by the Administrative Staffs, who, while supplying the retreat with food and ammunition, had more than 60,000 non-combatants and Labour Units to carry away to safety, with huge masses of stores, and large numbers of agricultural implements. More than 250 bridges had to be prepared for destruction, as an army which settles down on a defensive policy must have all things ready to frustrate the foe's efforts to advance.

C

Consider, too, how easy it is to set far too much store by merely material defences, such as trench systems, just as our mediæval ancestors thought far too much of armour, till at last they could neither move with ease nor get up without help if they fell on their backs.

Gough's defences, to my view, were not of a sort either to be distrusted or to cause our men to lean on them overmuch. Better defences could not have been made in a scamper against a time too short; and most of our men * had worked so hard upon them that they knew by heart the material agencies which would help them through the worst days. They could not say among themselves: "These places won't give Fritz a chance." But they could say: "If we stick it all right, these places should help us to do the trick." And this mood is certainly the best one for great resistance.

A forerunner and teacher of Napoleon dwells upon the useful and necessary lesson that good troops ought always to feel themselves superior to their field works; because they are sure to lose grit when they play second fiddle to the protection given by inanimate things. The Chevalier du Teil, who in 1778 published an excellent essay on artillery, and who was an artillery officer in the regiment in which Napoleon was to be a lieutenant, put into plain words the danger of depending too much on trenches: "It is admitted by instructed and experienced officers that any defence based solely upon entrenched positions is absolutely contrary to all grand views to the true and solid principles of the art of war, and in short that this method has never been that of the great generals."

Let us be glad, then, that no rear trench on Gough's overstretched front had a look that caused our men to feel too easy after grave losses and days of excessive fatigue and pain. To keep awake and alert became as hard as to hold off the attack, and a reaction into ease of mind would have sent our men to sleep at wrong moments. The Somme was only about four feet deep, and wreckage of blown-up bridges made pathways across it; so jaded brigades—sometimes they were gassed as well as jaded—had onerous night duties.

§ III

If it was a help to our men to feel far more dependent on their own efforts than on material defences, it was also a help

---

* Not all, unluckily. Several divisions were newcomers, and thus heavily handicapped.
† "The French Army before Napoleon," Spenser Wilkinson, p. 71.

A NEW FRONT: DEFENCE AND ITS LIMITS 19

to them that they were tied loosely, not tightly, as our foes were, to the machine named scientific warfare. The German, keen and enterprising while his routine keeps in gear, is apt to lose edge when his leaders' plans get entangled; and many German divisions cannot be crowded together in an assault without causing at last much confusion. Brigades of different divisions get jumbled together, and break-through becomes necessary to give the mass freedom of movement and deploying value.

To make second-rate compromise serve our turn is one of our national whims, or habits; and in adversity it is a great friend to our troops. The FIFTH ARMY was obliged to make shift, for its men had had no experience in the art of retreating; unlike their Commander, who served his country during the retreat from Mons, as well as in the first battle of Ypres.

Do civilians know what retreating means? Not many, and it is a nut to crack how to make clear in words the worst peril—namely, that gaps form inevitably unless enough reinforcements are at hand along the whole line. When a salient is formed by the act of thrusting inwards some miles of battle-front, the line around the salient is plainly much longer than the salient's width at its base; and thus an army in retreat, if it forms a salient, extends its lines ever more and more, while casualties make it ever more unfit to resist attack from greatly superior numbers. Yet a fine retreat must go on bending without breaking. It must not halt long enough to be overwhelmed by numbers. Can we compare it to stretched elastic which grows weaker as it grows longer? Yes; but not to a *single* piece of elastic, because a retreat is made in many stretching pieces called battalions, brigades, divisions, and corps. Each of these units is a piece of humanized elastic, likely to be broken by excessive stretching to fill gaps. Later we shall see that Gough had few reserves, and that his losses on the first and second days were very severe. So the stretching was always far too much to be safe; and the foe made this danger more perilous by attacking the points at which divisions and corps and armies were joined together. Yet our young troops, recently civilians, though handicapped also by a lack of pre-battle training (as Haig has pointed out), were not swallowed up by a veritable cyclone of scientific warfare. In spite of mistakes, they made shift so well that we civilians ought to be very grateful and very humble.

Take eleven wooden matches to represent the divisions in line, and three others to denote the reserve infantry, adding a match cut into three equal parts for the cavalry.* Draw a long line on a sheet of paper, and put the eleven matches upon it close together. And now begin to rehearse the retreat, forming a salient that grows deeper and deeper. Very soon you will understand all about natural gaps, and the need of many reserves, even if no casualties enfeeble the divisions.

Let me ask you to take up these matters into your understanding. Try to think of them till you see them as pictures; then you will follow the retreat with awe, and with other heart-searching emotions. Perhaps you will come to the humbled opinion that most men of our race need either military or naval discipline to make them effectual as friends to their native land, partly because their general outlook is too insular for their world-wide Empire, and partly because their civilian dislike of discipline runs into fads and sentimental illusions. As a people we need what we hate—discipline, with its unity of action.

Side by side with all these important matters, which help to give a massed impression of the influences at work in war, let me ask you to feel the growling of airplanes that practise for the coming battle, and that go forth after dark, whenever a ground mist does not prevent them, in order to spy on the foe's night movements. Many times before the battle began they flew low during the evening over hostile defences and dropped flares; but they could not see German troops and guns in the act of being moved up with all possible stealth, nor could they hear the German soldier songs which night discipline could not stop. These songs troubled Ludendorff, whose anxiety caused him to expect more stealth from his men than hundreds of thousands were able to give in their crowd-moods. What a picture it is—Ludendorff in his Headquarters biting his nails because troops passing by night through villages towards the battle front break suddenly into song, while overhead British airplanes drop flares!

Careful plans were drawn up for launching the FIFTH ARMY airplanes on a given signal to counter-attack the foe's infantry, and batteries, and roads, and bridges. Every target was mapped in the plans, then studied carefully by those who were chosen to assail it with bombs. Never before had this method of employing air flights been used on anything like such a grand scale, nor organized with so much skill and completeness. Later it was copied by other British armies.

* The three divisions of cavalry in our FIFTH ARMY equalled in manpower the average rifle strength of an infantry division.

Ludendorff and his Generals were equally active with their airplanes, and with results which came as a surprise to many British soldiers; but not to Gough, who never undervalued the foe's initiative and perseverance. The airmanship on both sides during the battle was as keen and good as are first-rate football teams in a cup tie—strained to the utmost, intrepid, full of resource and cunning. In some points, as in contact patrols, the German airplanes had an advantage over our own, according to FIFTH ARMY officers. They discovered our new fronts swiftly, with the result that heavy guns were soon in action against our new positions. German infantry lighted flares as soon as they were asked to do so by their air-scouts. Briefly, the German training in these things was excellent. Ludendorff speaks of this training (vol. ii., p. 577):

"In order to provide aircraft support for the infantry, special battle aeroplane flights were formed. As had hitherto been done by individual airmen, they dived down from great heights and flew along at a low level, attacking with machine guns and light bombs the infantry lines, the artillery, and, as the practice extended, the enemy's reserves and transport columns, as well as columns of troops coming up from farther in the rear.

"Originally intended to be an 'auxiliary' arm to the infantry, these battle-flights were finally given important tactical tasks. Thus the air force gained a new field of activity of the greatest importance. Airmen, in the course of their duties, were not only reconnaissance troops who had to fight; they were not only bomb-carriers for destructive work far in the foe's rear, but they had also, like infantry, artillery, and all other arms, to take part in the fighting on the ground. Like the other combatant forces, they were a destructive arm in the great battle on land. This, indeed, became their main object, and the aerial combat was only a means of attaining it."

Who can explain why newspaper propagandists told the British people that German airmen in March, 1918, were bunglers? One writer said:

"The Germans intended to overwhelm us when the great attack began, at which moment Richthofen and all the circuses of the air duly made their number. But meanwhile our men had so established their ascendancy over the insufficiently trained young entry of the enemy that not even the appearance of the German stars could alter matters. The enemy had at least 1000 aeroplanes on the scene when the attack began, but their training was inadequate, while ours was better than ever, and though the fighting has been as usual mainly over the German lines, all the advantage has been with our men."

This propaganda, being far and away too excessive, was as harmful as the zeal with which British pressmen throughout the war magnified hugely the German casualties till nothing said by newspapers on the foe's losses was believed, except by those who preferred any sort of over-sanguine fudge to an unpleasant fact. To belittle a foe's training and courage is a stupid act if you wish to do justice to your own men. The writer from whom I have just quoted must have known that he had gone much too far, because he ended his remarks by throwing a chill on any over-confidence which his falsely triumphant picture might produce in simple readers :

"At the same time it must be said that in a great action of this ultra-modern stamp we see the Air Force in better perspective, and realize that, good and valuable though it be, it does not alter the general course of events. To arrest a great attack, as we now see, our airmen must number thousands instead of hundreds, and the old Nelsonian maxim that numbers alone annihilate is shown to be as applicable to the air as it is to the land and the sea."

In a quotation from Ludendorff (p. 21) we have seen what German airmen were trained and expected to do, and those over the FIFTH ARMY'S front were thoroughly enterprising: so it is necessary for us to connect this fact with every phase of the ordeal through which our troops battled their way. My researches do not leave me to believe that the airmen on either side gained ascendancy over the other. Both sides had so much work to do both in and from the air that they had no leisure in which to think of duelling for superiority. British airmen were handicapped by two circumstances. First, as soon as French reinforcements began to arrive our air flights were worried because the French horizon-blue uniforms resembled from above the German field-grey ; and as these French uniforms were usually behind the British fighting front, air scouting for information became difficult, and now and then erroneous. More than once news was sent to the Army's H.Q. that German troops were active in the British rear, French horizon-blue having been mistaken for German field-grey. Next, through nearly three whole days German airmen could concentrate mainly on the battle itself because the Allied reinforcements came up slowly and gradually, while our own airmen had to divide their power between the battle and the vast German reserves, who, whether second and third line troops or last reserves, thronged the German rear till the battle was nearing its end. Ludendorff says that his troops suffered heavily from airplane bombing, especially those who were mounted; and from the first day onward our own troops were greatly harassed by the same new weapon.

On the second day, for instance, the South African Brigade was very much troubled by German planes. Dawson, their Brigadier, says:—

"The retirement of the artillery had been going on in the meantime, but the enemy's planes to the number of about thirty were causing the teams considerable annoyance. They were also continually flying along the trenches, firing at the infantry."

Another Brigadier, Robert White of the *Sixty-first*, writing of the same day, says:—

"During the afternoon fighting in Beauvois the Germans had some twenty aeroplanes hovering over the village and diving with extraordinary daring almost into the streets. Of these, two were shot down by our men at very close rifle range. I am inclined to think that this occurred right along the line."

It has been very unfair to our troops deliberately to hide what German aircraft did against our infantry and artillery. Truth still remains in the War with her eyes bandaged and her tongue tied. Surely it is time that she should be restored to Peace with her eyes uncovered and her tongue free to tell what she knows. In March, 1918, pressmen and officials forgot, unhappily, that a great nation in a time of danger should prove by her words and by her acts that she is genuinely great, and therefore above untruth.

Even at G.H.Q., apparently, there was an inclination to undervalue the foe's airmen. Early in the battle an official summary of news stated that their morale had not improved because they flew low! How could they use machine-guns in the fighting on the ground, or be alert in contact patrols, if they flew high?

And now that we have seen that the airplane training, both British and German, was usually thorough, let us note some other things in the routine of preparation. Plans were drawn up and issued for a swift garrisoning of all positions, by reserves as well as by line troops; and all arms were rehearsed several times, by day and night, in moving up to and occupying their posts and positions. As early as March 12, the "Prepare for Battle" order was issued; then reserves moved up closer, all resting guns were put into position, artillery fire was opened on hostile roads, and known batteries, and communications.

There were also two other FIFTH ARMY orders—"Prepare to Man Battle Stations" (when all troops got ready at once to leave their dugouts and billets), and "Man Battle Stations," when they went to their trenches and redoubts, and the strange whispering hush, with a sudden laugh here and there, began to settle down on a waiting defence.

These orders were rehearsed again and again, and the British soldier being an original person, perhaps they bored him a good deal: for a Division General tells me that his own troops, after a night rehearsal of "Man Battle Stations," were snappy when daybreak came. The foe had not attacked, you see; and they felt somehow that, after all their toil through a night without sleep, "Fritz had scored off them." What a joy it is to meet with this touch of British grumbling!

CHAPTER III

FORESIGHT, AND GOUGH'S MANIFESTOES

§ I

WHAT is the greatest quality in preparations for a battle? Forethought, foresight, vision. As early as February 3, 1918, in a conference at Catelet, Gough warned his leading officers that danger might come from across the Oise—an unpleasant prediction because this river hitherto had been an effective barrier along 16,000 yards of uneven front, and French statesmen had used this fact as an argument when they insisted on an extension of Haig's line by more than twenty-eight miles If 16,000 yards of this total distance needed no more defence than a line of far-scattered outposts, the French Ministry had reason to be urgent in their policy, though it was opposed by some French Generals as well as by Haig, whose combatant strength chanced to be at a low ebb, while Norfolk and Ireland were alert with reserves.

Two passages in the official dispatch suggest that G.H.Q. and Gough thought of the Oise in different ways, and that G.H.Q.'s way was not the better one. The first passage runs as follows:

"From Gouzeaucourt to the Oise River at Moy, forty German divisions were set in motion on the first day. An event which, having regard to the nature of the ground, was not considered probable, was that the enemy would be able to extend the flank of his attack in any considerable strength beyond Moy. The rapid drying of the marshes, due to an exceptionally dry spring, in fact enabled the enemy to attack this lightly held front with three fresh divisions, in addition to the three divisions already in line." *

Why was this flank attack considered improbable by G.H.Q.? The dry weather began at the end of December,

* "Haig's Dispatches," vol. ii., p. 185.

1917, and continued till the outbreak of Ludendorff's offensive, apart from a few showers. So its effect on marshes and on the Oise's depth and width were known; and on February 3, before any marsh was hardened, Gough foretold a riverside attack because Oskar von Hutier and the EIGHTEENTH GERMAN ARMY had been put into the line from the River Omignon to a point facing Vendeuil, and Hutier's character and past actions were warnings to be studied. So Gough said to his leading officers at Catelet :

"It should be impressed on all subordinate commanders that although things are quiet at present, the storm may come, and in view of the fact that the battle of Riga was opened by the enemy [Oskar von Hutier] forcing the passage of the Duna, that section of the line guarded by the Oise should not be considered as immune from attack."

And now let us read the second passage from G.H.Q.'s dispatch :

"On the extreme right, the valley of the River Oise, normally marshy and almost impassable during the early spring, was, owing to the exceptionally dry weather, passable for infantry almost everywhere, and formed no serious obstacle. This applies equally to the valley of the River Somme, which in the latter stage of the battle was easily negotiated by the hostile infantry between the recognized points of passage. A much larger number of troops would therefore have been required to render the defence of these rivers secure. *These forces, however, were not available except at the expense of other and more vital portions of my front, and as the exceptional weather conditions could not have been foreseen by the enemy at the time when the preparations for his offensive were undertaken, there was a strong possibility that he would not be able to take advantage of them.*" *

In an earlier part of his dispatch (vol. ii., p. 184), Haig runs counter to himself, when speaking of Gough's forty-two miles front :

"Over ten miles of this front between Amigny Rouy and Alaincourt were protected by the marshes of the Oise River and Canal, and were therefore held more lightly than the remainder of the line; but on the whole front of this [FIFTH] ARMY the number of divisions in line only allowed of an average of one division to some 6750 yards of front."

Gough held definite opinions, as we have seen; and it is

---

* My italics; the wording is very important, "Haig's Dispatches," vol. ii., p. 217.

worth notice also that his conference at Catelet on February 3 should recall to memory another important date.

"By the beginning of February," says Ludendorff, "the attack was fixed to commence on March 21, although the situation in the East was still quite obscure. The military situation, however, made a decision imperative. Later we could always make changes, but we should be unable to make a fresh start."

Are we to suppose that changes would not be made in Hutier's attitude toward the Oise when continuous dry weather gradually made the river fordable and some of its marshes a pretty firm pathway? Still, as we shall see, politics at home ruled over Haig's distribution of defensive power. Owing to the need of men, there was only a choice between bad compromises; all sorts of shifts had to be adopted; though they were known to be perilous.

For all that, one may venture to see something questionable in G.H.Q.'s words: "These forces were not available except at the expense of other and more vital portions of my front." Surely vital things are vital; there's no real need to give them a comparative and a superlative. It is with sectors of a battle front as it is with vital organs of the human body; when one perishes, of what use are the others? Around this question, or one akin to it, as we shall see, Ludendorff's mind revolved when he formed his immense plan of campaign.

What this campaign would be was another question discussed on February 3, at Catelet, and Gough's forecast was to a big extent accurate.

"The main attack may be expected against the THIRD and FIFTH BRITISH ARMIES, with Amiens for its objective."

This prophecy was based on five reasons. At that date noticeable German preparations had not been made elsewhere, and good divisions were being withdrawn from the German line facing Gough's front and Byng's. While these good divisions were passing through a thorough training, they were being reconstituted in their old corps. Within an eighty miles radius of St. Quentin sixty-four German divisions were in line, and thirty-nine in reserve, besides about fifty farther away. It would have been perilous to think that present quiet did not foretell a storm. Above all, Hutier's presence was a warning. The great General who had captured Riga and whose methods were original, masterful, swift and fierce, was unfit to be put as a mere feint along a span of front vital to the safety of France. So Gough wrote to G.H.Q., and at Catelet he said:

"Von Hutier, who carried out the attack at Riga, has been put in opposite to the FIFTH BRITISH ARMY front. In the case of the Riga attack, he relied completely on surprise. All the troops for the attack were kept seventy miles away from the front and collected in the forward area within five to eight days before the attack. The actual battle was preceded by a six hours' bombardment only, no trench mortar or gun emplacements being previously prepared."

What if Hutier endeavoured to repeat on the Oise, and between Mayot and the river Omignon, his rapid surprise tactics? What if he succeeded? Suppose his onslaught to be a complete surprise.

Gough considered this peril, and spoke of it in the conference at Catelet, hoping that "Corps Commanders would go very carefully into all details of measures that would have to be taken," notably, "how long it would take to move up reserve divisions." He added:—

"As the enemy are sure to shell all back roads with their long-range guns, divisions must realize that they will have to pass through heavy shelling on their way up; and reconnaissances should be made with a view to preparing tracks suitable for artillery when avoiding cross roads. All officers from Platoon Commanders upwards to be taken to the spot in order to decide on the positions of their headquarters, and to know them beforehand."

Again, the foe might use a new gas, so gas drill and thorough inspection of box respirators, etc., were obligatory. And it was necessary to test from day to day the foe's intentions. With this object in view, Gough outlined a scheme for destroying German roads within a thousand or fifteen hundred yards of the German front line. Every Corps Commander was to choose certain roads and then destroy them along a span of about a hundred yards. This was to be done deliberately, but not with such unanimous accord as would attract suspicion to its main object. When a Corps Commander had gapped the roads which he had chosen, he was to get them photographed every day by his airmen. If the roads were repaired at once, and with anxious care and speed, it might well show that Ludendorff intended to attack.

§ II

We pass on to moral influences, prime things in war. First-rate pre-battle appeals, at once inspiriting and prophetic, are uncommon. Here are two examples. The first one is a manifesto addressed by Gough to Divisional Commanders and Brigadiers:—

"HEADQUARTERS,
FIFTH ARMY,
January 25, 1918.

"DEAR ——, I enclose a paper I wrote by way of showing our young officers and our men what the general situation now is, and the necessity for a renewal of our Courage and our Resolution. I particularly wanted to point out also how every one can help by maintaining a cheerful spirit all round.

"But, on second thoughts, I realize that these appeals from Army Commanders do not carry so much weight, because they lack the essential personal touch. Young officers and men will listen to and believe their seniors whom they personally know or see, but a mere name carries very little weight.

"The only officers, therefore, who can make these appeals with success are the Divisional Commanders and Brigadiers, who can speak to all their troops, and whom the latter personally know and trust. I therefore decided merely to send you this paper, and I would be very obliged if you would speak to your officers and men on these lines when you get an opportunity. I am sure there is no greater service we can do at this moment for our Country than to show our troops exactly what the situation is, and what is necessary if our future is to be safeguarded.

"The spirit which should animate us all, not only out here, but at home, is that expressed by Abraham Lincoln, in the American North *v.* South War, which had then been going on for about four years:—

"'We accepted this war for one object, a worthy object, and the war will end when that object is attained. Under God, I hope it will never end until that time.'"

SECOND MANIFESTO: ISSUED BY GOUGH TO HIS ARMY,
JANUARY 25, 1918.

"Having at their disposal a large number of divisions released from the RUSSIAN front, there is a probability that the GERMANS will employ them in striking a blow at the Allies on the Western front in the hopes of gaining a decisive victory.

"They are openly stating that blood must be spilt like water, but that it will be worth it, as the coming battle will be the last battle of the war; and after that will come the longed-for German peace with all the world under their heel, including, and more particularly, our own beloved Country and People.

"A great deal of this is being said to raise the hopes and morale of their men, who are war-weary, and to stiffen their resolution, but there may well be real intention to attack behind these words.

"Should such an attack come on us, I am confident that it will find all of us and our neighbours ready and united in their resolve to defeat it; but this in itself is not enough to ensure success unless all have striven to the utmost beforehand to render success certain by concentrating all their endeavours on making our defences such that, however sudden or strong the attack may be, it will, without fail, be broken by the efficacy of our defences as well as by the gallantry of our troops. In view of the uncertainty as to when this attack may be launched, each day is of importance and should be taken full advantage of. Every trench dug, machine-gun emplaced, length of wire put out, may prove of vital importance in holding up the enemy.

"There is no doubt that this attack, if it should come, will be the climax of the German effort, and if all the necessary preparations have been made to meet it, and each officer and man welcomes it as all German counter-attacks have been welcomed in the past, then it will cause them as heavy sacrifices and as bitter a defeat as they suffered in any of their great attacks, such as the first battle of YPRES, or VERDUN, and such a blow may be given to the German Pov. r that Peace will indeed come, but the Peace which is the oni · acceptable one to the Allies, a Peace which as the result of victory will ensure our women and children security.

"This is, therefore, the great crisis of the war, but it is also one of the great crises of the world's history.

"Are Liberty, Honesty, Truth, and Courage, for which our Fathers fought and died and which they handed down to us to keep as an example to the whole world, are these great British virtues to go down in ruin before the brutality, the ruthlessness, the deceit and cunning of the German?

"I know I can with confidence voice the spirit of British soldiers when I say—NEVER.

"Our Country took up this struggle in order to maintain great and noble ideals as well as to defend the safety of our homes, of our people, and all that is most dear. We began the war with enthusiasm. It is only natural that, after three and a half years of this terrible struggle, many of us feel weary and would be glad of Peace—but only of the Peace that secures all the great ideals for which we have suffered and fought. Enthusiasm may die down, but DUTY remains. Duty and grit have carried our race through all struggles in the past.

"It is essential that we should all realize what still lies in the balance—the safety of our homes, of our women and children, our industries, our Country; the ideal of justice and liberty on the one side, and on the other, with the certain loss of all these, lie poverty and slavery to the Boche for all Europe.

"In this coming struggle we need have no doubts if we are all nerved and ready.

"Although the Boche Armies still stand firm to all outward appearance, like a dam against a flood, there has been a very great deal of disintegration going on which we do not yet see. The blows, defeats, and losses they have suffered have lowered the courage and spirit of the Boche soldier greatly, but their people behind them are still more stricken and shaken. When the dam finally will burst, one cannot say, but when it does, it will probably go with great suddenness.

"What is now required are gallant and cheerful hearts, putting our utmost energy into all work for improving our defences; and when the time comes, showing a grit, determination, and pluck which will inflict bloody losses in the Boche ranks and give their troops a shattering blow.

"We must not only keep cheerful here, but it is important that *all* officers, however junior, and all the men should try to keep the People at home equally cheerful, confident, and patient. Officers and men out here must realize one great fact in such a struggle as we are engaged in, and that is that it is not only the Armies which are fighting, but the whole people, and that as the disintegration of the German strength will almost certainly begin by the breaking of the will and discipline of the German people before it goes deep into their army, as happened in RUSSIA, so it is essential to help and support and cheer our own People at home.

"In thus addressing you, I think it is necessary to recall

to our minds our great ideals and the immense consequences in the future that victory or defeat now carries with it, and, while I wish to express my confidence in the gallantry, discipline, and firmness of the officers and men to shatter any Boche attack, I wish to remind them that our ideals and our security are not yet assured by the collapse of the Boche, and that it is important and necessary that we should all show a resolute spirit, one of confidence in the future and in ourselves, one of cheerfulness, and one of energy.

" Finally, I would call to your memory—you, the soldiers of to-day—the great deeds that have been performed in the past by the Regiments to which you belong—deeds which speak to us from the book of History, from the old church walls of ENGLAND—deeds in foreign lands against many different foes, but always the same cause, for—

Freedom for our Country.

"This trust now lies with us—the soldiers of the Regiments of to-day. Let us emulate our forefathers; and, when the time comes, let it find us ready, and so prepared that we shall place such a crown of glory on those past deeds that our sons will say: 'Well done, you soldiers of 1918: you proved yourselves men and won the great cause with a smile on your lips and a song in your hearts. The Battalion is proud of you.'"

CHAPTER IV

HAIG AND LUDENDORFF: THEIR CONTESTS IN PRE-BATTLE AFFAIRS

IN the meantime Ludendorff was training three large armies with which he hoped to win a conclusive victory; and then, swiftly, and as secretly as possible, he united them to his line troops facing Byng and Gough, while menacing other areas, both French and British.

As many German units arrived at their fighting stations just in time to begin the battle, Gough and Byng did not know till they were assailed how much force would be active against them at any point. A great offensive had been foreseen, but its distribution of power was hidden, and thus very worrying to those who waited.

Even if Haig had been able to place large reserves behind all threatened spans of his fighting front, Ludendorff's onslaught would have been more formidable than any other which German troops had undertaken. In comparison with its power and skill the first advance to the Marne would have seemed only a crude rehearsal, and the Verdun campaign only a fumbled bleeding away of vitality.

To be British is to be irrational, and Haig, in his time of greatest danger, had no choice but to be too politically British, since he had not men enough to safeguard all his known responsibilities; known, we must believe, to statesmen in London as well as to soldiers in France. That very sinister handicap that weighed against the Expeditionary Force in 1914, was pressing again ominously both on and behind our troops in France. To be short of reserves is tantamount to having a foe in the rear, placed there by statesmen, who alone, with sanction from Parliament and the people, can supply the nation's armed forces with enough power.

Haig had to guard 125 miles of vital front with fewer men than Ludendorff assembled on March 21 against fifty-four miles. "In all," Haig relates, "at least sixty-four German divisions took part in the operations on the first day of battle, a number considerably exceeding the total forces composing the entire British Army in France."

Ludendorff gives fifty-nine as the complete number of British divisions;* also he knew that they, like his own divisions, were cut down to ten battalions apiece. His knowledge of Haig's weakness was equal to Haig's knowledge of the increased German power. Between November 1, 1917, and March 21, 1918, the number of German divisions in the west had risen from 146 to 192: an increase of forty-six. Let us suppose that every division in this increase had the same strength as our *Ninth*, whose units happened to be better manned than the average strength of FIFTH ARMY battalions, 402 officers and 12,039 other ranks. This assumption means that Ludendorff reinforced his western front with 18,492 officers and 553,794 other ranks.

Allied journalists magnified hugely the number of men brought by Ludendorff to France from Italy, Rumania, Galicia, the Bukovina, and Russia. Would that this exaggeration, habitual in propaganda, had caused the Lloyd George Coalition, not to mass troops on the East Coast of England, as in Norfolk, but to supply Haig with enough combatant strength! Then the FIFTH ARMY would not have been a Jimmy Wilde who would be obliged to fight through a week against a German Carpentier!

Ludendorff assailed it with by far his greatest vigour while thrusting nearer the coast with very large, though lesser, forces. In this way he made a great concurrent battle on a continuous line which would become of decisive value to his plans if the much bigger southern attacks could crumble the St. Quentin defence and then break through at chosen places with operative force and purpose. Mere local rents and tears would be of no use to his ample strategical aims. They could be patched. Certain spans of defence must be annihilated, and swiftly, else reinforcements would arrive.

Gough knew in a few hours that enormous odds were active on his whole front against his few divisions, while Byng was hard set along only 18,000 yards of his line. This minor grapple may be called the battle of Bapaume-Arras.

Byng's front in all was 46,000 yards wide (26⅖ miles), spanning south-eastward as a whole from a point just south of Gavrelle to the south base-angle of Flesquières salient, about half a mile north of Gouzeaucourt. Byng had seventeen infantry divisions, including the Guards, ten in line,

* One division too many, fifty-eight being the total number.

seven in support, and opposed to them were twenty-four German infantry divisions, fifteen in line, nine in support. Clearly Byng was well manned for scientific defence with the most recent weapons from entrenched positions. The only perils he had to fear were the hazards of war, those chance blows, often like blows from a malign fate, that come as frequently in battles as they do in boxing.

A mystery has been thrown over the number of divisions in our THIRD ARMY, with the result that writers have been misled into errors. In several articles I have given the number as nineteen, two divisions too many, while Sir F. Maurice, in his vivid epitome of "The Last Four Months," gives only fifteen, two divisions less than the correct number. The G.H.Q. dispatch would have prevented much misunderstanding if it had announced in 1918 the full strength of Byng's Army, just as it published the full strength of Gough's.

As for the reinforcements along the THIRD ARMY'S front, map evidence shows that the *Forty-second* DIVISION was in support east of Adinfer on the evening of March 23. Next day, in the evening, the *Sixty-second* was in support west of Arras, and by nightfall of the fifth day the *Twelfth* was active hard by Fricourt. On March 26 the *Fourth* Australians entered the battle, together with a New Zealand division; and the bulk of Gough's northern Corps, under Congreve, reinforced Byng's right from Bray-sur-Somme almost into Albert. There on the seventh day the *Third* Australians did good work.

North of Byng—north from Gavrelle, that is to say—was the BRITISH FIRST ARMY, under Sir H. S. Horne, whose southern wing, on March 28, played a very useful part in Byng's battle.

Gough's front was nearly 75,000 yards wide (42 miles), about a third part of the whole line occupied by Haig's full combatant strength. It ran south-east from its union with Byng's right down to La Fère, then south-west to Barisis, a village south of the Oise, between the forests of Coucy and St. Gobain. On this wide front across the heart of France there were only fourteen infantry divisions and three divisions of cavalry. The cavalry in total man-power equalled another foot division. They were in support, and their positions when the battle began are shown in my large map of the approximate Order of Battle, British and German.

Eleven infantry divisions were in line, and after the first day, Gough had three infantry divisions in reserve. On

March 21 two of them were not present because G.H.Q. waited to see whether Gough would need them. The *Twentieth*, after a journey of seven hours, arrived in the evening of March 21, while the *Fiftieth* did not reach the battlefield till about the early morning of March 22. It nearly arrived too late, through no fault of the FIFTH ARMY'S.

Gough, then, began the battle with eleven infantry divisions in line, one foot division in support, and some of his cavalry. Immense forces were massed against him, forty-three infantry divisions, apart from others not yet in close reserve. And other great odds also were to ravage Gough's front—odds in guns, and machine guns, and trench mortars. To quote from the official dispatch :—

"The forces at the disposal of the FIFTH ARMY were inadequate to meet and hold an attack in such strength as that actually delivered by the enemy on its front."

Connect this fact with another—that Allenby had under his command in Palestine about 150,000 white troops, though "in India Sir Charles Monro's expansion of the Indian Army was well developed, and a steady stream of Indian troops for service in Palestine was assured. We should, therefore, have incurred no risk whatever in the East by sending Haig at the beginning of 1918 a considerable reinforcement of white troops from Palestine. Not a man, however, was moved from the East to reinforce Haig until after the German blow had fallen and our armies had suffered the most serious reverse which befell us during the whole course of the war."*

Why was Byng well manned while Gough and his officers and troops had to encounter the greatest ordeal against odds to be found in the long history of British battles? Some persons believe that favouritism was shown by G.H.Q. towards Byng. They forget that Byng's front was nearer to the coast and thus had less room for a retreat. North of Byng the battle front ran closer and closer to the coast till no land at all could be lost without instant peril to the seaports; and G.H.Q.'s rifle strength being at a low ebb, it was thought better to impose risks on Gough and his troops than to run them along the northern and northernmost areas. Besides, German preparations for attack astride Menin Road were known to be far advanced, and exceptionally dry weather had hardened northern land which, as a rule, was unfit for an attack during March and April. Perhaps a little ground might be lost without much danger in the Lys Valley, though some French

* "The Last Four Months," Major-General Sir F. Maurice, p. 19.

northern collieries were in this army area, as well as important tactical features by which our lateral communications were covered. Only south-east of Arras, and notably along Gough's front, was there room for a retreat; and even here an operative break-through—a wide enough span of defence overwhelmed, annihilated—would be a disaster not to be weighed and measured till its travelling mischief were known completely.

For instance, what would happen if the main German effort were along the area between Sensée River and Péronne, towards the sea? "If this blow succeeded," says Ludendorff, "the strategic result might indeed be enormous, as we should separate the bulk of the English Army from the French and crowd it up with its back to the sea."

Or, again, what if the foe achieved his annihilating break-through south-west of St. Quentin? Here a well-fed advance—south-west, north-west, and also due west—would have no definite limit, other than that enforced by fatigue and by such reinforcements as the French could hurry feverishly into action—two infantry divisions without guns by the evening of March 23, and a division of cavalry. No matter where a swift and complete break-through came, the British position south and north of it would be most precariously damnable, since Ludendorff had men enough for huge turning movements; and as for an advance due west after such a catastrophe, it would have found on Gough's front just enough reserves to be brushed aside. No wonder G.H.Q. was in the position of a gambler who, before risking his last gold, tries to brace himself by forming as hopeful an estimate as he may venture to form about his chances! Consider this passage:—

"The extent of our front made it impossible with the forces under my command to have adequate reserves *at all points threatened. It was therefore necessary to ensure the safety of certain sectors which were vital, and to accept risks at others* . . . ." *

Would our northern and northernmost areas be safe if Gough's defence, which would bear all the risks, were annihilated at one of several sectors? No. Their safety would be cancelled, as Ludendorff knew. So the safety of Haig's whole line was no firmer than the strength of its weaker places, *plus* good generalship at these places. The Tay Bridge was quite safe in places, but a gale wrecked 3000 feet of it, and the rest became futile.

* "Haig's Dispatches," vol. ii., p. 216.

G.H.Q. continues:—

"In the southern sector alone it was possible, under extreme pressure, to give ground to some extent without serious consequences. . . ."

As G.H.Q. was placing all the risks on Gough's forty-two miles of front, a third portion of the whole British line, why speak of his giving ground to some extent under *extreme* pressure, and without serious consequences? To what extent, for instance? Is it not with extreme pressure that attacking Generals hope, and hope logically, to annihilate defence along known weak sectors?

G.H.Q. goes on:—

". . . . give ground to some extent without serious consequences, over the area devastated by the enemy in his retreat in the spring of 1917. The troops holding this latter part of the front could fall back to meet their reinforcements, which need not necessarily be pushed forward so far or so rapidly as elsewhere. . . ."

I cannot feign to be convinced by this reasoning, which is completely antagonistic to the precision employed by architects and engineers when safety has to be considered side by side with the force of thrusts. G.H.Q. has no guess what weight of well-trained attack will be hurled against "troops holding this latter part of the front"; nor whether this weight, at present unknown, will include squadrons of tanks. Yet G.H.Q. assumes that these troops will fall back to meet their reinforcements; but will they do this all right, no matter what or how much the pressure may be? It is dangerous reasoning to suppose that reinforcements "need not necessarily be pushed forward so far or so rapidly as elsewhere. . . ." A wise old axiom says that reinforcements should be kept near the troops in the line of battle.

By reasoning in a way that invites criticism, G.H.Q. draws public attention away from the main point of all: namely, that political authority has left Haig at a low ebb in numbers and in training also. As war means casualties among the young and strong, risks imposed by insufficient means of defence cannot be stated in words too stark.

The dispatch continues:—

"Moreover, the southern sector could be reinforced with French troops more easily than any other portion of the British line."

Here is another assumption in support of which no pre-battle hopes or arguments could be at all useful, because

Ludendorff had only to glance at his map in order to see that French reserves were near to Gough's right and centre, and were thus a danger to the German plans. From this fact Ludendorff would pass on to the inevitable question: "By what means can French reserves be kept away from the St. Quentin front, at least for several days?"

Haig ends by saying that he "considered it unsound to maintain a considerable force of British reserves south of the River Somme, while it was yet unknown where and to what extent the enemy would commit his reserves."

Here, in brief, is the policy of compromise chosen in France because greatly impoverished rifle strength made gambling with peril a game to be played boldly.

Little by little this policy will be judged by events, always final as military critics. At present only two or three points need a little attention. Norfolk was well manned with troops and not at all nervous. A friend of mine was amazed by their number in the Norwich neighbourhood. How does this alertness look side by side with gambling compromise in France? Such compromise in great war, as history proves, is likely to be useful only when its employers are confronted by generals of no importance. Position maps, and maps of a whole front can be read as correctly by capable foes as by a G.H.Q. which is obliged to put incalculable risks into plans of defence; and were Ludendorff and his Staff at all likely to misread the north-westerly run of Haig's line towards the Channel Ports?

If Ludendorff is not the greatest soldier produced by Prussian training and ambition, he can be placed on a level with the greater Moltke, for the work done under the direction of his G.H.Q.—done in Russia, Rumania, Italy, and France—is hard to parallel in magnitude and in consequences. At present his qualities as a General are undervalued by Allied critics, as Napoleon's were undervalued when Napier was assailed because he dared to see them correctly; but even those who sneer at Ludendorff as "a mere tactician, a very poor strategist," cannot fail to look on it as a tragic misfortune that G.H.Q. should have been compelled to take risks which could not be hidden, since Ludendorff knew the total number of Haig's divisions, and the weakness of Gough's wide front; knew, too, how Haig's reserves would be affected by sectors near and nearer to the coast; and, again, what Pétain and the French feared most of all from a great offensive.

With these particulars before his mind, Ludendorff could go ahead with the development of his plans by means of cunning in wide-stretching preparations.

CHAPTER V

OTHER PRE-BATTLE CONTESTS OF MIND, WITH SOME OF THEIR EFFECTS

§ 1

A LARGE map in this book gives the whole battlefield as it was on the morning of March 21, 1918, before the foe let loose his thoroughly trained storm divisions. It enables us to see (*a*) what Ludendorff learnt from the front line's westerly course northward from La Fère to the north of Lens, and (*b*) why he massed troops at some places more formidably than at others. The map shows the twenty-one line divisions under Gough and Byng, and their reserves, but not their reinforcements. Facing our line troops are the huge German armies with their reserves, but not with their reinforcements.*

* Otto von Below commanded the SEVENTEENTH GERMAN ARMY, and Von der Marwitz the SECOND. They employed in all the same number of troops, 28 divisions each, including three which they used turn by turn. From first to last Hutier and Gayl employed 35 divisions, including the *Third* Bavarians and *Fourteenth* Reserve, which belonged to Boehn's Army when the battle began, and threatened Gough's extreme right along the Barisis sector. As regards reinforcements, I offer for criticism what at present I believe to be approximately accurate. In Otto von Below's reinforcements there were seven divisions, probably: *Twelfth, Thirty-eighth, Forty-first,* and *Hundred and Eighty-seventh; Fifth Bavarian* RESERVE, *Twenty-first* RESERVE, and *Twenty-third* RESERVE. Marwitz's reinforcements, seven divisions: *Twenty-sixth, Fifty-fourth, Third Naval, Guards Ers.* DIVISION, and three from Below's first-line troops, *Fourth, Hundred and Eleventh,* and *Hundred and Nineteenth.* Hutier's reinforcements, ten divisions: *Twenty-third, Fourteenth, Fifty-first, Fifty-second, Two Hundred and Forty-third, Tenth* RESERVE, *Eightieth* RESERVE, *Seventh* RESERVE, *First* Guards, and *Two Hundred and Forty-second* DIVISION. Next, as regards German mounted troops, I can gain no information as to their total strength; so I cannot say whether they were more or less numerous than the men in Gough's three cavalry divisions. On the first day it was reported to the *Eighteenth* that a post in Vert Chasseur Valley had been captured by German cavalry; divisional mounted troops, probably, who had been sent forward to keep in touch with the advance. There is no other record of German cavalry in the *Eighteenth's* experiences. Ludendorff made no attempt to use cavalry in huge turning movements, as Budenny has employed them frequently in Russia's counter-blows against Poland.

March 21st 1918

Approximate Order of Battle

Byng's Army, 26¼ miles of front; ten divisions in line and seven in support. Opposed by twenty-four divisions.
Gough's Army, 42 miles of front, eleven divisions in line, and ro. in support. They rifle-power of four infantry divisions. Opposed by forty-three divisions

MARCH 21ST, 1918: APPROXIMATE ORDER OF BATTLE, BRITISH AND GERMAN

There was no need to continue the front line beyond Lens, because any reader can see that less and less land could be given up with safety near and nearer the Channel Ports. To Ludendorff this matter must have been as trite as A B C; so he had to find out how he could use most aptly for the development of his central aim those weaknesses in Haig's strategical position which were revealed plainly in the map, and those other weaknesses which he had learnt by other means—namely, the total number of Haig's divisions, their reduction to ten battalions apiece, and the very inadequate rifle strength on Gough's over-stretched front.

What, then, was his central aim? Allied writers have summed it up variously. About six months before Ludendorff's book was published, I formed my own reading from his order of battle, the disposition and the movements of his armies, when considered in their relation to the north-westerly run of a British battle line which from the first lacked equipoise, since its defence was too weakly armed in some places and well armed in others. No revealing evidence could have been better than this, and I find that the reading I got from it is confirmed by Ludendorff's comments on his central aim. What he desired most of all, as less costly in losses and thus most inspiring to his troops and to the German civil population, whose temper had enfeebled greatly, was a continuous advance to go on for several months, unfolding its scenes and acts at different places as the plot of a well-written tragedy is developed to a climax by a master playwright. If long breaks divided the acts of his tragedy, each act would be a new beginning; his troops would have time to lose their confidence, their ardour; German civilians would grow suspicious, and perhaps seditious, in the midst of their hunger; defence and attack would renew their strength together, and American troops would pour into France. This last consideration must have put nightmare into Ludendorff's days, since he was going to gamble with the whole of his reserves, while we and the French could look forward trustfully to the arrival of vast American armies.

Ludendorff confirms this reading. During his preparations he thought much of the U.S.A., and ran the risk of interfering with the German Naval authorities by pressing for more and more submarines in order that the U-boat campaign might be directed simultaneously against two objectives—seaborne commerce and transports with American troops. The sea being so spacious and wireless telegraphy so accurate and swift in the transmission of warnings, he considered that hunting for American transports ought not to be done by submarines withdrawn from relentless attacks on mercantile marines. Some Reichstag deputies wrote to him and said that more submarines could and should be built. Consider a few brief quotations from Ludendorff's book:

"The question was: What will be the rate of supply of submarines in the spring of 1918? Will the submarines, even if they have been unable to damage England decisively, have so far reduced tonnage that the new American troops cannot come over in a short time, and will they be able to strike at American transports while engaged in destroying hostile tonnage generally?" (vol. ii. p. 538) . . . "The American danger rendered it desirable to strike in the West as early as possible; the state of training of the Army for attack enabled us to contemplate doing so about the middle of March. At that season, too, horses would find some grazing which, in view of the shortage of forage, was a necessary consideration" (vol. ii., p. 544). . . . "About New Year, 1918, the opinion of the [German] Navy was as optimistic as ever. I had, however, become more sceptical, and felt obliged to count on the new American formations beginning to arrive in the spring of 1918. In what numbers they would appear could not be foreseen; but it might be taken as certain that they would not balance the loss of Russia; further, the relative strengths would be more in our favour in the spring than in the late summer and autumn, unless indeed we had by then gained a great victory" (vol. ii., p. 539).

A great victory! Ludendorff regarded this as essential not only because of the power that could come from more than a hundred millions of U.S.A. subjects, but also because his own partners, including social, political, and industrial Germany, were anxieties that increased from week to week. Statesmen were slack in releasing reservists from munition factories, but not slack in asking for specialist workmen from the armies; were lethargic towards skrimshangers, wastrels, slackers, and other dregs; and seeds from the Russian revolution were being imported by many a soldier from the Eastern front, while German civilians here and there got similar seeds from gnawing privation. Turkey was the one partner that seemed to be in earnest, but she was weak and out of gear, and in need of more German battalions than Ludendorff could supply. Bulgaria had occupied all the land that she desired to keep, so her interest in the war had waned, and Ludendorff knew that she could be trusted only so long as he and his troops won victories. He adds, too, that in Bulgaria there had always been many persons in sympathy with the Entente. But as he was in need of men he could not be tactful all along the line towards Bulgarian sentiment. Indeed, he ruffled it by moving Bulgarian troops to Macedonia in order to release a few German formations (vol. ii., p. 544).

As for Austria-Hungary, after the loss of 1,800,000 men in prisoners alone, their Army was so worn, and so short of recruits, that it needed a new German backbone, which could not be supplied. Luckily, too, Ludendorff was obliged to withdraw from the Italian front the six German divisions—a fact to be remembered with gratitude when we recall to memory the way in which through several days the Austrian Piave offensive hung in the balance. Then it collapsed, and a great wave of disappointment, most helpful to ourselves, shook Germany from end to end, and put out the last flickers of battle temper in that hotchpot of discordant ethnology called the Austro-Hungarian Empire.

"In 1917," says Ludendorff, "we had already received an intimation from the Imperial and Royal Government that the [Austrian] Army could go on fighting for only a limited period; we might anticipate something similar in 1918. We had to take into consideration that Austria-Hungary might actually arrive at the end of her military power. It was clear that her political power would not last one hour longer. Nothing but the Army held the Dual Monarchy together."*

This forecast was proved by events to be true, though we are all unwilling to admit how very untrustworthy from the first was the ramshackle main partner in Germany's habitual aggression. To admit this plain fact side by side with the defeat of Russia, Serbia, Rumania, and the invasion of Italy, is to put a most distressing bitterness into truth. And Germany's other partners had recently been defeated in great war; another hateful thing, since it throws into higher relief the resistance shown by sixty-eight millions of Germans—a resistance supported by Allied blundering, pre-war and wartime. Still, Ludendorff was shackled by all these matters while he and his Staff were developing their plans for 1918. Hence they must be stated here, and frankly weighed and measured. Again, German railway trucks were scarce, so they had to be used mainly for military needs, and not to bring some ease to a hunger-stricken Empire.

* Ludendorff, vol. ii., pp. 539-40.

Never before in armed warfare had such a tremendous gamble been undertaken as a last resort. Ludendorff's only hope was to strike with his complete power while Haig's rifle strength was weak and before the new American armies could be brought across 3000 miles of sea. If he could annihilate chosen portions of the FIFTH ARMY, while crumbling all the rest of its lean vigour, the American troops would arrive too late; and if he failed to do this his advance must be at least great enough at selected places to set in motion other offensives, else long breaks between the battles would nullify, to a great extent, the effect of each battle on the Allied resistance, while the German armies would have to renew themselves from returned wounded, and not from fresh drafts. On February 13, 1918, in an audience at Homburg with the Kaiser and the Chancellor, Ludendorff said :—

"The battle in the West is the greatest military task that has ever been imposed upon an army, and one which England and France have been trying for two years to compass Yesterday I spoke with the Commander of the SEVENTH ARMY ; he told me that the more he thought about this task, the more impressed he was with its magnitude. This is how all responsible men in the West think.* I believe, too, that I, who have to furnish the Field-Marshal with the foundation on which he bases his request for His Majesty's decision, am more than any one impressed by the immensity of the undertaking. It cannot be successfully accomplished unless the authorities who conduct the war are relieved of all intolerable shackles, unless the very last man is employed in the decisive conflict, and is animated, not only by love for his Emperor and his native land, but by confidence in the strength of the military leadership and the greatness of our country These spiritual forces must not be underestimated, they are the foundation of the greatest deeds. They must be strengthened by the energy of our action in the East. The Army in the West is waiting for the opportunity to act. We must not

---

* This anxiety is a thing to be noted, because British propaganda was constantly referring to German boastfulness, forgetting the horrible tragedies that came from Allied over-confidence. Even Sir F. Maurice tells his readers that " the Germans were more confident and boastful than they had been any time since their first victories of August, 1914." In my studies I have found considerably less boastfulness among the Germans than among the Entente Powers. The amazing trench systems introduced by the foe denote consummate caution, not over-confidence ; and what German General would have chosen to leave a vital front in need of men, as our Government did ? The over-confidence produced by the first battle of the Marne weakened the Western Allies through three years.

imagine that this offensive will be like those in Galicia or Italy; *it will be an immense struggle that will begin at one point, continue at another, and take a long time; it is difficult, but it will be victorious."* *

But what if this continuous campaign were baffled in the first battle by Gough and his officers and men, aided by Byng's troops? On Gough's front of forty-two miles there was all the room that vast odds required—or seemed to require —for annihilating blows. But a General has always to consider the possibility of failure :—

"The crown of success would be an operation in which we could bring to bear the whole of our superiority. It was our great object. If we did not succeed at the first attack, we should have to do so at the next; by then, indeed, the situation would have become less favourable—how much less favourable would depend upon the rate of arrival and value of the Americans, and on the losses which both sides sustained. Everything was based on the assumption that we should do well in this respect, and although, of course, I expected our own Army to be weakened, I hoped it would be less so than that of the enemy. By continuing to attack we should still retain the initiative. More I could not aim at. I reported to the Emperor that the Army was assembled and well prepared to undertake the biggest task in its history." †

Haig speaks of the foe's excellent offensive training, and Ludendorff hoped that this thorough training would keep in battle its main characteristics—disciplined and combined initiative among all ranks, extended order in all onsets; swiftness in settling down on defence as soon as attack came upon a steady, strong resistance fitted to cause great losses; and readiness on behalf of the ruck divisions to follow their storm troops fearlessly, aided by the profusion of guns, machine guns and mortars which had been collected close behind the foremost lines, and now and then placed even in advance of the jumping-off ground. Each division had a company of medium trench mortars. These weapons were made as mobile as possible, and were allotted as required to battalions, together with flame projectors, which could be used at the shortest ranges against cellars, dugouts, and blockhouses. Ludendorff says of his artillery:—

"For the advance of the infantry in offensive battle concentrated preparation by massed artillery was of the utmost

* Ludendorff, vol. ii., pp. 587-88.
† *Ibid.*, vol. ii., pp. 588-89.

importance. It was necessary to bring up twenty to thirty batteries, about a hundred guns, to each kilometer (eleven hundred yards) of front to be attacked. No man had ever credited such figures before; still less had anyone ever thought of the quantities of ammunition hurled on the foe. These were indeed massed effects! And yet the battle area was so vast that even these quantities of steel did not destroy all life; the infantry always found far too much to do. These masses of guns and ammunition had to be got up close to the foremost lines; only thus could they engage targets far behind the foe's front line without having to change position as the battle progressed. At the same time, they had to be covered from view, both from the front and from the air. . . ." *

As about a hundred guns were brought to bear on each 1100 yards of Gough's front (*i.e.* a little less than 75,000 yards), we may multiply one hundred by sixty-eight, and say that the artillery power against the FIFTH ARMY was about 6800, since Ludendorff employs the words "*about* a hundred guns to each kilometre of front to be attacked." Trench mortars, light, medium and heavy, are not to be included in this "massed artillery." The Austrian gunners and guns proved of little value, happily, for the ammunition brought with them soon ran out; then they were withdrawn.

What enormous contests of mind and will went on both between the German leaders and those who caused hitches, and also between the German munition factories and our own! The more we think of them, the more strenuously we should ask for a full answer to the question why Haig, in his hour of greatest peril, was left unsupplied with enough rifle strength, though he was handicapped by a battle front whose weak points and strong points were revealed to all students by correct maps.

§ II

After studying these maps, the foe's Higher Command came to the decision that it must increase the soldierly and watchful solicitude felt by Haig for the Channel Ports and for the French northern coalfields. By increasing this solicitude, by turning it into anxiety, apprehension, or misgiving, reinforcements could be withheld from Gough's front, in order that they might guard districts very much nearer to the coast, where

* Ludendorff, vol. ii., p. 577.

no British retreat ought ever to be allowed by Haig. And to Ludendorff and his colleagues it must have been equally essential to increase the natural and soldierly nervousness felt by Pétain and the French for Reims, Champagne, Verdun, and Paris. By no other means could they sterilize through several days the French reserves, while titanic assaults were being delivered on the known weakness of Gough's army.

Little by little, and with great care, the foe began to display an acceleration of work from Flanders to the Oise, also on both sides of Reims, and elsewhere. Concerning the need of feints in his preparations, Ludendorff writes :—

"It took weeks, and required considerable foresight and the most detailed preliminary work to concentrate the troops in a confined area, bring up by rail the tremendous quantities of ammunition and other stores of all sorts, carry out the work allotted to the troops themselves, such as preparing battery positions, screening roads, constructing anti-aircraft shelters, and preparing gear for crossing the trenches, and finally to deploy for battle. Of course all this increased the danger of discovery. It was therefore necessary to commence dummy works on the fronts remote from the attack, which, as a matter of fact, served as the basis of attack later on. But the bulk of the available labour troops were required on the front of attack at an early date. The preparations on other fronts could not be extensive, but there was some chance of misleading the enemy, and the deception was to be completed by skilfully conducted defensive measures . . .*

"Feints and preparations for further attack were made between Ypres and Lens, by the group of Crown Prince Rupprecht; by the German Crown Prince's group, particularly between Reims and the Argonne; by the new-formed group of von Gallwitz, on the old battlefields of Verdun; and by the group of Duke Albrecht, between Saarburg in Lorraine and Ste. Marie-aux-Mines, and also in the Sundgau." †

Nothing half-hearted entered into the foe's widespread feinting and preparation, which appealed as strongly to the French G.H.Q. as it did to Haig's, stimulating anxiety in both. British and French airmen reported on the increased activity behind the German front, and by the close of February, 1918, it was clear that although hostile preparations advanced

* Vol. ii., p. 589. An attack must prepare also for self-defence, since it may be assailed by surprise.
† Vol. ii., p. 592.

elsewhere, they were particularly noticeable opposite Gough's front and Byng's, on both sides of Reims, and between Lens and Ypres.

Pétain became very wide awake in his great solicitude for Reims and the Champagne, and even for Belfort; so he kept his reserves far back so as to be able to use them there without delay should a need for them arise. Hence he could not send reinforcements to Gough, apart from perhaps two or three inferior divisions, till he was sure that Ludendorff's onsets against Gough and Byng were not great feints to prepare a way for a smashing main blow against French lines. To quote from G.H.Q.'s dispatch :—

"For some time prior to the 21st March, it was known that the enemy had been making extensive preparations for an offensive on the Reims front, and that these preparations were already far advanced. . . . The bombardment on the battle front [March 21] had been accompanied by great artillery activity on both sides of Reims. It could not be determined with certainty that this was a feint until the attack upon the British had been in progress for some days. The enemy might have employed a portion of his reserves in this sector, and the knowledge of this possibility necessarily influenced the distribution and utilization of the French reserves." *

This, no doubt, is convincing; but we are told also by G.H.Q., in the official dispatch, that Pétain and Haig made a pre-battle bargain for the main reinforcement of Gough's front with French reserves, should a great crisis develop there; and in battles against great odds the first phases of the attack are the most likely to produce disaster, together with a very urgent need for reinforcements ample enough in number and with their full equipments, military and administrative. Plainly, then, the pre-battle agreement between Haig and Pétain was a hostage given to fortune. It had no real value as a preparation for prompt and adequate support.

On the French side of Gough's front, then, Ludendorff made real his pre-battle aim—an aim, also, with two purposes. He had made it impossible for Pétain to send enough help to Gough as soon as a grave crisis came; and, if with his huge superiority of strength he could overpower Gough's right, he had another front ready for a forward thrust, while Hutier's left and Gayl's four divisions, aided by Boehn's troops in the

* Haig, vol. ii., p. 218.

OTHER PRE-BATTLE CONTESTS OF MIND

St. Gobain sector, pressed on rapidly to Chauny and towards Pontoise and Noyon.*

Hutier's southern boundary crossed the Oise at Pontoise, while his northern boundary was through the Omignon valley to and along the great westward-going highway

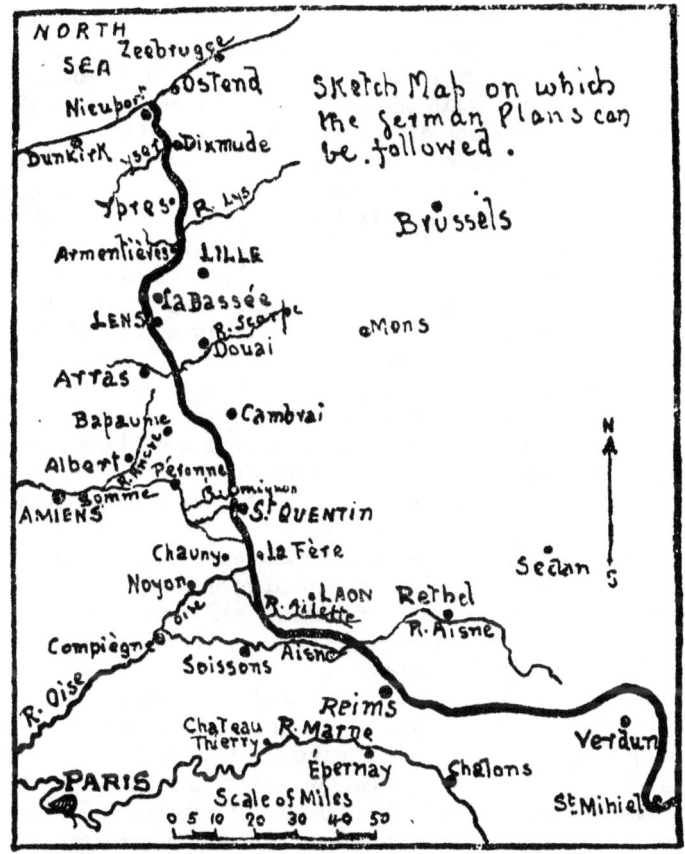

running from Vermand to Amiens. So it is easy to see what Hutier and Boehn wanted to do with their joint and immense forces, twenty-five divisions, and ten divisions used as reserves during the battle. There is, or there seems to be, reason to say that Gayl's troops were a semi-detached part of Boehn's army, whose *Third* Bavarians and *Fourteenth Reserve*

* See the map showing the German armies in position.

threatened Gough's liaison with the French north and south of Barisis.

The map considered in its relation to Hutier's power and Gayl's four divisions suggested to me that Ludendorff desired to extend his attack across the Oise below Chauny and in the Pontoise sector. Several military experts ran counter to this belief; but now I find that Ludendorff* anticipated the broadening of his attack both towards the Oise's farther bank and also towards Arras. How could he have failed to anticipate the possibility of these movements? On the first and second days, if he swallowed up Gough's very thin right wing, the way would be opened for a very swift drive to the Oise south of Chauny, and also south-east of Noyon; and if Hutier and Gayl reached this river while their troops were ardent and fresh and powerful, they could try to cross the Oise south of Chauny, and also to pass down the Oise valley to Compiègne, aided by Boehn's right wing, under Wichura, from the neighbourhood of Manicamp.† If these aims could be made real, Ludendorff would be able to manœuvre into action all his prepared strength on both sides of Reims; and a moment might arrive when Gallwitz might be let slip either against Verdun itself, or in a flanking movement to compel a withdrawal from the fortress. Gallwitz was in immediate command both of his own THIRD ARMY and also of Army Detachment "C."

Of course, nothing less than a complete break-through—a deep span of front annihilated—could open such a great and swift flanking movement south-west and across the Oise. Still, vast odds are collected and let loose to produce annihilation along chosen sectors.

Briefly, the south-westerly evil within the possible range of Hutier and his colleagues was not limited to the act of driving a wedge between Gough and the French. A thorough break-through south-west of St. Quentin would have extended this scope incalculably. Two other offensives might have been fired off by it, and the more trouble Hutier and Gayl caused among the French south-west and south-east of Noyon, then of Compiègne, the easier it would be for the remaining troops to forge ahead—on one side to Montdidier and

* Vol. ii., p. 552.

† During the retreat General Butler, of our 3rd Corps, must have thought of these dangers, for on March 26, at about four a.m., he warned his cavalry through Brigadier Portal that strong patrols were to be sent to Sempigny and Pontoise, and that the foe was to be prevented from crossing the Oise.

Pierrepont on the other, moving shoulder to shoulder with
Marwitz's left wing, towards Amiens and Abbeville.

Hutier chose leading officers whom he had tested, placing
Lüttwitz with the 3rd Corps on his northern boundary, and
Oetinger south of him with the 9th Corps. Then in southerly
succession came Webern's 17th Corps and Conta with the 4th
Corps. On March 21, between the Omignon River and our
lines south of Vendeuil, about thirteen miles, Hutier had
eleven divisions in line, and eight, if not nine, in near support,
as well as four reserve divisions on a complete war footing,
but not in my map. These were the *Twenty-third, First
Guards,* and *Seventh* and *Tenth* RESERVE DIVISIONS. Add to
this vast power Gayl's flanking force of four divisions in the
La Fère sector, and Boehn's two divisions along the St.
Gobain lines. What was the British force that opposed these
German legions till the first French division came up at
breathless pace, without guns and without administrative
equipments? It was a force of seven infantry divisions,
aided by two of cavalry, and hardly one of the units had a
full complement of men. Yet its bravery was maligned,
pitilessly slandered, while Ministers were received with loud
applause at public meetings. Are nations easier to hoodwink
than children?

The minor grapple also, under Marwitz, had very great
strength, as my map shows. On March 21, seventeen of its
divisions were massed against Gough along a front of about
twelve miles, while the remaining four faced Byng's right
around the exterior arc of Flesquières salient,* inside of which
G.H.Q. and Byng had placed no fewer than three divisions.
I wish I knew why. The salient was far too narrow and too
shallow for a big fight; it could be ransacked with a criss-
cross of German gunfire; and its defences, both natural and
military, were very formidable, what with a captured portion
of Hindenburg's line and Highland Ridge, not to speak of
other defences. It is impossible, then, to omit asking whether
this British salient, as formidable as it was narrow and shallow,
really needed a crowded protection from three divisions?
Later we shall see how puzzling this question is both tactically
and strategically.†

The German troops massed north and south of the salient

---

* We shall see that these four of Marwitz's divisions had a very strong reactionary effect against Gough's left, so they should be included in the power
that pressed against our FIFTH ARMY.

† See pp. 139, 140, 141, 157, 158, 159, 161, 165, 166, 167.

prove that the foe intended to follow the routine which is necessary when a small and strong salient—a sort of pocket Hercules—might easily beat a surprise front attack.* His aim was to leave the body of the salient alone while he tried to cut his way through near the base-angles, in order to break in behind its rear defence line and to capture its garrison. This routine was particularly dangerous because the salient's north base-angle at Demicourt was over four miles to the north-*west* of the south base-angle near Gouzeaucourt, as you will find by drawing an upright line from Demicourt southward. Now, as the distance north-west between Gouzeaucourt and Demicourt was and is only about 6½ miles, this point is very important. No wonder Ludendorff collected twelve divisions—six in line, six in support—on a front of about five miles north-west of the salient, partly to strike towards Bapaume, partly to take the salient's rear as their objective, while north of them another cluster of divisions extended to the River Scarpe! No wonder, too, that Ludendorff in his book shows how eager he was to cut off Byng's three divisions within the salient!

We shall see that this pressure on Byng caused complications among these divisions, and that soon these complications had varied unwelcome effects on Gough's left. Luckily, Ludendorff seems to have underestimated the number of divisions in Byng's forces; he knew they were more numerous than Gough's; but if he had known their full number he could not have expected all that he did expect from Otto von Below. It is Haig, in fact, not Ludendorff, who shows the very grave trouble caused by Below's chance blows, aided by Marwitz's extreme right.

G.H.Q., according to the official dispatch, believed the principal German attack would fall between Sensée river and the neighbourhood of Bapaume-Cambrai road; and although this great northern thrust had no more force than that of Marwitz south of Flesquières salient, yet Byng's seventeen divisions on a narrow front were not excessive owing to the great peril which would have come if the attack on the second day had captured Bapaume, with its road running southwest to Albert, and had crossed the Arras-Bapaume road westward.

Draw an upright line south of Bapaume and you will find that it passes about four miles west of—*i.e.* behind—Péronne. This fact alone shows how greatly Ludendorff was aided in

* Ludendorff's book confirms this map evidence.

his designs by the north-westerly run of the battle line coastward, and also how necessary it was to have a big defensive power to protect Bapaume and the northern rear of Flesquières salient. When I tell you that the boundary uniting Gough and Byng passed just south of Manancourt and Combles, you will see at once how bad it would have been for Gough's left if Bapaume had fallen on the second day. Would it have fallen then if Byng's front had been as thinly manned as Gough's?* I believe the answer Yes will come to any frank mind that studies Haig's dispatch side by side with a large map; so there's no reason for us to agree with the many critics who have questioned the need of giving the THIRD ARMY so many troops per mile in excess of Gough's. The thing to be deplored is that the same number per mile could not possibly be given to the FIFTH ARMY. Then Gough on the first day would have had thirty divisions with which to oppose the German forty-three.

Study that semi-salient extending from the Sensée river to Bapaume-Cambrai road; note how it thrusts the German power on a broadish front menacingly towards Bapaume and Ervillers. Then turn to page 154 and note how pressure from this north-westerly bastion affected the salient on March 21.

Moreover, in the northern battle the inner wings of Below's and Marwitz's equal armies were ordered not only to cut off the salient from behind, they were ordered also to take the strain off each other in turn, and to push through between Croisilles and Péronne; but the realization of these aims needed such a sequent unity of success that its miscarriage would be brought about by any among the bigger hazards of war. Ludendorff, for instance, could not foresee the incomparable defence of the Scottish *Ninth*, Gough's left flank division, which, again and again, was of great help to troops both north and south of it—a fact long concealed and even now but little known.

Though the northern battle was very great, and though from the fourth day it became through two days and nights the more dangerous, because the THIRD ARMY'S centre was broken, presumably by a chance blow, and its southern corps had ominous gaps between its divisions, as Haig has described,

---

* Remember, the average length of front held by each THIRD ARMY division in line was about 4700 yards, while each FIFTH ARMY division in line had to guard some 6750 yards of front. Remember, too, that Byng's reserves were much larger than Gough's.

yet we must never forget that the most perilous blows were struck through four days by Gayl and Hutier in the south, and that Hutier and his colleagues had always more powerful forces than either Marwitz or Below. And it is also necessary to remember that Hutier's reinforcements, ten divisions, equalled the number of French divisions hurried into the battle between the third and eighth days, gunless, and sorely handicapped by other hindrances to success.

Two other facts also must be stated. First, Ludendorff himself chose the EIGHTEENTH GERMAN ARMY, Hutier's, as the one through which he could express his own influence in the most convenient way (vol. ii., pp. 591–92) :

"For the decisive operation the SEVENTEENTH * and SECOND † ARMIES were to remain under the orders of the Army group of Crown Prince Rupprecht. The EIGHTEENTH ARMY joined that of the German Crown Prince. Remembering the November campaign in Poland in 1914, I meant to exercise a far-reaching influence on the course of the battle. That was difficult if it was being conducted by one group only; every intervention was only too apt to become mere interference from above. It was desirable to make the fullest possible use of the resources of the group of the German Crown Prince, and this was facilitated by the organization adopted. . . . "

This group extended to Reims and between Reims and the Argonne. Hutier, then, was to be the first of this group, apart from Boehn's right wing, to take part in the great offensive; and the best artillery officer in the whole German Army, Colonel Bruchmüller, was given to Hutier's H.Q. as Artillery General. Ludendorff speaks of him ardently, and says that Hutier's artillery was completely imbued with Bruchmüller's spirit.

But we must not suppose that Ludendorff was overconfident. Indeed, he was ill at ease. He did not know how much strength had been added to those portions of the British front which for a longish time had aided him in his plans by being weak. "The weakest part," Ludendorff says in his book, " was on both sides of St. Quentin. . . . Whether this weakness would continue I could not know." ‡ As a consequence, doubts were troublesome. To cause and increase

---

* Below's Army.   † Marwitz's.
‡ Vol. ii., p. 590. He adds : " Tactics had to be considered before purely strategical objects, which it is futile to pursue unless tactical success is possible. A strategical plan which ignores the tactical factor is foredoomed to failure. Of this the Entente's attacks during the first three years of the war afford numerous examples."

OTHER PRE-BATTLE CONTESTS OF MIND 55

uncertainty has remained the essence of war, despite airplane vigilance and other new sorts of spying.

One doubt very harassing to Ludendorff was the weather.

"At noon on the 20th," he writes, "G.H.Q. had to face the great decision whether the attack was to commence on the 21st or be put off. Every delay must have increased the difficulties of troops, crowded together close up to the enemy. Already the tension was very hard to bear. The psychological pressure of the mass was urging them forward.

"And yet our artillery relied on gas for its effect, and this was dependent on the direction and strength of the wind. I had to rely on the forecast submitted to me at 11 a.m. by my meteorologist, Lieutenant Dr. Schmaus. Up till the morning of the 20th, strength and direction were by no means very favourable; indeed, it seemed almost necessary to put off the attack. This would have been very hard to do. So I was very anxious to see what sort of report I should get. It was not strikingly favourable, but it did indicate that the attack was possible. At 12 noon the ARMY GROUPS were told that the programme would be carried out. Now it could no longer be stopped. Everything must run its course. G.H.Q., higher commanders, and troops had all done their duty. The rest was in the hands of fate . . ."*

* "My War Memories, 1914-1918," by General Ludendorff, vol. ii., pp. 596-7-8. Hutchinson & Co.

CHAPTER VI

WAS THE FOG A HINDRANCE TO THE FIFTH ARMY'S DEFENCE?

ONE thing in the second battle of the Somme is described by both sides as a very great hindrance; and thus we must try to see, as warily as we can, whether it hampered one side more than the other. On March 21 and 22, from dawn till midday, or a little later, a thick white fog enveloped the battlefield, hiding the fight from airmen, blotting out signals from scouts on land, and masking the fire of artillery, rifles, and machine guns. German artillerymen knew not which parts of our line held up the German attack; they could continue the routine of their creeping barrage, but they could not aid when their infantry was in difficulties, nor could they "spot" those of our guns which had been removed to alternative positions as in Maxse's ground. More important still, the foe's artillery could not bring concentrated fire to bear on those places where our machine gunners were lodged underground in masked pits fifteen feet deep. Surely this fact was a great help to our defence. Ludendorff speaks admiringly of our hidden machine guns, and notes the losses that they produced. Yet no good thing has yet been written by a British soldier about the thick fog which hid rents in our battle front on the mornings of two terrible days, March 21 and 22. From Haig himself down to the youngest subaltern who wrote letters home, runs a firm conviction that all the military drawbacks caused by fog were active against Gough and Byng. It is easy to understand why one-sided views are set astir by great perils, but history is like an auditor, it must be free from bias in order that its profit and loss accounts may be correct.

If Ludendorff and his Generals could have assailed through a fog with large squadrons of tanks, as Foch and Haig did on that most famous day, August 8, 1918, I could easily share the British belief that fog allies itself with the attacking side; but a huge infantry onslaught, dependent on combined action along nearly forty miles of continuous front, apart from Byng's, has

WAS THE FOG A HINDRANCE?

to be looked at differently in its many various relations to fog. Both sides were afraid of killing their own men with shells and machine-gun fire; neither could see how the battle was going, and German storm troops could not be seen by the masses behind them. No doubt the foe was aided by fog over no-man's-land and into our forward zone; but a sufficient number of smoke shells might have been almost equally effective for this purpose, and at any moment, in answer to signals, a smoke cloud could have been put where it was wanted. Hidden by a fog from smoke shells, Austrian troops got across the Piave, which may be regarded as a more troublesome barrier than no-man's-land and a forward zone ravaged by a creeping barrage, behind which the foe advances.

It is said that the foe could keep his direction in the fog by following three things: his own barrage, our communication trenches, and the belts of wire guarding our support lines. Yes, with difficulty; but, on the other hand, could the advance get up speed, could it go forward with that momentum which lifts men into the fury of attack and hides from them the extent of their losses? Did our own men, when they moved over familiar ground to their battle stations, find that the fog did not delay them? They were greatly inconvenienced, as we shall see. To move across cratered country in a fog must have been a blind, chilling business; and when, after delayed and long effort, Hutier and Marwitz got beyond the range of their barrage, their difficulties in the fog must have become greater, for no mass of men could see fifty yards to right or left or ahead. Officers must have been perplexed; cohesion in the assault must have been more or less haphazard; and no Boche could have been sure that the advance was general enough to be undangerous to his own battalion.

A war correspondent of the *Vossische Zeitung* said of the first day's fight that the widest stretch of country was won southwest of St. Quentin, "*although during the morning hours a thick mist, which only the midday sun cleared away, disturbed our operations. Curtains of mist gathered so thickly that men serving the field artillery, advancing behind the infantry, could hardly see their horses. Nevertheless there was no pause. Batteries had to take their new objectives under fire without direct and precise observation, and the infantry always in the fog, and unaided by methodical artillery preparation, had laboriously to win positions and sectors. Yet the movement continued and trench after trench was taken.*"
True: but the first day's results were so disappointing to

Ludendorff that the official bulletin ran as follows: "Between Cambrai and La Fère we have penetrated into portions of the English positions." No more than that!

Later George Wegener, of the *Cologne Gazette*, complained: "Through the mornings of three days, for the most part in thick fog, positions had usually to be taken by hand-to-hand encounters." This means that flanking and enveloping movements were harassed and confused by dense white mist; and those three days made up the first and most important phase of the battle. Moving heavy artillery through a fog over cratered and entrenched land must have been attended by many hitches and delays: and the distribution of food and ammunition to such hordes of advancing men must have been baffled also by foggy weather along such a wide front.

For in considering this military problem we must remember that width of battle-front is exceedingly important in its bearing on an attack through fog. Along a comparatively narrow frontage rapid and combined movement through a fog, aided by a thorough creeping barrage, would be far and away less difficult, and the fog itself might well be invaluable to the assailants, as it was in 1916 to Nivelle's famous counter-attack at Verdun. Ludendorff's front being very wide, swift and sure co-ordination, in accord with pre-arranged plans, was essential everywhere; it belonged to the essence of his huge aims. What he feared most of all was a ragged and disjointed advance—the very thing likely to be caused by fog on a spacious and extending front.

He declares in his book that fog impeded and retarded German movement and prevented the superior training of his troops from reaping its full advantages. This superior training is a fact; it is referred to by Haig as well as by other British officers. "The majority of the German divisions," Haig relates, "had spent many weeks and even months in concentrated training for offensive operations, and had reached a high pitch of technical excellence in the attack." If this excellence had been aided by the fog—not locally here and there, but in large aspects and results—surely the German onset with a huge superiority of numbers would have travelled much farther than it actually did reach on the first day. Ludendorff ends his brief reference to the fog by saying: "This was the predominant opinion about it, but a few thought it an advantage."

The main point of all is the one of co-ordinated speed and momentum, of swift, incessant, and increasing impetus. The

German leaders had formed two decisions: first, that their assault must be made on a very wide front because small salient-making was local and futile; next, that a great many divisions were necessary to crumble the western front, and then to break through at chosen places, and that the initial slaughter would be very grave. So they prepared the German people for huge losses. Nothing less than gambling hugely in casualties could have a chance of solving the western problem—how to break through, how to annihilate chosen portions of a deep defence which has been crumbled all along the line.

If a misty dawn had been followed by a bright, clear, windless day, the attack would have had what the soldiers call ideal weather, and the full weight of its tremendous power could have been hurled with gathering speed against our slender human lines, aided by smoke clouds placed where they were necessary. Thank God, no such thing was possible in a fog, which turned the assault into a series of local operations, all blindfolded and very difficult. And the foe was prepared to pay in blood the far higher initial toll that clear weather would have imposed upon the fury of rapid movements, his purpose being to overwhelm by numbers and to advance far on the first and second days. What early gain of the first day was pushed on rapidly and with increasing force? None: not even Essigny, Maissemy, and Ronssoy. Let us, then, be thankful that fog, though a hindrance to us in many matters, was, in the main, a boon to our defence, delaying and confusing the attack and giving our commanders time to form ripe decisions and to fall back with power. After the first two days, for example, Maxse lost no guns, though he felt in full measure the batteries and batterings of Hutier's legions.

The foregoing arguments were written long before Ludendorff's book appeared; they run counter to opinions hitherto published by British students and British officers. Fog has been deplored as a friend to the German assault. Why should any one assume that a great many divisions can attack in a fog without being jumbled up together and delayed?

General Gough writes on these matters:—

"The next point in your letter is the fog. A very difficult and thorny point! My opinion is that at first, say, for a couple of hours, fog was a great disadvantage to the defence. Had it not been present, many of our machine-guns, very skillfully hidden, would have taken a terrible toll. It is possible—but, considering the immense superiority of the German numbers, hardly probable—that this toll might have repulsed the attack. But as soon as the foe had broken through the first lines of resistance and was pushing on, he must have found that command, co-operation, and communication became inceasingly difficult. Then—so I think—it is quite true that fog was a very serious hindrance to the Hun. How could he go ahead for a decision—a big decision, and a rapid one?

"In war, where all is uncertain, and where so many influences are unceasingly at work, it is foolish to be dogmatic; but my summing up is this. If the day had been clear and the attack had got through the first line of defence, losing hugely more than it lost in the fog, the German skill in the movement of masses of men would have had opportunities to exploit rapidly the first gains. Ludendorff's object was not a limited one; it was unlimited and supported by enormous pushing power backed by vast reserves; and in all unlimited war aims, swiftness in execution is necessary throughout an attack. Can we be certain that the Germans would have been stopped by their first losses on a clear day? Their numbers and their training make it impossible for us to say Yes to this question. On the whole, then, it may be said that the fog favoured our FIFTH ARMY."

PART II

THE BATTLE IN ITS MAIN ASPECTS

CHAPTER I

GERMAN SHELLS AND BRITISH REDOUBTS: THE FIRST DAY OF
OSKAR VON HUTIER'S ATTACK

§ I

HUTIER was disturbed twice during his final arrangements. In the evening of March 19, no fewer than three thousand gas drums were fired from projectors into St. Quentin, with a wind towards Germany behind them; they caused much confusion. A whole regimental staff was put out of action, as we learnt afterwards from German prisoners.

Next evening, at ten o'clock, after our guns had poured in a great many shells, two companies of Warwickshire troops—Shakespeare for ever!—raided the German trenches beyond Fayet, partly to get a few prisoners, and partly to learn how much the foe's ordinary line troops had been reinforced. Fifteen Germans were captured, and three German regiments, nine battalions, were found on a span of front formerly held by one regiment, or three battalions. More valuable still was the news that in five or six hours Ludendorff would open his attack. This warning was made known at once to all Headquarters, British and French.*

When the noise of our Warwickshire raid had rumbled itself away, a wonderful quietness came, a deepening hush, with eery loneliness. Then a thick ground mist began to rise, damp and clasping; it gathered like teased cotton wool around sentries and outposts. The peace of nature before the strife of men has been often unforgettable, as it is in the hours preceding Wellington's battle on the Douro; but the night before the second Somme battle, with its uncanny stillness and its fog, has a poetry all its own, with underlying melancholy, as if a conscience in war listens while old Death

---

* Ludendorff says, I believe with truth, that on March 18 or 19 two Germans deserted from a trench mortar company and gave information to us of the impending attack.

silently prepares a shroud for the brave men who are going to be slain.

An officer of the *Sixty-first* writes :—

"The night was extraordinarily quiet. . . . I turned in early, about 11 p.m., after telling my signallers to call me at 4 a.m. if nothing happened earlier. I slept well; and at 4 a.m. on the 21st not a sound was to be heard. The line reported all quiet. I went upstairs out of the dugout. A dense ground mist and a light north-west wind. I went back again to bed, and at 4.40 I was wakened by a terrific bombardment. . . ."

Sir Hubert Gough, in his headquarters at Nesle, was awakened also by the same noise. Information was sought by telephone, and a few orders were given. Afterwards nothing more could be done till infantry fighting began. So the General went back to bed and slept, for there would be time for only short half-hours of sleep after the bombardment had passed into its creeping barrage, and it was important to keep as fresh and cool as possible.

Earthquake voices grew louder and louder as twenty or thirty batteries along each kilometre of German front poured shells by the thousand into our defences, particularly between the Rivers Scarpe and Oise, while high-velocity guns aimed at railways and roads far behind. Many communications were cut, many guns were knocked out; and let us try to make real to ourselves the fact that the twenty-one divisions in line on the fronts of our FIFTH and THIRD ARMIES had each either two or three battalions under shell-fire in the forward zone.

As for the business of manning our battle zone, which began a few minutes after the bombardment started,* men groped through fog to their stations with shells screaming and bursting all around. A curt oath, followed by a hoarse cry through clenched teeth, came here and there from a wounded man; or some one fell with a peculiar, double-sounding thud, a rifle here, a body there, and no movement afterwards. Earth and stones and volcanic smoke fumes spouted into the

---

* For some time this movement had been heralded by the "Prepare for Attack" order. This was a piece of Staff work confined to the FIFTH ARMY preparations, and it kept the whole defence alert, like the outposts constantly manned in all zones of defence. Quex writes of March 21, 1918: "Had not the 'Prepare for Attack' warning come in, I should have been in pyjamas, and might possibly have lain in bed for two or three minutes, listening quietly and comfortably while estimating the extent and intensity of the barrage. But this occasion was different, and I was up and about a couple of minutes after waking. Opening my door, I encountered the not unpleasant smell of lacrymatory gas. . . ."—*Blackwood's Magazine*, October, 1918, p. 429.

GERMAN SHELLS AND BRITISH REDOUBTS

fog as big new craters were scooped by explosions in and between many thousands of old ones.

One garrison, there is reason to believe, did not reach its battle station. It set out for Contescourt, but did not arrive there, according to a battery commander whose guns were in this sector. And at Contescourt the Germans got into our battle zone, and made their way by twos and threes down woody swamps of the Somme valley. Who knows how many of our men were either killed or wounded before breakfast by shell-fire?

If either Nelson or Wellington could have been present, he would have been appalled by the unimaginable hellishness invented since his day by science in slaughter; but mankind being a creature of custom, routine, convention, all in war is right except the unfamiliar.

The *Thirtieth*, west of St. Quentin, at the usual hour, sent out a couple of patrols, each a platoon strong. One was a patrol from the Second Wiltshires. Out it went into the gathering white mist and disappeared: it was never seen again. The other patrol had men from the Sixteenth Manchesters; and at 4.40 a.m., when German shells began to seek for the lives of men, it was in no-man's-land, and so cut off. Then our counter-bombardment started, and the patrol found itself between two fires. But it took its chance nonchalantly —or shall we say cigarettefully?—dodging from crater to crater; and after seven o'clock it made its way back into our forward zone, where it fought all day long; and then, with half of its men lost, it withdrew into and through the battle zone. Was it all that remained of the Sixteenth Manchesters? From eight battalions in the front zone of Maxse's Corps, less than fifty men returned. All had fought to the very last.

The bombardment fell on many wide spans of front, striking broadly east and north-east of Reims, and also here and there between the Scarpe and Lens. Our positions from south of the La Bassée Canal to the River Lys were profusely shelled with gas, and battery areas between Messines and the Ypres-Comines Canal were actively engaged. Dunkirk was bombarded from the sea; and Ludendorff in his first bulletin made astute reference to the firing duel in Belgian Flanders, on both sides of Reims, in the Champagne, along the Lorraine front also, and at Verdun. "Our artillery," he said, "continued its destruction of enemy infantry positions and batteries before Verdun."

These were diversions to detain the Franco-British

reserves. South of the Scarpe as far as La Fère, the shelling, carefully disciplined, was in deadly earnest. Byng's Army grew taut and keen throughout its ten line divisions: and Gough's Army, which started with about 66,000 infantry in first line, and about 16,500 in reserve, was ready. Owing to the fog, our airmen could not go out to attack all enemy batteries in action and troops on the move.*

While the artillery work continued, many German divisions trudged from anti-aircraft shelters to their places in the storming line, or from villages in the rear to their support stations. Now and then a British shell tore gaps in the marching ranks. Secret night marches to the battlefield must have tired a big percentage of men in each battalion. Divisions chosen to begin the battle were disposed variously for attack, but the formation most often used was this: two regiments in the front line (six battalions) and a regiment (three battalions) in divisional reserve. A regiment was echeloned in depth, having, as a rule, two battalions in first line. It was reinforced in numbers more or less strong with elements from the following units: companies of storm-troops, companies of pioneers, companies of flame-throwers, and mine-throwers, and cyclists; also one and a half extra machine-gun companies. A brigade's reserve seems to have had an independent detachment of two cyclist companies and an assault company. Half an hour after the attack began, and at arranged times through about three hours, a division's artillery—twelve field batteries and six heavy batteries—were to be moved forward.

During five hours of intensive bombardment every unit in these German forces moved in the white fog, learning from officers how the shelling advanced through its seven stages or periods. Every fixed target was known to the German gunners; its position had been accurately mapped and its range correctly measured; the errors of each German gun had been noted and tabulated, and allowed for when firing, like errors of the day caused by wind and atmospheric density. In this way it was possible to determine, by means of simple tables for any gun at any time, how much should be added to, or subtracted from, the normal elevation of any target. Of course, maps had to be faultless, and among the necessary

* But since March 10, two hours before dawn every day, airplane patrols of the FIFTH ARMY had reconnoitred the German front system as far back as a general line, about three miles east of our outposts. Flares were employed, but it was impossible to see German movements along roads.

GERMAN SHELLS AND BRITISH REDOUBTS

preliminaries was the determination trigonometrical and topographical of all battery zero points on the ground. The most watchful care had to be shown in marking targets on maps, as determined by sound-ranging, flash-spotting and aerial photography. What infinite patience! Ludendorff says that this new artillery procedure set gunners by the ears, particularly the senior gunners, but that " it fulfilled all expectations." He exaggerates, for a good many of our guns had been moved to alternative positions not yet discovered by the enemy.

At first, for two hours, the German gunners searched for our guns; then for thirty minutes, going through three periods, one half of the bombardment fired gas and high explosive shells into our infantry positions, while the other half went on with its attack on our guns and mortars. Afterwards, through a hundred and forty-five minutes, special parts of our infantry defences were ransacked by every German gun that did not belong to the counter-battery groups; and hundreds of mortars, heavy, medium, and light, took part in a crescendo of studied fire ; light mortars beginning to bark thirty minutes before a creeping barrage started to travel from our outposts up the forward zone to our line of redoubts at the far end and farther west.

We must linger over this routine because it was the most important factor in the foe's opening assault. Ludendorff thought of it with great anxiety during his preparations, and his chosen storm troops practised with a barrage of live shells, in order that they might learn to keep close behind a creeping protection which exploded violently. They were trained to advance in a thin wave constantly renewed from behind. In all the German training loose formations, with infantry group tactics carefully worked out, were compulsory. Ludendorff said : " We must not copy the Allied mass tactics, which offer advantages only in the case of untrained troops." As it was quite impossible for him to foresee what form the fighting would take when his infantry emerged from the protecting barrage, anxiety caused him to be present at various exercises and to converse with many regimental officers. He discovered that it was not at all easy for his troops to adopt the open formation which he held up to them as essential. Right up to the middle of March every moment of time available for training was urgently needed for attack rehearsals, in which every infantry group was expected to act with swift initiative.

The barrage caused the greatest worry :—

"It was evident that the closer the infantry could keep to the barrage, the less time the English would have to leave their dugouts, and the more chance there was of surprising them in their dugouts. Consequently the barrage must not advance faster than the infantry could follow. This pace had to be fixed beforehand, for, in spite of hard thinking and experiments, it had been impossible to discover any means of controlling the barrage. The nature and state of the ground had also to be considered, as regards their effect on the infantry's advance and the consequent pace of the barrage. Stronger lines required a more prolonged bombardment, and the barrage had to dwell on them longer. So it came about that an advance of one kilometre (eleven hundred yards) required as much as an hour. It was always a great misfortune if the barrage got ahead; the attack was then held up only too easily. It could not be brought back again without great loss of time, and the infantry suffered losses which it was the duty of all commanders to avoid." *

In these time matters, happily, fog was a great help to our defence, impeding the attack when it passed over trench systems and over ground profusely cratered with shell-holes, while the routine barrage thundered onward. As the range increased shorter range guns dropped out, so the barrage grew thinner and thinner, till at last, beyond extreme range, it ceased, leaving the fog-bound attack unprotected. Some artillery was moved up as rapidly as possible to support a further advance, but hitch after hitch was inevitable, happily, in such a fog and across ground which in peace manœuvres, aided by broad daylight, would have been indescribably difficult.

A regular scheme for bringing up a large force of artillery and even larger masses of ammunition had been prepared, but Ludendorff says that often too many guns were pushed up compared with the ammunition that could be brought in wheeled vehicles over shell-holes and the German and British systems of trenches and wire. Vast quantities of gear were needed to bridge the defensive belts. No one could see what was happening fifty yards away; and, happily, few German divisions knew anything about the country ahead of them. They had been trained to show initiative anywhere except in a fog. Even our own men felt lost on ground that they knew perfectly. Thus, at 6.15 a.m. the commander of one battalion, the 2/Fourth Oxford and Bucks Light Infantry,

* Ludendorff, vol. ii., p. 579.

GERMAN SHELLS AND BRITISH REDOUBTS 69

had a baffled adventure. He was in the forward zone of the *Sixty-first*, holding Enghien Redoubt with a company. He had orders to leave his redoubt if a great deal of gas collected there; and gas becoming worse and worse, he went out in the fog to see whether he could move his company to Champagne trench, a better spot. Though the Colonel knew by heart every nook and corner in his neighbourhood, he lost his way before he had gone fifty yards; and it took him about fifteen minutes to find his way back. He and his men remained in the dugout, with gas blankets put down, knowing that the Germans would not attack until they believed all gas had cleared away. But an officer went up frequently to put his ear on the bombardment.

At half-past seven gas shelling ceased, and Enghien Redoubt was pounded with high explosives from four batteries. Shell after shell exploded, above all in the quarry, a space about fifty yards by sixty.

Nearly two hours later there were barrage symptoms eastward that an attack through the fog had begun to play at blind man's buff with Destiny. How soon would it reach the line of eight redoubts ending the forward zone of Maxse's Corps? Would the attacking troops have courage enough to keep close to this exploding barrier of projectiles? Every one underground in Enghien Redoubt made ready for a rush upstairs.*

The barrage passed over: and when our men came up they had to grope their way to their lonely posts.

To be unable to see more than a few yards was a great ordeal—sometimes too great—when a company of young troops in a redoubt was divided between many isolated posts, and attack came all at once from many quarters, with the hiss and ping of bullets. A brave officer, Lieutenant Bassett, fell, shot in the head. Not a German could be seen; and for several minutes the garrison groped with strained eyes into the fog, and breathed almost as swimmers do when tired and cold.

Near the quarry was a sunken road connecting Fayet on the east with Holnon on the south-west; and suddenly, close by, some fifty Boches climbed out of this road. Bullets welcomed them; and about five-and-twenty went down. The rest sought seclusion in the roadway. But Fayet had fallen, and just before ten o'clock the foe entered a part of Enghien Redoubt, capturing the sandpit.

* I have drawn a detailed map of Maxse's Corps, as well as a text-map of the *Sixty-first's* front.

At once a bombing reprisal was arranged. It went briskly, led by Captain Rowbotham, and the sandpit was our own again. Only five posts now remained in the enemy's hands; the rest of Enghien was Oxford and Bucks.

Soon after eleven o'clock the Germans tried their luck with bombs, assailing from three sides, and with a skill that looked menacing. But our men had warmed to their work; their hearts were in it, for now they were freed from the cold, clammy demon that rules over most young soldiers when the blood is iced before battle by lonely waiting and a troubled consciousness of past joys and present dangers. Set firmly in a proper fighting vein, cool, firm, and fierce, they stopped the attack, then drove it back.

Foiled, the enemy persisted, surrounding the whole ground included in Enghien Redoubt and its posts. A rear post, No. 12, only about three hundred yards from Holnon village, was in the thick of it, till a Vickers gun shot more than fifty attackers. They could be seen through the fog, these dead or wounded men, huddled into wire entanglements. No wonder a German war correspondent wrote of the blasts of death that blew around the Holnon district. Twelve hours later, when the war correspondent of the *Berlin Gazette* visited the scene, wounded men were still there in long lines, Germans on one side, our own men on the other; and near by, in the sunk road, was a terrible wreckage of guns, and horses, and dead soldiers. For both sides had fought their best, each in its own way. German platoons and companies came on as blurred targets through the fog, and hour after hour handfuls of British troops held them at bay. Self was lost in duty: *and this fact was equally active all along our firm line of redoubts.* Tommy had no time to cry: "Outnumbered again! Why? Isn't this war nearly four years old?"

Towards midday the fog began to shred upwards, uncovering Enghien. At any moment enfilade fire might commence from the rear. What was happening to the Fifth Gordons in Fresnoy Redoubt, two thousand yards northward? And to the 2/Eighth Worcesters in Ellis Redoubt, about a thousand yards due south. Germans had passed between these strongholds; but had they settled themselves in Holnon village? If so, nothing but a barrage from our eighteen-pounders could save the quarry garrison at Enghien from shots in the back.*

Some one must visit Holnon before the fog dispersed.

* See the Map on page 71.

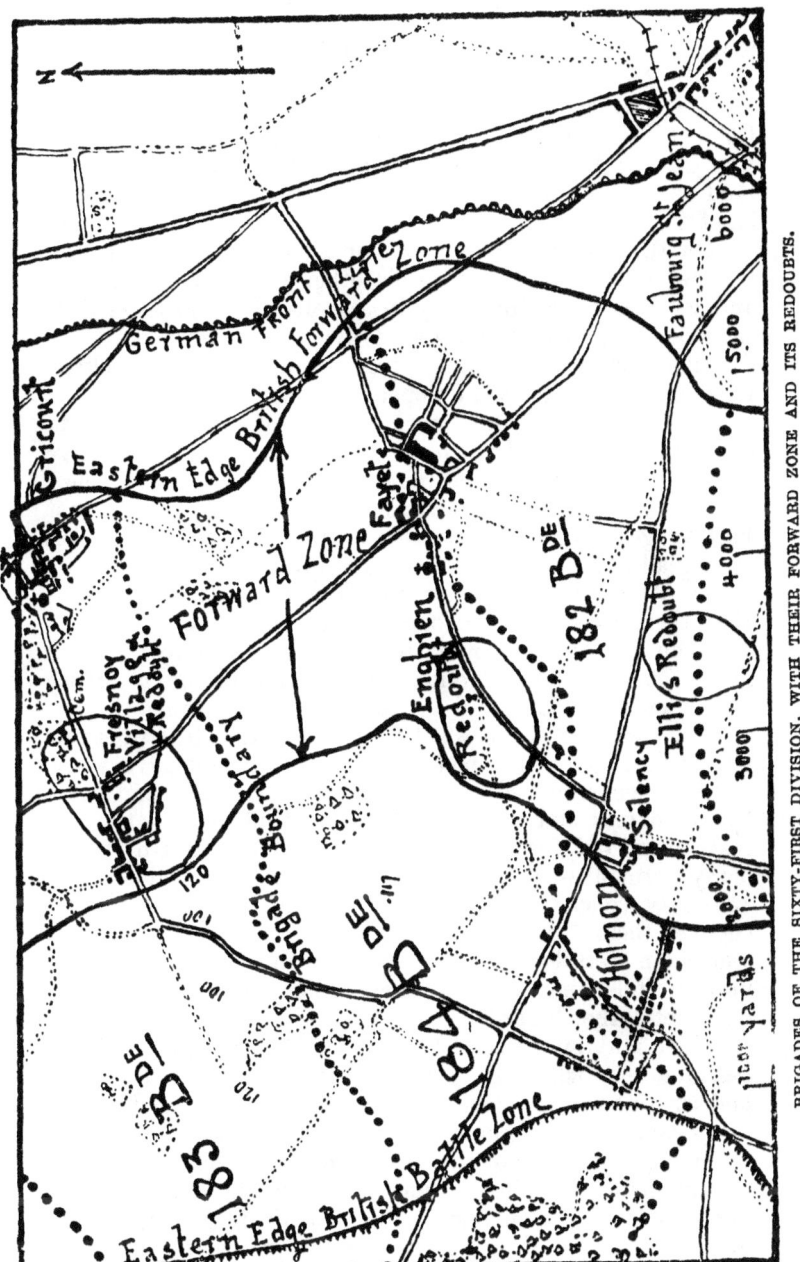

BRIGADES OF THE SIXTY-FIRST DIVISION, WITH THEIR FORWARD ZONE AND ITS REDOUBTS.

Some one—but who? The only other officer at Battalion H.Q. in Enghien, Lieutenant Cunningham, had been so busy, with a bravery all of a piece with Chinese Gordon's, that Colonel Wetherall thought it would be unfair if he did not go himself. So he chose two men and stole across the strip of land separating No. 12 post from Holnon. The village was empty.

On their way back one of our men was shot, while the Colonel was captured, with his other companion. Captors and captives made their way to a shell-hole; and there they sat peaceably until a quarter to five in the afternoon. The Germans chose many things from their prisoners' pockets, but found no use for the Colonel's watch.

Cigarettes they liked very much, yet were willing to share them with their owner; and Tommy also might have one if his Colonel did not mind. There was no unkindness, but just a compulsive communism in a shell-hole while a vast battle raged. Many bullets were flying about, and the Boches were glad to regard two prisoners as quite enough for a day's peril. At a quarter to five one German went away, while the others took their prisoners to the rear, passing between Enghien and Ellis Redoubts towards the Faubourg St. Jean at St. Quentin. All at once, about fifty yards off, a British 6-inch shell exploded, and another was heard coming.

The Germans ran forward to a shell-hole. Their prisoners ran back to an old trench, there to begin new adventures. They were surrounded by Boches, who moved here and there by companies and platoons. Yet all went well until they reached our old line between Holnon and Round Hill, where many Germans were busy on the toil named "consolidating"; and busy so close together that it was impossible to pass between them. An hour toiled through its long seconds. It seemed an eternity. At last a platoon finished its work and moved off, leaving a gap through which an escape could be made into other hazards.

Near midnight the Colonel reached Attilly, his brigade headquarters, where he got his first drink since daybreak, and where he learnt that Enghien Redoubt had made a big name under Cunningham. Not till half-past four in the afternoon did the position there become hopeless. Then Cunningham, completely surrounded with overwhelming numbers, sent a telephone message to his Brigadier, seeking final orders. On the château side his quarry was enfiladed. What was he to do?

MAXSE'S CORPS, WITH ITS FORWARD AND BATTLE ZONES, ITS BRIGADES AND BATTALIONS, AND THE GERMAN CORPS AND DIVISIONS

The Brigadier, Robert White, having praised a great defence, told Cunningham to cut his way out after destroying the telephone gear. Parts of the redoubt were strewn with German dead, and its garrison, in proportion to its number of men, had suffered as heavily. Game to the last, it began to cut its way through, and just a few machine-gunners, with Lieutenant Richards, had fortune for their friend, reaching our battle zone more than a mile westward. And Cunningham? He was captured and, I fear, wounded.

Similar great deeds, let us remember, were achieved by the other redoubts. Enghien is only an example. Thus the Second Wiltshires did their duty with thoroughness in the Epine de Dallon, like the Sixteenth Manchesters in Manchester Redoubt; and on the front of our *Thirty-sixth* DIVISION two Ulster battalions were among the bravest of the brave, the First Royal Inniskilling Fusiliers repulsing not less than twelve attacks on Fontaine-les-Clercs Redoubt, and the Royal Irish Rifles holding on till half-past five in the afternoon, when only thirty men remain unwounded. Some of these Royal Irish swam the canal at night, and did well in another fight next day. And next day the Inniskillings also went on with their grapple, after troops on their right had been withdrawn under orders. A noble defence, by which every attack was beaten off. At about three p.m. the officer in command sent back a small party, whilst the rest fought grimly to the end.

A Victoria Cross was won in Manchester Redoubt by Lieut.-Colonel Elstob, D.S.O., M.C., an officer in whom courage was true genius. The official account of his inspired bravery says: "During the preliminary bombardment he encouraged his men in the posts in the Redoubt by frequent visits, and, when repeated attacks developed, controlled the defence at the points threatened, giving personal support with revolver, rifle, and bombs. Single-handed he repulsed one bombing assault, driving back the enemy and inflicting severe casualties. Later, when ammunition was required, he made several journeys under severe fire in order to replenish the supply.

"Throughout the day Lieut.-Colonel Elstob, although twice wounded, showed the most fearless disregard of his own safety, and by his encouragement and noble example inspired his command to the fullest degree. The Manchester Redoubt was surrounded in the first wave of the enemy attack, but by means of the buried cable Lieut.-Colonel Elstob was able to assure his Brigade Commander that 'The Manchester Regiment will defend Manchester Hill to the last.' Some time after this post was overcome by vastly superior forces, and this very gallant officer was killed in the final assault, having maintained to the end the duty which he had impressed on his men—namely, 'Here we fight and here we die.' He set throughout the highest example of valour, determination, endurance, and fine soldierly bearing."

After one o'clock, when the fog cleared away, airmen on both sides became very active. Our own, as usual, were very brave; on several occasions during the battle they prevented a hostile attack from developing; and as to the German airmen, they did not go in search of air-fights, their business being to help their infantry and to collect accurate news. Haig says: "Later in the day, as visibility improved, large numbers of low-flying aeroplanes attacked our troops and batteries."

Their low-flying contact patrols, aiding the attack, found our new fronts too swiftly; and their use of signal flares came from careful practice. FIFTH ARMY officers write and talk with frank respect of the foe's airmen.

§ II

As early as midday, March 21, Hutier had found weak places in our thin line. Southwards he captured Essigny and Benay, striking Butler's left flank and threatening to turn Maxse's right; and northward, along the Omignon valley, he hit the right wing of Watts's Corps and began to turn Maxse's left, capturing Bayley's Hill and Maissemy, and moving toward Villecholles and Vermand, so as to reach the straight main road to Amiens. In the afternoon it was arranged that Watts should try to retake Maissemy after Maxse had pushed the enemy from a commanding position on the high ground between Maissemy and Holnon Wood.*

This attack began at 6.10 p.m., the 2/Fourth Royal Berkshires ascending the highlands from Hill Redoubt towards Maissemy Ridge. The heroic Colonel Dimmer, V.C., another man of inspired courage, was leader. Unfortunately he led on horseback, and was shot through the head at a very short distance from the German trenches. His groom also was killed and his horse. Mainly because of Dimmer's death, a bitter loss, the attack failed, and the Berkshires withdrew towards Marteville.

* Butler = 3rd Corps; Maxse = 18th Corps; Watts = 19th Corps.

GERMAN SHELLS AND BRITISH REDOUBTS

Let it be remembered that every infantry brigade in action was composed of two, and not four, battalions, one battalion having been lost with the forward zone, and in February, 1918, all British infantry brigades had been cut by a battalion apiece. By this diminishing economy, which came from the Army Council, nothing at all good was done. As soon as the battle began every Brigadier felt the need of a fourth battalion for counter-attack. The whole system of *roulement* was disordered, and no battalion liked to leave its own brigade and the traditions won by it during the War.* And another point of equal importance must be stated candidly. Several of Gough's divisions had been with him only a very brief time. The *Fiftieth*, for example, was allotted to the FIFTH ARMY only about a week before the battle began, and it remained far in the rear, and also under G.H.Q.'s orders, till the 21st of March. This was a great handicap, as the *Fiftieth* had no chance of learning to feel at ease in the systems of defence.

Every soldier in a defensive battle should understand not only the relative value of the lines to be held, but also, of course, what will happen if the foe captures or outflanks a dangerous portion of any main line, and there are no reserves to drive him out. When divisions are hurried into action from a long distance, they cannot learn these things; they are aliens in the defensive zones.

G.H.Q. was fond of moving divisions from one corps to another. This was keenly felt all through the war. Divisions were thrown into battle, offensive or defensive, under corps commanders who did not know them; and, of course, these divisions were unacquainted with their new chiefs, who had varying methods. And they were supported by strange artillery—another weakening influence. The Australians did so well mainly because they maintained the corps organization and knew their commander and their gunners. Much strength would have been added to the FIFTH ARMY if every one of its few divisions had been in its ranks for three or four months.

When evening came the position was more menacing. Hutier had pressed some hundreds of yards—from four to six

---

* Haig's criticism is pointed: "Apart from the reduction in fighting strength involved by this reorganization, the fighting efficiency of units was *to some extent affected*. An unfamiliar grouping of units was introduced thereby, necessitating new methods of tactical handling of the troops and the discarding of old methods to which subordinate commanders had been accustomed."

—to the west of Essigny; had advanced towards Clastres and Lizerolles; had entered the northern outskirts of Hinacourt, and was near to Ly-Fontaine; also he was aiding Gayl, whose attack south of Vendeuil had made considerable headway, capturing Fargniers, then Quessy, and pressing close upon the Crozat Canal, which Hutier desired to cross on the first day.

The deepest of these German gains was about 7500 yards, less than five miles; but, although Hutier's advance was far short of the German plans, it threatened Maxse from north and south, and imperilled Butler's very long front, bringing our southern defence to a crisis.

An exceedingly great strain had been borne, above all by the *Fourteenth* and *Eighteenth* DIVISIONS.

So much inaccurate information has been noised abroad about Essigny that the principal facts must be given here. On March 21, the Urvillers sector was held by the 41st INFANTRY BRIGADE of Sir Victor Couper's Division, the *Fourteenth*. This brigade united Butler's left to Maxse's right, and it fought under P. C. B. Skinner, D.S.O. The Eighth Battalion King's Royal Rifle Corps was in front line, the Seventh Battalion Rifle Brigade in the battle zone, and in support was the Eighth Battalion Rifle Brigade, under Lieut.-Colonel Prideaux-Brune. The foe at about noon invaded the battle zone and took Essigny, but was held up by the Eighth Rifle Brigade on a line which had been prepared before the battle. This line ran from the railway cutting about 400 yards west of Essigny station along the ridge from 500 to 600 yards west of this important village. Here the battle swayed till nightfall, the Eighth R.B. holding steadily from about noonday, and recapturing the Brigade H.Q. Of the nine battalions forming the 41st, 42nd, and 43rd BRIGADES, *Fourteenth* DIVISION, only three were left with a strength of more than a hundred each. The 41st BRIGADE suffered very heavily, two battalions—the Eighth K.R.R. and Seventh R.B.—being wiped out, apart from certain details left behind in the Transport Camp at Clastres. At eleven p.m., March 21, the Eighth R.B. was ordered to retire to a portion of the Green Line * (behind the Crozat Canal between Jussy and St. Simon); and this movement was carried out with great success, thanks chiefly to good rearguard work by Captain the Hon. A. Tennyson, killed a few hours later (March 23) when leading a brilliant counter-attack

* Green Line = the rear system of defence; so-called because of the colour used in technical maps.

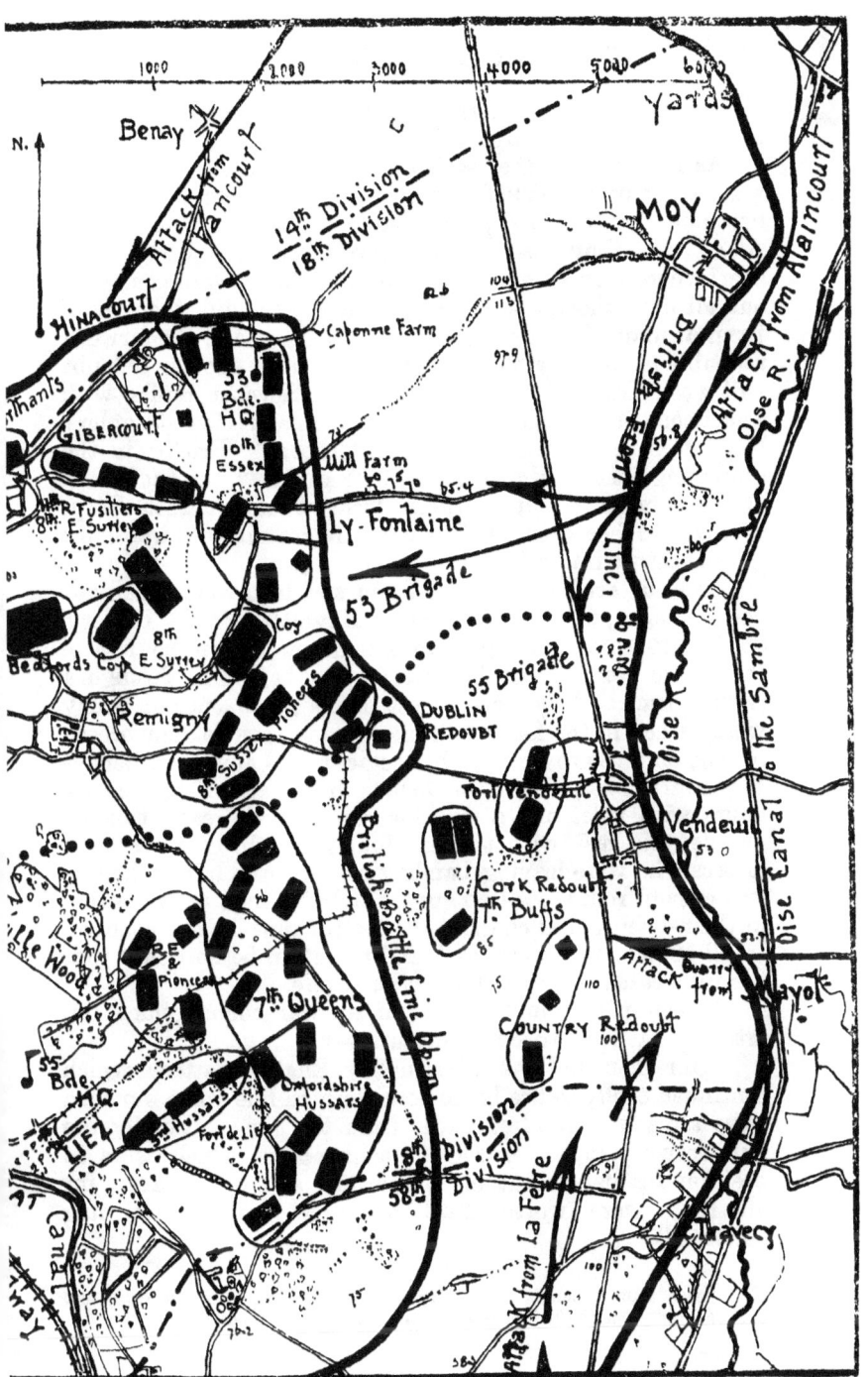

FRONT OF THE EIGHTEENTH DIVISION AT 6 P.M. OF MARCH 21.

at Flavy-le-Martel. For the rest, the foe did not enter Clastres till after 2 a.m. on March 22.

As for Lee and the *Eighteenth*, though they had a very wide front of about 9500 yards, stretching from a point just north of Travecy to a point that faced the German line at Alaincourt, they managed to keep their deep battle zone everywhere, and several strongholds in the forward zone held out all day, though four German divisions did their best. Even at midnight rifle-fire was heard from one of the forward redoubts manned by the Seventh Buffs; and another redoubt —it was "Dublin," headquarters of the Seventh Buffs—with a garrison of cooks, pioneers, sanitary men, and a few stragglers, beat off several attacks in the afternoon.* Briefly, in the grapple against the EIGHTEENTH GERMAN ARMY, the *Eighteenth* DIVISION was to our southern front what our 18th Corps was face to face with St. Quentin. It resembled a well-built groyne thrust into a high tide.

And our artillery? Its officers and men were usually as good as their guns. Thus Captain Haybittel of "C" Battery, 83rd BRIGADE, R.F.A., put up a fight by which the left of the battle zone of our 3rd Corps was kept safe through a critical time. About noon most of his guns south of Benay were rushed in the fog, yet he managed to remove their breech blocks, and also to form up his detachments along the Benay-Hinacourt road, where he held a bitter attack for several hours with rifles and a machine-gun. At the same time he guarded his rear with two machine-guns, firing at German masses who were leaving Lambay Wood. And later, when he was cut off from these two guns, Haybittel took up a position in their defence and checked the foe till nine in the evening. In all 1900 rounds were fired, and there can be no doubt that the foe's casualties must have been severe.

A Kiel paper published from its war correspondent an artillery battle-picture full of truth:—

"Our men tell me of a heavy English battery which continued coolly to fire behind our German line when our men were already a hundred yards from the guns. Finally the gun crews jumped to some machine-guns which were in position for defence at close quarters, and blazed away for all they were worth until overcome by the storming columns."

* These four divisions were Gayl's *Two Hundred and Eleventh*, and Costa's *Thirty-fourth, Thirty-seventh*, and *Hundred and Third*.

§ III

For the rest, a battle line with damaged flanks needs infinite care. Happily the body of our defence—Maxse's Corps—remained powerful all day. Its battle zone, with fifteen redoubts in it, was almost intact. There was a flaw at Contescourt and another at Roupy, but as yet neither caused much anxiety.

At Roupy and Savy, where German tanks led the attack, at first with success, Williams fought finely with the *Thirtieth*. At midnight the Seventeenth Manchesters and Second Bedfords held the whole of their battle positions, while the Second Yorks, after a hard struggle against big numbers often renewed, had lost no more than their front and support lines, retaining their keep. Two hours later our lost trenches in this sector were recaptured by the Nineteenth Battalion of the King's Liverpool Regiment, apart from a small span of ground in the front line on both sides of the St. Quentin-Roupy road.

Williams had twenty-four machine-guns well posted in his battle zone, and their teams had deep dugouts, from most of which the guns could be fired. They suffered little from casualties during the bombardment: and their turn came when the foe, after pushing patrols forward, assailed the battle zone, coming on in waves sometimes, and sometimes in small columns that bunched.

Into these large-moving targets our machine-gunners fired, one gun using in all about 12,000 rounds, and two others about 35,000. Attack after attack was shattered, and the many Germans who clustered into the quarry on the northeast of Roupy had terrible experiences, bullets ripping through them and strewing the ground with many dead and wounded. Yet the German attack did not give in. It went below ground into trenches, or sought shelter behind ridges, and rallied itself for another grapple.

If Gough had had reserves enough to replace the first day's heavy casualties, and also to drive Hutier from Maissemy, Essigny, Benay, Quessy, and Fargniers, our position would have been quite good; but, as Haig says, "the forces at the disposal of the Fifth Army were inadequate to meet and hold an attack in such strength as that actually delivered by the enemy on its front." The position being very bad after the day's losses, Gough came to a decision as painful as it was wise. He decided to withdraw his 3rd Corps—Butler's—

behind the Crozat Canal, and to move the right division of Maxse's troops behind the Somme as far as Fontaine-les-Clercs. His right would be overwhelmed if it stood still with its back close upon the canal. It must bend at once, but could it stretch with safety? Had it men enough?

At present Butler's Corps had only a cavalry division in reserve, and it had lost a great many men. Few reinforcements could be expected with absolute certainty, because there might be an attack north of the La Bassée Canal, where the enemy had made preparations, and because another offensive was prepared on the Reims front.

"It could not be determined with certainty that this was a feint until the attack upon the British had been in progress for some days. The enemy might have employed a portion of his reserves in this [Reims] sector, and the knowledge of this possibility necessarily influenced the distribution and utilization of the French reserves." *

Even if circumstances were favourable, British divisions could arrive only one by one and at intervals of two or three days. French reinforcements would come as soon as possible, but arriving hurriedly from afar they would not have their guns and transport, and at first their signal and staff organization would be sketchy or improvized. Handicapped by this want of necessary equipment, they would be face to face with Hutier's enormous pressure. How, then, could they do justice to themselves? Still they would lose no time. Our Allies never hoodwinked themselves when they employed the word "vital" in military phrases. They knew that every part of the Franco-Flemish front was vital, because, if any part of it were overwhelmed, the effect on other parts would be disastrous.

As Germany's power began to crumble away as soon as the Bulgarian front was shattered, so the Allied power in the west would have crumbled away if any part of its front had been annihilated; and French officers knew that Gough was perilously undermanned on a front forty-two miles wide spanning the heart of France.

To many Frenchmen the battle against Hutier is known as the battle of Picardy, and such in truth was its geographical importance.

No doubt the first day's results were a failure to Ludendorff and Hutier, who neither crossed the Crozat Canal on the south nor reached Vermand with their right wing;

* Haig's Dispatch.

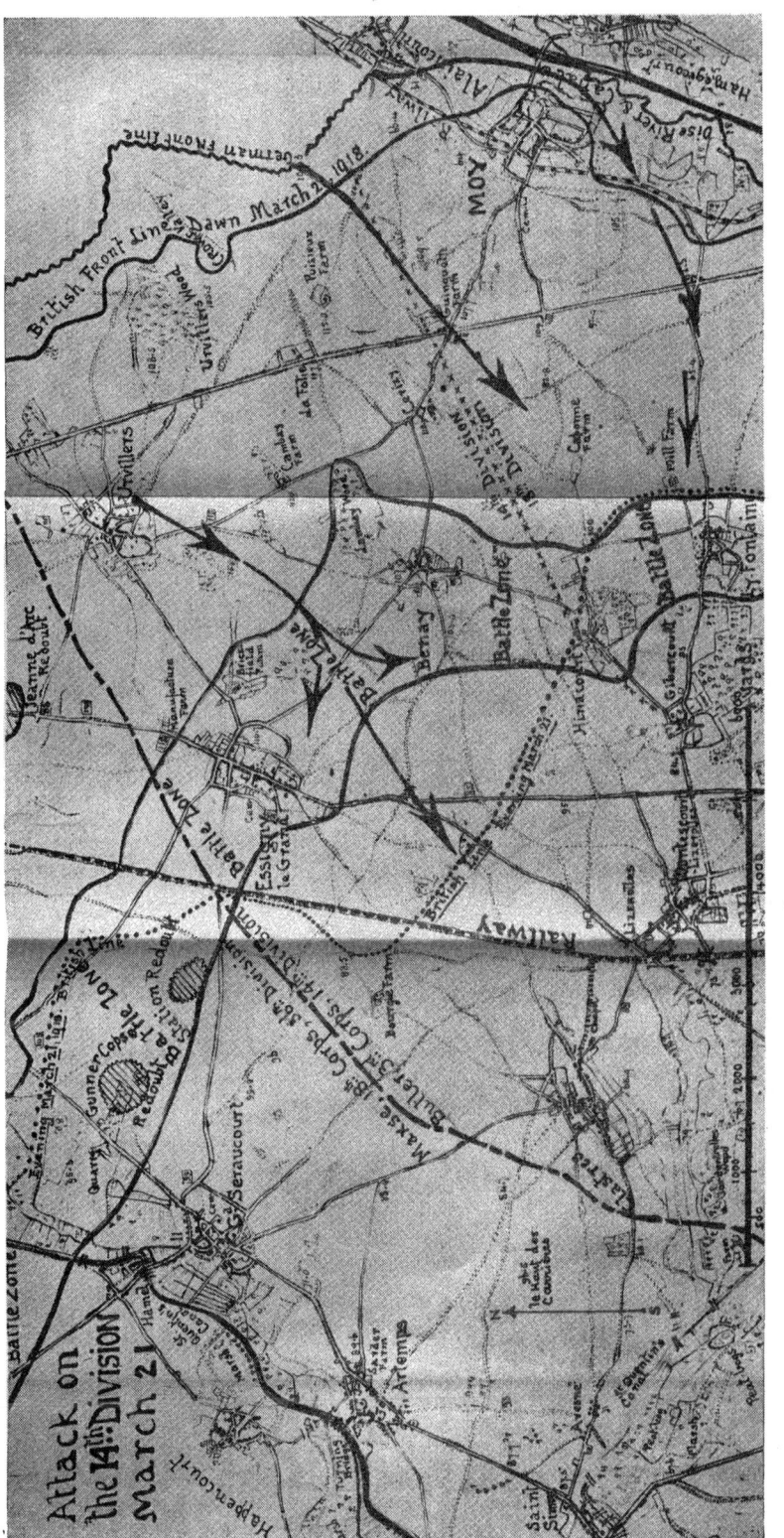

HUTIER BREAKS THROUGH THE FOURTEENTH'S BATTLE ZONE, BUT FAILS IN HIS EFFORTS TO CROSS THE CROZAT CANAL

but yet it was a tragical day to us, the attack having penetrated at those points which were most upsetting to the balance of our defence, while imposing very severe losses on our slender brigades.*

Gough was aided greatly by Butler, whose judgment was cool, clear, and firm; and Butler's divisional commanders also were undismayed by their attenuated front of 30,000 yards, a front only 16,000 yards less than that which was guarded by the whole of Byng's Army. Yet little honour has been paid to Butler's Corps.

Few persons think under the form of visual conception; so few persons *see* that when only three infantry divisions, aided by some excellent cavalry, have to hold in a great battle 30,000 yards of vital front, their responsibility through a critical day is tremendous, and even terrible. That Butler and his officers handled their brave troops well is proved by the fact that the enemy was unable to press far beyond Essigny and Benay, though these strategical villages were captured at about midday.

As for the withdrawal by night across the Crozat Canal, it went off well, and eased an excessive strain after grave casualties.

* Ludendorff believes that losses in a retreating defence are heavier than those of an advancing attack, partly because all prisoners taken are as dead to their sides for the rest of the war. He says that his losses in the autumn of 1918 were much heavier than those which he suffered in his 1918 attacks. And Général Mangin has given French figures to prove that it is more costly in casualties to lose land than to gain or regain it. But surely this matter depends to a great extent on the speed of an advance, very slow progress, as in the muddy and bloody Ypres salient, being much more harmful to storming troops than a rapid advance would be, above all after an operative breakthrough.

CHAPTER II

HUTIER'S ATTACK MOVES ON TO BE BAFFLED

§ I

IF we wish to see great magnitude in focus, and correct perspective, we must move away from immense things till their details combine into groups and masses, becoming not more noticeable than are twigs and leaves in the foliage of noble trees. As a landscape painter is concerned with the beautiful varied charms of foliage, not with leaves, so historians, if they know their art, pass from items into the great sweep and bulk of those generative happenings which gather slowly to a climax and then break up into new and rival movements, whereby the future will be shaped. But details of war touch the heart so keenly, while moving the bias of patriotism, that few persons wish to see recent big battles largely and truthfully, each in its own amplitude, with the root causes of its vicissitudes.

Apply these reflections to Hutier's attack. Of what does the main story of this attack consist? Are we to see how the fight raged from hour to hour and day to day? No. Daily bulletins amplified make a diary of the battle, so congested with scattered details that each day is a lesson in the anatomy of war, not an act in a vast drama. Officers go to school to this diary, pondering over minutiæ, noting lessons, and tabulating them for methodical use in the training of platoons, companies, battalions, and divisions.

We studied the first day for two reasons. Hutier expected to make big gaps north and south of Maxse's Corps, and the first day of an offensive usually governs later events. On March 21, Ludendorff and his agents missed their stride in many places while doing about a half of their planned day's work; and before they could recover from the first dismay caused by this circumstance, General Gough, by night, had withdrawn his endangered right behind the Crozat Canal and some miles of the Somme, putting a perilous new beginning before his foes, who had learnt what their losses had been and how their legions had been disordered by fog and overthronged fighting. By good fortune, too, the second day was foggy till about one o'clock;* so our damaged lines were hidden, and a storm of machine-bullets ravaged the attack when Hutier's men, after many terrible attempts, managed at last to cross the canal, sometimes on rafts, and to gain a shallow firm footing on the western side. And in another matter the fog was as a grey-white shield to our defence. It prevented Hutier's infantry from seeing their storm troops.

Note carefully this fact about storm troops; it is very important. The British Higher Command had copied many things from German war, but they had not copied what our foes regarded as the most valuable agency in their attacks—the energetic use of storm companies and divisions: men specially brave and trained, and proud of themselves. Their purpose was twofold: not merely to storm and to be physically fit for grave stress and strain, but also to be seen by the masses behind them and to inspire emulation, as officers do by leading and showing the way. They were ordered to go on and on till they encountered a line of resistance; and then, after sending up white lights, were to strive hard to hold firmly till the masses arrived, or enough men had made their way by threes and fours to their support. They obeyed this planned routine, and our officers—who hate cant as much as they like pluck—admire the German storm troops.

In the use of storm troops there are some disadvantages, no doubt, since they are the cream of a nation's bravery; and most British and French officers believe—and the French have employed storm troops—that the cream should be kept *in* the milk. But we are dealing here with German actions. Our enemies had a faith in storm troops that increased, partly because they wished to avoid excessive losses among young levies and their officers; and it is also true to say that better soldiers than the German storm divisions did not appear during the war.†

* The fog in all its bearings on the battle is considered in Part I.

† Ludendorff, when regretting his half-success in the Lys Valley, which followed the events of March, 1918, places among the causes the fact that his men were not storm troops. It is quite probable that if we had employed special assault companies and divisions, the losses among our invaluable subs.—potential Wellingtons, many of them—would have been less wasteful and heart-searching. Germany began to lose too many officers as soon as her armies were reduced by attrition to a militia recently trained. In every

Yes, but storm troops advancing in a fog? What would they be to the masses behind them? Like electric lights in a fog—a guiding influence half useless. The ruck of Hutier's divisions saw them not; so their casualties were the more serious to Hutier and the more helpful to our defence, the ruck of attack becoming ever more of a ruck as fresh storm troops became fewer and fewer. Not once in the first three days was the ruck of Hutier's divisions led by storm troops at top speed and momentum against any chosen place of our frayed lines; and this great good thing we owe in part to the game of blind man's buff that the attack had to play against shells, bullets, trenches, shell-holes, barbed wire, and in part to the fact that *no stage of our retreat was put off too long, and the advance became leg-tired, rattled, and irritable with baffled hopes and efforts.*

In three days our men fell back a very considerable distance. Hutier advanced with his right wing to and along the Vermand-Amiens road as far as the Somme, west of St. Christ and Brie; a distance of 26,500 yards. His centre reached the Somme between Falvy and the west of Ham; a distance of 29,000 yards in the deepest place. His southern advance had formed two bridgeheads: a shallow one south of Ham and the Somme, and a deep one west of Crozat Canal.

The crossing at Ham, March 23, was a nasty blow. On the previous night, when our front troops were withdrawing to the Somme, a gap formed in their line in the neighbourhood of Ham, and the foe, following closely, entered the town during the early morning. Before midday bodies of German infantry, at first only in small numbers, got across the river between Ham and Pithon, where the bridges had not been completely destroyed. In the afternoon, these forces became strong enough gradually to press back our troops, till a spirited counter-attack by the *Twentieth* and *Sixty-first* about Verlaines restored the situation in this locality. To the east of this point, heavy fighting took place both around Ollezy, which the *Thirty-sixth* regained and held till a late hour, and also around Aubigny and Brouchy. The attack was reinforced, and at last, before night, these villages fell into the enemy's hands.

We turn now to the German bridgehead west of Crozat

---

period of the war the Allied casualties were too high, too extravagant while the German were not; and hence the question of storm troops is certain to be restudied by historians.

Canal. After capturing Jussy. the foe had tracked our withdrawal westward 6000 yards; after crossing the canal at Liez, he had followed us 10,500 yards; and southward he had captured Villequier-Aumont. In the south, also, aided by Gayl, he was pressing down to Chauny. To meet this grave threat, some French troops arrived on the third day, coming at full speed, without their guns and administrative equipment. Their business was to help our reinforced cavalry and the long-suffering *Fifty-eighth,* whose elastic units had urgent need of help.* Chauny was on the way to Manicamp, and Hutier hoped that Gayl and the German SEVENTH ARMY, after a complete break-through, would be able to thrust south and south-west from Manicamp, in conjunction with the same pressure from his own troops both in the Noyon region, and also south of the Oise at Varesnes and Pontoise. Altogether, then, on the evening of March 23, when the first phase of the battle ended, the situation was dramatic. We had lost three positions, our forward zone, battle zone, and incomplete rear lines. But land lost bravely and without strategical disaster is not a hostage given to defeat; it is an investment placed with skill in compulsory prudence, and recoverable. And now let us note what had happened to Hutier's best men, whose loss could not be recovered by him and Ludendorff.

First, then, Hutier had thrown already into his first line efforts to break through not less than fifteen of his own divisions and Gayl's four, nineteen in all, with their storm troops; and his losses, though not even half so great as our propagandists declared (as if to make the German advance look superhuman), must have given him many disquieting hours. When very large armies are taken from the ordinary manhood of a country, they have in them the defects of ordinary manhood, containing so many men who need incessant watching by junior and non-commissioned officers that severe losses among the best men, picked fighters, cause much anxiety even when an advance keeps to its time-table, and when the general casualties do not exceed the forecasts of military auditors, who have studied earlier offensives

* On March 22, troops of this division did invaluable work, when the foe tried to cross the Crozat Canal on rafts, under cover of machine-guns and trench-mortars. At one p.m. he made the passage at Quessy, and went on towards Vouel, until Cator held him up at Tergnier. It was not until evening, after many costly efforts, that he captured Tergnier, less than a mile west of Crozat Canal. What could have been more valuable to the Allied cause than was this prolonged resistance at a most critical time and place? Equally valuable work was done by the *Eighteenth* DIVISION and by the *Second* CAVALRY.

and have tabled in averages the killed, wounded, and missing.

To employ in first-line fighting during the first three days nineteen highly trained and trusted divisions, and to see many thousands of shock troops vanish into the fog to be killed or wounded, must have been very harassing to Hutier and his commanders, whose time-table had not been kept. Their advance, too, long before it had reached Noyon, the first of their prime aims, was becoming clogged by the ruckmen, among whom were many who liked to dally in shell craters.

As the advance covered a great many square miles of land, straggling was easy. Men of combative temper went forward as naturally as boar hounds do, while the dead level of German manhood had abundant opportunities to split up into differing elements: an element that looted food in villages and tried to find liquor; an element of prudence that got a stitch in its side and was glad to keep it there; a fussy element that wanted to be in force when prisoners were taken to the rear; and a blunt, dull, almost candid element that wished to be a scattered rearguard to an advance, having no willingness to win and wear the B.M., or Bandage of Merit, a surgical dressing.

Among the causes given by Ludendorff for his half-success in the Lys Valley, you will find the complaint that his troops often wasted time looking for food.

"The way in which the troops stopped around captured supplies, while individuals stayed behind to search houses and farms for food, were serious matters. This impaired success and showed poor discipline. It was equally serious that both our young company commanders and our senior officers did not feel strong enough to take disciplinary action and to seize sufficient authority to enable them to lead their men forward without delay. The absence of our old peace-trained corps of officers was most severely felt. . . ."

The German troops who fought against Gough and Byng were specially trained, unlike those who attacked in the Lys Valley, but since they had long felt many effects of the Allied blockade, the food which they captured in their advance must have been a great attraction to those among them who wished to be laggards; and Ludendorff says bluntly that they were "checked by finding provisions." He complains, too, that "numerous slightly wounded made things more difficult by the stupid and displeasing way in which they hurried to the rear."

Human nature in battles will show its wondrous variety and its national variations, above all when bitter fighting continues for a long time; and discipline tries to weld all dross elements into that level body of good homespun which, though it soon gets "fed up with fighting," has a firm sense of duty and a pride always ready "to stick it out."

It is with these varying constituents of ordinary mankind, stiffened and led by the heroic minority, that a story of great war has to deal, unless we have uncandid minds which turn away from truth. Every nation in the war believed that her own troops were the bravest of all, and took care to make no printed references to any dross elements in her own armies, though courts of inquiry and published reports of their verdicts are invaluable as a national tonic and training. No leader in the field, whether a sub. or an army commander, can forget without danger, that the upper stratum of troops, the heroic minority, has always to struggle in big battles not only against the foe but also against the lowest strata of its own comrades; and for this reason, when in a fight against unusual odds a defence baffles an attack ably planned and well led, we may be sure that dross elements became far more active in the advance than in the retreat, owing partly to graver losses among first-rate divisions.

According to Ludendorff, German infantry groups were often lacking in enterprise, and often their co-operation with companion arms had failed. They "found special difficulty in reorganizing themselves for defence at the close of their attack, and above all in recognizing when no further success was to be gained by continuing the assault. ... At many places machine-gun posts had given us [the German troops] an undue amount of trouble, and so caused delay." This candour is refreshing after the camouflage which became habitual among all the belligerents.

Even on March 22, Hutier had to draw upon his second line, the *Fifth* Guards displacing Webern's *Two Hundred and Thirty-eighth* near St. Simon, for example, and the *Fifth* DIVISION relieving the *Eighty-eighth* among Lüttwitz's first-line men. Not a good start, seeing that Hutier's first line on March 21 had in all eleven divisions, apart from Gayl's force. Next day, when the resistance was local, rather than incessant and general, Oetinger had to bring up his one support, the *Two Hundred and Thirty-first*, to attack on the west of Ham towards Eppeville; and the *First* Bavarians, piercingly ransacked by our machine-gunners at Jussy, asked to be withdrawn, but asked in vain, its support division, the *Tenth*, being already active on its right. Now Ludendorff desired particularly that the first-line divisions should fight on through several days unrelieved, in order that second and third line troops might be kept fresh and fit for swift operative movements after a break-through at one or other of several chosen places.

Hutier's cyclone, then, had been split up by rude blasts from a destructive counter-wind, while a battle was growling through its first phase or period, without arriving at any point at the hour set down in Ludendorff's plans.

Have we got Ludendorff's time-table? This question is asked frequently, and the answer to it is that there were *two* time-tables probably, one advertised to cheer up the German troops, and one known to superior officers alone. It would have been very foolish if Ludendorff had said to his men: "You'll meet with such a fierce resistance that you won't be able to take much on the first day." Surely he would stimulate their confidence by saying: "You are splendid fellows, and I expect you to go far on the first day." In a French study of Hutier's attack we read: "L'objectif de la première journée était, semble-t-il, d'atteindre au Nord le cours de la Somme, au Sud le canal du Crozat; mais en fin de journée ces objectifs sont loin d'être atteints." No doubt the first day's work in the south was to cross the Crozat Canal on the line Fargniers-Liez-Jussy-St. Simon; but the present writer cannot believe that in the north Ludendorff and Hutier really expected to reach the Somme between Brie and St. Christ. This expectation was too much at odds with western experience to be put into a confidential time-table; and the pressure of Hutier's right—evidence worth trusting—showed that the purpose in the minds of officers was to reach Vermand and our Green Line offshoot running north on the east of Caulaincourt, Pœuilly, and Bernes. It took a couple of days to attain these objects, so on March 21 the attack lost fifty per cent. of time.

Worse still, perhaps, from Hutier's point of view, were two other considerations. If he arrived at Noyon without annihilating a big part of the defence, or without enough storm troops and other picked men, a drive down to Compiègne would be impossible; his losses might easily destroy the offensive value of his masses by having in them a percentage far too high of born fighters, specially equipped by long practice. Then his army would need, at least, a month's rest for the training of new storm troops and new machine-gunners, another *élite* body; and a month's rest would throw out of gear Ludendorff's main purpose, a continuous campaign, while enabling the Entente Powers to rally from their first round, and to bring over American troops.

Besides, the retreat was drawing nearer and nearer to reinforcements, nearly all French south of the Somme, but including the British *Eighth*; while Hutier's communications lengthened over cratered land, and railways torn up, over roads blasted into holes, and scores of bridges blown into ruins. Thanks to thorough preparation, only six or seven bridges during the whole retreat were left at all fit for the enemy's use, like one at Chipilly, where the charges failed to have the necessary effect; or, again, like the railway bridge at Pithon, east of Ham, which, I believe, was under G.H.Q. orders in the demolition scheme. Much gallantry was shown during the demolition of bridges. At Tugny there were eleven bridges, and in one, the safety fuse having failed, Second Lieutenant Knox lit an instantaneous fuse with a match—and escaped almost unhurt. One bridge at Falvy, blown up at 4.30 p.m. on March 23, had the leads cut by German bullets; but Sergeant Crossley repaired them under fire—and the bridge went up all right. Maxse's Corps prepared seventy-three bridges for demolition, and only five were disappointments; two of no consequence at Falvy, and two light railway bridges, which, though burnt, were still of use to infantry; fifth, a double steel lattice girder at Ham, in which, probably, the gun-cotton slabs failed to detonate.

Close upon two hundred and fifty bridges were destroyed by our FIFTH ARMY, so Hutier and Marwitz had no end of hindrances to get over, and always when they were most eager to hurl divisions into a hand-to-hand grapple. Land gained must have been an increasing burden to Hutier while he tried vainly to make real the ideal of great attack—annihilation at chosen places of a crumbling defence.

All these matters belong to the prospering side of Gough's retreat; and now we must be as frank towards dangerous aspects. Take our British feeling for retreats. When have we been taught to regard them as an essential and inevitable part of long wars? Neither we nor our armies have received enough cool good sense in this particular, with the result that the occasional necessity of bending to avoid breaking is not accepted as a matter of course, as we accept an enforced change of plan in a game of chess.

In this matter, as in many others, the most "popular" British newspapers were a curse, teaching their readers to think that every advance was a victory and every retreat a defeat. The propaganda of jubilant lies after Passchendaele, like the premature ringing of joy-bells after the first phase of Byng's blow at Cambrai, was to my mind hysterically un-British, and a very bad preparation for the spring of 1918.

Our troops hate a retreat so ardently that, as I have said before, no division will ever admit that it is obliged to fall back; it blames a division on its flank, and says to its officers: "We could stay here as long as you like, sir. Are we in the air again? Damn!" In these or in similar words, Tommy makes known that he is adding to the wear and tear of a bad time by chafing over a useful and necessary thing, the noble art of wise retreating.

He should be as proud of his ability to retire ably as to advance finely, since an attack foiled by an able retreat is to the defence as a big victory of the second grade. Every foot blister should be as a medal to him—a proof and recognition of his duty done under orders, and for a purpose thought out with that mingling of caution and temerity which belongs to armed strife as to financial gambling. But in a time of head-lined journalism all day long, when even the taking of a ruined village in local fighting is profusely annotated, troops are misled by a propaganda that confirms them not only in their natural desire never to go back, but also in the shame they feel when the need of giving ground comes upon them in war as in football and boxing.

In these sports candid criticism on all points has ever been welcomed publicly, while in life or death war defence and attack are usually left unaided by that degree of reasonable fault-finding which gives value to praise and admiration. Why? Would our troops have harassed themselves during a retreat if they had felt sure that people at home would grasp the need of their withdrawal, and would cheer as gladly as do the crowd at a cup tie when goal is relieved and a rushing attack baffled?

No such enthusiasm welcomed the second battle of the Somme, except from those tamed pressmen at the front who wrote glibly their too familiar columns for a censorship well known, while the official bulletins showed fear of the battle's maps, and the War Office issued a fondled report of its own making.

Even to-day, essential moves in the retreat are questioned

sometimes, and sometimes condemned, though they had a marked effect on Hutier's failure to achieve the main pivotal parts of Ludendorff's plans. On March 23, for example, Gough retired from that unfinished line which guarded the Somme from a point east of Rouy-le-Grand, north-eastward to Monchy Lagache and Hancourt, thence north as a portion of the Péronne bridgehead.

In Part IV. of this book, where some controversies are stated and examined, these matters are shown in various aspects. Swiftly and bravely Gough had to make one of those decisions which historians reconsider from age to age, and always with a new zeal. There were many reasons why he would stand firm if he could, but they were cancelled as influences by one fact, a fact to be put into blunt words. Watts could not promise to make a firm successful stand; his corps was in physical condition to be overthrown by a last grapple against superior force renewed by fresh divisions. And some other troops, overstrained almost to breaking-point, needed rest—all the rest they could get—on guard west of the Somme.

Behind the Somme our men took breath; they "got their second wind," and gained invaluable time for the incoming of slow reinforcements. Malcolm's division, for example, whose brave Lancashire brigades suffered perhaps heavier losses than any others, guarded the crossings along the Péronne sector from about noonday on March 23 to about dusk on the 25th—with about 1500 rifles only, so severe had the losses been in the *Sixty-sixth* DIVISION.

§ II

In the evening of March 25, Hutier closed upon Noyon, only to find that he had not enough power to strike south and south-west while keeping a firm pressure along his westward-going front. He made an effort, and then moved on towards Lassigny, Canny-sur-Matz, and Montdidier, turning towards the French a lengthening flank. This was a bad second best, and its development to March 28, when his line ran south and west of Montdidier and north to Marcelcave, brings us to the end of Hutier's battle, in so far as the most of Gough's remaining troops are concerned.

Two other phases came, extending the fight to April 4; they were settling-down phases, and confirmed the work done mainly by two British corps, Butler's and Maxse's, aided by the right wing of Watts's troops. The bantam-weight amateur had foiled the heavy-weight professional, causing so many bruises and wounds that his own battered condition did not seem to matter much.

Let us see what Hutier's position was from March 24 to the evening of March 28. He had bled all of his second-line divisions and a part of his reserves. On March 24, when his northern wing crossed the Somme, he called to the front at St. Christ the *Sixth* DIVISION, and the *Two Hundred and Sixth* went into action towards Voyennes. Two days later, the advance continuing by Chaulnes and Rosières, and all second-line men being engaged, a reserve division began to fight. It was the *Two Hundred and Forty-third*, and probably it relieved one of Lüttwitz's, the *Hundred and Thirteenth*.

The central part of Hutier's attack met with fierce opposition across the Somme. He was obliged to employ the *Ninth* DIVISION; and two units from Army Reserve were soon in battle, the *Tenth* RESERVE on March 25, and the *First* Guards on the 27th.

As for the left wing, perhaps its movements may have been more difficult, particularly after reaching the Noyon-Roye road. On March 25, the German *Thirty-third*, Conta's group, which had been in second line north of Jussy was united to the *Thirty-fourth* and *Thirty-seventh*, to screen a movement towards the north-west made by the *First* Bavarians and the *Hundred and Third*, who were to become active again in the neighbourhood of Lassigny.

By the evening of March 28, Hutier had employed twenty-two divisions, apart from Gayl's and Boehn's; his reserves were already like a half-empty barrel of wine that leaked; and anxiety had caused him to summon several units from calm sectors of his front, the *Third* Bavarians arriving from St. Gobain, and the *Fourteenth* DIVISION and *Eightieth* RESERVE coming from Lorraine and Champagne.

To understand how bitter these facts must have been to him we must remember that Hutier told his first-line troops of March 21 that they would have to fight for several consecutive days without being relieved, and he warned his Corps Commanders also not to draw hastily on their supports and reserves.

As Ludendorff says: "The German Supreme Command attached decisive importance to the attack being continued for a period of some days by divisions in the first line." He adds: "I opposed the view that these units already on the second or third day should be relieved by divisions of the second wave. At the beginning of the war we had fought for weeks at a time without relief. Our existing troops, it is true, were no longer capable of such a performance. But even so, there was no need for such frequent reliefs as many would have liked to see." *

And what was Hutier to do with his wide flank extending from Montdidier to the south-east of Noyon and thence to Chauny? To make such enormous efforts, and yet be unable to follow the Oise a few miles to Compiègne! To take Montdidier only to be worried by the Avre bridgehead! To come within gunshot of Amiens—and then to stand still, baffled, completely spent!

As Ludendorff says in his book, the strategical situation was by no means favourable, though as yet a final opinion could not be given on its outlook, as the German operations were still in their first stages. "The Avre bridgehead," he writes, "was a special difficulty in the tactical sense. The advisability of giving it up was discussed. But as this would have shown the enemy that we had abandoned any further attack on Amiens, we kept it. . . . Strategically we had not achieved what events of the 23rd, 24th, and 25th had encouraged us to hope for. That we had also failed to take Amiens, which would have rendered communication between the enemy forces astride the Somme exceedingly difficult, was specially disappointing. Long-range bombardment of the railway establishments of Amiens was by no means an equivalent. . . ."

Ludendorff's candour is manly, and it helps every one to appreciate what Gough's generalship and British fighting had achieved when Hutier's power was most formidable, and before any French reinforcements had its full equipments, either military or administrative.

It was always, or nearly always, a British order that did most effectively at the right moment an essential thing. On the sixth day, for example, while two French divisions were withdrawing south-west, and taking with them Nugent's Ulstermen and Maxse's artillery, a remnant brigade of our *Twentieth* fought a very valuable delaying action as it fell back to the line Fresnoy-Villers-lès-Roye-La Damery, and Le

* In plain words, there was no such system of divisional "leap-frogging," as British war correspondents attributed to Ludendorff's tactics in this battle.

Quesnoy. The last village was the most westerly. It had for its garrison two officers, two Lewis guns, and about a hundred men, all footsore, begrimed with dust and sweat, and haggard from battle strain as from a fever. Captain E. P. Combe was in command. All day long—a day of sunshine—this handful fought against a stiff advance, checking the foe till six in the evening, when only nine of our men and their leaders were left. Yet they decided to fight another round, and this miniature Waterloo went on till orders were received for a retreat by night north-west to Beaufort. Meantime, greatly helped by this most gallant stand at Le Quesnoy, other men of the *Twentieth* freed themselves from a difficult position and moved on unmolested.

§ III

To guard his flank from a possible attack by Franco-American troops, Hutier was obliged to fight on until the Lys battle began. His northern wing, as early as March 26, instead of continuing its direct push towards Amiens, began, I believe, to bend a little towards the south-west; and between March 29 and 31 all-round efforts on his extended front implied that he was seeking for a weak spot in order to convulse the Entente's line, which stiffened slowly but surely. What remained of his reserves, five divisions in all, were thrown into action—not as a body of shock troops to break through, but as distributed striking power, to aid an assault along the whole front between Noyon and Moreuil * With these reserves he used every unit fit to attack, with five divisions which had been withdrawn and reorganized. But his efforts gave either local gains or mere flashes in the pan; and then, through four days Hutier was obliged to reshuffle his pack before he played a renewed game.

Thwarted, yet still eager to separate the British and French forces, he decided that he would make his front narrower by handing over his northern divisions to Marwitz,† and receiving from Marwitz in exchange two units from the reserve, the *Second* Bavarians and the *Fifty-third* RESERVE. Then, on

---

* Note that the *Twenty-third* DIVISION was active in the direction of Moreuil; that the *Fifty-first* RESERVE, like the *Fifty-second* DIVISION, fought on the north of Montdidier; that the *Two Hundred and Forty-second* was thrown in at Orvillers, south-east of Montdidier; and that the *Seventh* RESERVE was engaged at Plessis de Roye.

† Four divisions in all: *Eighty-eighth*, *Twenty-third*, *Fiftieth*, and *Two Hundred and Forty-third*.

April 4, he and Marwitz struck together, the greatest blow coming from their sphere of union, though the battle ran from Moreuil down to Montdidier; but not much was achieved.

The morning attack, begun at seven o'clock, was repulsed by the British right; but on the northern wing, immediately south of the Somme, our men were obliged to retire behind le Hamel and Vaire Wood. During the afternoon another thrust struck the British right, causing a dent in the neighbourhood of Hangard Wood, while on the French front some ground was lost on both sides of the Avre.

Contrary to Ludendorff's orders and training, waves of attack came on in dense formation, and these targets felt the full force of our machine-guns and artillery. Just north of the Somme the *Third* AUSTRALIANS turned their artillery on the foe's attack across the river, and, firing over open sights with excellent effect, were very helpful.

As a whole Hutier's final effort was a failure. It did not lessen any of his anxieties. Indeed, Boehn seems to have supplied him with troops, for I believe that two of Boehn's divisions, the *Forty-seventh* RESERVE and the *Two Hundred and Twenty-third*, were sent to be in support near Roye.

These particulars are very important. They prove that Hutier could not recover from Gough's retreat and its results. It was during the first four or five days that Hutier shot his bolt and missed his mark. His aim was to overwhelm while his storm divisions were fresh and confident, and before reinforcements could reach our meagre long line running from the Omignon valley down to Barisis.

These special divisions of the foe's first line had been trained by Hutier himself in the neighbourhood of Fourmies-Chimay, his H.Q. being at Avesnes, and by means of careful propaganda he had raised the ardour of his whole army to a high pitch. A French study of the battle says with truth: *

"*Tous les prisonniers interrogés ont déclaré qu'ils avaient été soutenus par la certitude de la victoire et de la fin prochaine de la guerre.*"

Weigh these words well. Hutier's army entered the battle to win a complete victory and to end the war. Then fog and heavy losses and brigades jumbled up together threw chill

---

* "Les Opérations de la XVIIIe Armée Allemande (Armée Von Hutier) du 21 Mars au 5 Avril, 1918." Grand Quartier Général des Armées du Nord et du Nord-Est. État-Major. 2e Bureau. No. 20,419.—A helpful study with excellent maps.

after chill upon its impassioned confidence, its ardent self-belief; and then —— ? May a student venture to express his belief that Hutier confounded Gough with Haig? To my mind there is no doubt on this point.

Haig's character in war is evident in all its actions. It is a very cold and a very unbending resolution, unmoved by those Napoleonic impulses which come from imaginative fevour at a white heat; and Hutier's conduct shows that her thought constantly of this character, till Gough's fire and swift flexibility had baffled him several times. At all costs, on the evening of March 21, Hutier ought to have pressed his attack west of Maissemy and west of Essigny and Benay, and also in the Crozat Canal region from Fargniers north-westward; but he paused to take breath, evidently believing that the British would be too obstinate and that he would be able to deliver a decisive blow in the morning after his brigades had been disentangled.

Fortunately, we were not unbendingly obstinate. Gough withdrew his right, and in the morning Hutier had to attack the Crozat Canal through a thick fog, noisy with our machine-gun bullets, while west of Vermand he found our newly arrived *Fiftieth* DIVISION.

Even then both Hutier and Ludendorff continued to think much more of Haig's character in battle than of Gough's, taking their cues too confidently from that doggedness for which British troops have always been famous, and which Haig revealed in full measure during the Somme campaign of 1916 and later in the Ypres salient.*

A paragraph in Haig's dispatch suggests that he would have taken decisive risks along the Péronne bridgehead.† No doubt the central portion of Ludendorff's offensive showed a leisurely confidence after breaching our Green Line close by Nobescourt Farm, and also at Caulaincourt. This great error in generalship aided our troops invaluably. It is explained only by the assumption that Hutier and Marwitz expected our men to stand for a conclusive grapple east of the river. Happily, Gough had a plan as simple as it was effectual. Knowing the physical condition of his men, he refused to

---

* British Empire casualties in the Ypres salient—July 31, 1917, to November 4, 1917—were 12,580 officers and 246,257 other ranks. What if these troops had been used with the Italians against Austria? The deepest advance on a narrow front, from July 30 to November 26, was about 5½ miles, from Hill Top Farm, Wieltje sector, to N.E. of Passchendaele.

† The paragraph in question is quoted in Part IV. of this book.

HUTIER'S ATTACK MOVES ON TO BE BAFFLED

keep his bantam-weight force where the heavy-weight professional could overpower it by incessant blows at close quarters.

A great many persons have said that although Hutier and his commanders handled their masses of troops with a skill which invites the most careful attention, yet they failed to bring their battle to a well-defined ending. No doubt this criticism is true. The immense attack came as a cyclone and blew itself out in gusts of dwindling violence; and note well that what may be called the last gust did not come from Hutier's army. It came from Boehn's, and on April 6.

On this date Boehn attacked on the Oise's left bank from Chauny to La Fère in the direction of Coucy la Ville, and also farther south. His object was to push the French across the Oise-Aisne Canal in order to give some security to Hutier's long south flank; and this aim he made real. For all that, not much ease was given to Hutier; week after week his long south flank was there; and Foch gathered troops and made very strong positions below Noyon and thence to his Montdidier sector. The foe noticed this menace, and made preparations to ease the strain on Hutier. On June 7 Boehn was to attack with the SEVENTH GERMAN ARMY south-west of Soissons, while Hutier with the EIGHTEENTH was to strike simultaneously between Montdidier and Noyon. Happily, this combination could not be brought about, as Hutier could not finish in time his artillery preparations. The attack was postponed for two days; and we have still to learn why our Allies, who were well prepared and in excellent positions, did not crush Hutier's onset. Once more the foe failed to reach Compiègne, but he formed a protective salient all the way from south-east of Montdidier to south-east of Noyon. The attack broke through a most difficult trench system, advancing almost as far as the Aronde, and resisting heavy counter-attacks along the Méry sector. South of Noyon this bulwark salient passed over formidable high ground just west of the Oise. Consider, then, what the Allied position would have been in March if Hutier and Gayl had crossed the Crozat Canal on the first day, with the way open both towards Chauny and towards Noyon!

Again, if we ask ourselves why Hutier's cyclone blew itself out in gusts of dwindling violence, we come face to face with a fact which is apt to be forgotten by those who write in the Press about strategy and tactics; namely, that the most important thing in war is not the brain shown in tactics and strategy, but the varying limit set by nature to the physical endurance of good troops. Hutier's men became almost as tired as our own; and on March 27 they would have been in a most perilous plight if we had possessed five or six fresh divisions with which to enforce the spurs of a thorough counterstroke into their broken-winded sides.

When from day to day they were held off at arm's length from that break-through for which they had been specially trained, their confidence and fighting fervour became flat and lukewarm. It was noted by British officers who were captured, and who were taken east through Hutier's rear, that German second-line troops and reserves, advancing towards the battle front, did not regard an advance as a victory; they moved without marching discipline and without ardour. Their tails were not up! Their blood was not on fire with that peculiar tonic heat which a genuine victory circulates from heart to heart through a whole army.

And this dull mood behind Hutier's battle line was natural, inevitable; it marked a reaction that settled down upon his men after intense hopefulness had been thwarted again and again by Gough's bending obstinacy, which I compare to a good yew bow. The big advance, without a genuine success, was always very difficult, and also too costly; and constantly ahead of it, and unbeaten, was the British line of remnant brigades, and the gradual coming of Allied reinforcements.

From the third day our *Twentieth* was helped greatly by two Canadian batteries of the motor-machine-gun sort; on March 26 seven hundred American engineers joined Maxse to dig themselves in on a line covering Demuin; and as for the French troops, from dawn of the third day, gradually, and in great haste, they began to arrive, without guns, and with no more rifle ammunition than they carried. No brave men could have been more sorely handicapped. It was impossible for them to be adequate, effectual. Yet somehow, anyhow, they were put in authority over our own officers and troops! This was done officially on the fifth day south of the Somme, before Foch was appointed to Supreme Command; but earlier it was active in a piecemeal fashion, and always with bad results.

Perhaps nothing in this battle is more distressing, or more controversial, than the act of putting British officers and men under French commanders before the French troops were à *pied d'œuvre*, on a complete war footing, with all necessary equipments, both military and administrative. Thus to swop

HUTIER'S ATTACK MOVES ON TO BE BAFFLED 99

horses in mid-stream in the presence of Hutier's immense power——! What will historians think and say? In Part IV. of this book there is a chapter on this peculiar use of reinforcements, by which much confusion was caused, and which came, among other things, from a lack of self-control *outside* the battle, partly among those statesmen who had kept far too many troops in the British Isles.

For the rest, some writers misinterpret Ludendorff's aim in Hutier's attack. One of them says :—

"The German object was not a specific break-through, but a general crumbling. What wrecked this object was that Ludendorff got the break-through, but not the crumbling."

I see no reason why the Muse of History should stand on her head. Very high casualties prove that the FIFTH ARMY'S incessant peril was general crumbling. Yet Hutier strove vainly with all his might to prove that numbers alone annihilate.

In this fact we find decisive proof that Gough's orders were correct, and that they were carried out well by his officers and men. Hutier can have no excuse to offer. His army was first-rate; he had plenty of time before French reinforcements began to come up, and there was room enough along his front to break through a thin defence; to break through operatively, in wide-sweeping movements opening out like a fan.

CHAPTER III

THE CENTRE FIGHTING NORTH AND SOUTH OF THE VERMAND-AMIENS ROAD

§ I

ON March 22, soon after midnight, our *Fiftieth* DIVISION arrived at the Somme and began to detrain at Brie, feeling stiff, unwashed, and ungummed. Its North English troops, coming from the district west of Rosières, had started an evening journey after a brisk march had put too much sweat into their shirts; and imagine patience in troop trains! Has it not been described as "strap 'angin' all in a bloomin' 'eap without any bloomin' straps"?

G.H.Q. had kept this division too far off from the weakest part of the British front. Two days before the battle Gough wanted to move it up, together with the *Twentieth;* so he appealed by telephone to G.H.Q. With what result? The C.G.S. viewed his request as a desire to use the reserves too soon. In other words, the C.G.S. ran counter to a military maxim which says that when Generals expect to be attacked, they should keep their reserves at hand and entirely fit for battle. To keep them at a long distance from the front is to invite disaster. If G.H.Q. had listened favourably to Gough's appeal, the *Fiftieth* and *Twentieth* would not have been thrown into action under very adverse conditions.

In a great hurry, and with much fatigue, the *Fiftieth* had to reach those swirling borderlands north and south of the Vermand-Amiens road, where Hutier and Marwitz united their attacks, striving with the utmost energy to separate Watts from Maxse, while Watts was in trouble northward near the Cologne River, where he and Congreve had to encounter flanking pressure from the south-west of Ronssoy and Templeux le Guérard.

Neill Malcolm and Daly had done wonders only to find that their thin divisions had burned too much in the furnace of battle. Lancashire lads of the *Sixty-sixth* * had shown tenacious mettle, fighting as Lancashire archers used to fight when English longbows were feared throughout Europe: but soldiers all of gold pay themselves away in long necessary efforts to do overmuch.† There had been far too much strain from the Omignon valley to the River Cologne—a nasty name for a French river when seven German divisions on a front of about five miles have been active for a whole day against two undermanned British units. Both defence and attack cursed the fog; and when the fog cleared away and uncovered the attack all muddled up in the valleys, our machine-guns were more than enough to dismay the German jumble, that never seemed to know how much success it had won, and certainly it was very slow to profit by its gains. Benign fog!

For a considerable time on the second day there was a frowsiness in the attack that came from yesterday's troubles. A German prisoner told Colonel Lloyd of the Ninth Manchesters that Marwitz had no intention of attacking in the north sector of Malcolm's front; enemy troops were digging trenches there; and a wounded German officer declared that German casualties from German gas had been very large on the first day, as the assault had begun too soon. If the German officer had attributed the German gas casualties to *our* shelling of Hargicourt, he would probably have been right, as the German gas when the attack began was too weak to put men out of action.

* Malcolm's Division.
† The *Sixty-sixth* fought continuously from dawn, March 21, till the night of March 30-31, and its casualties, counting also the spent and sick, were perhaps the heaviest of any. Its men proved that competitive industries and bellicose trade unions befriend the old British liking for blows, bruises, and battles. On the sixth day, for instance, the *Sixty-sixth* was so short of officers that its depleted companies were merely improvised small teams, but yet they held on with a grip little slackened, as though fighting were as natural to them as that automatic panting of their lungs that gained for them air enough to keep them alive. Even when they seemed to be far gone in locomotor ataxy, they contrived somehow to make good hobbling counter-strokes, as on the afternoon of March 30. Perhaps the best episodes of their fighting were: (1) On March 21, a cavalry counter-attack to Carpeza Copse, and the holding of this copse until a withdrawal on the second day; (2) the recovery east and north-east of Hervilly at about 11 a.m. on March 22, which at the right moment delayed the German advance to the Péronne bridgehead at Nobescourt Farm; (3) holding the exits of Péronne and the village of Biaches (this in conjunction with Feetham and the *Thirty-ninth*); (4) Harbonnières, invaluable as well as memorably picturesque; and (5) the last spurt in a counter-blow near Hangard, when its fagged men advanced as far as a brigade of fresh Australians, and forgot afterwards to blow their own trumpets. Their total casualties during the operations were nearly seven thousands, apart from the sick and spent.

But these favouring circumstances were counterpoised by our own losses and anxieties. Daly's men were badly hit, like Colin Mackenzie's left;* and thus the centre of Gough's Army was in danger. The *Fiftieth* could not be too quick, since it had been kept too long by G.H.Q.

From Brie to Caulaincourt and the Green Line offshoot is a march along the straight road towards Vermand; a march by night of eight miles, if you please, and through another fog dense enough to have a strong clasp on things and persons. Martin's Brigade marched to the Péronne bridgehead near Hancourt, where its men had a short rest in some huts. Afterwards they took up their position in the main Green Line. Their left rested near Boucly, and their right was held by the Fifth Durham Light Infantry, under Major A. L. Raimes, who had his headquarters in Nobescourt Farm, like Neill Malcolm, who commanded the *Sixty-sixth*. The main Green Line, an essential part of the Péronne bridgehead, was about five hundred yards east of the ruined farm, and about the same distance north of it, as the line at this point formed a semicircle.

Soon after ten o'clock the Fifth D.L.I. was lent for a time to Neill Malcolm, who employed it to guard his left flank against any attack which the foe might attempt from the north of Roisel. In the afternoon, at about half-past two, the *Sixty-sixth* was ordered by its Corps to fight a rearguard action and to withdraw through the *Fiftieth*, who would hold Green Line. The brigade groups and attached troops and cavalry were to assemble at Buire, Courcelles and Doingt, but the *Sixty-sixth's* divisional artillery was to be left under the command of the *Fiftieth*.

This withdrawal was not attacked. It went smoothly, and was completed before midnight. The *Sixty-sixth's* headquarters left Nobescourt Farm at one o'clock, and, four and a half hours later, opened at Doingt.

Already the losses in each brigade of this brave division were estimated as from 40 to 50 officers and from 1200 to 1400 other ranks. These were severe casualties, for the *Sixty-sixth* entered battle with an average strength per battalion of not more than 20 officers and 600 rifles: or 60 officers and 1800 rifles in each of the three brigades,

* The *Sixty-first*. A special order of the day, April 18, recorded the fact that since March 21, this division had fought against fourteen German divisions, had identified three other units by contact, and on one afternoon had taken prisoners from three different airplane flights.

Equal and similar losses also had been suffered by the *Twenty-fourth*, so that our 19th Corps had urgent need of the *Fiftieth*.

In all the *Fiftieth* had a wider front to guard than that which is given in the official dispatch; it exceeded 10,500 yards by much. South of Martin's Brigade was Rees's, that guarded the Green Line offshoot from the north-west of Bernes to a point just north of Pœuilly, where Riddell's Brigade of Northumberland Fusiliers carried on the defence southward to the wooded Omignon River near Villévéque. Undulating and timbered country aided the Boche. Long belts of spinney and weald ran east and west, hiding an inquisitive push which at midday would squeeze us from Vermand and begin to press westward.

At about eight o'clock Brigadier Riddell had his men hard by their battle stations. With his three battalions, about 1800 rifles and some 800 stragglers, it was his duty to hold 5000 yards of very shallow trench, and yet have men enough for counter-attacks. How was this duty to be fulfilled?

Civilians have a very cloudy notion as to the span of front which a small body of troops should be able to keep secure. Experienced officers believe that 1500 yards of front in a battle zone is all a battalion can hold; and then it must be supported by many more guns than our FIFTH ARMY had in March. A famous Corps Commander writes:—

" I still think the forward zone should be as lightly held as possible, and I would put a battalion even on 3000 yards of front there, and the other two battalions of a brigade each on a 1500 yards front in the battle zone. Thus the brigade would be in depth. But we need on the spot in each brigade a fourth battalion for counter-attacks. As for the prevalent idea that reserves can be marched for miles and miles on the day of battle to be handled by some genius on the spot who can foresee somehow where his jumping-off place will be for his counter-attack by a battalion—all this may be splendid in theory, but it doesn't work out in practice." *

* G.H.Q. has still to explain not only why two-thirds of Gough's infantry reserves were absent during the first day's battle, but also why the official dispatch declares that they were present. Consider this quotation : " The THIRD ARMY disposed of eight divisions in line on the front of the enemy's initial attack [from Sensée River down to Byng's union with the FIFTH ARMY], with seven divisions available in reserve. The FIFTH ARMY disposed of fourteen divisions and three cavalry divisions, of which three infantry divisions and three cavalry divisions were in reserve. The total British force on the original battle front, therefore, on the morning of March 21, was twenty-nine infantry divisions and three cavalry divisions, of which nineteen infantry

Counter-attacks might decide the day. Compared with neighbouring troops, such as Colin Mackenzie's southward, Riddell's Northumberland Fusiliers had not yet turned a hair; so a great deal was expected from them. It would be well to have a whole battalion for counter-attack, and its best position would be at Tertry, a village just a mile or less behind Caulaincourt, and guarded by such bog and marsh as the Omignon has made in this part of its course. The Fifth Fusiliers were put in reserve east of Tertry, while the battle-line on our right was held by the Fourth Battalion; and northward, on our left, the Sixth was hard at work digging.

Fog continued; but at one o'clock, or thereabouts, it thinned away, and parties of Daly's Division retired through Riddell's lines, nearly all gassed and every one of them dead stiff and weary. Two hours later, when the Brigadier was visiting his front line east of Caulaincourt, some German planes came growling nearer and nearer till at last they were able to drop bombs on his defence and to open fire from their machine-guns.

British planes were so busy attacking the German rear and reserves that none was seen by the Northumberland Fusiliers before March 24. Then, during a hot retreating march from the neighbourhood of Misery to Foucaucourt, some growled above the Fusiliers, giving the Boche reserves a spell of rest. Meantime German airplanes had been very active against our battle troops.

The Fusiliers could not have been pleased when they read in the official bulletin of March 22, how "the enemy's attacking troops and reinforcements on the battlefield offered most excellent targets to the pilots of our low-flying machines, who

---

divisions were in line." As only a part of Byng's front was assailed on the first day, this quotation omits two THIRD ARMY line divisions, while giving the whole of Gough's, including absent reserves, two infantry divisions. I note, also, that two of Byng's support divisions were *not* available on the first day, the *Forty-first* being west of Albert, in the Baizieux sector, and the *Thirty-first* farther off still, in the north-west at Frévillers. Yet G.H.Q. expected that the main German blow would fall between Sensée River and the neighbourhood of Bapaume-Cambrai road. The *Thirty-first* was not even in Byng's land. Support divisions were kept much too far from their battlefronts, because G.H.Q. wished to move them to other sectors if Gough and Byng were not hard pressed. The need of more men being a harassing anxiety, this attitude towards four support divisions can be understood; but yet it was one of those manifestations of excessive caution which put danger after danger into chosen risks. If Gough was to bear all the risks, certainly he needed all his supports close by his battle zone; and the fighting value of Byng's seven support divisions was greatly impaired because two had to be hurried up from a long distance and thrown tired into the battle.

THE CENTRE FIGHTING 105

poured many thousands of rounds in them, causing innumerable casualties." This reads like journalism prepared for a democracy feared by craven officials, for British soldiers do not speak lightly of a foe's "innumerable casualties," particularly when their own losses are perilously high. Besides, the German air flights throughout the battle were as enterprising as our own; from day to day, then, overhead, we must hear not only our own airplanes, but also the growl of large hostile flights, with the purring swish of dispersed bullets from machine-guns.

§ II

A few minutes after the German airplanes appeared over the Northumberland Fusiliers, our patrols were heard firing. A creeping attack had begun to stretch its legs. Riddell got back to his horses just in time to see a company of British machine-gunners coming forward to "putt-puttr-putt." In a few minutes our whole line was ablaze. Boches in waves could be seen advancing towards our Sixth Northumbrians, who were using their rifles and Lewis guns with unflurried rapidity. Time after time a wave came in, and broke; eddied, and went back in a swirl, leaving behind it, upon or close to our wire, a litter of killed and wounded. Twice the attack got through; and twice the Sixth Fusiliers delivered a noisy counterblow, recovering lost ground and taking prisoners. It was a most gallant affair—gallant on both sides. An officer writes:—

"Meanwhile, working through woods on the Omignon, Boches had crossed the river south-east of Caulaincourt; and coming through a gap which we understood was to be held by another division on our right, he got round our right flank."

Hence a sound of firing over there, in the neighbourhood of Caulaincourt church. Near the church Colonel Robb had posted his reserve company. He had his headquarters in a large mausoleum at the north-west end of Caulaincourt. He left it at once and joined his reserves; took them forward charging; and, by Jove! the turning movement recoiled, and bunched, and jostled back over the Omignon!

But when you are short of men, every good thing is offset by something bad. A call for help came to Robb: the left part of his line was in trouble; and help could not be given. Every man was in action: and none could be withdrawn.

How many troops had we in Ireland? And how many in England?

An hour before civilian England enjoyed the cosiness of afternoon tea, the Fusilier's Brigadier—" a grand fellow in a fight," another General tells me—was feeling somewhat the worse for wear. Five bullets had passed through his saddle wallet, another had ripped through his coat, and his groom's mare had a nasty head wound. The bullet through his coat had ended a search for death plump against a safety razor case. Such is war, scientific war. A bearded brigadier would have been either badly wounded or killed.

Over there, through a clump of trees east of Caulaincourt-Pœuilly road, another attack came on; and at the same moment northern Caulaincourt was taken. Two companies of Fifth Fusiliers were let slip, and got their stride at once, the left company crossing the road north of the village. How well it charged among the trees . . . with Fritz in retreat! Every one cheered as much as Englishmen ever cheer; and was it not a sight worth cheering?

Northward the Sixth Fusiliers were holding nearly the whole of their original line. On their right they had been obliged to give up some ground to a point about a mile south of Pœuilly. Caulaincourt had gone from us, but the Brigadier was still in telephonic communication with the mausoleum, which he knew was in German hands. A message came asking him to send reinforcements. If he could and did all would be well. What officer sent this message? The German refused to give his name. There were five British batteries of 18-pounders about a thousand yards off, and the Brigadier turned them on to Caulaincourt and its mausoleum. Did the Boche at the wire's end get his answer?

Shortly afterwards our guns began to ransack the woods about Caulaincourt and east of the Sixth Fusiliers. Shells burst in among a close attack with excellent results, causing many casualties east of Pœuilly, as Colonel Robinson could see.

And now we must see what had happened to Martin's Brigade. As soon as the *Sixty-sixth* was ordered to withdraw behind the *Fiftieth*, like the *Twenty-fourth*, the Fifth Durham Light Infantry returned to the main Green Line about five hundred yards east of Nobescourt Farm. On its right was one of Rees's battalions, the Fourth Yorks. The foe followed quickly, and at five p.m. these two battalions were heavily attacked. The Fifth Durham Light Infantry did great execution with their Lewis guns and rifles, but a portion of the main Green Line was lost, and Nobescourt Farm itself was nearly captured. The advance got so close to it that the C.O. of the Fifth Durham Light Infantry felt that his headquarters "was almost in the actual firing line." In preparation for a last stand, every available man was posted—signallers, servants, and other odds and ends—but the attack was not pressed at once after Green Line had been reached and manned. Captain J. K. M. Hessler, who commanded B Company, was killed while fighting most gallantly, and Lieutenant Scott was wounded and captured.

In the meantime the Fourth Yorks had fared worse, losing the C.O. and a Major and the Adjutant, all killed. The Colonel died while leading his reserve company in a desperate counter-attack. It was badly hammered, this brave battalion, and was pushed out of Green Line, but not so far as to outflank Nobescourt Farm, which Major Raimes kept as his headquarters till one a.m. on March 23.

Hitherto it has been believed that the farm itself was captured by the five o'clock onrush. A report to this effect was sent to 19th Corps, whose Staff passed it on to the FIFTH ARMY. Gough himself called up the Corps and threw doubts on the report, but was assured that the report was authentic.

How did this misunderstanding arise? There were two possible, if not probable, explanations:—

1. The Green Line system was connected with places near to it. Thus the official dispatch says: "By 5.30 the enemy had reached the third zone at different points, and was attacking the *Fiftieth* DIVISION heavily between Villévéque and Boucly." Now Boucly was nearly 500 yards west of the main Green Line, and Villévéque was about the same distance south-east of the Green Line offshoot. So a report could say: "The bridgehead has been broken at Boucly," and yet Boucly itself might be all right. Similarly, a report could say: "The bridgehead is broken at Nobescourt Farm," though the farm itself had not yet fallen.

2. I believe I am right in saying that the Nobescourt Farm sector was in the area of Rees's brigade of the *Fiftieth*, but the Fifth D.L.I., Martin's Brigade, occupied it after returning from the work it did in the morning for the *Sixty-sixth* DIVISION. It follows that divisional headquarters would appeal to Rees for news of Nobescourt Farm.

In any case, the foe had settled himself in the main Green

Line in the neighbourhood of this farm, and his front line was close to the huts which had been set up in the farm's ruins. A counter-attack failed to dislodge him, and this breach of the main bridgehead had to be considered side by side with three other circumstances. One of them was the loss of the Green Line offshoot south-east of Pœuilly; another was the grave loss in casualties which had stricken the undermanned 19th Corps; and the third was the fact that, with no reinforcements at hand, and with the *Fiftieth* overstretched on a front of nearly 14,500 yards, renewed counter-attacks were undesirable. It became necessary to readjust the *Fiftieth* on a new line.

By nightfall of the 22nd Riddell's Northumberland Fusiliers held a line immediately west and north of Caulaincourt, then along their original line east of Pœuilly, where their front was drawn back a little to the road north of Pœuilly in order to meet Rees's men, whose right had been driven in slightly. The Fusiliers had lost the Green Line offshoot south-east of Pœuilly, but they were well established in their new position, and at about nine p.m. their right nearly obtained touch with the *Twenty-fourth* near Monchy-Lagache, and therefore near the main line of the Péronne bridgehead. The Fusiliers being west of Caulaincourt and the *Twenty-fourth* about 2500 yards to the south-west, Riddell's right flank was open; and the gap had to be filled with all spare officers and men of the brigade staff.

About midnight orders were received to withdraw in line with the *Twenty-fourth*, and by dawn the Fusiliers reached their new position immediately west of the Tertry-Bouvincourt road. Many men were set to dig trenches in ploughed fields, while many others had a hot breakfast. With equal success, too, Rees had slipped back by moonlight, and as for Martin's Brigade, the Fifth Durham Light Infantry withdrew at three a.m. of the 23rd, and was placed in brigade reserve behind the Sixth and Eighth Durham Light Infantry, who were in line east of Cartigny.

Riddell's withdrawal was timely, partly because of the breach of the Péronne bridgehead east of Nobescourt Farm, and partly because at six p.m. on March 22, all artillery had been sent back to a line south of Mons-en-Chaussée; so it could not have covered the Caulaincourt-Pœuilly position. This tactical error had its origin in a false report which reached the Corps headquarters that Pœuilly had been lost. This village stands on high ground and commands the country

THE CENTRE FIGHTING

to the south and west; it was used as headquarters by the Sixth Northumberland Fusiliers until four a.m. on March 23. The bridges at Caulaincourt and Tertry had been blown up.

No one liked the new battle position—a dead flat plain stretching from it westward, with no cover anywhere until Mons-en-Chaussée and its clump of trees on the southern end varied a dreary monotone.

Soon after dawn Fritz opened fire with his forward machine-guns, and an hour later our men were ordered to fall back to the railway line east of Athies.

"Watching this movement from high ground north of Athies, it resembled a set-piece at Aldershot, one company retiring in perfect order covered by the fire of another, while an officer commanding the Sixth Fusiliers controlled the 'field day' with his whistle."

The retreat had not far to go, its destination being the Somme's west bank. Here the Northumbrians were to occupy an entrenched line and "to hang on like grim death to a dead nigger." They were in fine spirits, though they resented their retreat. Fritz followed with caution, remembering his losses and not yet knowing that our artillery during the night had been withdrawn across the Somme. There was only one bridge by which Riddell's Fusiliers could cross this river—the one at Saint Christ, south of Athies. To cover the crossing it was necessary to hold with rifles and machine-guns a small village named Ennemain, perched up on highlands that overlooked the country for some miles in every direction. Fritz could advance unseen in one place only—east of Athies through the wooded valley. Just east of Saint Christ bridge, again, high ground commanded Ennemain.

To this ground the Brigadier sent four machine-guns, the last that remained; ordered his Fifth Northumbrians to hold Athies and Ennemain, while the Fourth and Sixth Battalions slipped back among thick trees on the Omignon's bank in order to reach their new position and to cover from the west Saint Christ and its bridge.

This bridge was under fire from German heavies, but for some reason or other the shelling stopped just when the Fourth Northumbrians began to cross. Both battalions reached the west bank without casualties, the Sixth with its left on Brie bridge, and the Fourth covering the bridge at Saint Christ.

A game of bluff had scored very well. While the brigade was crossing the river enemy troops crept with great caution towards Athies and Ennemain. Losses throw an icy chill over an attack when movement is not rapid enough to carry the unhit away from the killed and wounded. There is so much mystery ahead, above all in foggy weather, that human nature during an impeded attack is likely to "see in every bush a bear"; to-day's bear being a machine-gun.

Leaving Captain Proctor's company as a rearguard at Ennemain, the Fifth Northumberland Fusiliers moved down the Omignon valley and made their crossing at Saint Christ; it was hard, plodding work that lasted ninety minutes. The men could hear that Proctor was hard set in a very brisk rearguard action.

This young officer's business was to make his foes believe that a whole brigade opposed the German advance; and Proctor managed to circulate this illusion. German battalions were deployed with great care for a combat of much importance. Then at last, a full two hours after noon, little Ennemain was rushed from east and north, and Proctor and his company were cut off from Saint Christ.

This hitch would not have mattered but for another. By some mistake the four machine-guns east of Saint Christ had been withdrawn. If they had kept to their posts—and they had no right to move without written orders—they could have covered Proctor back to the Somme. As it was Proctor had no choice but to withdraw to Falvy, after holding two German battalions with his tiny force, not more than eighty men.

On reaching the Somme at Falvy he found a bridge in ruins, but he got across all right under cover of darkness and rejoined his battalion, bringing with him about forty of his first-rate men. Thanks to his and their cool valour, Riddell's Brigade had time to arrange new dispositions and to settle itself for another brisk encounter.

In the afternoon, just before three o'clock, a few enemy scouts appeared on the Somme's eastern bank. It was time to blow up the bridge. Previously the Northumbrians had destroyed all stores that could not be removed from hutments on the east bank.

The Durham Light Infantry had equally stirring experiences. Thus, for example, the Sixth Battalion was ordered to cross the Somme by the Eterpigny footbridge. A route across country was taken towards this bridge, which was partly destroyed, and about three hundred yards long. As no gap was found in the undergrowth and marshland, the battalion turned aside through the Mesnil village, into which

THE CENTRE FIGHTING

the foe had already entered. As soon as Z Company, the leader, had reached the far side of the river, the other companies were attacked. They deployed at once, and, though driven towards the marshes, they checked the enemy and managed to cross the bridge with the loss of only two officers and about twenty men. For this episode Captain J. F. G. Aubin, M.C., was awarded the D.S.O.

At night, March 23-24, a creeping surprise attack tried to cross the river over piled wreckage of bridge materials damming a shallow channel. A few Boches got across—and were killed. Though this movement failed, there was a half-hour of real danger, some troops on the right being taken all at once by one of those unaccountable fears which the ancients attributed to Pan. Even Wellington's pet division, a body of veteran troops that never failed him and never suffered a defeat, the immortal Light Division, was seized one night in a wood with uncontrollable dread, and ran for dear life, not knowing why. Similarly, on the Somme a good many troops might have taken to their heels, carrying with them some Fourth Northumberland Fusiliers, but for Lacey Thompson, Captain and Adjutant, who at the right moment met the retreating men and set their minds in order.

After the incipient panic had been stopped, a quiet night passed through its misty moonshine into the dusk before dawn. Some reinforcements had been picked up meantime in the small village of Misery, where Riddell had set up his quarters, and where the Twenty-second Entrenching Battalion was lodged in snug huts.* It was without orders, and was glad to keep company with our Northumberland Fusiliers. It was reported to be 600 strong.

A cold daybreak, with another thick mist, began the fourth day of the battle.

It was Sunday—not a Waterloo Sunday, but a tragical one, on Gough's front and on Byng's. Once more Watts had to bear heavy losses and unusual pressure. But his men held the line of the Somme against many attacks. At one place only the assault gained ground, turning and pressing back their right, and pushing along the river from Ham, and gradually opening passages at Voyennes and Bethencourt. By two p.m. some units of the *Eighth* DIVISION—the first British reinforcements on the FIFTH ARMY'S front—had been pushed back west of Potte, two and a half miles from the Somme;

---

* The Twenty-second Entrenching Battalion being a long name, we will speak of it as the Twenty-second Battalion.

but from this point the Corps' line ran back north-east to the river, and remained firm against insistent blows.

On Sunday morning Riddell's troops were sore and stiff after another cold night. Their joints ached, and their whole bodies felt numbed. Another fog hung around everything, and before it had cleared off some battalions of the *Eighth* came up to the Northumberland Fusiliers;* they made a pageant of moving shadows that grew darker and darker in tone until bronzed faces could be seen. As soon as possible they took over Riddell's front, and the Northumbrians turned their faces towards Foucaucourt, where their Corps had its headquarters. Boche heavies were shelling all the roads, as though preparing for another assault.

After breakfast bright sunshine dispersed the fog, and it became so hot before noon that a route march was irritating. Not a breath of wind stirred—except that from bursting shells. A few men were killed, and among them was brave Captain Drummond.

At Foucaucourt the Brigadier found his new chief, Major-General H. Jackson. After food they went together to Estrées, headquarters of Neill Malcolm's Division, which held the Somme line from Brie bridge to Biaches. Several important changes were discussed and decided upon. Riddell's brigade was to support Malcolm on the high ground about Assevillers; while Rees and his troops were to be sent as a contribution to a scratch body of men wrongly known as Carey's force.†

Already Malcolm had been reinforced by the Fifth

---

* The *Eighth* DIVISION was a fine body of men commanded by Heneker; it came from St. Omer—a long distance. In the meantime several British units had reached the THIRD ARMY, and from places not so far away, I believe.

† Wrongly known, because Carey had not yet returned from leave in England. Gough gave the raising of this force to his Chief Engineer, P. G. Grant, whose work was to re-establish an old and untidy line covering Amiens from Moreuil, Demuin, and Marcelcave to the Somme. Colonel Harvey became Chief Staff Officer, and Captain W. Bosanquet, Gough's A.D.C., was Second Staff Officer. No Labour Battalions were put into Grant's force, but some tunnelling companies were, and some Army troops companies also; with some Field Surveyors, and about 150 volunteers from the Army Signalling Staff, as well as two companies of U.S. bridge-builders, a battalion of Canadian railway engineers, and all British officers and men who had returned from leave. This force impressed our foes and caused them to hesitate, particularly at Lamotte. At first rumour transferred to it the very dramatic work done by other troops along the Harbonnières line. General Carey disliked very much the wild talk that journalists, and other fanciful persons, collected noisily around his name. The work done, before Carey arrived, by Gough, Grant, and their two assistants, Harvey and Bosanquet, was passed over, and by the Prime Minister even—a very noteworthy fact.

THE CENTRE FIGHTING

Durham Light Infantry. Early in the morning of the 24th, it was ordered to take post on the Barleux-Biaches road and to be ready for a swift counter-attack if the foe succeeded in crossing the Somme near Biaches. No attack was made during the morning, but at six p.m. the Germans forced a crossing a little south of Péronne. D Company of the Fifth Durham Light Infantry was sent forward at once under orders from the Brigadier; it advanced twice, but was held up by machine-gun and rifle fire. Realizing that its task was impossible, it retired, and found a place in the line with Neill Malcolm's men.

The foe had lodged himself on only a narrow span of land, and made no immediate attempt to advance farther. Indeed, the night passed quietly.

§ III

Riddell moved his men to the east of Assevillers, and once more his tired Fusiliers began to entrench themselves, doing as much work before dark as under-gardeners would expect to do in a long, easy day.

Meantime, in the Péronne sector, Malcolm and his remnant brigades would have looked upon their situation as well in hand but for two or three circumstances. On a map Péronne and its exits looked very strong, but trees and undergrowths on both sides of the canal made the field of fire far from good, and the town itself offered the foe a covered advance to the river. The Corps' policy, from about 9.20 a.m. on Sunday. March 24, was to hold the river line in this sector until it became untenable. Then Malcolm was to withdraw to the line Herbecourt-Assevillers, with Feetham—a very good officer—on his left from Herbecourt to the Somme,* and Jackson on his right from Assevillers to Estrées †

It happened that serious mischief was being done to the *Sixty-sixth* by the short shooting of British guns north of the river, apparently from the direction of Frise. Shells exploded among Malcolm's machine-gunners, not only causing many casualties, but also disturbing the morale of men who had lost most of their experienced officers, both commissioned and non-commissioned.

Some other matters also must be summoned up before our

---

* Feetham, *Thirty-ninth* DIVISION. Feetham was often in the front line with his tired men, who were devoted to him.
† Jackson, *Fiftieth* (North English) DIVISION.

minds in pictures when we study the fight for the Somme crossings and our gradual retreat from this river. We must understand the German pressure above and below the borderlands; above, north of the Somme; below, from St. Christ to Voyennes, and south-east to Ham.

On Sunday, March 24, our enemies crossed the river at Pargny and kept their footing on the west bank making a gap between Heneker and Douglas Smith.* At nightfall the river line north of Epénancourt was held by us, but the gap opposite Pargny had been ripped wider, and Boches had settled themselves in Morchain. South of this point, Douglas Smith, his left flank in the air, had exhausted all his reserves in a sequence of brilliant and useful reprisals; and for this reason in the afternoon, he retreated to the Libermont Canal.

Next day, March 25, there was no improvement. Haig says:—

"South of the Somme the situation was less satisfactory. The greater portion of the defensive line along the river and canal had been lost, and that which was still held by us was endangered by the progress made by the enemy north of the Somme. All local reserves had already been put into the fight, *and there was no immediate possibility of sending further British troops to the assistance of the divisions in line.*"†

Yet on this day, March 25, Congreve was taken from Gough and put under the THIRD ARMY, and next morning he and his troops were all on THIRD ARMY land, apart from those at Bray. These happenings will be reviewed in their relation to the northern fighting.

Even if the French reinforcements could have arrived with all their equipments, their number on the 25th was not large enough to justify the transference of Congreve from FIFTH ARMY land to that of the THIRD ARMY *unless* Byng's position had become more critical than Gough's. Haig says of the outlook south of the Somme:—

"The French forces engaged were increasing steadily, and on this day our Allies assumed responsibility for the battle-front south of the Somme, with general control of the British troops operating in that sector. The situation still remained critical, however, for every mile of the German advance added to the length of front to be held, and, while the exhaustion

---

* W. C. G. Heneker, the *Eighth* DIVISION, a first-rate fighter; Douglas Smith, the *Twentieth.*

† My italics. "Divisions in line" *south* of the Somme; remnant divisions, remember, and reinforced by only one British division, the *Eighth.*

THE CENTRE FIGHTING

of my divisions was hourly growing more acute, some days had yet to pass before the French could bring up troops in sufficient number to arrest the enemy's progress." *

There was also a gap between Maxse and Watts; it was widened by hostile attacks at Licourt; and Nesle was captured, while northward Watts' right was slowly pushed back in the direction of Chaulnes. Marchélepot was burning, but, east of Villers Carbonnel and Barleux, our border troops at midday were still holding the line of the canal, and their greatest danger was—not the German pressure, with its adroit vigour, but—their lack of renewed strength, of fresh brigades, numerous enough to stiffen adequately our defence from the Biaches neighbourhood of Péronne southward to Epénancourt.

How strange it is that although the great Amiens road and its borderlands were plainly the centre of the main battle, not only because Hutier and Marwitz struck together with their flank groups, but also because the borderlands northward extended to the Somme's southern bank, and southward to Chaulnes, Rosières, Caix, and the River Luce, yet, somehow, our guardianship in this area, through lack of enough reinforcements, had to be borne from day to day by a Corps very weak in numbers, Watts's. One thing only—a circumstance that seems providential—saved Watts, preventing his defence from being frayed through and broken before relief came in what may be called the Hangard line, some 14,000 yards from Longueau, the threshold of Amiens.

Two of Congreve's divisions—a small body of South Irish and gallant Feetham with the staunch *Thirty-ninth*—happened to be south of the Somme on March 25; they remained with Watts, and the *Thirty-ninth* did invaluable work, as we shall see. Now, on the evening of the 23rd this division—or the most of it—was north of the river; next evening it was on the opposite side and guarding our line north of Malcolm's Lancashire troops.

What an escape! If on the 25th it had been north of the Somme, it would have gone to Byng, and in twenty-four hours, or less, would have been on THIRD ARMY ground with Watts's *First* CAVALRY and Congreve's *Ninth* and *Thirty-fifth* DIVISIONS, and other troops.

Are you perplexed by these matters? I am. Their bearing on the central fighting grows much stronger as the retreat from

* Vol. ii., p. 204. Let me ask the reader to keep very carefully in mind these quotations from the G.H.Q. dispatch. Their bearing on later aspects of the battle is varied and memorable.

Péronne towards Amiens becomes more difficult and perilous. There is only a narrow strip of land between the Somme and the great Amiens road; in one part—from north of Proyart north-westward to Cérisy—it dwindles to about 4000 yards; and at this very part the greatest danger came into the borderlands from across the river, because Byng retreated more rapidly to the Ancre and the Somme at Sailly-le-Sec than Watts retreated before intense German pressure.

Unless readers understand these points, they cannot possibly appreciate the priceless value of the work done in the borderlands, still under Gough's orders, happily, from that moment of the fifth day when the river crossings along the Péronne sector became insecure.

The small bridgehead west of the canal, which the foe had made by crossing from Péronne's Foubourg de Paris, was not dangerous, though troublesome; our positions around the hostile posts were all right, and a company from reserve had been sent forward to reinforce them. But at about nine a.m. on the 25th bad things occurred at Eterpigny, four thousand yards south of Péronne, where the Pioneer Battalion of the *Fiftieth* was acting under Heneker.* Covered by an intense barrier fire, mainly from machine-guns, the enemy made his crossing and advanced. The barrage sprayed upon the Pioneers, causing them to lose confidence and unity, and to retire in clusters through Barleux towards Assevillers.

As soon as this bad turn of events became known, the Fifth Northumberland Fusiliers advanced south of Barleux, while the Sixth remained in reserve on the western outskirts of this village. Some of Heneker's own troops were busy also, together with a few of Malcolm's, and Eterpigny was swept clean again. But it could not be held owing to a rapid sequence of troubles.

At about ten a.m. Heneker heard that the right of his centre brigade had been pressed back, and about the same time his left brigade was breached. He put into the fight all his reserves, but reports said that the attack had pressed through Licourt, 2500 yards west of the Somme canal, and about 5000 yards south-west of St. Christ. At Eterpigny, too, a new crisis came. Germans began to move south-west on the road to Villers Carbonnel, and they were active also in Barleux valley. Now this eager thrust west of Brie took the attack once more to the Amiens highway.

* *Eighth* DIVISION.

THE CENTRE FIGHTING

A defensive flank was formed by Brigadier Borrett;* it spanned north of the road running east from Barleux to Lamire Farm; and Riddell sent two battalions of his Northumbrians to hold the spur south-west of Barleux and to intervene between Barleux and Villers Carbonnel.

A considerable amount of German fire—artillery, machine-gun, and trench-mortar—poured into our forward positions between Lamire Farm and La Maisonette, causing many casualties.

Some of our men retreated to the high ground between the Orme de Barleux and La Maisonette; the majority would not budge; and their reserves moved about on the slopes of the crest-line, sometimes on the rear slopes, at other times not, according as the hostile artillery fire increased or decreased. Through the afternoon fighting was very brisk, and the outlook was that of a fight pretty well balanced. The attack had gained some points, but with a disconcerting difficulty. Yes, but events north and south of the borderlands were untoward, and shortly before six o'clock the FIFTH ARMY's policy became known. Watts was to retire as soon as it was dark upon Estrées, Assevillers, and Herbecourt.

The German attack was handled cleverly, so it persevered, and just after sunset it scored a point, turning the right flank of the Fifth Northumberland Fusiliers.

As for the units of Malcolm's Division, they were about the strength of companies, and so mingled together after many counter-strokes, and frequent interchanges of intrepid help, that a very perplexing question had to be answered. Was it possible to withdraw from the battle to new positions?

There appeared to be only one way of untying this military knotted skein. Riddell had one battalion, his Sixth Fusiliers, a company of the Fifth, and six machine-guns belonging to the Tank Corps. A company of Fifth Fusiliers took up a line south of Barleux; machine-gunners held the eastern edge of Barleux; and as for the Sixth Fusiliers, they prolonged their line by deploying over high ground through a network of old trenches to the north of this village. Meanwhile the Fourth Fusiliers at Assevillers had been ordered to collect all stragglers, to give them food and water and ammunition, and to post them along the line between Assevillers and Herbecourt.

At 7.30 p.m. the *Sixty-sixth* began to withdraw through

* *Sixty-sixth* DIVISION; he commanded three remnant battalions of Lancashire Fusiliers.

these lines, and by eight o'clock Germans were trying to enter Barleux! The Northumbrians held their ground for an hour. Then our machine-guns were withdrawn; every one got ready for a retreat; and when they fell back, at 9.30 p.m., a few riflemen were left behind to fire Véry lights and to keep up a continuous fusilade. All went well. In less than two hours our men were back in the old trenches at Assevillers, and Véry lights were still shining up from Barleux, while rifle shots marked the line of our rear-guard. Meantime the *Sixty-sixth* had reached unmolested its new quarters, and Riddell's Northumbrians were all right. They had had but few casualties. Not a man had been left in enemy hands.

It was on the same day, March 25, remember, that an event in the THIRD ARMY had an increasing influence on the movements of all troops under Watts. At 1.45 p.m. Gough received a message from Byng's Army that its centre would retire during the night behind the river Ancre, and that Congreve's Corps would pass from its own ground in order to form Byng's right from Albert to Bray inclusive. Now Bray-sur-Somme was more than six miles behind Gough's left, and to guard this big span of river with his few exhausted troops was a responsibility as urgent as it was sudden and unexpected.

It had to be considered also in its relation to his right flank, where the French, and the British troops mixed with them, were hard-pressed. Butler's Corps reported that after very heavy fighting on the wooded spurs and ridges east and north-east of Noyon, the Allied line had been driven back. In the evening Noyon fell, and both British and French troops east of the town were ordered to withdraw southward across the Oise. Thus the right flank was far from safe; and now the northern flank also was weakened and threatened. But the main problem was clear and simple, as main problems are usually in war. An army when undermanned and outnumbered must concentrate all its power; to disperse its units is to invite disaster, above all when they are spent with fatigue; so Gough directed Watts to fall back during the night to a line running from Hattencourt to Frise, and to guard the Somme from Frise to Bray, where touch with the Byng-Congreve forces would be made. This narrowed the riverside front by about two miles, Byng's right being still about four miles behind Gough's left, despite Congreve's help. The uncertainties of war!

§ IV

The Northumberland Fusiliers, after some hard bludgeon work, were ordered to withdraw from Assevillers; but how? This townlet stands high, and the foe could watch it from a distance of three or four miles. He had another attack in preparation, and there was no fog. But smoke would be as useful as fog if it were thick enough; and between Fay and Estrées, happily, were many military huts with tarred roofs, and these were fired. By good luck, also, a friendly wind blowing from the north-east carried thick smoke in rolling clouds to the south-west, hiding all movements. An officer says:

"We repeated the same tactics at Foucaucourt—a small town of huts. It was here that an old sapper was found in the act of locking up a shed in which an engine pumped water to supply two large tanks and about a hundred feet of horse-troughs. The old man intended to join our retreat. As he showed great reluctance to break his engine I smashed its important parts with a hammer. When last I saw him he was looking at the damage done, and muttering: 'There'll be trouble over this.' Men behind the lines have very little knowledge of war."

We have reached the sixth day of battle. German airplanes flew low over Foucaucourt, and but for the smoke cloud they would have seen our transport moving westward, heralding another stride in a gradual retreat. Rosières-Vauvillers was to be Riddell's next line for a stand. Engineers were busy there, with some infantry reinforcements, digging trenches. The Northumbrians needed food and rest, and there would be neither if they failed to reach their new line in good order.

Words cannot portray the incessant and compelling squeeze which German tactics applied here and there on very painful places of the FIFTH ARMY'S elastic front. An art student said: "Sometimes we were pressed out into a retreat as I used to press out pigments from a tube; and sometimes we were like stags at bay, with yelping hounds all around us. The very devil!" That the twentieth century A.D. should have made war vastly worse than it was during the miscalled Dark Ages is one of those differences between pretty phrases and ugly facts over which Satan must chuckle as gladly as old Falstaff does over sack and wit and humour. Machine-guns alone are so base-hearted in the progressive genius which evolved them into their present halting-places of devilry, that the profuse blood shed by them stains our age indelibly. For all that, Ludendorff is right when he says that during the War the light machine-gun, ceasing to be an auxiliary weapon, became the true "infantryman," while the infantryman of 1914 and earlier had dwindled to a "rifle carrier."

The evolution of weapons has ever been from worse to worse in its effects on living persons and on living things. Many novelties regarded as crimes in one war have been customs in the next—customs evolving towards something worse. Consider the horror that Julius Cæsar would have felt for machine-guns!

Sprayed often by machine-gun fire, the Northumberland Fusiliers continued to go back, covered by a ding-dong action by rear-guards. Unhappily, the Fifth Battalion lost two whole platoons just east of Foucaucourt, in one of those gallant combats that occurred in many places. And the *Sixty-sixth* DIVISION—or, to be correct, its heroic remnants—had in the afternoon a grim struggle near Framerville, a small town which the foe turned from the north by passing round a Northumberland rear-guard.* But the rear-guard fought on, playing its hot part well; it saved Hill 109 west of Lihons and kept a noisy front of fire north-westward towards Framerville.

Four hours earlier, at noon, the main body had reached the cross-roads south of Vauvillers; had asked for their dinner, had received it and eaten it; and then, smilingly, had fallen asleep anyhow, anywhere, under a coverlet of genial sunshine from a beautiful spring day. What will he not do, the British soldier, if his manly appetite is not offended.

* The Framerville positions were bad and distressing. There is a report that the B.G.G.S. of the 19th Corps will never forget how he tried to get in touch with the Army by means of a telephone line which, unknown to him, had been cut by a bomb. He wished to obtain leave to withdraw from Framerville, so report says, and for half an hour—it was about 4 a.m.—he spoke with a despairing persuasion.

CHAPTER IV

THE CENTRE FIGHTING—*continued*: FRAMERVILLE, CÉRISY, HARBONNIÈRES, AND OTHER COMBATS

§ I

STIRRING events clustered. In the afternoon of the 26th the Germans took Framerville, less than a mile south of the Amiens road and only 30,000 yards from the city. They must be ousted. What troops were fit for this counter-stroke? Malcolm's were in the grapple, and suffering from parched fatigue; just then they could do no more; so the Fourth Northumberland Fusiliers were chosen, and Jackson and Riddell walked to the north end of Vauvillers to encourage the attack.

On the south-east of Framerville there was much confusion. A few hundred men from two spent divisions, after fighting almost without sleep through five days and four nights, had been shattered in a hot fight, and were hobbling back, confused rather than disordered, through the protective ranks of the Fourth Northumberland Fusiliers. Colonel Anstey, a staff officer of the *Fiftieth*, comforted the broken men, and cheered the Fourth Fusiliers, who rushed Framerville under a hail of machine-gun bullets from the church. In the church German machine-gunners were found, safe and insolent, till a few of our engineers entered the building and threw them neck and crop from the tower window.

Framerville was retaken apart from its north-west corner, protected by German machine-guns in Rainecourt. In this neighbourhood villages are very close together, and each was a bastion or redoubt on the nearing way to Amiens.

At dusk on the 26th our order of battle was as follows. Feetham with the *Thirty-ninth* manned the Proyart sector; southward, just west of Framerville and north-east of Vauvillers, was Malcolm's front, with the Northumbrians continuing the line south to Rosières, where Heneker's men were in line, with remnants of Daly's brigades in the Warvillers neighbourhood south-west. During the night, March 26–27, our left was drawn back from the northern outskirts of Proyart until it rested on the Somme north of Mericourt—a townlet only about 2000 yards to the south-east of Chipilly, and so close by the riverside district into which the Germans entered on Wednesday morning, March 27.

More than any one else, then, the *Thirty-ninth* was affected when the foe made his crossing to Cérisy.* It fought hard and well, but Watts's troops, let us remember, were in a dangerous fix. Their front was too wide, and every part of it was vital to Amiens; they longed for their cavalry, which had gone to the THIRD ARMY, and also for fresh faces, the coming of new rifle-strength. To have the foe behind you is a startling experience when the foe is also before you, and by dark, March 27, the Germans from Cérisy had marched 5000 yards south-west to the great Amiens road, and had taken Lamotte, a village projecting south of the Amiens road from the south-east of Warfusée-Abancourt.†

Now Lamotte is about 9000 yards nearer Amiens than the Proyart-Framerville line. East of it, then, all British troops and guns were outflanked perilously.

Somehow, too, news of the British withdrawal from Chipilly happened to travel slowly. A leading officer under Watts heard of it only at 3 a.m. on March 27, when a situation report was received from Sir W. N. Congreve; and all the reserves that he could scrape together were two armoured cars and about 300 men, with six Lewis guns.

What was to be done? Gough measured the crisis coolly and quietly, declining to exaggerate the hostile force south of the river, and hoping that a counter-stroke would drive it out. On the 27th, then, all day long, while a fluctuating battle raged along the Proyart-Rosières frontage, German troops were behind our tired men. It was like Alexander Dumas at his very best. Episode after episode had in it the elements of great adventure. For example, the South Irish Division, already dwindled to a small body of men, ceased to exist as a fighting unit. Cavalry north of the Somme, at Gough's request, pushed a division across the river at Corbie and took Hamel on the flank of the foe's invasion. This

---

* By 3.15 p.m., Wednesday, March 27, the Germans had crossed from Chipilly to Cérisy after repairing the bridge.

† Lamotte-en-Santerre, not to be mistaken for Lamotte Brebière, 5000 yards to the east of Amiens.

THE CENTRE FIGHTING

happened in the afternoon; and the foe—almost as exhausted as our own men—was impressed by this prompt action, and also by Grant's Force * in entrenched line from Marcelcave to the west of Lamotte. He seemed to fear a counter-blow.

§ II

In a series of pictures I wish to show the main events of this day—a very critical day for Amiens—and one that every one of us should be glad to remember. Suddenly, and only just in time, two scratch battalions arrived, Kingham's and Little's; and Little is one of those instinctive soldiers that our race produces, with much help from manly games and sports.

On the third day of battle Little was in a quiet spot of the Lake District, travelling home on leave. A newspaper came; it showed plainly that the great show had begun; and as Hargicourt was mentioned Little knew that his own battalion, the Fifth Borderers, was fighting. He caught the first train for Folkestone, and arrived there the following morning. A fog! Boats were not running. Little crossed as soon as he could, and at seven p.m. on the 25th, with the help of trains, lorries, and his legs, he reached Corbie, and got from the O.C. of the Reinforcement Camp a body of stragglers, and some other troops, about six hundred in all, and six and twenty officers. At two a.m., on the 26th this improvised force set out from Corbie. The creed of Too Late, endemic in British politics, had not found its way into this true soldier!

As soon as it was daylight a halt was called, in order that the leader and the led might learn to know each other. Some experienced officers were present, and to each of four captains Little gave a company. No one knew exactly where Malcolm's troops had reached in their retreat, but some transport men who passed him in the road gave Little a clue; and later in Lamotte he learnt that Malcolm was at Harbonnières.

The battalion marched to Harbonnières, and at once found work to do. In the dusk, March 26, it was taken to relieve those jaded Lancashire men who were in line west of Rainecourt, their left touching the Amiens road at that point south-east of Proyart where troops of the *Thirty-ninth* held

---

* On the evening of the 27th Grant returned to his own work, and Carey supplied his place.

the Beet-Sugar Factory. The Beet-Sugar Factory! How romantic this detail will be a hundred years hence!

Little's arrival was a godsend; and about the same time Kingham's little scratch force arrived. Evening sunlight after a dark day.

At last Malcolm's three brigadiers would be able to take a genuine night's rest. Officers were very scarce, and in the morning—that eventful Wednesday, March 27—the *Sixty-sixth's* infantry, whose effective strength was considerably less than that of a normal brigade, were under Lieut.-Colonel Woodcock, commander of the machine-gun battalion, with Little virtually in control of the front line.

Ardent, inspired leadership would be needed in the front line; and it was there, and elsewhere. Malcolm, Jackson, Little, Riddell, Woodcock, Whitehead, Hurlbatt, Gell,—how well they fought, and how bravely they were seconded! But it was touch and go.

At six a.m. a company of Kingham's force was sent to reinforce Little. During the night the Northumberland Fusiliers had taken over the defence of Vauvillers, aided by 120 men and 5 officers of the Fifth Durham Light Infantry, and their left flank was in touch with the *Sixty-sixth* on the cross-roads north-east of Vauvillers. South of the Northumbrians, in front of Rosières station, were other troops of the Fifth Durham Light Infantry; at and below Rosières were Heneker's men : * and a big attack upon Rosières began at nine o'clock and extended along the railway line.

Between ten and eleven the adventures of Little's force began. Troops on its left—tired men of the remnant South Irish, I believe—under a strong south-westerly pressure from the Proyart district, were broken, and went back until they were out of sight. Then some Lancashire men on the right had to yield before a pressing thrust, and they went westward and out of sight. Little's forward companies were exposed to enfilade fire, and were ordered to come back about two hundred yards. During the movement they were badly shelled by some field artillery, and sprayed also by machine-guns; but in a fine manner they took up their new positions.

Then with one company Little "refused" his left flank, and soon afterwards, with some Lancashire men, he was able to form another defensive flank by drawing back his right. But if counter-blows were not struck soon and keenly, the position might become critical. For this reason Little went

* *Eighth* Division.

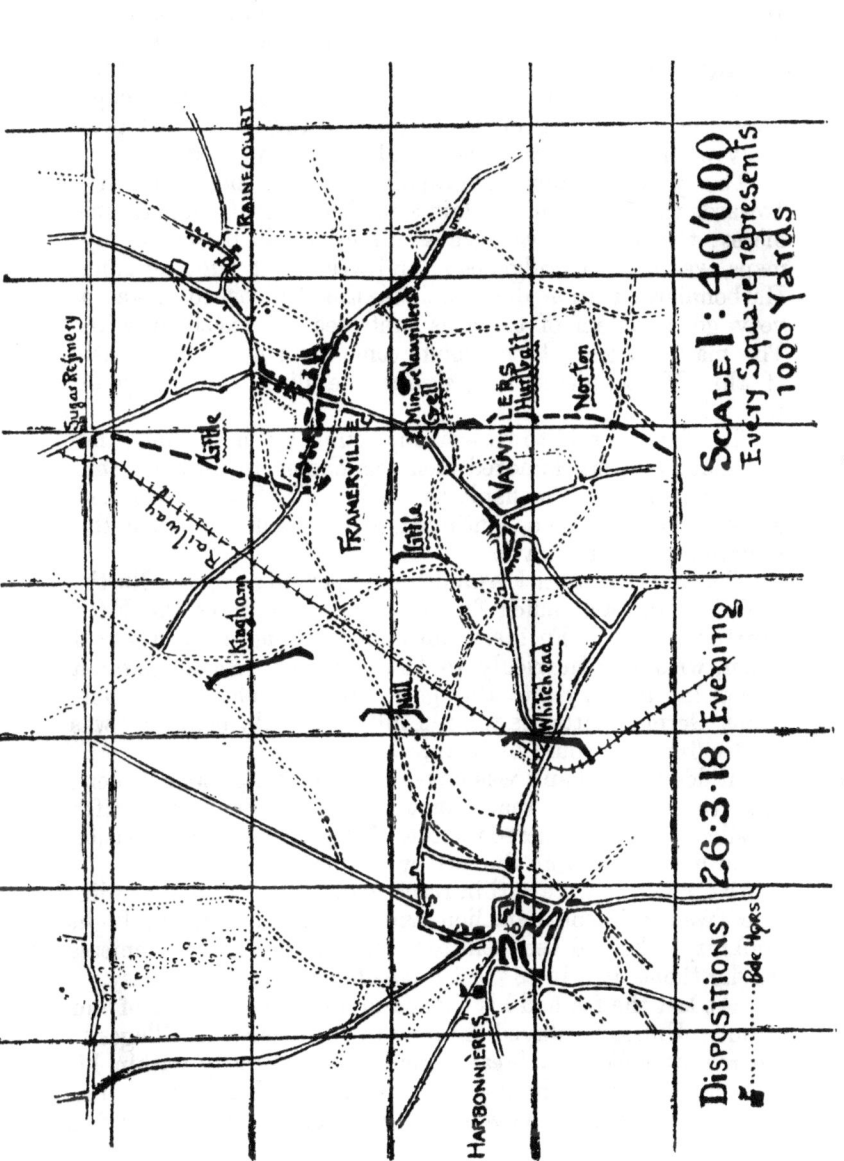

MALCOLM'S FRONT AFTER COLONEL LITTLE'S ARRIVAL.

west for help; and meeting the Brigadier of the Northumberland Fusiliers, just east of Harbonnières, he explained the situation, and the Brigadier hurried away to get a counter-attack set in motion on the left. Then some of our troops were seen assembling on the right, and they were told precisely where they were wanted, and what they must do.

The greatest danger appeared to be the northern one. Towards the east an open plain stretched away from Harbonnières; the light railway, whose direction will be seen in my maps, was a good bridgehead; and west of it, running from Harbonnières station due north to the Amiens road, was a very good system of trenches protected by excellent wire. The main dangers, then, would come from north and south of this Harbonnières line, *unless* the dire uncertainty of war interfered.

The foe was said to be working round by the Somme, and Kingham with six hundred men was chosen to form on this north side a defensive flank to Little. The South Irish, and a few Lancashire men, continued to fall back, and soon the situation was very grave.

Concurrently a brisk assault developed all along the Northumbrian line and much farther afield; and next the Fifth Northumberland Fusiliers, misunderstanding a provisional order, withdrew hurriedly to Harbonnières. Eager German troops led the way into this gap; and soon along the whole front, German batteries were in full blast. Harbonnières was under fire, and would be scrapped by shells.

Riddell's left flank was enveloped; his centre was broken; and through shells that burst in Harbonnières, his Fifth Fusiliers made a scattered retreat. What nastier local situation could have come from the lottery of war?

No reserves were within reach apart from two weak units; the Twenty-Second Battalion, and the Eighth Durham Light Infantry, who had been sent to the north-west of Harbonnières to dig themselves in to meet a possible attack from Cérisy.

At last the foe had his chance to annihilate a span of our front. Unless he stayed too long in the clustering villages to search after food,* a break-through seemed easily within his power; but not without a scramble and much bayonet work.

Riddell ordered the whole brigade staff to turn out and to

---

* In Ludendorff's book there are two or three remarks on the way in which his troops were attracted by Allied provisions. As for drink, wine, simple *vin ordinaire*, may have been found, now and then, in our deserted dugouts, and other drink too, we may assume, in the canteens that we left behind.

rally all stragglers, and then to go forward to Harbonnières' eastern limits. A telephone message told the Twenty-Second battalion to drive with a swift counter-blow past the left of the Sixth Northumbrians; and the D.L.I. were directed to advance round the north of Harbonnières.

While the brigade staff assembled under Captain Bell and Lieutenant Brown, stray men of the *Sixty-sixth* were collected. A small scratch body was raised, including remnants of the Field Companies, some Royal Engineers, and the Signal Staff of Hunter's brigade. Shells meantime dropped here and there upon Harbonnières, to detonate into spouting bricks and mortar, tiles, slates, and odds and ends of timber.

Riddell was on horseback near Harbonnières church, sheltering below the tower. A few yards away were two dead men, with three dead horses; and on the church steps, drooping and alone, sat a little old withered nun. She would not leave the church steps, this old nun, but hid herself when efforts were made to rescue her. As soon as possible she came back, with a firm feebleness; and why should she have wished to live on when her world on earth were those clustered villages close at hand which were disappearing one by one?

She did not look up when the brigade staff went by on their way to battle, marching in fours, and singing: "Good-by*ee*, Good-by*ee*, there's a silver lining in the sky*ee*!" A shell burst just before they turned into the square, dressed in all sorts of kit, just as they had left their work. Cooks' sons, and dukes' sons, and sons of a belted earl; clerks in spectacles, sappers, signalling officers, staff officers in red caps, and men who cleaned saucepans: all were there, and with them some tired, grim Northumbrians eager to rejoin their fellows. They went eastward with a swinging stride, these mixed symbols of a free-and-easy empire; went eastward with that doggerel upon their lips and in their minds a new and strange gladness, for this day in their lives made all the others worth while. Soon they were out of sight; but now and then, between reverberating shell explosions, a word or two of their song could be heard. "Good-by*ee* . . . Sky*ee*. . . ." And the little old nun did not move.

Riddell touched his horse and rode off at a gallop to the Lihons road, on his way to that part of the light railway which ran south-east. Here his odds and ends were gathered for their counter-stroke, with other men.

It was a good line, being on the reverse slope of a hill and thus unseen by German officers.

The Fourth Northumberland Fusiliers could be heard fighting west of Vauvillers, while the Sixth Battalion hammered away along the light railway almost as far south as Rosières. To save a break-through a swift and extraordinary blow was essential. Could it be given? Only the brigade staff were fresh and fit; but if the troops failed in their exhausted condition, Heaven alone knew what would be the final result.

From his horse Riddell could see more than those on foot. When the foe was about three hundred yards away he ordered the advance: and forward for fifty or sixty yards the men ran in extended line; halted, lay down, and then——? They let the foe have it with rifle and Lewis gun. The German attack was in eight or ten waves. No need for the right of our Sixth Fusiliers to advance. With half-a-dozen machine-guns this battalion splashed the waves with raking bullets: and one leading wave after another fell prone. It hesitated; then it turned, and eddied back into the supporting waves. Here was the moment every soldier looks for! Riddell ordered his whole line to go in with its bayonets, and then galloped his poor old artillery horse in order to ring up his guns by telephone.

The guns, ready and alert, brought down their barrage just east of the Rosières-Vauvillers road and right on top of several supporting enemy waves. The effect was magical. Our foes trooped away like crowds on a racecourse, and our own men went on; sometimes as far as their line of the morning, and sometimes farther. Vauvillers was retaken, partly by Lancashire men under Lieut.-Colonel E. A. Gell, and partly by Northumberland Fusiliers. The advance actually passed Little's line; but no sooner did it stop than the Boche attacked again, and then—then our own men hesitated. They were spent. They turned about, and began to fall back, while Little's troops raked the Germans with enfilade fire.

Meantime, advancing round the north of Harbonnières, the Devonshires from the *Eighth* DIVISION, aided by some men of the *Fiftieth*, had recaptured Framerville. This was a fine counter-blow; and, let us note, it was accompanied by eight machine-guns taken out of tanks which arrived only just in time, like Little and Kingham. Only just in time! And the troops in the British Isles? How many precisely did they number? More than 200,000?

What a day! About sixteen miles from Amiens the foe had had an opportunity to break through. His attack was

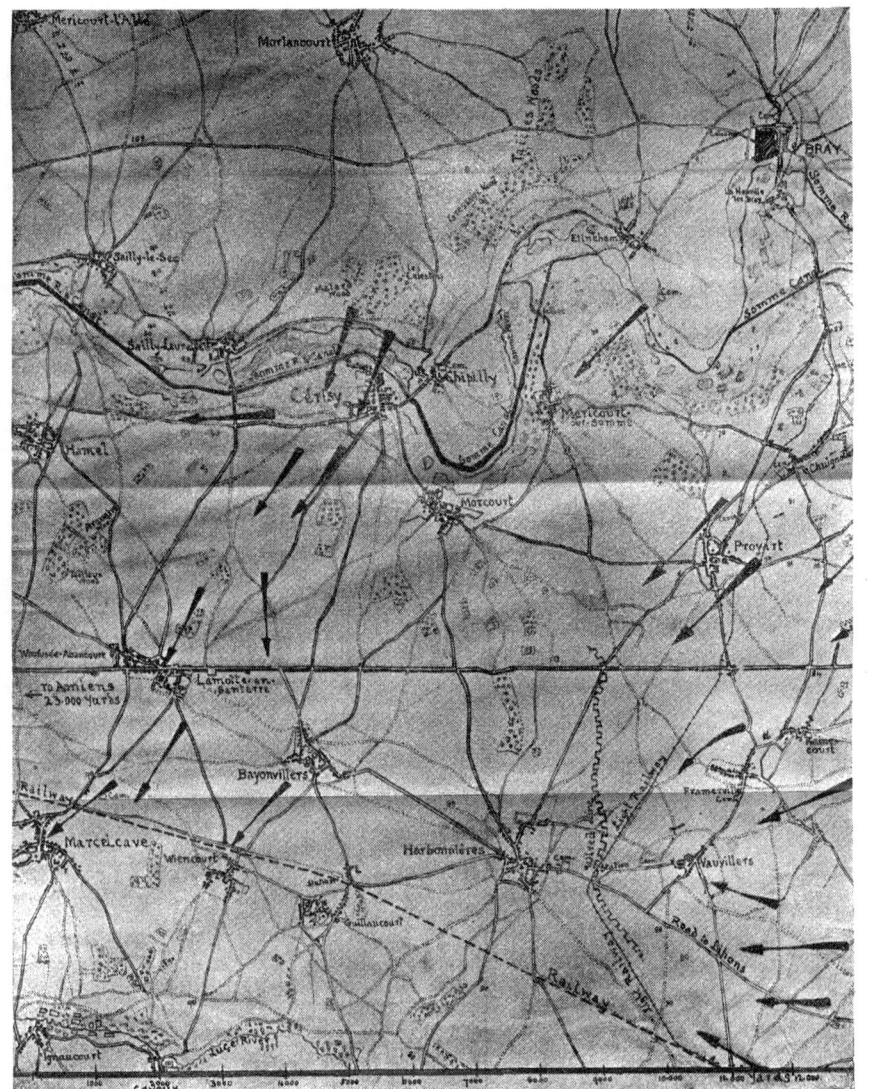

THE CERISY DRAMA AND THE VERY IMPORTANT COMBAT OF HARBONNIERES

clever and brave. Yet he had failed. And our own success was incomplete because most of our men were overdone when they went into action, with the result, inevitably, that they reached a point of exhaustion beyond which their will-power could not carry them. This happened to Riddell's Northumberland Fusiliers. They had been completely successful, taking prisoners and machine-guns, and driving the foe back in disorder. But they were short of ammunition. Ammunition was on its way to their front line when the men who had done so well at Vauvillers began to retire towards the light railway from which the counter-attack had set out. At Rosières the right flank held fast; and Northumberland Fusiliers, with a battalion of the *Eighth*, made a fine effort to recover Vauvillers. To ask exhausted troops to go forward yet again was to court disaster. So it was decided to hold the light railway and to reorganize all forces. Riddell and Little collected a lot of men who had fallen back, and echeloned them behind Little's right. Afterwards the situation remained unchanged till nightfall.

The day's fighting had been costly. Riddell's Fourth and Fifth Fusiliers had not more than two hundred rifles between them; and the Sixth Fusiliers had lost their gallant commanding officer, Colonel Wright, who was seriously wounded, like Captain Lacey-Thompson of the Fourth Northumberland Fusiliers. And losses were bitter and heavy in Malcolm's small force; they included Lieut.-Colonel Hurlbatt, killed— a fine officer, whose death was as much deplored as that of Dimmer and Elstob earlier in the battle.

Meantime, in Harbonnières, the little old withered nun remained alone and in action. "She was seen once more," says an officer, "on the church steps as usual, but dead, a merciful shell having opened for her the gates of that Other World she had lived her life to see."

§ III

At eleven p.m. Corps orders were received for another short withdrawal at six o'clock next day. Six hours later this order was cancelled by another. Our men were to take up the line Caix-Guillaucourt-Wiencourt and dig in, with some French troops on their right and our *Thirty-ninth* on their left. This change of policy had to be carried out in a few minutes, and written orders alone would be accepted by officers. Now it happened that the brigade Staff was in two parts—one *hors de combat*, the other almost in collapse through fatigue. And yet, somehow or other, the work was done before we civilians in Britain had got out of bed.

Though the work done at Harbonnières was (on this centre front) the most satisfactory of the whole retreat, giving the Boche such a thorough hard blow that he was in no condition on the 28th to resume at once his adventures there, I see no reason to doubt, as many do doubt, the expediency of this new withdrawal. Exhausted men after yet another hard fight suffered a reaction which a cold night increased; platoons and companies were jumbled up together and in need of being restored to their individual party spirit; and the Cérisy episode was not yet ended, so it was the main thing to be considered by those who had many divisional fronts to review when they came to fresh decisions. The Cérisy episode at one end of a battle front and an increasing menace to Montdidier at the other, with danger spots between them; this was the general position; and only persons on the spot could realize what the enemy had suffered in his failure at Harbonnières.

The Guillaucourt-Wiencourt line was used as a halting-place only, because troops at Caix, between ten and eleven a.m., were unsteady, and reported that their right was turned. An effort was made to establish a defensive flank from Cayeux to Wiencourt; but the jumbled companies and platoons were unfit for this job; and slowly during the day the retreat continued to the general line Ignaucourt-Marcelcave.

Mischief begets mischief, and Watts and his troops were feeling more and more the need of their *First* CAVALRY DIVISION, and of those other FIFTH ARMY men who were guarding THIRD ARMY land. Throughout the retreat in the borderlands, north and south of the Amiens road, in other words, there was an intense yearning for such information as divisional cavalry would have gathered. A troop of horse would have done wonders, stopping rumours by the dozen and anxieties by the score. As our ancestors got rid of archers long before their use had become an obsolete contributive aid, so we have disbanded too soon the divisional cavalry, as a great many officers have learnt from bitter experience.

On March 28 an effort was made to recapture Lamotte. The day before Maxse's men had been relieved by General Mesple's French Corps, and one remnant division, the intrepid *Sixty-first*, Colin Mackenzie's, was brought up in 'buses from the south to counter-attack against Lamotte. The southern part of the assault was to be done by its jaded men, while cavalry * would attack from the west. Colin Mackenzie had only about 2400 rifles left, and not a man was yet in a fit condition to undergo another fiery ordeal. Yet one and all behaved with the greatest gallantry, though they had to advance across flat, open grassland with no cover and without artillery support, for one 18-pounder is not artillery. The attack began at about noon, and a good bit of progress was made, unhappily to no purpose, for the Germans had many machine-guns in Lamotte and Bayonvillers. At about four p.m. Lamotte retaliated, the Boche beginning to shell Marcelcave more heavily than usual; and as he was expected to attack from Lamotte in order to get in behind Marcelcave, some of Colin Mackenzie's men were ordered to line the Marcelcave-Villers-Bretonneux railway on a front of about 400 yards, with their right on Marcelcave facing north. Just at dusk the foe attacked Marcelcave, aided by a good deal of artillery; he advanced in two parties on each side of the railway, coming on at a wide extension in about six waves.

After the village fell, a new defence was dug 600 yards west of Marcelcave, rain falling heavily, and veterans of the *Sixty-first* passed a quiet night there. The foe was nearly as tired as our own troops; and if the Allies could have employed four or five fresh divisions for a simultaneous attack, great and necessary things could certainly have been done. They might have regained the Somme in a single day. Either on this evening, or on that of the 27th, Gough called up the C.G.S. to Haig and expressed these views. Instead of fresh troops, spent men were thrown into the cauldron, as when Douglas Smith, whose division † was reduced to about 1000 rifles, was sent to reinforce Watts. It took line about Mézières and helped on the 28th to succour Daly's few remaining heroes.‡ Even the *Fourteenth* and *Eighteenth* were brought up to the Amiens front after their grapple against Hutier, so pitiless in its consequences was the tragical need of more men. Will civilized nations in a time of war ever impose a fitting punishment on those statesmen who fail to supply enough troops? The best punishment would be immediate banishment to the front battle line. To preserve the statesmen that fail while sacrificing the flower of youth and bravery cannot be less than horrible folly.

It was also on March 28, before midday, that Riddell

---

* The *First* CAVALRY, now returned from north of the Somme.
† The *Twentieth*, Maxse's Corps.
‡ *Twenty-fourth* DIVISION, Watts's Corps.

began a bitter experience. Our left was in the hands of men who, in seven days and nights, had managed to steal not more than about eight hours of sleep. They had dug trenches without number, and in their marches and counter-marches, attacks and counter-attacks, had covered certainly not less than sixty miles. Suddenly they were assailed when they were in the act of scratching shelter for themselves in dusty, ploughed land and in fields of young wheat. They were defeated; and if we gallop north out of Caix along the Guillaucourt road, accompanying the Brigadier, we shall see what happened. We breast a hill and reach the top. Below is a deep broad valley. On our right, along the valley's western side, and also over that hillock near the small wood on the south-east of Guillaucourt, scattered troops are falling back. They run all doubled up as men do under machine-gun fire. Close at hand bullets flick up little spurts of dust from ploughed fields, and we gallop into these fields and think of the retreating men, not of advancing bullets. Some men rally at once, though German machine-gunners have taken the wood south-east of Guillaucourt, and their fire in enfilade is a hail of torture.

But on our left, happily, our own machine-gunners are all right, hidden on a hill crested by a small wood. Their fire rattles most comfortingly into purring bursts. Yet the attack comes on; it is only about eight hundred yards away, and its aim is to reach a crest overlooking the valley and Caix. Then Caix could be turned into a shambles and our centre and right, enfiladed, would be untenable.

Below us on the south, sheltered by a steep-sided bank, men of our Twenty-second Battalion are at dinner, and have no guess of the surprise about to break upon them. We have about seven hundred yards or so to gallop, but we cry to them as we ride: "Fall in! Fall in!" They sit in extended order under the bank, and their officers hear us. They fall in, in two ranks, and then they are told that at all costs they must reach the hilltop before the German advance. First they scramble up the steep bank. And then—then a surprise. All of a sudden the notes of a hunting horn come thrillingly from behind us, near the Harbonnières road. It sounds to "the pack," and General Jackson himself is huntsman. "Forrard away!" we cry, every man Jack of us, for do we not belong to the Don Quixote of nations and empires? "Forrard away, then!" Up the hillside we go, but not so fast as the men who dined so comfortably. These good fellows reach the crest first—and back to Guillaucourt the Boche retreats.

We have saved the hill: but enemy machine-guns hammer away from that copse south-east of Guillaucourt, and many a good man is killed. Our left, too, is in the air, so a couple of platoons are sent west along the Caix-Guillaucourt road into the woods to join hands with the *Thirty-ninth* DIVISION.

The *Sixty-sixth* retreated somewhat south-west until it reached Hangard. On March 29 Neill Malcolm was wounded at Domart, and A. J. Hunter assumed command of the division. On this day, too, at Demuin, General Feetham was killed, I grieve to state. At all times he thought of and for his men, and knew when his presence among them under fire would ease their strain during a critical time. He was in the first line among his men when death came to him. He and his division, the *Thirty-ninth*, are remembered with gratitude by the survivors of two corps—Watts's and Congreve's. Next day Brigadier Borrett was wounded; and thus to the last the *Sixty-sixth* was in the fire. Its final fight, a counter-attack, came almost within reach of capturing a battery of German field guns, and many machine-guns, and from two to four hundred prisoners. Seldom have exhausted men made an equal effort.

In the afternoon of March 30, two attempts were made to recapture the old Army line between Aubercourt and Marcelcave. One of them—at about 5 p.m.—was an Australian attack; it regained touch with Colin Mackenzie's right, but was held up before it reached Aubercourt. Earlier, soon after three o'clock, Brigadier Williams of the *Sixty-sixth*, from about 2500 yards south-east of Marcelcave, set a counter-stroke in motion after collecting all the men that he could find. Colonel Little was among the leaders, and he says:—

"It was a fine show, just within an ace of being a huge success. It was wonderful to see the lines, hastily got together, advancing under a perfect hail of machine-gun bullets and shrapnel. I was on the left with some two or three hundred men, and I saw something I had never seen before, namely, Hun gunners firing over open sights at us and running about feeding their guns. In a red-brick building were four machine-guns spitting fire, with any number of others dotted about."

Despite this unusual fire, the thin advancing line did not stop. On the left it recaptured about two thousand yards, but presently it reached a forward slope and came under a heavier fire still, which our men found impassable. Colonel Little wished to go on, so eager was he to reach the German battery. On the right, too, the advance was held up by machine-guns, firing from the high ground north of Aubercourt. At last, after suffering severe casualties, the fight ended. Our men were pressed back again to the Hangard line, which ran northward from the village to Hangard Wood.

Later, at 8 p.m., the *Sixty-sixth* was relieved by the *Eighteenth* DIVISION; its various fighting units, apart from transport, had a total strength of about 2376 men, with some 107 officers.

§ IV

In this neck-or-nothing warfare, skeleton companies were obliged to counter-attack with the spirit of battalions and skeleton platoons with the spirit of well-manned companies.

Riddell's withdrawal drew closer and closer to the high ground near White House and the two roads, Amiens-Roye, Demuin-Moreuil. This neighbourhood was reached on March 29, the day on which the enemy attacked from the Avre to Demuin. It was also on this day that the few unwounded troops of our *Fiftieth* were joined to remnants of the *Twentieth*.

For three days these genuine soldiers fought under Douglas Smith. Once they were driven back towards Amiens perhaps half a mile; but after the first enemy rush they stood like rocks. And not only did they break attack after attack—they regained some lost ground. How they did it was astounding, so small was their number and so complete was their fatigue. At last, on April 2, they were relieved by the remains of the *Fourteenth*, 3rd Corps, which had been brought from Hutier's southern battle for yet another ordeal. Then they limped their way to Longueau—and a prolonged sleep.

Since March 22 they had been buffeted by the waves of Hutier's right, and had felt many bad swirling reactions from the doings of Marwitz and his divisions. Were they proud that they had helped to stalemate an enormous plan of campaign as ably designed as the best in military history? Not yet. They had overpast the fag-end of their strength, these Northumberland Fusiliers, and wanted to sleep now that duty did not forbid rest.

On their way to Longueau, hard by Amiens, they met

THE CENTRE FIGHTING

French Poilus by the thousand going east with brisk confidence; and a great many British and French guns boomed into thunderclaps of defiance, warning the foe that Amiens had locked gates not to be forced.

Ludendorff in his book says :—

"Strategically, we had not achieved what the events of the 23rd, 24th, and 25th had encouraged us to hope for. That we had also failed to take Amiens, which would have rendered communication between the enemy's forces astride the Somme exceedingly difficult, was specially disappointing. Long-range bombardment of the railway establishments of Amiens was by no means an equivalent."

CHAPTER V

THE NORTHERN ATTACKS: PRELIMINARY POINTS AND QUESTIONS.

§ I

THE northern fighting came from two combined offensives:
1. The northern portion of Marwitz's Army, extending from Cologne River up to the Bapaume-Cambrai road, at the north base-angle of Flesquières salient.
2. The battle of Bapaume-Arras, in which Otto von Below attacked Byng's centre and left.

My subject being the FIFTH ARMY, I shall speak only of those influences which passed from Byng's front to Gough's, and from Gough's to Byng's. When writing of the THIRD ARMY I shall quote as often as I can from Haig's dispatch, partly because a writer is always assumed to be too friendly towards his own subject, and partly because many persons continue to repeat the slander that "the Byng Boys would not have lost a yard but for Gough and his men, who let them down badly."

Here and there new facts will be given; and inferences will be drawn both from Haig's evidence and from Army maps. Some questioning criticism will be offered for impartial debate: and let us make it a point of honour to be equally frank towards both armies as both should be kept on the same level towards our patriotism and fair play.

One useful and necessary thing is to keep always before our minds the boundary by which they were united. I show it in a correct map, in order that readers may see at once its vital importance to both armies in their hazardous retreat and in their liaison troubles.

For some reason or other the official dispatch neither shows this boundary in a map nor describes it in words. Even in the re-published dispatch, as edited by Haig's private secretary, Lieut.-Colonel J. H. Boraston, this all-important

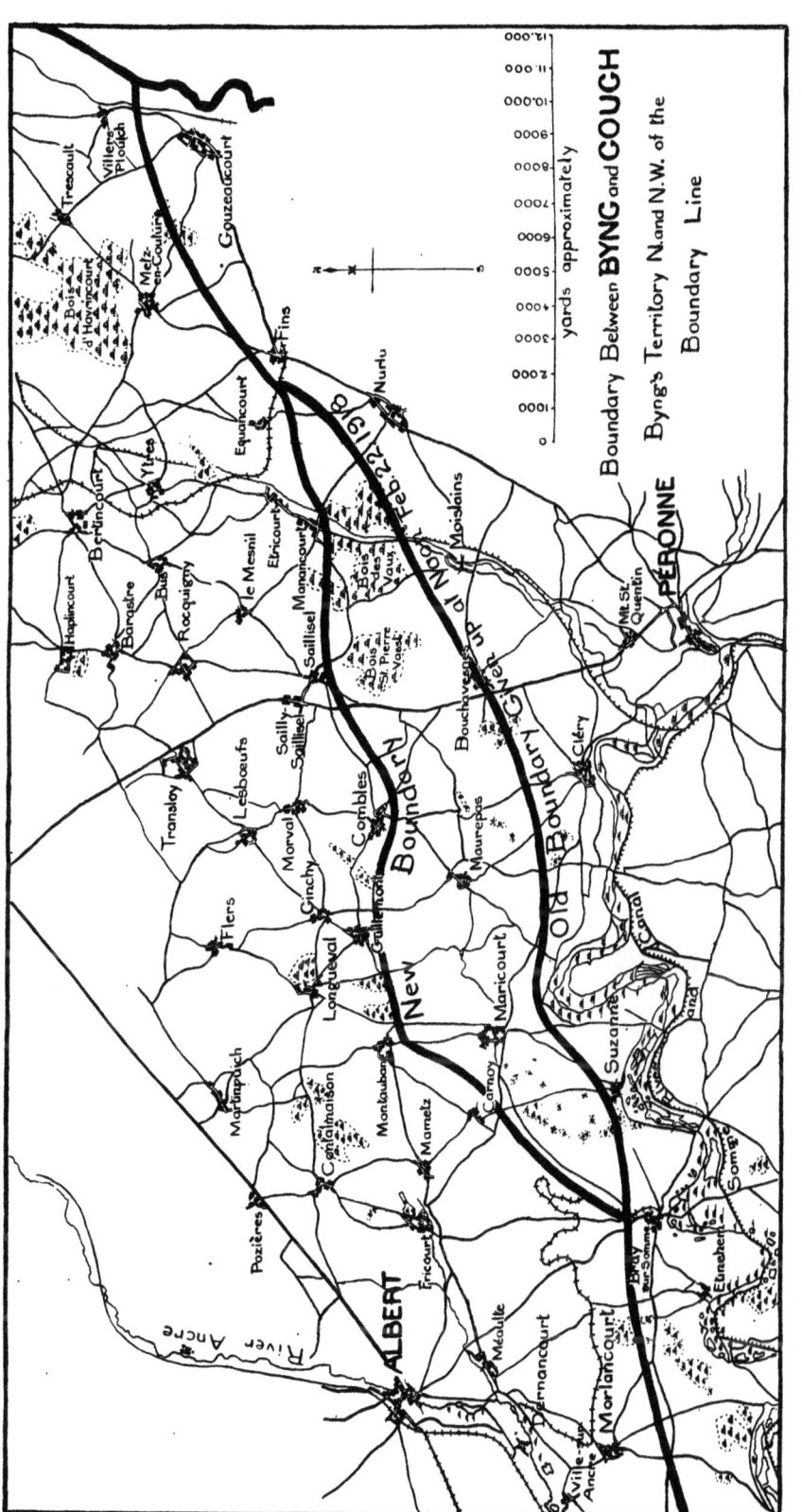

THE NORTHERN ATTACKS

boundary is not given completely. Turn to the second volume of Haig's book, and between pages 202-203 you will find a large coloured map, in which the boundary is given correctly to a point south of Guillemont and no farther. Yet it ought to have been given in full to the south of Montauban, and thence sharply south-west to Bray, as in the entirely accurate map which I am able to give. As a consequence all is vague in the boundary districts. No reader unacquainted with official maps can see when Byng's right keeps liaison with Gough's left, or when troops from Gough's left have to guard a strip of Byng's land. I note also that the dispatch becomes too indefinite as soon as Congreve, with the bulk of 7th Corps, is transferred from Gough to take over land from 5th Corps, THIRD ARMY.* The *Ninth* DIVISION is praised for a gallant combat at Méaulte, near Albert, for example, but we are not told why Gough's left flank division, on the morning of the sixth day, had to fight about four miles within Byng's area. I have no inkling why the précis-writers at G.H.Q., when preparing notes for the dispatch, were so nebulous in these important particulars, because G.H.Q. itself attached so much value to the boundary uniting Gough and Byng that a revised boundary was planned, and on February 22, 1918, at noon, the old boundary was given up.

In my map both boundaries are given, and we must study them carefully at once because the battle cannot be grasped fairly unless we learn them by heart. Note these points:

1. The new boundary from north-east of Gouzeaucourt to a point south of Montauban is gentler as a whole in its south-western course, and thus as a whole it is an easier boundary for Byng's right to follow.

2. From south of Montauban to a point a little north of Bray-sur-somme, the boundary runs steeply down to Bray, forming a very narrow one-division front immediately west of Bray. This riverside front would be held by Gough's left flank division, the *Ninth*, aided by a reserve, and all troops south of the *Ninth*, would cross the Somme at Bray to reinforce the centre battle, north of the great highway to Amiens. All this *would* be done if Byng's right retreated

---

* In the coloured map given in the second volume of Haig's book between pages 202-203, the stopping of the boundary a little south-west of Guillemont marks the point at which the bulk of Gough's northern Corps reinforced the THIRD ARMY, whose right and centre were in great peril; but this fact is left unexplained.

firmly along its southern boundary. If it failed to do so, and retreated under pressure due west to Albert, FIFTH ARMY troops would be drawn deep into THIRD ARMY land, and Gough's defence south of the Somme would be starved of reinforcements coming from north of the river. This would be a dangerous misfortune, because, as we have learnt from Haig, G.H.Q. had no more reserves ready to send south of the Somme; all local reserves had already been put into the fight: every mile of the German advance added to the length of front to be held; and, while the exhaustion of our 19th Corps was hourly growing more acute, some days had yet to pass before the French could bring up troops in sufficient number to arrest the foe's progress.* Hence it was essential that Byng's right should follow its southern boundary firmly to Bray-sur-Somme, in order that many of Gough's troops might cross the river into the centre battle.

3. The new boundary increased Gough's responsibilities at the very moment when he required more troops, not more territories. A big expanse of new ground runs from west of Fins down to Bray. It includes the Bois des Vaux, the Bois St. Pierre Vaast, Bouchavesnes, Maurepas, Maricourt, and their neighbourhoods. No doubt this new land on Gough's left supplied rear room for manœuvres, an invaluable thing when an army is well manned; but obviously weakening when insufficient rifle strength grows less as casualties increase.

4. The old boundary, note with care, is probably the better one, for its bold run south-west to Bouchavesnes afforded Byng the opportunity of forming—with as much help as possible from Gough's northern Corps, under Congreve—a strong flank looking south-east on any German effort to reach Péronne, if only he could hold his ground in front of Bapaume. Such a flank, even if it were not pushed forward to Moislains and the Mt. St. Quentin, would be the best of all guardians for Péronne; it might cancel the loss even of the Péronne bridgehead. The line of the Canal du Nord and the River Tortille was obviously the best rear line for this flank pressure. Hence it would be interesting to know why G.H.Q., after altering the boundary, did not set apart enough reserve strength to hold a firm flank along the line (let us say) of Gouzeaucourt, Fins, Nurlu, and on towards Péronne.† Consider what we owed in

---

* See the quotations given from Haig in Part II., chapter iii., pp. 114, 115, of this book.

† After-thought suggests that perhaps G.H.Q. thought that it had done

the Lys battle—which followed at once the events of March, 1918—to the firm flank running north-west from Givenchy to Clarence River. It was this steady, stalwart line that baffled Ludendorff's efforts to capture Hazebrouck and to throw us back on the coast. Gough had no men for a virile flank running south-west from Gouzeaucourt; the utmost his left could do was to keep a reserve battalion at the boundary in Dessart Wood; and as for the THIRD ARMY, it had on the boundary, between Equancourt and Manancourt, only a very thin brigade of the *Second,* while no fewer than three divisions were placed, with G.H.Q.'s approval, in the narrow and shallow Flesquières salient. Here is another point which puzzles me incessantly. . . .

The salient, much too small for a big battle, was not at all likely to be assailed by a front attack because its defences, both natural and military, were very formidable, what with Highland Ridge, and a captured portion of Hindenburg's line, abundant wire, many well-hidden machine-guns, and other defences. Ludendorff's aim, inevitably, was to cut off its garrison; and hence the salient itself, thrusting a blunt negro-nose towards Cambrai, was a thing of secondary value, which, indeed, might be turned into a trap. The useful and necessary things to consider were the defences across the base of it, and a very powerful system of trenches to guard its north flank, base-angle, and rear; next, a not less powerful protection for the south flank and rear. Why, then, place a crowded garrison of three divisions *in* the salient? Is it not quite true that strength at the wrong places means perilous waste in battles, while at right places it wins victory?

Even in peace manœuvres three divisions could not be moved easily after dark from a place so cramping. The few roads would become over-thronged; here and there a wheeled thing would break down and block the way; and as for those troops who had to go steeply south-west from the Villers Plouich sector to Equancourt and Manancourt, they might easily get into hitches and scrapes. In actual war all difficulties were multiplied vastly. Haig tells us that Byng's right remained till the evening of March 22 on Highland Ridge and in the Hindenburg line, with the most southern troops holding Villers Plouich as a bastion. We are not told why these defences were held so long, when the position both

so. Certainly Byng's was very much the stronger British army per yard of ground, and Byng had to deal merely with the German secondary attack. Perhaps G.H.Q. believed that he had troops enough to meet all exigencies.

north-west and south-west of the salient had been menacing all day; but we do learn that in the evening of March 22 the foe made a heavy flank attack against Villers Plouich as well as a delaying onset at Havrincourt. These German movements were repulsed, but nothing could have been worse for a retreat south-west. The foe followed vigorously through the night, and, as we shall see, Byng's right was pressed away from its liaison with Gough.

Hitches occur in all complicated retreats, and never should they be magnified; but from time to time they must be noted, not because they are blameworthy, but because of their effects. Till Byng and G.H.Q. explain the whole of their policy towards Flesquières salient, no student, military or other, can understand either the absence of enough reserves along the boundary or the presence of so many troops in the salient. Some persons assume that as the salient was won in a battle which had a misfortunate final phase, both G.H.Q. and the THIRD ARMY valued it overmuch, in accordance with that natural habit of mind which magnifies anything done with great difficulty. There's no need here to have views on this point, as the main object here is to state problems and to see whether they are foes or friends to that equipoise which defence needs when it is assailed.

§ II

When we look at the boundary in its relation both to Flesquières salient and to the whole retreat, we must keep always before our minds a principle of war which may be accepted as a permanent axiom. If two military forces make a continuous line in a battle, like Byng's force and Gough's, and if one is strong while the other is weak, the stronger force should regard it as an obligation to hold and keep firm union with the weaker. The reasons:—

1. When the strong force fails to do this, the weak one has to extend its flank into the strong one's ground; so its weakness is weakened—a terrible fact when it is fighting against great odds, while the strong one has less pressure to hold off.

2. If the strong force, like the weak one, has odds against it, firm union with the weak one is equally imperative, since the weak one is less fitted to bear overstrain; and if the weak is overwhelmed in the boundary districts, the strong force has its flank rolled up and its rear invaded.

3. Hence it is an act of self-help for the strong force always to keep enough reserved strength at the boundary, and to do all in its power to reinforce its weak neighbour at necessary moments.

Sound principles in war are obvious common sense; hence they fare often in battles as trite good aphorisms do in everyday life—badly. What need would there have been for FIFTH ARMY troops on THIRD ARMY land if the stronger army had retreated in time from Flesquières salient and had held either a firm flank or a firm course along the boundary?

In a question of this important sort a writer of history cannot beat about the bush; so it is necessary for me to say that I have sought in vain, both in official maps and in authentic written evidence, for prompt and effective liaison movements by the units of Byng's right.

Yet every one must have met THIRD ARMY men who have said: "Our right flank, you know, was uncovered by Gough." To receive reinforcement from Gough, and then to bring this allegation against him, is somewhat contradictory. North of the Somme troops from the FIFTH ARMY held much more than their own ground till they were relieved, mainly by Australians. Here is a fact, and a fact is neither cancelled nor hurt by a thousand arguments.

The précis-writers at G.H.Q. seem to have forgotten this platitude, for at one point they accepted a view gathered from Byng's southernmost division—a view expressed by all units when they are obliged to retreat, namely, that their flank was left in the air by their neighbours. In other words, the *Forty-seventh* DIVISION, 5th Corps, THIRD ARMY, declares that its flank was left in the air by the *Ninth* DIVISION, 7th Corps, FIFTH ARMY; while the *Ninth* blames the *Forty-seventh* for the same routine misdeed. Which of these allegations is correct? G.H.Q. takes sides with the *Forty-seventh*, paying no attention to the presence of the *Ninth's* left on land which ought to have been held by the *Forty-seventh's* south brigade. Further, G.H.Q. has passed over in silence the frequent and pointed warnings sent by Gough's left to Byng's right. So a student is naturally perplexed and surprised.

As G.H.Q. has published errors in this matter, and as historical truth is our aim, I give a chapter in Part IV. as a refutation. But a quiet statement of facts must go hand-in-hand with the recognition that précis-writers are liable to blunder here and there while striving to reduce into order a chaos of details; and when a Commander-in-Chief, with vast current affairs pressing upon him, has to compile a long dispatch on a battle several months old, errors made by précis-writers pass into an authoritative document. For all that students cannot help being troubled by the way in which all boundary matters are treated in the dispatch. Readers are not told that even such important places in the defence as Combles and Morval are within Byng's sphere, though bad events happen there, and the *Ninth's* Highlanders try to restore a very menacing situation.

One point more. As it is necessary for a strong army always to hold strong liaison with a weak one, so in a weak army it is essential that the component units should strive unceasingly to protect the land within their own boundaries and to keep strong union with one another. No unit has men to spare, and hence it cannot send help to a neighbour without impairing its own weakness. Here is another commonplace that adds drama and pathos to the interchanges of help that Gough's units gave to one another, while Marwitz was aiding Otto von Below.

Ludendorff hoped that these German officers would take stress and strain off each other turn by turn, and that they would manage to push through between Péronne, Bapaume and Ervillers, while the central and southern offensives overwhelmed a very thin defence before Allied resources could arrive.

§ III

Let me ask you to examine my map of the whole battlefield with the massed German armies in their approximate order of battle. It is clear that Otto von Below's power, redoubtable as it is, must be regarded as a minor one, compared with the odds which assailed Gough. Below and Marwitz employed in all twenty-eight divisions each, including three that they shared together. These three divisions were the *Fourth,* the *Hundred and Nineteenth,* and *Hundred and Eleventh.* Marwitz had thirteen in first line, eight in support, and seven in reinforcements, while Below had twelve in first line, nine in support, and seven in reinforcements. Only four divisions in the Marwitz groups, when fighting began, were in line against Byng; they were those around Flesquières salient; and soon they became as troublesome to Gough's left wing as they were to Byng's right. So the

THE NORTHERN ATTACKS

whole of Marwitz's attack weighed upon a half part of our FIFTH ARMY, and its northern divisions helped to carry southward, or south-westward, disturbing influences from the gaps and gains made by Otto von Below.

As a whole the aspects of Marwitz's attacks compose a wonderful battle, not so terrific as Hutier's but certainly as full of lessons and warnings.

They had five aims :—

1. To make Marwitz's left wing an increasing help to Hutier in order to break through north and south of the Vermand-Amiens road;
2. To break through also north and south of the Cologne River, at the point of union between Amyatt Hull's South Irish and Neill Malcolm's Lancashire troops;*
3. To strike between Tudor and David Campbell† in order to unbalance the whole defence of both;
4. To separate Tudor's left wing from Gorringe's right,‡ and thus to let in travelling mischief behind Byng and Gough.
5. To support with his right flank division, the *Twenty-fourth* RESERVE, a cluster of divisions forming Otto von Below's extreme left.

If we look at these five aims in their relative co-ordination, we find that No. 1 belongs as much to Hutier's right as Gayl belonged to Hutier's left; and that Nos. 2, 3, and 5 were mainly agencies to ensure the largest measure of success to No. 4.

In other words, to break through near the boundary line dividing Gough from Byng was the main purpose behind Marwitz's great northern attack. At this point a genuine break-through would give scope for two very big turning movements; even a partial success would keep British reserves from being hurried south against Hutier, and it might aid Marwitz and Below in their wish to take Bapaume and Arras at a moderate cost in casualties, while preparing for a contributory battle in Ludendorff's plans to be fought on the Lys.

Aims 2 and 3 in their effects, if they were made real on the first and second days, would throw out of gear the whole

---

* *Sixteenth* and *Sixty-sixth* DIVISIONS.
† *Ninth* and *Twenty-first* DIVISIONS.
‡ Sir G. F. Gorringe; *Forty-seventh* DIVISION, 5th Corps, THIRD ARMY, whose right wing was in touch with Tudor's left on the boundary between Byng and Gough.

defence which the *Ninth* had prepared as the guardian of Gough's left and rear.

Within its own territory, too, the *Ninth* would protect Byng's right, but not, of course, without adequate support from its neighbour. Happily it was a powerful division, with a commander of impressive character and uncommon good gifts as a soldier. Not yet have Tudor and his men received much credit for their work, except from the foe, who had many reasons to speak of their brigades with wondering respect. It is a thousand pities that Byng did not place the GUARDS DIVISION on his extreme right; then the *Ninth* would have had a collaborator as great as itself, and many a good result would have aided the defence.

Both infantry and gunners were aided by some special training. For nearly six weeks they had been out of the line, and through half of this time had been exercised in sham open warfare. In the circumstances, then, the *Ninth* was fortunate; and after its brief training there was work enough with spade and pick to teach its men to know their defences and to keep their sinews from being slackened by dugouts and trenches. One and all were entirely fit. Their order of battle:

Left Front, the 26th (Highland) Brigade commanded by Kennedy: Eighth Black Watch, Seventh Seaforths, and Fifth Camerons; 74 officers and 2593 other ranks; an average of 864 rifles per battalion, including "details"; so the brigade of three battalions was only 407 men below maximum strength. This was too many for such a huge battle, but the *Ninth* was lucky in its numbers nevertheless. Sir F. Maurice certainly is right when he says, concerning Haig's fifty-eight divisions, " hardly a battalion, a battery, or a squadron had its full complement of men" in March, 1918.*

Right Front, a fine South African Brigade, commanded by Dawson; 91 officers and 2718 other ranks; an average of 907 rifles per battalion, including "details."

Divisional artillery had 107 officers and 2452 other ranks; the Ninth Battalion Machine Gun Corps, 37 officers and 753 other ranks; and as for the reserves, in the Ninth Seaforth Highlanders, Pioneers, there were 24 officers and 857 other ranks; and the 27th (Lowland) Brigade, commanded by Croft, consisting of the Eleventh and Twelfth Royal Scots and the Sixth King's Own Scottish Borderers, possessed 2636 men and 69 officers.

* "The Last Four Months," p. 19.

FRONT OF THE NINTH DIVISION AND THE ENTRENCHED LAND NORTH AND SOUTH OF IT

The total man-power, with artillerymen, machine-gunners, and pioneers, was 402 officers and 12,039 men. The total rifle-strength, including pioneers, was below the maximum by 1195 men. For all that, what a blessing it would have been if this man-power had been present and active in every division of our FIFTH ARMY.

Each brigade in the battle front employed one half of its forces to defend the forward zone and one half to guard the battle zone. In the forward zone men were to fight as in forlorn hopes; no counter-attack on a large scale would be made to rescue them or to recover what they had lost. Their battle zone was the main theatre; artillery posts were chosen principally for its protection; and if the foe broke into it, and no order for a withdrawal came, counter-blows were to be struck with full strength.

The Corps Commander, General Congreve, was very well satisfied both with the *Ninth* and with his Corps' defences. His front was too deep and too wide to be manned all through, so it was held by a series of strongposts or redoubts, with guns and machine-guns covering all intervals. On the left, and also on the extreme right, where deep valleys lay, the field of fire was pretty bad; elsewhere it was very good and widespread. As for strongposts, taken from left to right, they were Gouzeaucourt village, St. Quentin Ridge, and Gauche Wood,* Chapel Hill and Vaucellette Farm, Peiziére, Epéhy, Malassise Farm, and Ronssoy. Behind these there were other strongposts in every zone. The defences were called from front to rear the Red Line, Yellow Line, Brown Line and Green Line. This last was heavily wired, but shallow, here as elsewhere. Still, it had some mined dug-outs, like the other lines.

* These three were in the *Ninth's* area.

CHAPTER VI

THE JOINT ATTACK BY MARWITZ AND OTTO VON BELOW: THE FIRST DAY'S BATTLE

§ I

ON March 21 the salient itself was almost a haven of rest. Near the northern base angle the *Seventeenth* was active with its left wing, and there was a tepid raid of perhaps two battalions against a part of Gorringe's line; but from the upper base angle north-westward to the Sensée River, between eight and nine miles, a very grim conflict was active all day long. Otto von Below's left and centre were at work, crashing with nine well-armed divisions, and Byng, north-west of the salient, on these eight or nine miles, had to throw eight divisions into fierce action: the *Third, Thirty-fourth, Fortieth, Fifty-ninth, Twenty-fifth, Sixth, Fifty-first*, and *Nineteenth*.* Marwitz had four divisions around the salient, watching the British three inside: the *Seventeenth* on the British left, the *Sixty-third* in our centre, and in the south, forming liaison with Gough's left, the *Forty-seventh*, London Territorials. As the northern part of the *Seventeenth* was in action on the first day, Byng had 8½ divisions inside the fighting. Along equal spans of front Gough had never more than 3½ divisions, usually less, though the odds against him were a great deal heavier.

It is commonly supposed that on March 21 the German armies employed many of their second-line troops. This error is circulated even by Lieut.-Colonel John Buchan, in his excellent book on "The South African Forces in France" (p. 170):—

"Against nineteen British divisions in line Ludendorff had hurled thirty-seven divisions as the first wave, and before the

---

* The *Twenty-fifth* came during the day from Bapaume, and the *Fortieth* from a point on the River Crinchon, about seven or eight miles south-west of Arras. It went to the St. Leger sector, a danger spot.

dark fell not less than sixty-four German divisions had taken part in the battle—a number much exceeding the total strength of the British Army in France."

I wish Ludendorff had been mad enough to act in this preposterous manner. His first-line divisions were very numerous and so close together that they could not attack through a whole morning of thick fog without getting their units into much confusion; and his new tactics had for their central aim the art of getting the man-power of massed formations without offering thick targets to hostile fire. So his first-line divisions were trained to advance in a thin wave with the men in open order, and constantly renewed in strength from the rear. Those brigades who had to follow the slowly creeping barrage were practised behind a barrier fire of live shells; and as Ludendorff desired above all things to achieve his purpose with the smallest possible loss in casualties, he opposed energetically the use of second line divisions during the battle's opening phase. To crowd into action more and more divisions would ruin inevitably his firm belief both in open order and in highly specialised bodies of troops welded by practice into the common pack of carefully trained ordinary riflemen. On the second day, here and there, a second line division was called into the first line, but even these few exceptions were so at variance with Ludendorff's tactics that they must have been a bitter disappointment to him. Note in his book how eager he was always to keep his men in open order and to fight through several days with the first-line divisions only.

Otto von Below's nine divisions on eight or nine miles of front must have lost in the fog their open order; and in meeting eight British divisions during the day, in a new Waterloo fought between forces of almost equal strength, their losses must have been unusually severe. Indeed, Ludendorff says that Below's losses were too heavy on the first two days, and that his capacity for later work was impaired by those losses. Byng, too, must have suffered severely, for heavy losses are inevitable when almost equal powers keep at death-grip through two terrific days. As for the northern part of the salient, Byng's *Seventeenth* had against it Marwitz's right flank division, the *Twenty-fourth* RESERVE aided by Below's left flank division, the *Hundred and Nineteenth*.

By midday on the 21st Byng's battle zone was entered at several points, but fortunately not astride the Canal du Nord, running about midway between Havrincourt and Hermies, and thus of vital need to the salient's garrison. Not much general progress was made here, thanks to Robertson and the *Seventeenth*; but farther west Doignies was lost, and Louvaval also, and the battle zone had been stabbed at Noreuil, and Longatte, and Ecoust St. Mein.

Ludendorff imagines that Otto von Below's troops lost the protective barrage, but this view is contradicted by the rapid advance against a very powerful defence.

"Fighting in and in front of our battle positions continued with the greatest intensity throughout the afternoon and evening," says Haig. "On the THIRD ARMY front, our line in the Flesquières salient had not been heavily attacked, and was substantially intact. Beyond this sector, fierce fighting took place around Demicourt and Doignies, and north of the village of Beaumetz-lez-Cambrai. In this area the *Fifty-first*, under G. T. C. Carter-Campbell, was heavily engaged, but from noon onwards practically no progress was made by the enemy. A counter-attack carried out by two battalions of the *Nineteenth*,[*] G. D. Jeffreys commanding the division, with a company of tanks, recovered a portion of this ground in the face of strong resistance, and secured a few prisoners, though it proved unable to clear the village of Doignies.

"Lagnicourt fell into the enemy's hands during the afternoon, and heavy attacks were made also between Noreuil and Croisilles. At one time, hostile infantry were reported to have broken through the rear line of our battle positions in this sector in the direction of Mory. By nightfall the situation had been restored;[†] but meanwhile, the enemy had reached the outskirts of St. Leger and was attacking the *Thirty-fourth*, under C. L. Nicholson, about Croisilles heavily from the south-west. A strong attack launched at five p.m. against the *Third*, under command of C. J. Deverell, north of Fontaine-les-Croisilles, on the left bank of the Sensée River, was broken up by machine-gun fire."[‡]

[*] A support division brought into action by a menacing situation; and so were two other divisions, the *Fortieth* and *Twenty-fifth*. On the second day Byng had twelve divisions in action: *Third, Guards, Thirty-fourth, Fortieth, Fifty-ninth, Sixth, Twenty-fifth, Nineteenth, Fifty-first*; and three in the salient. On the third day, from the Scarpe down to the neighbourhood of our FIFTH ARMY'S boundary, fifteen divisions were fighting: *Fifteenth, Third, Guards, Thirty-fourth, Thirty-first, Fortieth, Fifty-ninth, Forty-first, Twenty-fifth, Nineteenth, Fifty-first, Second, Seventeenth, Sixty-third, Forty-seventh*.

[†] This fact shows the value of abundant reserves on the spot. Gough's troops as a rule had to counter-attack with numbers tragically small. But the break-through towards Mory is very remarkable.

[‡] Vol. ii., pp. 188-190. Note the leverage pressure from south-*west* against Croisilles, a very important stronghold.

JOINT ATTACK BY MARWITZ AND VON BELOW 149

Correct maps show what this information means. On March 21, along a narrow span of eight or nine miles, Byng lost almost the same varying depth of land as Gough lost on his very wide front, as at Chapel Hill, Ronssoy, Le Verguier, Maissemy, Holnon, Savy, Contescourt, Essigny, and Quessy.

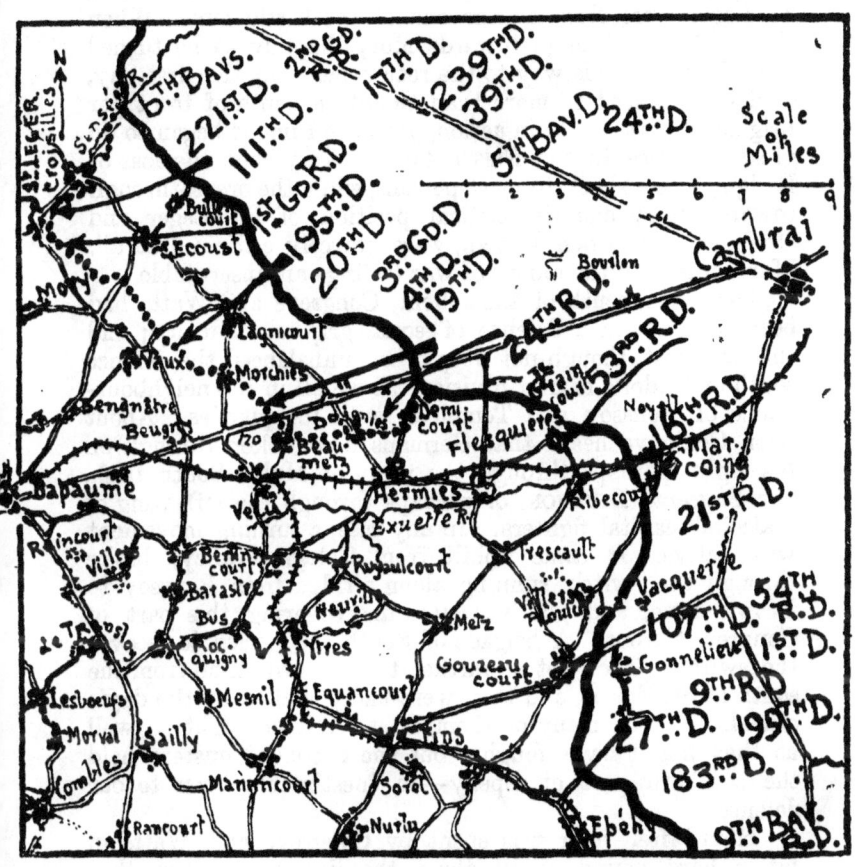

FLESQUIÈRES SALIENT, MARCH 21, 1918, WITH THE GERMAN DIVISIONS, AND THE LAND LOST BY OUR THIRD ARMY NORTH-WEST OF THE SALIENT.

Of course, an advancing battle line cannot be given at all accurately, since it alters from hour to hour; and it should be measured from the attack's starting point, and not from the defenders' line. My map on p. 149 gives the line from which Byng's troops were pressed back, not the line from

which the attack set forth on its adventures. South of St.
Leger—in the Ecoust St. Mein sector—the hostile advance
was about 6000 yards; along the Bapaume-Cambrai road,
about 4700 yards; and the loss of Doignies, with German
pressure to the outskirts of Beaumetz and Morchies, menaced
Flesquières salient, enforcing a withdrawal.* Morchies and
St. Leger were close by the end of the battle zone. When
the foe broke through towards Mory, happily to be turned
back, he was on his way to the rear zone. On the first day,
evidently, Byng lost more than Gough in depth of front per
brigade of man-power in action, yet false rumour began to do
great injustice to the FIFTH ARMY. Very soon the loss of
Essigny was a shock to most persons, while the break-through
towards Mory and the critical position of St. Leger and
Croisilles, even when known, were scarcely criticized at all.
Many things in the moods of war feelings are inscrutable.

Meantime, south of the salient, Congreve and Watts had
been hard set in a defence of equal grip and ferocity; and
the land lost, though not deep,† had unbalanced the defence
south of Tudor's barrier division, above all in the neighbourhoods of Ronssoy and Templeux with its quarries. About
noon Congreve heard that Germans had broken through on
his right, perhaps through the right of Hull's South Irish,
our *Sixteenth* DIVISION, or perhaps through the left wing of
Malcolm's capital fighters. In any case, a turning movement
was active. It came uphill from Cologne valley, broke
through the switch running along a ridge from Ronssoy to
Brown Line, and got into our guns covering this part of
Congreve's front. A brigade of South Irish tried to recover
the switch. They got no farther than Brown Line from the
south of St. Émilie, and they were badly shaken by the day's
ordeal. A good many of them, I fear, did not fight as well
as they might have fought; but the Second Munsters held
the southern part of Epéhy—an inestimable boon to our
defence.

Hour after hour was spent by Congreve and Watts in
bitter hard pounding all along the line, apart from that

* At Ronssoy the South Irish lost about 4700 yards; at Maissemy the
Twenty-fourth went back about 5750 yards; and as for the *Fourteenth* at
Essigny, from 7000 to 7500 yards is the estimated loss.

† Indeed, the defence by units below strength in our 19th Corps was
astonishingly good, but very costly in casualties. On a front of nearly
13,000 yards Watts had only two infantry divisions, aided by the *First*
CAVALRY, which on March 21 was brought from the Péronne sector into the
fighting area north-east of Vermand.

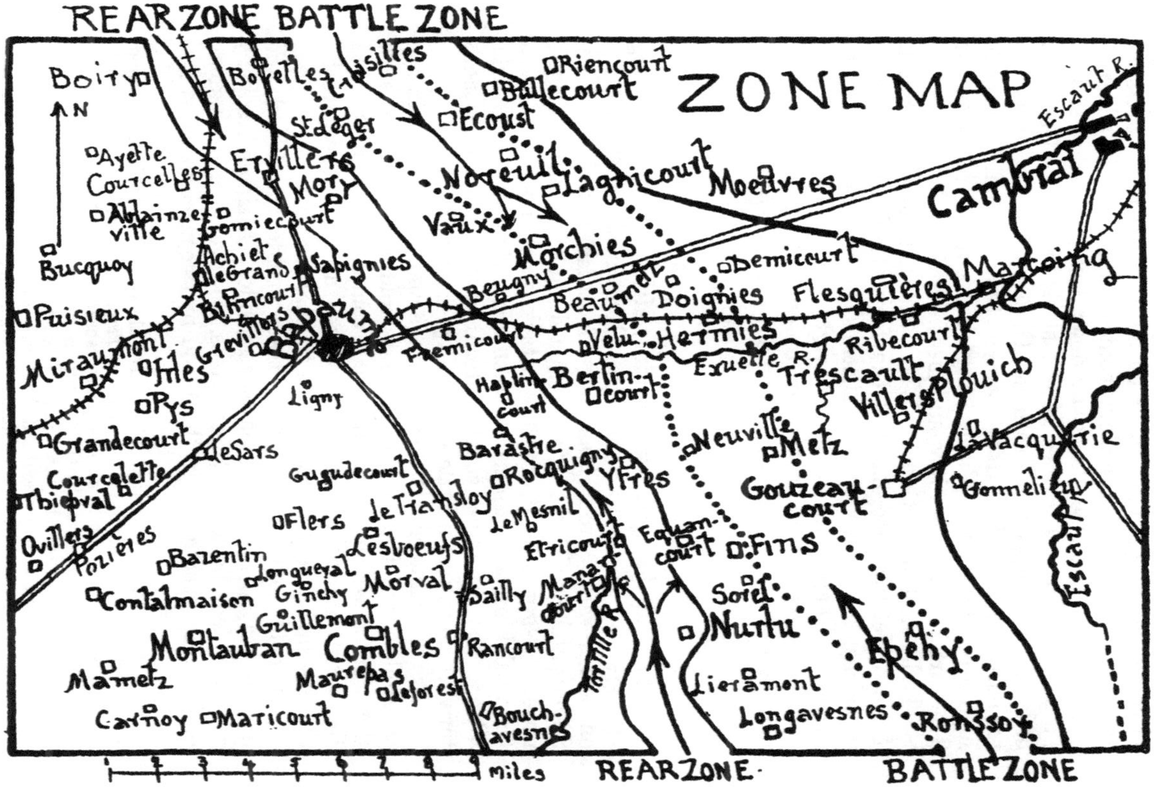
ZONE MAP
REAR ZONE
BATTLE ZONE
REAR ZONE
BATTLE ZONE
N
Boiry
Boyelles
St. Léger
Ervillers
Mory
Ayette
Courcelles
Ablainzeville
Gomiecourt
Bucquoy
Achiet le Grand
Sapignies
Bihucourt
Puisieux
Miraumont
Irles
Grévillers
Pys
Ligny
Grandecourt
Le Sars
Courcelette
Thiepval
Ovillers
Pozières
Bazentin
Longueval
Contalmaison
Ginchy
Guillemont
Montauban
Combles
Mametz
Maurepas
Carnoy
Maricourt
Riencourt
Bullecourt
Ecoust
Noreuil
Lagnicourt
Moeuvres
Vaux
Morchies
Beugny
Beaumetz
Demicourt
Doignies
Flesquières
Frémicourt
Vélu
Hermies
Ribécourt
Haplincourt
Bertincourt
Trescault
Villers Plouich
Barastre
Rocquigny
Ytres
Neuville
Metz
Gueudecourt
Le Transloy
Flers
Lesboeufs
Morval
Le Mesnil
Etricourt
Equancourt
Fins
Gouzeaucourt
Gonnelieu
La Vacquerie
Sailly
Manancourt
Rancourt
Sorel
Nurlu
Épehy
Liéramont
Longavesnes
Ronssoy
Bouchavesnes
Cambrai
Marcoing
Escaut R.
Escaut
Exuette R.
Tortille R.
1 2 3 4 5 6 7 8 9 miles

portion of Tudor's front which faced Gouzeaucourt and northward. Here no serious attack was made, as Ludendorff's purpose was to unsettle Tudor by indirect means.* Pressure west of Ronssoy and Templeux continued, and as the advance appeared to have made headway down Cologne valley and to be fixed in parts of Brown Line east of St. Émilie, Congreve ordered two brigades of Feetham's Division, the *Thirty-ninth*, to entrench a switch from Brown Line at Saulcourt over high ground east and above Longavesnes to the north end of Tincourt Wood, where it would meet the Green Line.

Tudor lost only Gauche Wood, but not until the South African defence had maimed the foe's attack; and on two occasions the brave South Africans helped Campbell † to recapture Chapel Hill on Tudor's right flank. These brilliant combats must be described, in order that their full worth may be known to those who have not studied them closely.

§ II

At about five minutes to nine, after the foe's creeping barrage had begun to herald the German storm troops, fog on the *Ninth's* front was more freakish than elsewhere. Some patches of light—" as from a flight of blushing angels unseen "—got into it, for the attack used a smoke screen from belching trench mortars when advancing against Gauche Wood, the extreme south-eastern corner of the *Ninth's* forward zone, just a little south of Quentin Redoubt.

The foe came on with true courage and thorough training; scrambled into the Wood, at first from the east, and now the South African garrison—" B " company of the Second Regiment, under Captain Garnet Green, a cool and resourceful officer—had a very stern grapple to pass through.

It held four strong posts, three inside the Wood and one in the open on the south-west side. A single company was divided between these posts, so every man had to do his very best, aided in the Wood by two machine-guns and

* Tudor = *Ninth* DIVISION. Please keep always in mind that the German policy was to break their way through the *Twenty-first* and the South Irish, or *Sixteenth*. Two results of this policy were that the *Ninth's* right was constantly being uncovered by the *Twenty-first's* left, while the *Twenty-first's* right was being uncovered by the *Sixteenth's* left. Always to remember this crumbling stress and strain south of the *Ninth* is essential to a right understanding both of the *Ninth's* magnificent work and also of the enormous pressure against Gough's northern corps.

† The *Twenty-first* DIVISION.

a detachment of the Brigade Trench Mortar Battery under Lieut. Hadlow.

If an assault had come from the east alone, there would have been less cause for anxiety, a direct attack being a simple matter of "bludgeon work," or "damned hard pounding," to use Wellington's descriptions; but it got between the South African outposts north of Gauche Wood, crossing Lancashire Trench, and entered from the north over Somme Alley, another trench. Several posts were surrounded.

This enveloping thrust was patient and skilful,* like the defence, which fought with a will under Lieutenants Bancroft and Beviss. At last Bancroft was overwhelmed. Only one of his men escaped. But Beviss had better fortune. His troops—about half of a platoon—fought their way back to Captain Green and took up their defence again. As for machine-gunners, and those who served light trench mortars, they held on till they were either killed or captured.

When Green knew that his foes were active on three sides, in overpowering numbers, he withdrew his men sullenly from Gauche Wood to join the fourth post in the open ground on the south-west. Oncoming Germans lost their open order, they were close together. Perhaps the screen of smoke and mist made them reckless; in any case Lewis guns ripped holes at point-blank range in their bunching waves. So numerous were their losses that they did not try to get beyond the Wood's western edge. Instead, they began to dig themselves in, though in full view of the next British line.

Many Germans in the Wood could be seen also from the Quentin Redoubt, and the garrison there, a company of the First South Africans, fired at them with Lewis guns and rifles. Then Dawson, the South African Brigadier, ordered the whole of his artillery to ravage the lost ground; so the foe's position there became an awful blend of earthquake with bursting volcanoes. Still, Gauche Wood was lost. Green's company went into battle with 150 or 160 men; it came out with only 35 or 40.

Northward, all day long, there was little stir. Kennedy's Highlanders were not attacked, as Ludendorff's aim was to outflank the *Ninth* from the south by crumbling a way rapidly

---

* Captain Green, in a telephone conversation, told Dawson, his Brigadier, that "the German officers were leading their men magnificently, and were coming on absolutely regardless of danger." He added, "We've killed a hell of a lot of them."

through the *Twenty-first* and *Sixteenth*. The *Twenty-first*, Campbell's men, at about noon, lost Chapel Hill, and as this mishap outflanked the South African Brigade, Dawson gave immediate help. He turned southward those of his men who held Lowland Support (the rear trench of Yellow Line), west of Chapel Hill, forming a good flank on the enemy's advance; and early in the afternoon a reserve company of the Natal Regiment was sent to stiffen this flank. It encountered the Germans on the hill's northern slope; there was a bomb fight, and neither side could progress.

At this moment the South African forward troops were about a mile east of the hill, dangerously outflanked. Southward the attack pressed on against the *Twenty-first* and *Sixteenth*, and then worse news came. After midday the foe got behind Yellow Line, and Genin Well Copse was assailed till some South African Scottish brought relief by means of flanking fire, aided by some machine-gunners who were stationed in the ruins of Revelon Farm. My map of the *Ninth's* whole front will make these facts clear, and will show also how insidiously perilous were the foe's efforts to crumble his way through the *Twenty-first* and Hull's South Irish, the *Sixteenth*. If those linked bastions, Epéhy and Peiziére, had not remained firm on their high ground, a big disaster would certainly have happened.

Just after dusk, two N.C.O. patrols, each with a corporal and two men, were sent out, and they brought in between them nearly fifty German prisoners, who, when they came forward and surrendered, declared that the German casualties had been appalling, as none could live in such a hot fire.

The main business for the South Africans was to retake Chapel Hill. Captain Bunce's company of the South African Scottish was ordered to do this noisy, scrambling work, and late in the afternoon, just after dusk, it overran Chapel Hill and took some trenches also on the south and south-eastern slopes. Then posts could be established between the hill and Genin Well Copse.

Although Tudor's unity with Campbell was protected by a firm grip on Chapel Hill, Lowland Support, Revelon Farm, and Railton, yet events in Cologne valley and north of it threatened his line of retreat south-west. Then at five p.m. a message from Congreve's B.G.G.S. brought the news that the 5th Corps, THIRD ARMY, would fall back by night to its Red Line, which was a continuation of Tudor's Yellow Line. This withdrawal would uncover Tudor's forward zone, and

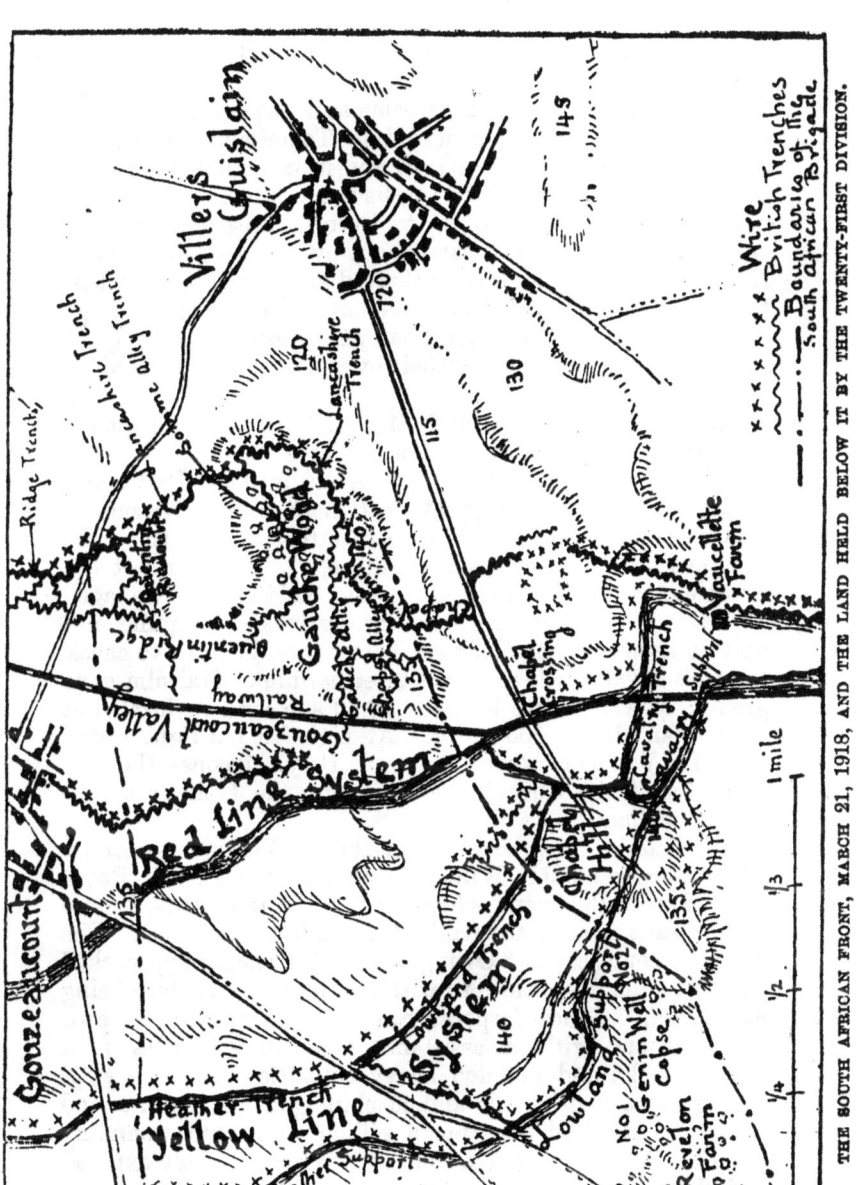

THE SOUTH AFRICAN FRONT, MARCH 21, 1918, AND THE LAND HELD BELOW IT BY THE TWENTY-FIRST DIVISION.

thus he would be obliged to retire with Gorringe's right wing.

This withdrawal may have come as a surprise to Gorringe and the *Forty-seventh*, as it did to Tudor and the *Ninth*; because at 4.40 p.m. the *Ninth* was in communication with the *Forty-seventh*, and no bad news was related. Indeed the news was cheery. According to German prisoners, the raid on the *Forty-seventh* was carried out by only two battalions! If the THIRD ARMY'S most southern division was not kept in touch during the day with events north of the salient, troops inside the salient's lower flank had an imperfect knowledge of the main events and also of their own position as affected by these events.

In any case, Below and Marwitz had done so much mischief that there was cause for anxiety.

Watts, with his intrepid but weak divisions, Daly's and Malcolm's, had done a great deal more than a reasonable country should have asked them to attempt. On the right they had lost Maissemy, a key village, and on their left the Templeux positions, strategical points, but they had managed by desperate counter-attacks, very costly and fatiguing, not only to keep the centre of their battle zone, but also to check the foe's advance where it was most harmful. Malcolm gave ground slowly, losing between 10.30 a.m. and nightfall not more than about 4500 yards. At nightfall his right rested near Le Verguier, where some of Daly's troops—the 8th battalion of the Queen's, belonging to the 17th Brigade—fought brilliantly.

A Victoria Cross was won in the Le Verguier sector by Lance-Corporal John William Sayer, of the Eighth Royal West Surrey Regiment, when holding for two hours, in face of incessant attacks, the flank of a small isolated post. The official account says: " Owing to mist the enemy approached the post from both sides to within thirty yards before being discovered. Lance-Corporal Sayer, however, on his own initiative and without assistance, beat off a succession of flank attacks and inflicted heavy casualties on the enemy. Though attacked by rifle and machine-gun fire, bayonet and bombs, he repulsed all attacks, killing many and wounding others. During the whole time he was continuously exposed to rifle and machine-gun fire, but he showed the utmost contempt of danger, and his conduct was an inspiration to all. His skilful use of fire of all description enabled the post to hold out till nearly all the garrison had been killed and himself wounded and captured. He subsequently died as a result of wounds at Le Cateau."

Equally brilliant and helpful was Major Whitworth's defence of Carpeza Copse, with a mixed force of cavalry and Manchester soldiers. It held the attack at bay until Malcolm was ordered to retire, on March 22. Whitworth died of wounds—to be gratefully remembered by all survivors of Gough's Army.

Though Watts's Corps, both infantry and cavalry, had acted as a strong breakwater, heavy losses, united to the disorganization caused by confused fighting in the fog, set anxious thoughts astir; for next day, early in the morning, Marwitz would certainly try to open gaps west of Maissemy and Ronssoy. Reinforcements! Here, as elsewhere, they were needed at once.

Congreve had kept Epéhy and Peziére in his centre, but both were doomed; and the loss of Ronssoy, united to bad events south of this village, presaged an early withdrawal to ease the *Sixteenth* and *Twenty-first* as well as the overstrained men of Watts's Corps.

Campbell's left had been so badly hit that Tudor was told to extend his right and take over Chapel Hill. This had been done already by two counter-attacks, but some Lincoln troops remained on the hill itself, and also between Chapel Hill and Revelon Farm. After dark they were relieved by the South Africans. Already, then, Tudor * was called upon by external events to widen his front southward into land not his own, and soon he had to extend northward also, and therefore into THIRD ARMY ground. The South Africans were reinforced with a reserve battalion, the Eleventh Royal Scots.

As soon as possible Tudor began to withdraw from his forward zone in order to keep firm liaison with Byng's withdrawal. The railway in Gouzeaucourt valley was held by an advanced guard until two a.m., March 22, and Red Line three hours longer. For some reason or other, Marwitz did not attack either against Tudor or against the flanks of Flesquières salient, whose garrison got back early to Highland Ridge, and thence westward along the Hindenburg Line to Havrincourt and Hermies.

Ludendorff must have known that these withdrawals were inevitable, since they were brought about by his own troops. Why, then, did he fail to harry them by night raids

* Tudor = *Ninth* DIVISION.

and attacks? No interference came from him; all was quiet apart from some sploshing detonations of gas shells in Dessart Wood. Why? An assault on the salient's southern flank, pressing north-west, belonged to the ABC of generalship; and on the evening of March 22, when a more important retreat was in preparation, Villers-Plouich *was* assailed, as we know, and with considerable force and bite. Havrincourt also was attacked north of Exuette River and on the Bapaume-Cambrai railway. We have much reason to be thankful that they were not set in action during the night of March 21–22. Ludendorff and Marwitz missed an opportunity, and their inattention can be explained in two ways only; that they misunderstood the alertness of Gough's generalship, and that our FIFTH ARMY's defence, and the huddle of brigades which fog and congested fighting had imposed on Marwitz, as on Below and on Hutier, had caused so much anxiety among German leaders that many local events were neglected, while some others could not be exploited.

CHAPTER VII

MARWITZ AND BELOW CONTINUE THEIR JOINT ATTACKS

§ I

THE second day, like the first, seemed to have no dawn. Its drama began in a fog, which compelled both sides, after a bitter cold night, almost without sleep, to warm themselves in another mixed game of hide-and-seek and blind man's buff with Destiny.

Here and there on Gough's widened front the morning attack was hesitant, dejected, slow; but it was wide-awake immediately south of the *Ninth*, and also in Otto von Below's pressure on Byng.

Let us see what happened north-west of Flesquières salient.

"Farther north," says Haig, "fighting was severe and continuous throughout the day. Shortly before noon the enemy attacked Hermies strongly from the north-west,* and repeated his attacks at intervals during the remainder of the day. These attacks were completely repulsed by the *Seventeenth*. Heavy losses were inflicted on the German infantry in the fighting in this area, the leading wave of a strong attack launched between Hermies and Beaumetz-lez-Cambrai being destroyed by our fire." [Our own losses, too, of course, were very severe, but in official dispatches our own losses are passed over in silence.]

"In the neighbourhood of Beaumetz the enemy continued his assaults with great determination, but was held by the *Fifty-first* and a brigade of the *Twenty-fifth* until the evening, Sir E. G. T. Bainbridge commanding the *Twenty-fifth* DIVISION. *Our troops were then withdrawn under orders to positions south of the village.* Very severe fighting took place at Vaulx Wood and Vaulx Vraucourt, as well as

---

* Note this geography. North-west of Hermies means that the attack south-west from Doignies was driving a wedge behind Hermies and narrowing the narrow salient, from which three of Byng's divisions have to retreat.

about St. Leger and north of Croisilles, *which latter village our troops had evacuated during the night.*"

My italics. The loss of Croisilles needs as much attention as the loss of Essigny or Maissemy. This applies also to Beaumetz, near the western edge of the battle zone, and about a mile north of the Bapaume-Cambrai railway. So, about seven miles from Villers-Plouich, there was heavy German pressure to the north-west; and far to the northwest, for if you draw an upright line due south from the centre of Beaumetz, you will find that it passes through the west outskirts of Ytres, and Ytres lies about six and a half miles west—by a little south—of Villers-Plouich. Further, when the defence fell back to the *south* of Beaumetz, turning its back towards the Bapaume-Cambrai railway, it showed that the attack was trying energetically to invade the salient's rear. With this keen pressure coming southward from the north-west, a retreat from the salient was becoming more and more difficult. In such close fighting between almost equal forces on a narrow frontage, both sides must have lost heavily. Who knows why the official dispatch glides over too many THIRD ARMY losses, while speaking with full historic frankness of the FIFTH'S? The dispatch continues:—

"At Vraucourt the enemy broke through the rear line of the battle zone and penetrated into the village. There he was counter-attacked by infantry and tanks, and driven out. Farther west, after heavy fighting, his troops forced their way into our positions along the line of the Croisilles-Hénin-sur-Cojeul road. On the left of this attack troops of the *Thirty-fourth* maintained themselves in St. Leger until the afternoon, when they fell back to a line of trenches just west of the village. To the north the *Third* DIVISION brought back their right flank to a line facing south-east, and in this position successfully beat off a heavy attack." *

Study this information on a good map, and at once it becomes evident that Byng, hard pressed all day long, would be obliged by night to recover balance by two withdrawals. The protective barrier looking south-east made by the *Third's* right wing was ugly and artificial, positions due north of it being outflanked; and for this reason Byng's troops withdrew from the remainder of their forward positions as far north as the Scarpe, taking up the rear line of their battle zone between Henin and Fampoux. The foe followed this

* Vol. ii., pp. 192-93.

MARWITZ AND BELOW CONTINUE THE ATTACKS 161

retreat, and early on Saturday morning, March 23, as the dispatch relates, he found a gap about Mory in Byng's new front and rear zone. Now Mory is only about four miles north of Bapaume, and Bapaume was to Byng what Péronne was to Gough, approximately. Below's men and Marwitz's right struck with great force, and unluckily fortune aided them.

From inside Flesquières salient Byng withdrew by night some 6000 yards in the deepest place. His line north and east of Hermies crossed the Canal du Nord and then went south through Havrincourt Wood to the east and south-east of Metz-en-Couture; but was it able to join hands firmly with Gough's left?

Before answering this question, let us note the equally powerful squeeze south of Tudor's lines. Friday, March 22, was a galling day. Between ten and eleven o'clock Marwitz began to thrust into some weak places, as into the gap he had made on the first day between Campbell's left and Dawson's South African Brigade. And St. Émelie fell, then Villers Faucon, and Epéhy and Peiziére had reached the fag-end of a noble struggle. North of Cologne River, then, was a distressing outlook; and south of it also, apart from Carpeza Copse and a brilliant counter-attack east and north-east of Hervilly, to be described later in a chapter on Episodes. At Le Verguier Daly's men were gripped with increasing force, but they did not retire till about noonday on the 22nd, when they were ordered to fall back from a position almost surrounded; and northward a converging danger from both sides of the Cologne menaced Roisel with envelopment from the rear. So in the afternoon our troops around Roisel were ordered to withdraw behind Green Line, between Bernes and Boucly, and to gain breath and some rest behind the *Fiftieth*.*

On Congreve's front all day long the main anxiety was lest Marwitz should get round the right flank which was stretched across the Cologne River. Two divisions, Hull's and Campbell's, had suffered grave losses. The South Irish infantry were reported to be only about a thousand strong, and Dawson's South African Brigade, fighting stoutly and almost incessantly, perished on the second day to nearly the same number of rifles. Already Congreve's reserve division, the

* A party of our cavalry held out in Roisel till the evening of the 22nd; mostly Seventh Dragoon Guards, I believe. The battle there had left them behind, and they were able to watch the Boche transport coming forward from Templeux.

M

Thirty-ninth, had lost its counter-attack value, since a wasting battle-front must be repaired and renewed. Shortly after noon the South African brigadier received orders to retire by 4.30 p.m. to Brown Line, and to be ready later to fall back on Green Line, about three miles more to the west. This withdrawal began well; but soon it was observed, and the foe in strength took up the trail. On he came, looking eagerly confident, till the Second S.A. Infantry sprayed over him with bullets at close quarters.

Meantime our Highlanders on Tudor's left were quiet; some of them patrolled Gouzeaucourt until midday, when it became known that the Army's policy was to fight rearguard actions to delay and ravage the foe's power. Tudor was to fall back to Green Line from north of Epinette Wood to the south of Equancourt. So his brigades were ordered to withdraw to their Brown Line by 4.30 p.m., and to begin three hours later to move back to Green Line.

Dawson was warned about the retirement to Green Line, but he did not receive the message in which the precise time of his leaving Brown Line was given. Somehow it miscarried; but, as Colonel Buchan has related, Dawson sent Captain Beverley, his Acting Brigade Major, to deliver the order to the battalions. Beverley went off on horseback, and before five o'clock all troops had their instructions, though Beverley's horse was shot under him.

It was a brave ride, for at four o'clock Brown Line was breached at Guyencourt; and although a prompt counter-blow just managed to check a venomous thrust, matters in this neighbourhood were very critical, and every one understood that a retreat south-west could no longer be made without difficulty.

Guyencourt was a redoubt village about 2000 yards south of Heudecourt and in the *Twenty-first's* land. After its fall, German storm troops turned northward and began to roll up our line to the South African right flank. In a twinkling, Dawson's three battalions, now enfeebled by heavy losses, were in great peril, threatened by envelopment. Could the advance be held till darkness would cover a withdrawal? As the boundary uniting Gough and Byng ran south-west, this German drive due west through Guyencourt imperilled the *Ninth's* retreat. What if the foe had men enough to go ahead for a decision—a big decision, and a rapid one?

Communication with Dawson became impossible. Yet platoons and companies never wavered, never hesitated.

Junior officers threw out defensive flanks and handled rearguard actions with a skill which Dawson will never forget. But for this veteran coolness in the junior ranks, the South Africans would have been trapped.

Some thirty German airplanes aided the attack. They flew low, and the putt-putt-putt of their machine-guns harassed the teams of our artillery, raked our trenches, and continued their efforts till about sunset. At this hour, in a flaring twilight, very noisy with explosions, observers at Sorel-le-Grand, west of Heudecourt, could see the foe dimly, advancing in full strength southward on their right flank. Sorel was noisy with our passing artillery, lame and bloodstained with our wounded, and in other ways thronged, as with details of departmental units retreating towards Green Line. For Heudecourt in the *Ninth's* own land had fallen, and the attack had only a mile or so to advance on Sorel. At all costs it must be checked.

Dawson climbed up a wall in Sorel to see the whole battlefield. Everywhere the countryside was an inferno wondrous and varied in contrasts of rival human efforts and of devastating flames and explosions. Heudecourt spouted like a volcano, and other villages were burning. Barracks and stores flared; ammunition dumps detonated; and Sorel itself was becoming a swirl of wind-blown smoke flashing with streaks of fire. Field ambulances were trying with beautiful courage to get the wounded away from Heudecourt, while batteries at thundering speed obeyed their orders, and fugitives of many sorts crowded the roads. Meantime, over there on the right, grey and menacing German troops pressed on, wave after wave, column after column. A more precarious position could not well be imagined. What could be done, then?

Dawson turned out his H.Q. staff and put it into trenches east of Sorel. Two companies of Eleventh Royal Scots took up a position south and south-west of Heudecourt; the Sixth K.O.S. Borderers manned high ground from Sorel south to Liéramont, about 3500 yards; some field artillery came into action also south of Sorel; and in this way the heavy, persevering onrush of panting Germans was stopped for a time.

Before a new thrust could be set in movement, our last guns went westward safely, and Dawson with his brave H.Q. made their way to Moislains some 5000 yards west of Green Line. All guns on the *Ninth's* front were saved except a forward anti-tank gun which was bogged, and ten pieces of field artillery, south of Sorel, the teams of which did not come up in time. So these guns were destroyed.

The South Africans, parched with a thirst which cannot be described, and aching everywhere with fatigue, beat off all attacks till 7.30 p.m. Then they were ordered to retire northward before striking west as the Germans had moved northward behind the South African front. The withdrawal was bravely managed, particularly by Colonel Christian of the Second Regiment, whose troops were most perilously situated. For the most part the withdrawal moved along the Brown Line to the Fins-Gouzeaucourt road, and then turned westward and marched to Fins, followed very closely by the German advance.

"B" Company of the Second Regiment had no chance at all. It began the day at the old quarry on the east of Heudecourt, and was destroyed, fighting to the last, with its intrepid leader, Captain Green.

It had been arranged that the Seventh Seaforths and Fifth Camerons should retire through Fins to Etricourt; but German storm troops got into Fins before the last Highland companies could pass through, and a roundabout way had to be sought in the darkness. A few Fifth Camerons did not receive the order to retire; it failed to reach them, so they stayed in Yellow Line until ten p.m., and then fought their way out and joined their battalion, bringing with them a German officer and seventeen prisoners.

By ten p.m., March 22, all divisions of Congreve's Corps had either manned or were nearing Green Line, and orders were issued to fight on this front. A certain amount of Corps artillery—about two brigades, mainly South Irish—had been lost; the rest was withdrawn safely to cover Green Line.

At the same hour a message from Gough made known the fact that Marwitz had *broken the Green Line about five hundred yards east and south-east of Nobescourt Farm,** in Watts's territory, and Congreve was directed to retire to new positions as soon as a serious attack was made on his portion of the Green Line. Congreve would be responsible for a front running from La Chapellette, south of Péronne, to the THIRD ARMY'S boundary, about halfway between Moislains and Manancourt.

He called together his Divisional Commanders to explain

* Pray note this breach carefully. Nobescourt Farm and the Green Line in this neighbourhood formed part of the Péronne bridgehead.

MARWITZ AND BELOW CONTINUE THE ATTACKS 165

the situation, telling them that since the battle was developing into a series of rearguard actions, it would be impossible for him to control scattered, rapid and local fights, apart from giving broad general lines, on which all must put up the sternest possible resistance. He must leave them to learn from events when a retirement was timely; but on no account were they to lose touch with units on their flanks, and Gough was very insistent on the need of holding close and strong liaison with Byng.

The story of this liaison in its opening incidents has to be told now, and I wish to make it clear, because it has been mistold, and also because of later events and their consequences. We are concerned with the boundary divisions—*Ninth* and *Forty-seventh*, and remember that the *Ninth* was in Gough's Army and served under H. H. Tudor, while the *Forty-seventh* served in Byng's Army under Gorringe. Further, the *Ninth* belonged to the 7th Corps, commanded by Congreve, and the *Forty-seventh* to the 5th Corps, commanded by Fanshawe.

If these divisions misunderstood each other and failed to fall back together with mutual support, hitches and scrapes would come, and Marwitz would be aided greatly by a disjointed British defence, as we have seen (p. 140). The stronger army ought to have been especially alert in this matter, wishing not only to help the weaker as much as possible, but also to prevent itself from being pushed away from its southern boundary. On Friday morning, March 22, the *Ninth's* H.Q. sent a Staff Officer to explain the situation to the *Forty-seventh*, and soon after midday a telephone message warned the *Forty-seventh* not only that the *Ninth* might be ordered to fall back from the Brown Line, but also that any withdrawal on the *Ninth's* part, being south-west along the boundary, would widen the front to be held by the *Forty-seventh*, which was on Highland Ridge, in the north-east, and seemingly at ease there.

After Tudor had received orders to retire upon Green Line, the Staff Officer returned from the *Forty-seventh* and the news he brought was disconcerting. The *Forty-seventh* was to retire to Brown Line only, and could not accept the responsibility of connecting its right on Brown Line with Tudor's left on the Green. In plainer words, Byng's right wing would neither fall back in line with Gough's northern corps nor hold a firm flank along the boundary. It left its flank and rear to be covered by the *Ninth* DIVISION, as though Byng's Army were much weaker, not much stronger, than Gough's. So the border problems were becoming too Gilbertian to be fit for the drama of a retreat.

As the *Ninth* had already widened its front southward, it would endanger itself if it took over lines north-eastward from the *Forty-seventh*. This important matter was discussed by telephone with Congreve, and in the evening it became known that the *Forty-seventh*, after all, would retire to Green Line. The question " When ? " was very important, since the German policy was to roll up the *Ninth* by destroying the two divisions south of it.

At 7.30 p.m. the *Ninth* telephoned to the *Forty-seventh* to make known the position of its own troops, and was told that a brigade of the *Second* DIVISION, THIRD ARMY—unfortunately, it was a weak one in numbers—was in reserve at Manancourt and Equancourt. Later, at 9.10 p.m., this brigade was placed temporarily under the *Ninth*. Here was a very welcome addition of strength, as already the *Ninth's* front had increased to about 7500 yards.

Despite this reinforcement the position remained very menacing. What would happen to the *Forty-seventh?* It was far in the north-east, and a heavy flank attack against Villers-Plouich had to be driven off before a retreat under pressure could begin. Also an attack against Havrincourt would hinder a retreat from the central portion of the salient. Fanshawe had remained too long on Highland Ridge and in Hindenburg's line. How is this lack of judgment to be explained ? Note first of all that two divisions in the salient, the *Forty-seventh* and *Sixty-third*, were not really assailed till the evening of March 22. Their defences were very strong, the attack and its cutting-off pressure were not close by ; so visible causes for anxiety were absent, while visible reasons for quiet confidence were present. And the next point to be noted is that Byng and his officers did not protest against the slanderous outcry—" The Byng Boys have been let down by Gough's men, who have been badly handled ! " As it is not in the nature of British officers to do wrong wittingly, we have reason to infer that Byng's right wing misunderstood its duty towards Gough's left, and that its ill-grounded accusations against Gough's left were accepted as facts by Fanshawe, Byng, and G.H.Q. Why, I cannot suggest, because I have no conjecture to offer. The accusations were refuted by the presence of the *Ninth* Highlanders in Byng's Land, as well as by the urgent warnings sent by the *Ninth* to

MARWITZ AND BELOW CONTINUE THE ATTACKS

its northern partner; and Byng's right ought to have remembered that Gough's divisions on the average had to hold nearly 50 per cent. more front than Byng's, though very nearly twice as many German divisions attacked Gough as fell upon Byng. Had these facts been understood, surely the THIRD ARMY could not have failed to connect itself with the weaker army by means of a strong and steady flank. To leave this work to the *Ninth* was to make a very perilous and bad beginning in a most hazardous retreat.

The necessary thing was to guard as much land as possible; so the *Ninth's* left flank was thrown forward to a point about a thousand yards north of Fins, while its right rested on the north end of Epinette Wood, about fifteen hundred yards south of Nurlu. At the north end of this front were men of the *Second* DIVISION; but when would they be able to secure touch with the *Forty-seventh*? Hope was expressed by 5th Corps that a complete liaison would be formed by 5 a.m. on the 23rd. Meantime there was a gap; and there was reason also to be anxious about the *Ninth's* south flank, as the German desire to cleave their way through the *Twenty-first* had not weakened in the least.

At midnight two things were certain on Gough's left flank. One of them was that enough timely warning had been given to Byng's right; and the other, that Marwitz's tactics were working towards a great climax both north and south of the *Ninth* DIVISION.

CHAPTER VIII

SOME POINTS AND CROSS-QUESTIONS RAISED BY THE FORE-
GOING CHAPTERS

§ I

THE breach of the main Green Line in the neighbourhood of Nobescourt Farm proved that the high pressure of the foe's attack was directed with skill, in order to cancel the worth of that sketchy system of defence called our Péronne bridgehead postions. So I have made a map—a correct one, I believe—to show clearly, among other important matters, what effects this breach had on the balance of our battle front. Thrust and counterthrust, poise and equipoise, these are things to be studied as carefully in fighting fronts as in architecture and engineering.

To retreat effectively against perilous odds is a search after stability, akin to that which occurs when a bridge has to be built across one of those rivers which rise into sudden floods and scour into the foundations of piers and abutments. The bridge-builder has to defeat this scouring onrush of waters, only he cannot move away from it as a wise General retires from excessive thrusts and concussions; but when a General is not wise, when he allows his army to be swallowed up by superior numbers, there is much resemblance between the disaster and an ill-built bridge which is carried away by storm and spate.

To bend like a yew bow, in order not to break like an unpliant stick, was the essential generalship which our FIFTH ARMY was set to obey while reinforcements were coming gradually into line. Apart from some gunless French infantry, with some French cavalry, in the south of Hutier's battle, no support could reach our fraying lines before Sunday morning, March 24. During Saturday and Sunday the *Eighth* DIVISION—the only British reinforcement that

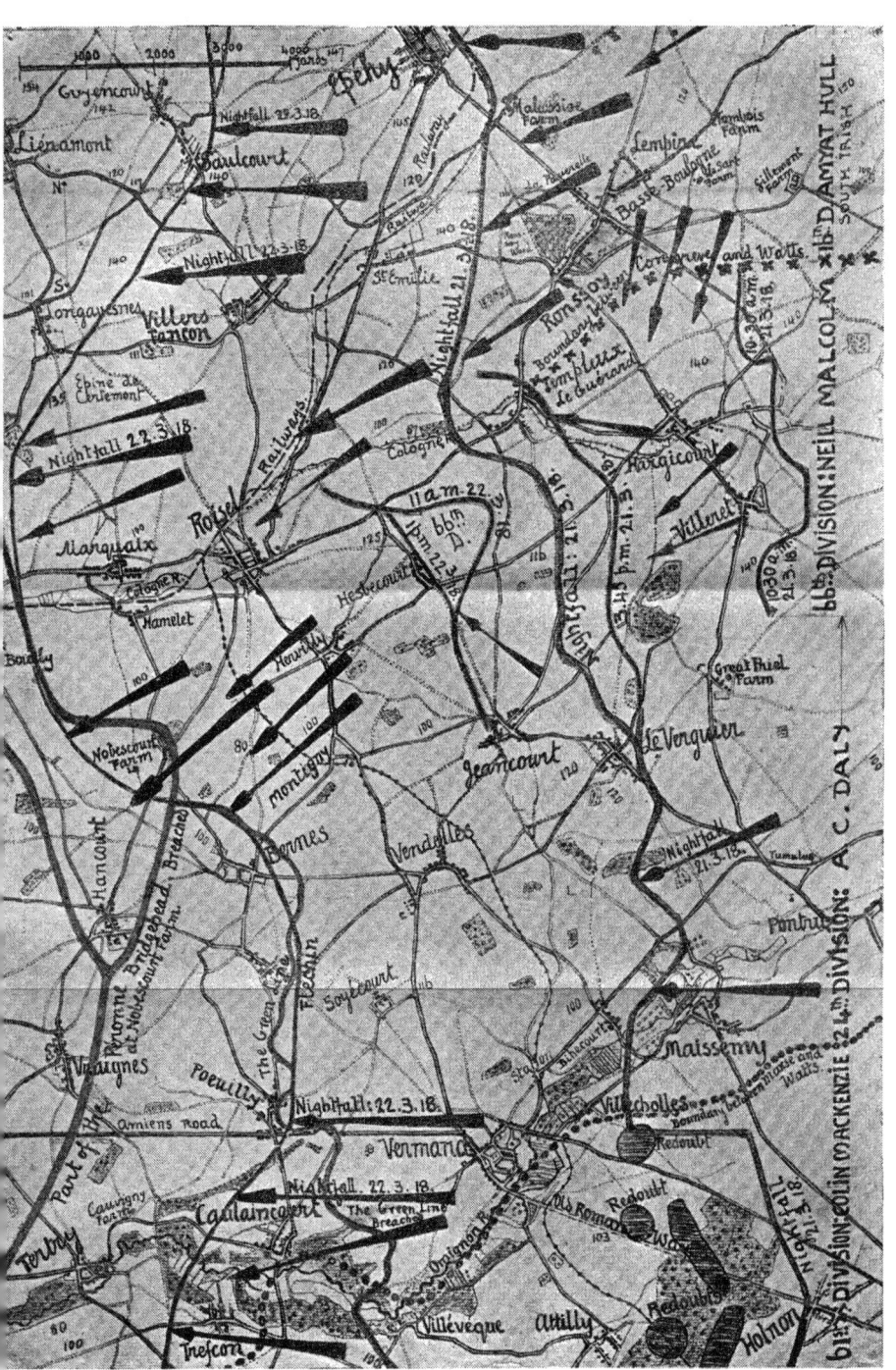

MARCH 21ST AND 22ND: GERMAN ADVANCE TO THE PERONNE BRIDGEHEAD NORTH AND SOUTH OF THE VERMAND—AMIENS ROAD

would aid Watts—would be detrained at and near Nesle; and about then G. M. Franks with the *Thirty-fifth* would begin to join Congreve.* But an immediate need of men for two big battles against perilous odds could not be made less acute by these coming events.

So at nightfall, March 22, the situation was critical, not that we had lost a great deal of land against Marwitz, or against Hutier and Marwitz on the borderlands north and south of the Vermand-Amiens road, but because menacing thrusts at dangerous places had upset the balance of our prepared defences, with the result that our weakness in numbers had for its companion a lack of structural fitness or equilibrium. I think here of another analogy. An arch too weak for its purpose must be dangerous enough in a bridge, but if you dislodge its keystone you know at once that a notice in red letters must be put up to forbid heavy traffic—above all during bad weather.

Now the Péronne bridgehead positions may be compared, without any extravagance, to an arch unfit for its office; it was good enough for a rearguard action, but far too unfinished and too thinly manned for a decisive fight; and the breach a trifle east and south-east of Nobescourt Farm may be compared, also without any extravagance, to a keystone badly damaged, if not indeed dislodged.

And another structural matter invites attention. German Commanders liked to attack slantingly from right to left— from north to south-west. Yet our corps and divisional boundaries, like the boundary line between Byng and Gough, ran in this direction, as a rule, so the foe had but to attack on a slanting front along one of our boundaries, while assailing due west on a sector a few miles south, in order to cause grave troubles in the retreat of our men.

It appears to me, then, that boundaries running due west might have been much better both for the resistance of an army dangerously undermanned, and also for the liaison between Byng and Gough. Attacks cutting across them in a south-westerly direction would have offered flanks to our counter-blows; and since the advance on the first two days was not rapid but slow, surely we should have had many chances of damaging the foe's exposed flanks. Laymen are too apt to forget that an advance has no comfort when the

* This excellent division came from the Ypres neighbourhood. If it had been sent southward much earlier in the battle, its value to the defence would have been doubled, if not indeed trebled.

defenders can turn against its right or left in a keen, swift counter-stroke.

If, now, you turn to my map, you will find it easy to apply these reflections. Two Corps boundaries are given, one between Congreve and Watts, and one between Watts and Maxse. Both run south-west; the former down to and along the Cologne River, and the Maxse-Watts line in a wavy course to the east and south of Trefcon.

The map relates also what happened on the first two days from Holnon to the north of Saulcourt, 21,500 yards away in the north-west. Four British divisions and their supports are in action; and let us remember that both cavalry and tanks have been very helpful to Watts, as in the counter-blow near Hervilly, about eleven a.m. on March 22. This good stroke was invaluable. It prevented the attack from reaching Green Line near Nobescourt Farm, and enabled the *Fiftieth*, after its tiresome journey and a forced march through fog, to take up its positions with its three brigades over-stretched along Green Line, while sending one of its battalions, the Fifth Durham Light Infantry, under Major A. L. Raimes, to help the *Sixty-sixth*, whose left might be assailed by a German thrust from the north of Roisel.

Five of Maxse's battle zone redoubts are shown by my map in the north of Colin Mackenzie's front; and note how they were outflanked on the first day by the pressure through Maissemy towards Villecholles. Next day this pressure carried the German advance through Vermand to the Green Line offshoot between Pœuilly and Bernes, 5000 yards; and south of the Vermand-Amiens road a part of the Green Line offshoot was overrun, and both Caulaincourt and Trefcon passed into German hands. Stability had gone from this portion of our structural defence.

Another part of the bridgehead positions faced the attack west of Tertry, east of Vraignes, and on both sides of Hancourt northward and north-westward. Just north of Hancourt we find Nobescourt Farm, which the foe nearly captured at five o'clock in the afternoon of the second day, after breaching the main Green Line some 500 yards away. Even if the Green Line offshoot had not been lost east of Caulaincourt and Trefcon, this breach of the Péronne bridgehead close by Nobescourt Farm would have enforced a night retreat from Villévêque, Pœuilly, Bernes, whose position below it on the south-east would have been dominated by this grave menace to the main bridgehead.

Watts * had not men enough to mend the bridgehead, his losses having been very grave; and it was clear to him that an effort to keep his ground east of the Somme would thrust his few and jaded troops into a very unwise forlorn hope. They would fight to the very last, but at last they would be routed by far superior numbers; and afterwards? . . . Then Marwitz and Hutier would be free to go ahead.

Watts, then, received sanction to withdraw behind the Somme; and this move, for another reason, was timely, a gap having formed between Watts and Maxse, leaving the remains of Daly's Division in the air about Croix Moligneux.

§ II

Though this withdrawal was helpful and essential, and though unfinished preparations had been made for it by G.H.Q., Gough's judgment is questioned by one set of critics and condemned by another. Neither set has an argument or a fact which was not clear to Gough and his Corps Commanders; but when controversial minds have fixed ideas, they make shift contentedly without new facts and fresh arguments.

Recently one such mind said to me: "A devilish bad business to lose the Péronne bridgehead! It hit our national prestige below the belt, and made us cut a very poor figure before our Allies! And on French soil, too! How many French bridges did we destroy, and what was their value in money and in traffic communication? Our men should have been firm—ashamed to budge!"

An unreasoning mood of this powerful sort goes its own way like the wind, and like the wind it has influence—often harmful. For this reason I return to this bridgehead question in the Part on Controversies, so as to show it in other aspects. Though G.H.Q.'s instructions were sometimes rather lax in their use of stereotyped phrases or in sentences that cancelled each other, yet, beyond all question, a retreat behind the Somme was looked upon as a likely and useful move when the Somme defences were planned, and many thousands of men were set to work upon them in a race against insufficient time.

Before the battle Gough had gathered from G.H.Q. instructions, both written and spoken, that since the crisis in man-power was a grave threat to Haig's widened front,

* Watts = 19th Corps.

too many risks in battle were not to be taken with the FIFTH ARMY; that its divisions were to be nursed as carefully as possible if a determined assault upon them were made by superior numbers; and that it might well be desirable to fall back to the rearward defences of Péronne and the Somme while linking up with the THIRD ARMY on the north, and preparing for counter-blows.

Certain matters, of course, belonged to the rudiments of common sense; as, for example, that the FIFTH ARMY, though dangerously weak in numbers, had to guard as long as possible the French flank on its right and Byng's flank on its left, *while receiving adequate support from these flanks.* Also it was obvious that the loss of Péronne, if this centre of communications became of operative use to the foe, would be very bad; hence an emergency zone was roughed in behind the Somme to Péronne, and thence north-eastward behind the Tortille River. But it was—and is—equally obvious to good sense that an army too weak in numbers cannot fight a Waterloo day after day, and that its Commander must learn partly from the condition of his troops, partly from the enemy's power and concussions, when his line must bend swiftly in order to avoid snapping into fragments.

To fight at all costs against superior power in a retreat is to hold on as long as you can without suffering disaster; and then to be clever in delaying actions while patching the gaps in your retreating and perishing divisions. It was thus that Gough and his Army fought through days and nights; and when cavillers declare that Gough nursed his Army overmuch and should have kept it longer at close grip with the German hordes, they show not only that they do not call up into pictorial presence before their minds what our men had to endure, but also that they are ignorant of what our men lost in casualties, though nursed as carefully as possible by their Commanders. When a Corps of five divisions loses in a battle 25,000 in casualties; when another of four divisions loses nearly 22,000; and when two other Corps have an equal average loss in their brigades, we know that they have borne to the full all that they could bear and that closer contact with superior numbers would have been criminal and fatal.

Indeed, there are times when I cannot help thinking that the retreat was not rapid enough. I say to myself, for example: "Between 10.30 of March 21 and one p.m. of the second day, our troops east of Hargicourt and Villeret were pressed back only about 5500 yards in the centre, and less than 7500 yards along the Watts-Congreve boundary. From the line east of Hargicourt south-west to Nobescourt Farm, which was nearly lost late in the afternoon of the second day is 10,500 yards. Was this very slow withdrawal in a staunch defence worth the drain of casualties that our brave men suffered? Watts had divisions much below strength, and their tenacity, shown so clearly on correct maps, bought its gradual giving of ground at a very high price."

In these questioning moods, too, as I have said before, I cannot help wondering also whether the system of defence chosen by G.H.Q.—a Forward Zone, a Battle Zone, and a Rear Zone, three defensive belts, sited at considerable distance from each other—were in keeping with what may be called the *genius* of modernized attack. Early on the first day, several times, the battle zone was turned by the loss of a village on its flank, as when Marwitz on the first day pressed beyond Ronssoy and Templeux, on the boundary between Congreve and Watts. Would it have been better to employ two forward zones with a strip of open country between them, and the battle zone several miles behind them? In the south—the battle against Hutier—the Crozat Canal would have been a part of the second forward zone; and in the centre and north, the Péronne bridgehead and its continuation into THIRD ARMY land.

These reflections are given here for the purpose of showing that when cavillers find fault with Gough and his Army, they let their ideas run in a rut or groove and pay no attention to cross-questions and other matters also. Hazard plays a part so incalculable in all battles, and above all in battles along very wide fronts, that students cannot review their opinions too frequently, making allowance after allowance for inevitable hitches.

CHAPTER IX

SATURDAY AND SUNDAY IN THE NORTHERN FIGHTING

§ II

WATTS, under cover of rearguards, got safely away with his guns and stores and impedimenta; but on reaching his positions behind the Somme, he had 18,000 yards of river line to guard by scattered posts, with small reserves at all known crossings. Rest, then, had to go hand in hand with a vigilance always wide-awake, and Rest did not get the best of the bargain. On the third day, late in the afternoon, enterprising Boche patrols picked their way forward and made several efforts to reach the right bank, only to be shot down by our gunners.

As soon as Watts retired from the Péronne bridgehead, it became necessary for Congreve to fall back, and he was directed to man a line extending from La Chapellette, below Péronne, to Doingt, guarding Péronne itself, thence north-eastward to Bussu and Aizecourt, and on to the Green Line at Nurlu and Equancourt. We have seen that the *Ninth's* vanguard reached Green Line on the evening of the second day, at about ten o'clock. Its rearguards, of course, were well ahead, and always on the look out for Byng's right flank troops of the *Forty-seventh*.

At 5.26 a.m. on Saturday, March 23, in a misty cold gloom, when our men were stiff and sore after another bad vigil, the *Ninth* received orders from its Corps to hold Green Line with rearguards only, and to draw the rest of its troops to the line of the Canal du Nord, north of Moislains, and the Tortille river south of this village. It was to help the movements of the *Twenty-first* whose left was hard pressed. As this move affected Byng's right, a warning was sent at once to 5th Corps, whose troops, as we have seen, had not fallen back in conformity with their southern ally. To recover from a bad start is often as difficult as to produce a masterpiece, and 5th Corps, by remaining in Flesquières salient to be assailed on

THE NORTHERN FIGHTING CONTINUED 175

the evening of the second day, made an unlucky start, which enabled the attack to worry its retreat all night in the manner most likely to push our two armies apart. To do this, and to envelop 5th Corps from south and north, was one of Ludendorff's prime objects; hence 5th Corps' right would have been wise if it had retired to Green Line with the *Ninth* Division, or if it had formed with enough troops a strong flank running south-west from Villers Plouich to Equancourt. By failing to do either of these things, it was pressed gradually away from its liaison with the *Ninth;* first to Metz-on-Couture, and then, during the morning of March 23, to Four Winds Farm, south-west of Ytres, about 3500 yards north of the boundary at Manancourt. Here the *Forty-seventh* fought very bravely in the open till nightfall, when it was pushed to the east of Rocquigny, still farther from its union with Gough's left.

Meanwhile the *Ninth* was harried by events of equal moment. Its withdrawal to the Canal du Nord was full of stirring episodes. The foe, covered by a barrage from guns and trench mortars, assailed Green Line. On our left, after a stern grapple, this attack was broken by Scottish Highlanders, but it did much harm on the right, capturing Epinette Wood, from which the K.O.S. Borderers got out with difficulty. Then both Highlanders and Lowlanders, aided by rearguards, began in broad daylight to withdraw, always under pressure; there was no artillery to cover them, as it had to be taken across the Canal du Nord; yet slowly, and skilfully, they carried out their movement all right, and the German losses were severe. By two p.m. the *Ninth* was in position behind the Canal du Nord from Moislains to the beet-sugar factory north of Etricourt, about 2750 yards within the Third Army's area. At the beet-sugar factory about 750 men of the *Second* Division continued the line eastward to about a thousand yards north of Fins, also in Third Army ground.

Before noon, at eleven o'clock, the *Ninth's* G.O.C. made an urgent visit to 5th Corps, Third Army, because the position was becoming much too perilous. The foe was trying to envelop 5th Corps, and the *Ninth* was struggling to prevent this envelopment, but its front had stretched to about 11,000 yards, so effective defence became more and more difficult and hazardous. The Highlanders were guarding land which ought to be held by the *Forty-seventh*, though they were needed urgently in their own ground. These matters were placed before the 5th Corps' B.G.G.S., who at once consulted

Fanshawe, the Corps Commander. Permission was granted to the *Ninth's* G.O.C. to order the *Forty-seventh's* right brigade to take over a part of its front—from north of Fins (V. 6, Central in the maps) to north of Equancourt (V. 4, Central). At about 11.15 this order was delivered, and I believe that this little strip of front was taken over by the *Forty-seventh*.

In the afternoon troubles became gregarious. After plodding efforts a German wedge was driven between the Lowlanders and Highlanders; then, southward, the *Twenty-first* was pressed back to the south of Bouchavesnes, uncovering the South Africans, who were posted on the Epine de Malassise, midway between Bouchavesnes and Moislains. How intense and incessant was the pressure which the *Twenty-first* had to grapple against! It shows how the German attack strove tenaciously from day to day to annihilate defence south of the *Ninth;* and also how the *Ninth*, both south and north of its own frontiers, had to be always alert and active. Not even Wellington's favourite troops, the unbeatable Light Division, ever behaved better than the *Ninth*. Yet Tudor's men have received no thanks from the THIRD ARMY, and but little recognition from the British people.

In a lecture delivered in South Africa, Dawson has related what occurred on the third day along his frontage:—

"All our ammunition and supplies were arranged in dumps parallel to the front, and the first result of the retirement was that all these advanced dumps had to be destroyed by us. As a consequence we could get supplies and ammunition only from the railway, which was a long way off. There was great difficulty in obtaining rations and ammunition. Tanks and aeroplanes could get no petrol, and machine-gunners could not get belts.

"The third British line was held by the reserve brigade, a battalion of the Highland Brigade, and 'details'; namely, those of the men who had not been taken into the battle were formed into a battalion and put in to hold the line. Details as a rule do not fight very well. We never get the best out of a man who is not in his own formation. Details will put up a scrap all right, but will not endure the absolute hell that they will go through with their own platoons and companies. But these details held the line, and held it very well. The Germans tried to get through. They came on platoon after platoon, and we shot them down at forty yards like tame rabbits. But the time came when the details had the order to retire; it was a bad order. It said, 'Retire as soon as you get this.' In five minutes the battalion of details was in full retreat, and once they got going like that there was no stopping them. The Germans, as soon as they saw these fellows going, got up and began to fire, but although within forty yards they were so excited that they could hit no one at first. Then they cut the wire, and after a few minutes they got the machine-guns and riflemen on the parapet, and did a great deal of damage to our details as they were retiring.

"The orders of the South African Brigade that day were that it was not to be in the front line, because it had borne the brunt of the fight the other two days. It was to be in support on the right. But the other two brigades, owing to the loss of the battalion of details, could not cover the front, so the South African Brigade had to go into the front line again. We retired slowly, in accordance with orders, until we reached the Tortille River. I went up some high ground on the left, and to my consternation found no infantry on the hill. I went back to the road, and while I was there, two officers and forty men belonging to the division on our right came along. I ordered them to go up and hold that hill. The officer in command said that he could not do it; his men were absolutely done. He said that these forty men were the remains of about three hundred, and that they had had no food whatever since the attack started two days before. I replied that I could not help it; the work had to be done. I promised them rations and rum, and supplied the rations and rum, and sent them up the hill with my brigade major to put them in position. Half an hour afterwards I went to see, and they had all gone. I ought to have recognized that they had had a bad time of it, and had reached that stage when troops were no longer reliable. In this stage there is only one way to hold troops—by the influence of an officer or non-com. with a stronger personality, who will use his fists, and if this does not work, will use his revolver."

Dawson watched the *Twenty-first* DIVISION retiring. Two thin lines of British were covering the retirement of the third, and following came wave after wave, and column after column of Germans to a depth of about a mile. It struck him as ridiculous to see these two thin lines of British troops keeping their end up, but all the same they had to withdraw. They went back till they were two miles in the rear. Then Dawson had a gap of two miles open westward on his right flank. If the Germans turned to the north they would cut off his troops. While he was wondering what to do, the details, who had retired with the transport, were sent back again, and he formed a line of posts to protect the gap on his flank.

Before sunset the G.O.C. visited Dawson and told him to retire after dark to a ridge just west of Bouchavesnes, while Lowlanders were to man the near or east edge of St. Pierre Vaast Wood. At all costs this line must be held.

Then the G.O.C. hastened northward to see Kennedy, his Highland brigadier, whose troops at two p.m. held a line from about a mile or less below Mesnil-en-Arrouaise to a point north-west of Etricourt, pretty close to a well-known beet-sugar factory. From this point, as we have seen, about 750 men of the *Second* DIVISION carried on the line to the north of Fins; but they found their hard job too hot, and before dusk they retired north-westward, without orders. No doubt bitter attacks in the afternoon were very trying. As soon as these men of the *Second* fell back towards Rocquigny, the Highlanders pulled in their line till it spanned a portion of Byng's land from about Mesnil to Saillisel's ruins just north of the boundary.

This was the position of affairs when the G.O.C. visited Kennedy, his Highland brigadier. What could be done? A safe retreat could not be made by twilight. It would be seen by the foe, who at once would strike. The Highlanders were completely stranded on THIRD ARMY land, with both flanks uncovered by gaps. After dark they could close down southward till their right joined the Lowlanders along the east edge of St. Pierre Vaast Wood, while their left rested still on Byng's land in front of Saillisel.

These ticklish movements by night were to be done by four a.m. on Sunday, March 24; and with help of rare good luck, accompanied by cool and swift leading, all went well enough, though at midnight, or thereabouts, the Lowlanders had to beat off a determined push. But for these night manœuvres, both Highlanders and Lowlanders might easily have shared the fate of their comrades, the South Africans, who on Sunday, March 24, were surrounded and overwhelmed because the *Ninth* had no reserves left, having been compelled by events to extend beyond its own boundaries.

Though the night manœuvres had reunited the Lowlanders and Highlanders, everybody knew that one danger had been exchanged for another, for if the 5th Corps, THIRD ARMY, did not close down rapidly, a gap would exist at four a.m.

THE NORTHERN FIGHTING CONTINUED 179

on Sunday between Saillisel and Mesnil. So a warning of this danger was sent at once to Gough.

§ II

If the *Ninth* DIVISION had mao a complete report of all particulars, no mistake could have been made by the préciswriters at G.Q.H. But chivalry interfered. Liaison troops in a time of peril should not fall back without orders; but those men of the *Second* were few in number, they had had a trying experience, and afterwards their brigadier was killed in action. So the *Ninth's* H.Q. made no complaints. But complaints were raised by the *Forty-seventh*, as by other THIRD ARMY troops, and some influenced the précis-writers at G.H.Q., and found their way into the official dispatch. The result is that the British people have been asked to condemn the *Ninth*, who warned Byng's left again and again, and then held some two miles of THIRD ARMY land. Such is human nature! We feel more or less unkind to those who humble us by helping us in a time of great need, while we are fond of those whom we help.

The dispatch says not a word of the earnest warnings which Byng's right received from Gough's left, including a personal visit from the Ninth's G.O.C. to 5th Corps in order to see Boyd, the B.G.G.S.; and the précis-writers pass over the boundary uniting Byng and Gough as if ignorant of its place in G.H.Q. maps.

The dispatch begins by saying that 5th Corps, THIRD ARMY, during the morning of March 23, continued its withdrawal, covered by rearguards who were heavily engaged. It fell "back from the Metz-en-Couture salient to the defences of the third zone about Ytres." Turn to my map of the boundary districts and note the position of Ytres. From its most southern point to the boundary below Equancourt is some 4500 yards, and the distance is about 500 yards more to the boundary below Manancourt. Further, Green Line passed east of Equancourt to the east of Ytres, and the *Ninth's* vanguard reached this line at about ten p.m. of the second day, keeping rearguards well ahead. Was it safe and right for 5th Corps to postpone its arrival at Green Line to the morning of the 23rd? It was warned by the southern events which compelled the *Ninth* to withdraw. It was warned also by events at Hermies, Beaumetz and Vaulx. Why, then, did it not pull out of Flesquières salient in order to retire with its southern partner, and to avoid the risks it ran of disaster owing to the enemy's success in the north? On the evening of the first day, when a withdrawal by 5th Corps, THIRD ARMY, uncovered the *Ninth's* forward zone, the *Ninth* retired at once with its neighbour. Surely this example was one to be followed, since firm unison between our two armies was essential? Yet the dispatch has not a word to say on those important matters. Nor does it speak of the very able way in which the attack was handled in accordance with Ludendorff's aims.

On the other hand, it declares that 5th Corps was pushed north-west because Congreve's troops had been withdrawn under orders from Green Line to the Canal du Nord, north of Moislains; a movement rendered necessary, as we have seen, by southern events. Even if 5th Corps' right had followed the boundary during the night, instead of going west to Metz-en-Couture and Ytres, this official statement would be aside from the main point—a belated retreat from the salient. Then we are told that the *Forty-seventh* DIVISION and the brigade of the *Second* made vigorous efforts to re-establish touch with the FIFTH ARMY!

We have seen what happened to that brigade of the *Second;* and anxiety about the *Forty-seventh* not only detained the Highlanders in Byng's land, it caused the *Ninth's* G.O.C. to visit 5th Corps.

One cannot help regretting that the boundary is forgotten in the official dispatch. Much misunderstanding arises from this fact. We are told how the *Forty-seventh*, on the fourth day, held the village of Rocquigny from sunrise well into the afternoon, beating off all assaults till the foe worked round their flank between Rocquigny and Le Transloy and forced them to retreat. A splendid fight; but something more should have been said. The *Forty-seventh* was far from its southern boundary. It ought to have defended both Morval and Combles.

§ III

At 2.50 on Sunday morning, March 24, the South Africans sent a message as follows to their G.O.C. :—

"*Twenty-first* DIVISION reports that Cléry * is in the

* Cléry-sur-Somme, a little more than 4000 yards south-west of Bouchavesnes, and about 5000 yards north-west of Péronne. A very important German success, but soon countered along Hem Spur by two battalions of

THE NORTHERN FIGHTING CONTINUED 181

hands of enemy, and that they are making a further retirement to gain touch with their flank."

The *Twenty-first*, from the first day, as we have seen, had been badly hit, and the German pressure continued to be so keen upon its left wing that it fell back more rapidly than the South Africans, whose retirement began at 9.45 p.m. of the 23rd. By three a.m., March 24, the South Africans—about 500 men in all—took up their positions north of the road running between Le Forêt and Rancourt. During the night, touch was obtained by the South African right with the left brigade of the *Twenty-first*, which had retired and then had advanced again. As for the South African left flank, it was in touch with a company of the K.O.S. Borderers, but not with the other Borderers who were in reserve south of Rancourt. A mounted patrol was sent out, as well as several infantry patrols, but all attempts to find the Lowlanders failed, the weather being foggy.

Before dawn a mishap came out of a false report. Our Highlanders, hearing that the Lowlanders had fallen back, which was false, withdrew to Bapaume-Péronne road to be in line with them; and the message reporting this move did not reach the G.O.C. till 7.5 a.m. About five hours lost!

As quickly as possible three tanks at Combles were sent to a front between Marrières Wood and Rancourt. It was hoped that they would fill the gap between the South Africans and our Lowlanders. They came too late. At eight o'clock the Lowlanders were attacked in front and on both flanks, the biggest jolts coming against the right flank; but at this point, happily, the Sixth K.O.S. Borderers, from south of Rancourt, delayed the turning movement long enough to let other troops retire from St. Pierre Vaast Wood and to take post covering Combles, where THIRD ARMY troops had not arrived.

Here a brisk stand was made for an hour or so; a brilliant rearguard action, but not so good, of course, as the very noble last stand of Dawson's five hundred.

In the part on Episodes, I give a full description of the South African Brigade's last stand, which, like the rest of the *Ninth's* defence, struck admiration into the German leaders. At a most critical time and place it stopped the German advance for a little more than seven hours, causing a great block of German troops, guns and transport. From west of the *Thirty-fifth* DIVISION, who had just arrived after a long forced march. When our country goes to war, always unready, her only safe Ally is merciful Providence.

Bouchavesnes to Aizecourt-le-Haut the road was packed with a double line of delayed German troops and equipments.

General Byng and his officers can never be grateful enough to the South Africans. Colonel Buchan says, very well:—

"It was no piece of fruitless gallantry. . . . Indeed, it is not too much to say that on that fevered Sabbath the stand of the [South African] Brigade saved the British front. It was the hour of von der Marwitz's most deadly thrust. While Gough was struggling at the river crossings, the THIRD ARMY had been forced west of Morval and Bapaume, far over our old battle ground of the Somme. The breach between the two armies was hourly widening. But for the self-sacrifice of the (S.A.) Brigade at Marrières Wood and the delay in the German advance at its most critical point, it is doubtful whether Byng could ever have established that line on which, before the end of March, he held the enemy," * aided by many troops from Gough's left wing, and by other reinforcements.

The foe understood what our *Ninth* had achieved.

"On the road to Le Cateau," says Buchan, "a party of British officers was stopped by the Emperor, who asked if any one present belonged to the *Ninth* DIVISION. 'I want to see a man of that division,' he said, 'for if all the divisions had fought like the *Ninth* I would not have had any troops left to carry on the attack.'"

The Highlanders also encountered many perils. They withdrew to a ridge south of Morval, on THIRD ARMY land, but their rearguard, about 150 Fifth Camerons, had their right flank turned. At first they retired to Lesbœufs, being unaware that the foe had broken through Byng's right flank and had taken Combles, Morval, Lesbœufs, along about 5000 yards of front; and then they marched to Flers and joined the 52nd Brigade, *Seventeenth* DIVISION. †

It was at 4.15 p.m. that the THIRD ARMY reported to Gough: "The enemy has broken through our right flank and has occupied Combles, Morval and Lesbœufs." Owing mainly to this disaster, Congreve's Corps, heavily pressed also along its whole front, fell back by evening to the line Hem-Maurepas. All that the Staff could collect of cavalry, Canadian motor

---

* "South African Forces in France," p. 191. Colonel Buchan puts a plain matter pointedly, unlike the G.H.Q. Dispatch, which glides over the South African defence in a few formal phrases and without examining its widespread influence.

† They rejoined their own unit on Monday evening, March 25.

THE NORTHERN FIGHTING CONTINUED 183

machine-guns, and the crews and guns of some tanks, were thrown out on the left to the north-west in the direction of Bernafay Wood;* and, though still not in touch with the THIRD ARMY, the exposed flank was more or less covered. But now our line behind the Somme made a very sharp angle westward from Péronne; it would be enfiladed and taken in reverse from the northern bank.

Haig relates how Byng was affected by the loss of Combles, Morval and Lesbœufs. The advance "threatened to sever the connection between the FIFTH and THIRD ARMIES and the situation was serious." "In view of this situation the 5th and 4th Corps, THIRD ARMY, were ordered to fall back to the general line, Bazentin-Le Sars-Grevillers-Ervillers . . . The withdrawal of the right and centre of the THIRD ARMY was carried out during the afternoon and evening in circumstances of great difficulty, as on the right flank bodies of German infantry were already between our troops and the positions to which they were directed to fall back. In this withdrawal valuable service was rendered by twelve machine-guns of the *Sixty-third* DIVISION Machine-Gun Battalion, in Lesbœufs. These guns held up the enemy's advance from Morval at a critical period, firing 25,000 rounds into the enemy's advancing masses, and by their action enabling their division to reach the position assigned to it.

"By nightfall the divisions of the 5th Corps had taken up their line successfully between Bazentin, High Wood, Eaucourt l'Abbaye and Ligny-Thilloy.† Before midnight the troops of the 4th Corps, who had carried out their withdrawal by stages in the face of constant attacks, were established on the line assigned to them west of Bapaume, between Le Barque and Ervillers. *Touch between the several divisions of the 5th Corps and between 5th and 4th Corps, however, was not properly established.*"

Note this last sentence with care. As the 5th Corps was separated from the 4th, there was a breach in the centre of Byng's Army; and as its own divisions were not in touch

---

* Bernafay Wood, east of Montauban, in Byng's area.

† Still far from the boundary: 5th Corps ought to have been at Montauban as well as Bazentin. Instead of Byng's troops at Montauban there were newly arrived units of the *First* CAVALRY, which, during the afternoon of March 24, arrived there, coming from Watts's undermanned Corps. The dispatch mentions the arrival of *First* CAVALRY units at Montauban, but forgets to say that Montauban was in Byng's area, and that an increasing strain was thrown upon Gough's left and centre by the disunity in Byng's 5th Corps. This disunity is described, but not its results on Gough's troops.

there is no difficulty in understanding why 5th Corps' right could not join hands with the *Ninth* DIVISION.

What remained of the Highlanders, after a stand on the Morval-Combles positions, which, as the map shows, was far in Byng's land, retired to the ridge south of Ginchy, also in THIRD ARMY land, and there took their revenge with machine-guns and Lewis guns, firing on masses of German troops who were advancing in column of fours along the road.

Many other experiences marked the fourth day, and among them was the origin of Colonel Hadow's force. At about five p.m., when some Highlanders were withdrawing to Maricourt, some three hundred of the Eighth Black Watch, under Hadow,' had their right turned and retreated northward. Around this body other men gathered until Hadow's force was two thousand strong. It served under Congreve, holding a position for two days—March 27 and 28—between Mericourt l'Abbé and Sailly le Sec; then it was relieved, and the Highlanders returned to their own division.

On the fourth day, again, Congreve began to receive the *Thirty-fifth* DIVISION as reinforcements. It came from the SECOND ARMY, and arrived mainly by battalions of different brigades, and there was no time to organize its units.

Troops of the *Thirty-fifth* detrained at Bray-sur-Somme, were hurried along the north bank of the river to support Congreve. Already the German advance had passed Cléry, and was pressing hard upon Tudor's and Campbell's remnants when these and some other reinforcements came upon the scene. The Fifteenth Cheshires and Fifteenth Notts and Derby did very well, counter-attacking with success; and afterwards a line was taken up from the river at Hem north into THIRD ARMY land at Longueval. For a moment danger in this sector was averted; but Marwitz very nearly made real the main purpose of his attack. To think of it is to grow cold. And the whole line north of the Army boundary had such an unstable form that it presaged few good things. Indeed, boundary troubles went on and on. At first they were caused by the fact that 5th Corps remained too far in the north-east; then, suddenly, 5th Corps went back too fast and was too far in the north-west. Hazard and hitches during a modernized retreat make a gambling hell unfit even for Milton's fallen angels.

On this Sunday, March 24, the *Ninth* was attached to the *Thirty-fifth* DIVISION, commanded by Franks, and the Twelfth Highland Light Infantry of the *Thirty-fifth*, less one company,

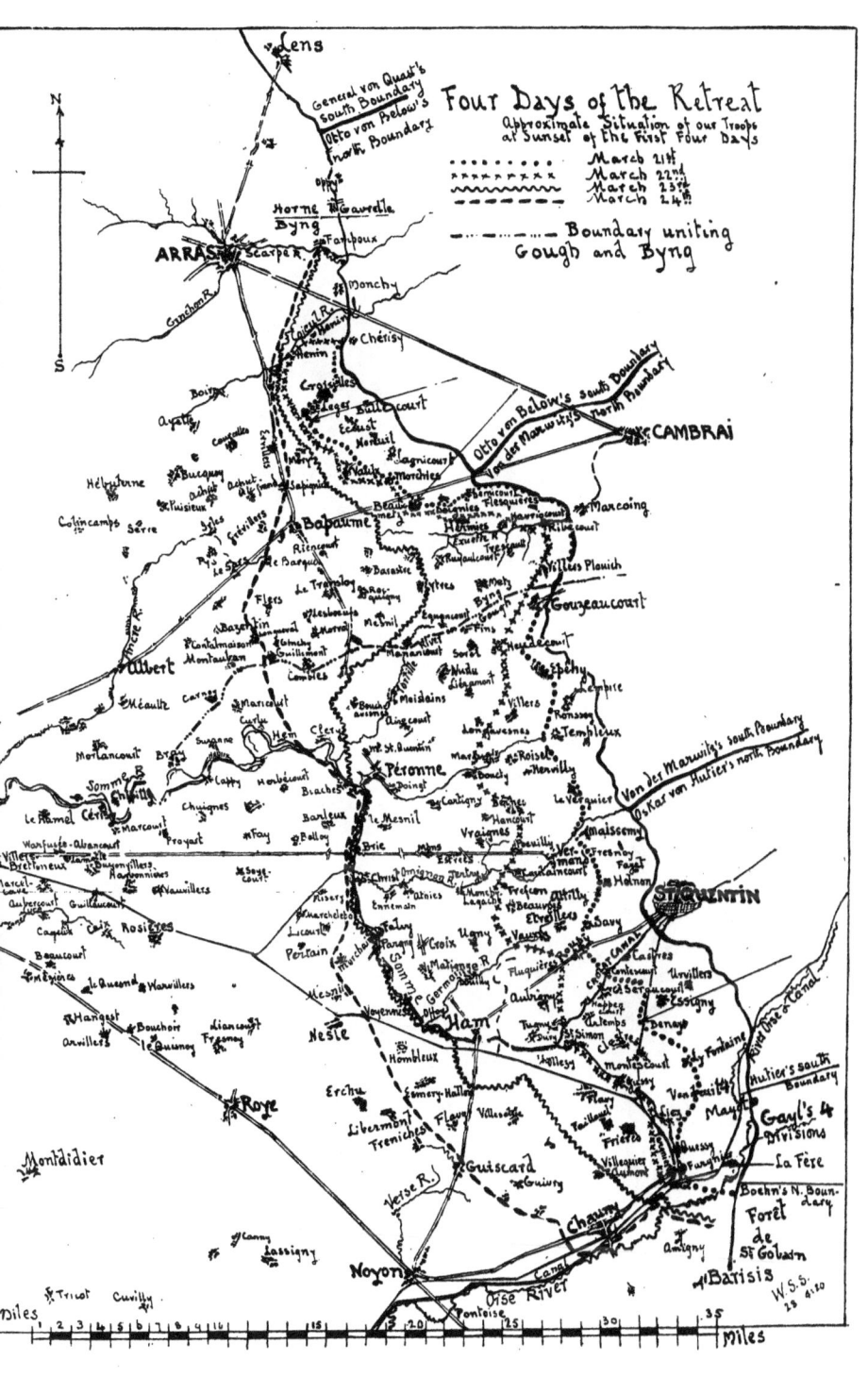

THE NORTHERN FIGHTING CONTINUED 185

reinforced the *Ninth*. At three p.m. the Twelfth Highland Light Infantry retook Maurepas, but held it only a short while as troops on the right were obliged to fall back between Hardecourt and Cléry-sur-Somme.

Again, students will note that the *First* CAVALRY at Montauban were not used as mounted troops. Campbell, of the *Twenty-first*, desired to use them mounted, but the Corps did not, and I believe could not, give him leave. In fighting of this nature G.H.Q. opposed the use of mounted troops, I believe. Dismounted men of the *First* CAVALRY did great work on the 24th and 25th, guarding the open left flank at Trônes Wood and Montauban; but is it right to believe that their value as mobile reinforcements would have been greatly increased if they had not been separated from their horses? Aided by machine-guns, and employed as genuine cavalry, they might have gained touch with Byng at Bazentin, closing the gap between the 5th and 7th Corps.

Between the second and fourth days a very welcome addition of power was collected by Congreve in Péronne: stragglers, leave men from England, and other odds and ends, four or five thousand in all eventually, and commanded by Lieut.-Colonel Hunt. Their first business was to put into a state of defence the line Suzanne, Vaux Wood, Maricourt, and Montauban; and they did good service both in their work and afterwards in defending their line. Later, too, Congreve collected another scratch force, this time in Corbie, and put it into the Old Amiens defences from the Somme to the Ancre, covering Corbie.

This collecting of " scratch " parties, which were rapidly organized into fairly homogeneous forces, was being constantly done by the Staff and Commanders of the FIFTH ARMY. Carey's Force, so called, is one among many examples, and a creditable proof of the activity, energy, and forethought shown by the whole defence. But for this general alertness the FIFTH ARMY could not possibly have held off the vast German power launched by Ludendorff. To hold off an attack of this magnitude and organization, and then to tire it into exhaustion were wonderful achievements. France and our own country do not yet understand in full what they owe to the FIFTH ARMY'S few divisions, but they are beginning to understand.

CHAPTER X

LAST DAYS OF THE NORTHERN FIGHTING

§ I

ON Monday, March 25, I regret to state, all FIFTH ARMY troops north of the Somme were transferred from Gough to Byng. They made up the bulk of 7th Corps, under Congreve, and in four-and-twenty hours they formed Byng's right wing from Bray almost to Albert, and thus on THIRD ARMY land, apart from Bray itself.

By good luck, as we have seen (p. 115), two of Congreve's divisions had passed south of the Somme; both were remnants, but yet invaluable to Watts, who was greatly harassed in the centre battle. The 7th Corps men who reinforced Byng were the *Ninth* and *Twenty-first,* remnants both, the *Thirty-fifth,* a newcomer and powerful, the *First* CAVALRY, and Hunt's and Hadow's Forces, important scratch bodies.

This act of swopping horses in midstream is too controversial for discussion here, so I have placed it in Part IV., together with a map which I have made to illustrate its effects. With his own troops Byng was unable to follow his southern boundary from Montauban to Bray-sur-Somme; indeed, his right never closed down into Montauban, so troubled was it by gaps between its divisions as well as by the breach between the 4th and 5th Corps.

Mishaps of this bad sort are likely to occur in all retreats, and these were very unfortunate because they threatened Amiens from the north-east. Ludendorff and his officers were very eager to break through north and north-west of Albert. Happily, Marwitz's guns and transport moved with great difficulty over the old Somme battlefield, and Otto von Below, after his grapple at close quarters against almost equal numbers, was exhausted, as Ludendorff declares. So it happened that the foe was out of gear at the very moment when our THIRD ARMY was passing through its most perilous crisis.

On March 25, the gap in Byng's centre became the greatest danger of all, and it remained so till early in the afternoon of the next day, when New Zealand and Australian troops prevented the whole Ancre line from being outflanked in the neighbourhoods of Bucquoy, Hébuterne and Colincamps. Even this timely relief did not save the town of Albert, which fell into Marwitz's hands during the night of March 26–27.

General Monash in his book gives a black picture of the position at Albert, but we must make allowance for his incessant bias. He is out to praise his own men and not to write cool history seen in true proportion and perspective. I do not know for what reason he overstates his views, because the British people and their newspapers praised the Australian troops unstintingly, even to the extent of being neglectful towards the backbone of the Allied cause in the West—unboastful Tommies enlisted in the British Isles and serving in line divisions. But although General Monash does not arrive at history, he enables us to feel the rumour-filled wrong notions that circulated while the battle was being fought; and we learn from him also how very false were the opinions formed by reinforcements who were hurried through forced marches till they came upon the British infantry retreating.

General Monash wants us to believe that Australian troops rescued Amiens. As a matter of plain fact, the Australian reinforcements had easy jobs compared with those that French reserves undertook in the south, that our *Eighth* DIVISION tackled grandly from day to day in the central battle, and that faced the *Thirty-fifth*, when its battalions came into the grapple one by one, breathless after forced marching.

We read how two brigades of the *Fourth* Australians, though over-tired by previous forced marching, came up on the 27th from the Basseux area to the high ground west and south-west of Albert. This town in the night had fallen, and the position was critical, mainly because the defence had been in battle since the 21st, but partly because the attack, though almost as tired as the defence, had a superiority of numbers.

General Monash says that the two Australian brigades formed an "already over-tired infantry," before they started their heavy route march from the Basseux area; but their fatigue did not come from days and nights of battle; in comparison with our line troops they were fresh and fit, and thus exceedingly welcome. Monash declares that their forced march—

"was more than justified, for the mere presence, in a

position of readiness, of these two Australian Brigades, did much to steady the situation opposite Albert, by heartening the line troops and stimulating their Commanders to hang on for a little longer." *

Monash likes touches of this latter sort. In his case, as in a game of bowls, bias acts at once and often too much. Consider another passage :—

"So far, the pressure of the enemy upon my front had not been serious. It was obvious that he had, as yet, very little artillery at his disposal. We had not, however, found our front totally devoid of defenders. During the forenoon [of the 27th], a few troops of our cavalry, and a force under Brigadier-General Cummings, comprising about 1500 mixed infantry, the remnants of a large number of different units of the THIRD ARMY, were slowly withdrawing under pressure from the advancing German patrols. These valiant 'die-hards,' deserving of the greatest praise in comparison with the many thousands of their comrades who had withdrawn from any further attempt to stem the onflowing tide, were now ordered to retire through my outpost line, thus leaving the Australian Infantry at last face to face with the enemy."†

I wish that General Monash had been with Byng's troops on March 21, and that he had fought on through the retreat till it reached Albert. Then the beginning of his book would have had focus, perspective, experience, sympathy, history, and, in fact, a very different character.

§ II

Harassed by gathering stress and strain, which came to their culminating point between Sunday and Tuesday, March 24 and 26, the THIRD ARMY was not master of its own movements till gaps in its front had been filled. If its right wing had been able to follow its southern boundary to Bray-sur-Somme, great good things would have happened, of course, because all FIFTH ARMY troops would have crossed the river at Bray into the central battle, apart from those who would have held the very narrow front east of the town while keeping liaison with Byng's right. The central battle needed reinforcement at the very moment when Congreve had to relieve Byng's 5th Corps from the south suburbs of Albert south-east to Bray.

There are writers who say that the FIFTH ARMY troops

---

* "Australian Victories in France in 1918," p. 30. † *Ibid.*, p. 29.

LAST DAYS OF THE NORTHERN FIGHTING 189

transferred to Byng were pressed back. Even Sir F. Maurice, in an oversight, has made this mistake, saying, page 42 of his book: "This new right of the THIRD ARMY was pressed back north of the Somme, and the FIFTH ARMY south of the river, finding its flank exposed, had to continue its retreat."

The mistake in this quotation is too big to be passed over in silence. On the fifth day 7th Corps fought splendidly, defeating a hard-pressed attack, and holding a line from the Somme through Maricourt and on to the north of Montauban. A menacing gap remained unfilled north-west of Montauban, because 5th Corps was passing through perils that increased. These perils gathered towards their climax during the day; and the breach in Byng's centre, between 4th and 5th Corps, became more threatening, with the result that Byng himself ordered 7th Corps to fall back after dark from the Maricourt line. It was this order that uncovered Gough's left south of the river, after 7th Corps, by defeating the foe's efforts to break through, had saved Amiens.

At this point, then, I wish to work into a drama some very striking contrasts from the official dispatch.

On March 25, north of the Somme, between the neighbourhood of Hem northward to Trônes Wood (some 3000 yards east of Montauban, and in THIRD ARMY ground)—

"all the enemy's attacks were held. Though their left flank * was constantly in the air, the various forces operating in this sector maintained a gallant and most successful resistance all day, counter-attacking frequently. Prisoners from five German divisions were taken by us in the course of this fighting, and the enemy's casualties were stated by them to have been abnormally heavy."

Congreve's troops achieved these good things, extending their left well into THIRD ARMY land and yet unable to find the 5th Corps' right. Those prisoners taken from five German divisions were captured mainly by the brave *Thirty-fifth*, commanded by G. M. Franks, after a combat so full of ups and downs that the very last reserve had to be used with the utmost vigour. For the tired attack, reinforced, had risen into good spirits, believing that it had a fine chance to break through north of Montauban and on the Maricourt line; and no doubt it would have broken through but for the *Thirty-fifth*, a recent reinforcement.

As the official dispatch does not make real to us the touch-

---

* Namely, towards the 5th Corps, THIRD ARMY.

and-go perils on the Maricourt line and north of Montauban, let us take a glance at the work done by the *Thirty-fifth*, the *Ninth*, and the *First* CAVALRY, remembering that a breakthrough, here, added to the increasing menace north of Albert, would have been fatal. By way of introduction we will consider this northern menace first:—

"At noon," says Haig, "fresh attacks developed in great force, and under the weight of the assault the right of the 4th Corps, with which the divisions of the 5th Corps were not in touch, was gradually pressed back.* The enemy gained Grévillers, in which neighbourhood the *Nineteenth* was hotly engaged; and also Bihucourt," † north-west of Bapaume.

In plain words, the foe was widening the gap in our THIRD ARMY'S centre; and by ill fortune, too, there was no stability south of Grévillers to the boundary at Montauban, apart from that which was formed by Congreve's men north and east of Montauban. Haig says :— ‡

"Between Montauban and the neighbourhood of Grévillers *our troops had been unable to establish touch on the line to which they had withdrawn on March* 24. After heavy fighting throughout the morning and the early part of the afternoon, in which the *Sixty-third* DIVISION in particular, under C. E. Laurie, beat off a number of strong assaults, *divisions commenced to fall back individually towards the Ancre, widening the gap between the* 5th *and* 4th *Corps*.

"During the afternoon the enemy reached Courcelette, and was pressing on through the gap in our line in the direction of Pys and Irles, seriously threatening the flank of the 4th Corps. It became clear that the THIRD ARMY, which on this day had assumed command of all troops north of the Somme, *would have to continue the withdrawal of its centre to the line of the River Ancre, already crossed by certain of our troops near Beaucourt*. All possible steps were taken to secure this line, but by nightfall hostile patrols had reached the right bank of the Ancre north of Miraumont, *and were pushing forward between the flanks of the* 5th *and* 4th *Corps in the direction of Serre and Puisieux-au-Mont*. In view of this situation, the 4th Corps fell back by stages

---

* Ludendorff declares that on the fifth day Otto von Below's Army was quite exhausted, and Haig in a footnote (vol. ii., p. 199) refers to this declaration by Ludendorff; so I do not understand this great pressure on the right of 4th Corps. Whence did this pressure come? From Below's exhausted troops?
† Vol. ii., p. 202.
‡ The italics are mine.—W. S. S.

during the night and morning to the line Bucquoy-Ablain-zevelle, in touch with the 6th Corps about Boyelles. On the right the remaining divisions of the THIRD ARMY were withdrawn under orders to the line Bray-sur-Somme-Albert,* and thence took up positions along the west bank of the Ancre to the neighbourhood of Beaumont Hamel."†

Turn to a map and sketch in this information, and at once it will be clear to you that the act of holding the Somme front safe from Hem northward to the north of Montauban was one of decisive importance. The *Thirty-fifth* was the groyne or break-water, but it was a newcomer which had arrived mainly by battalions of different brigades, and these battalions had to be used as soon as they arrived. On the tragical Sunday, March 24, for example, it was the Sherwoods and Cheshires who at daybreak arrived at Maricourt, under Brigadier Marindin, to be sent forward at once to retake Hem Spur. During Sunday other battalions arrived, the Seventeenth Royal Scots, who hurried to support Marindin; the Twelfth Highland Light Infantry, who were sent at once to help the *Ninth*, and the Nineteenth Northumberland Fusiliers, Pioneers. Several battalions, and among them the Fourth North Staffords, arrived after dark or during the night of the 24th–25th. Consider the feverishness of this reinforcing, nearly all the troops marching from 12 to 14 miles, because a desire to move them by 'bus could not be put into effective action.

By seven in the evening the *Twenty-first* was relieved by the *Thirty-fifth*, and what was left of them withdrew into reserve near Bray. By Congreve's order, the G.O.C. of the *Thirty-fifth*, G. M. Franks, took command of all 7th Corps troops, north of the Somme; namely, his own division, and remnants of the *Ninth* and *Twenty-first*, the *First* CAVALRY, and the scratch or improvised unit.

At six a.m. on the 25th our right sector from Curlu to the south end of Bois Favière was held by a brigade of the *Thirty-fifth* under Marindin. In the Maricourt defences were three composite battalions; and the *Ninth* with its supports guarded the left sector from Bois Favière to Bernafay Wood, just east of Montauban, and on THIRD ARMY land. The *Ninth's* supports were a mixture of units from the *Thirty-fifth*, two

* These divisions were Congreve's, drawn by events into land which the 5th Corps would have held but for its troubles. Note, too, that Bucquoy is in a position from which the whole Ancre line may be outflanked.
† Vol. ii., p. 208.

battalions from Pollard's brigade, and the Nineteenth Northumberland Fusiliers. Two battalions of the *Thirty-fifth* were in reserve.

All day long, till five p.m., fighting was very keen and sometimes very critical. In the morning persistent efforts were made by the foe to turn our left flank through the gap which Byng's troops were unable to fill owing to their grave troubles. Brigadier Legard with dismounted men of the *First* CAVALRY did some fine work on THIRD ARMY ground, shooting the attack at point-blank range, and holding out well from the south of Bernafay Wood to north-east of Montauban and thence westward some 2000 yards; while the *Ninth*, meantime, were hard pressed in front of Maricourt. Artillery barrage was directed to the north of Montauban from the east of Bernafay Wood. By noon a battalion of the *Thirty-fifth*, and all three battalions of the Cavalry Brigade, formed a defensive flank north of Montauban. About an hour later it was said that a brigade of Byng's *Seventeenth* was holding a line from north of Bernafay Wood to the south-east of Bazentin le Grand, and that the other brigades were reforming east of Fricourt. Touch with them could not be made, however, neither then nor later.

During the afternoon the whole of our troops passed through desperate combats. Favière Wood was lost and regained. Bernafay Wood was turned from the south-west when we lost the Briqueterie, but a counter-attack ejected the foe. In the south, on our right, British supports were thrown back off Curlu Spur as far as the Maricourt line, and a successful counter-blow was followed by another set-back. Reinforced, our men went ahead again and pushed the foe back from 500 to 700 yards.

Meantime the attack pressed from Hardecourt against the centre of our main position, and broke into Maricourt; but at 5.20 p.m., after bitter, fluctuating efforts, and after Franks had used up his last reserves, Maricourt became safe again, and our whole line from Bernafay Wood to the Somme was intact, and also very cheerful, for every man knew that the Boche had been badly beaten. In the final counter-attack had been pressed even the Brigade H.Q. of the 104th and 105th Infantry Brigades—officers, clerks, servants, signallers and runners, so short were we of men. After this really glorious combat, steel helmets were worn jauntily aslant on many heads; cheers rang out here and there; and then, suddenly, at about 6.30 p.m., chilling news came. The THIRD ARMY,

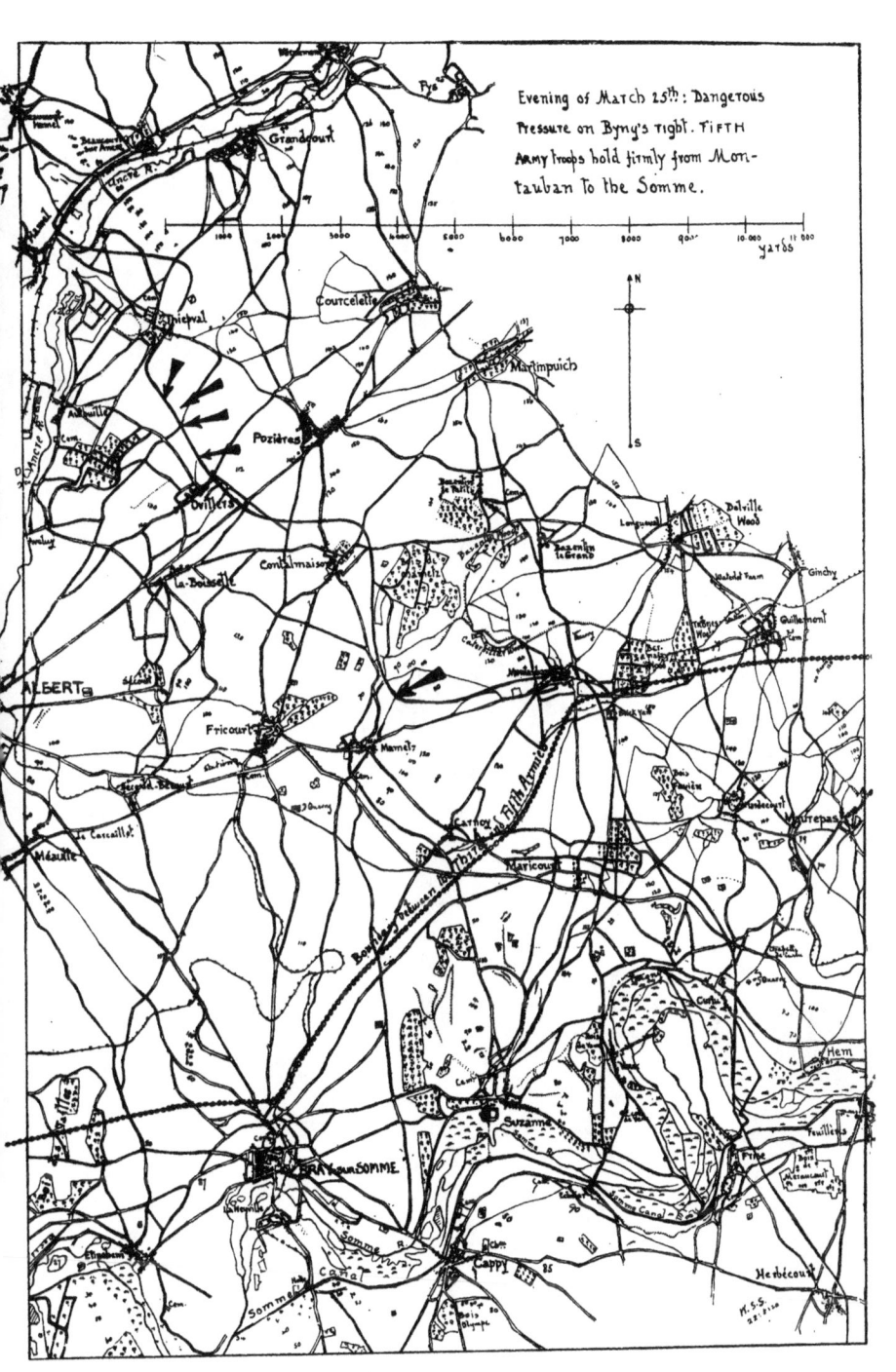

LAST DAYS OF THE NORTHERN FIGHTING

owing to troubles north and south of Albert, would withdraw Congreve's troops and transport to the Ancre, holding as a rearguard position the line Bray-Albert.

To stop a break-through and then to be ordered to fall back from the land just saved! There's no greater trial in a retreat, perhaps, above all when troops feel almost exhausted, and so parched that water has no appreciable effect on thirst. But it could not be helped. The position north of Albert was not yet relieved. There was "a dangerous gap about Serre," as Haig points out. On the other hand—

"considerable reinforcements had now come into line, and had shown their ability to hold the enemy, whose troops were becoming tired, while the transport difficulties experienced by him in the area of the old Somme battlefield were increasing. Other reinforcements were coming up rapidly, and there seemed every hope that the line of the Ancre would be secured and the enemy stopped north of the Somme" (vol. ii., p. 203).

Unfortunately, all these reinforcements on the THIRD ARMY'S front did not at once bring equipose to the battle line. Next day, March 26, was a very grave one north of Albert. Between Hamel and Puisieux, as Haig explains, the situation was not yet clear. "A gap still existed in this area between the 5th and 4th Corps"; and German infantry pressed through the gap and worked their way forward till they "occupied Colincamps with machine-guns," threatening to outflank the whole Ancre line by a south-westerly drive accompanied by a thrust west and north-west.

In Part IV. we shall see what happened afterwards when we study the transfer of Congreve and his troops to Byng's right wing, and the origin of the Cérisy episode by which the centre battle was affected so dramatically (p. 268).

To my mind it was nothing less then providential that G.H.Q., on February 22, 1918, altered the boundary uniting the two armies, greatly lessening that south-western slant which aided Marwitz so much by baffling Byng's right wing and by drawing Congreve deeper and deeper into THIRD ARMY ground. No other matter in the battle is *more* important than this to our two armies. But the superlative bravery of the *Ninth* DIVISION is equally important to them both. It is plain, too, that after the breach was made between Fanshawe's 5th Corps and Harper's 4th Corps, which was accompanied by the opening of gaps in 5th Corps, a retreat south-west by Byng's right was impossible. A general closing-up towards the north became necessary, in order to lessen gaps while falling back both firmly and quickly.

§ III

It was Congreve's Corps that felt with most searching pain the force of Marwitz's attacks, and its losses were very high, amounting to 25,000 men and 135 guns, of which 27 were heavies. These losses came to five divisions, not alone to the original four—*Sixteenth, Twenty-first, Ninth,* and *Thirty-ninth,* reinforced by the *Thirty-fifth.* The great barrier division, the *Ninth,* Scottish and South African, lost a general average of 38·47 per cent., including pioneers, machine-gunners, and artillerymen, but not including Royal Engineers. Officers killed, 23; wounded, 96; missing, 94; total 213. Other ranks killed, 279; wounded, 1625; missing, 2670; total 4574, apart from the sick and completely exhausted.*

The *Ninth* won great fame among German officers and men. Here is the testimony of Captain G. Peirson, who was captured while holding the appointment of Brigade-Major in the *Sixteenth* (South Irish) DIVISION :—

"After being captured at Lamotte, near Corbie, I was taken to the German battalion headquarters for examination by an intelligence officer. In the course of this examination the officer asked me if I knew the *Ninth* DIVISION; he said that the fight it put up was considered one of the best on the whole front; and particularly the last stand of the South African Brigade at (I think) Moislains, which, he said, was magnificent. Both men and officers fought to the last against overwhelming odds, the Brigadier himself being taken firing a machine-gun, whilst his Brigade-Major was killed beside him.†

"After this conversation I was sent to Le Cateau, and on the way many German officers spoke to me, and all mentioned the splendid fight put up by the South Africans. On reaching Le Cateau I met two British officers who said that while their party was being marched to this place they were stopped by the Kaiser, who asked if any one present belonged to the *Ninth* DIVISION. The Kaiser then said that had all divisions fought as well as the *Ninth* DIVISION he would have had no

---

* Among the "missing" were other dead and other wounded, of course.

† Brigadier Dawson has contradicted this statement about his having fired a machine-gun before he was taken. There was no machine-gun ammunition to fire.

more troops to carry on his attack with. The truth of this statement I cannot vouch for, and unfortunately I have forgotten the names of the officers, but Brigadier-General Bellingham and Lieutenant-Colonel Gell were both at Le Cateau at the time and heard the story.*

"On my way to Le Cateau I met between thirty and forty men of the South African Brigade working as prisoners of war close to Epéhy. They were in a very bad condition, as no rations were allowed them, and they had to exist on what the individual German soldiers chose to give them, and what they could find in the old trenches, consequently nearly all of them were suffering from dysentery."

Yes, the Scottish and South African Division was genuinely great, and the whole of Congreve's Corps, as we have seen, had a history full of value. Parts of it fought on till April 4, on which day Congreve handed over his command to the chivalrous Birdwood and the Australians.

§ IV

On March 27 it was clear that the cyclone let loose in the northern fighting had lost its reserve force and was dwindling away, just like Hutier's in the south. One reason was the very serious loss of men suffered by Otto von Below, who attacked on a narrow front against a British force not in the least under-manned for defence. His brigades, too, inevitably, during fogs, must have got into dense formations, offering excellent targets for many of Byng's machine-guns. Again, when an army on a narrow front has men enough for a defensive battle, the forces at death-grips produce a mortal fatigue, a prostration not to be borne without great effort by the very bravest, as the French and British found at Waterloo, which was a skirmishing brief battle compared with Byng's grapple against Below's left and centre and Marwitz's right wing.

Very fortunately, Marwitz's inner wing in its advance towards Albert was greatly harassed by old shell-holes and trenches, and at last stuck fast in the western edge of the Somme's old battlefield.

One part of Below's Army, the north or right wing, had been inactive, so on March 28, it was ordered to assail and take the high ground commanding Arras. The fight began in the morning, between seven and eight o'clock, and although

* Dawson heard the same story when a prisoner in Germany.

the attack was a minor one compared with Hutier's onslaught against Gough's right, it had a far-reaching object by which it is made memorable for ever. Arras and her heights were the north abutments of that British defence which, with French help, was hardening around the huge arc of the new German salient. If these abutments could be carried the least effect would be an effectual opening for Ludendorff's next blow—at Armentières and in the Lys valley; but a strong advance beyond Arras, with adequate turning movements, would throw the whole defence into backward-going action, while imperilling the Channel ports and, probably, unlocking the gates into Amiens.

The fight extended from Puisieux to the north-east of Arras, and when Below found that he was checked on his northern flank, he struck vigorously towards Arras along the Scarpe valley, hoping that he would earn freedom for the development of his plans. Happily, since March 23, this thrust had been foreseen; ample preparation had been made for it by Byng, aided by G.H.Q.; and though a slice of land was lost, no real structural harm was done to the brave defence.

Below extended the fight north of Gavrelle and struck our 13th Corps, forming the right of the British FIRST ARMY commanded by Horne. This fact is often passed over. Let us remember, then, that our FIRST ARMY with its right flank troops helped to defend Arras.

Germans declare that their troops were too slow in their attack, pausing too often and too long, though their original strength had been reinforced by three divisions; and Ludendorff himself, as though ignorant of the number of divisions in Byng's Army, blames Otto von Below's troops for the gradual miscarriage of his northern plans.

"Immediately prior to the assault," says Haig, "masses of German infantry with artillery in rear of them were observed drawn up in close formation on Greenland Hill, and were shelled by our artillery. North of the Scarpe, about Rœux, great execution was done at point-blank range by single guns, which we had placed in forward positions close up to our front line.* The enemy's infantry in this sector are reported to have advanced almost shoulder to shoulder in six lines, and on the whole front our machine-gunners obtained most favourable targets."

* The detachments of certain forward 15-pounder guns, after firing all their ammunition and destroying their guns, got away safely on bicycles along the main Douai road to Arras.

LAST DAYS OF THE NORTHERN FIGHTING

I find in our official maps of the German Order of Battle that Below's troops north of the Scarpe to his union with Quast at Acheville and Bouvrey were as follows, from north southward: *Two Hundred and Fortieth*, Acheville-Fresnoy sector; *Forty-first*, between Fresnoy and Oppy; *Fifth* Bavarian RESERVE, between Oppy and Gavrelle; and *Twenty-third* RESERVE, from Gavrelle * to the Scarpe. Four divisions in line on a front of about 6½ miles.

South of the Scarpe to Puisieux, about 15 miles, thirteen divisions, mostly battle-worn, were in line, as follows, beginning at Puisieux itself: *Twenty-fourth, Third* Guards, *Fifth* Bavarians, *Hundred and Ninety-fifth, Sixteenth* Bavarians, *Two Hundred and Thirty-ninth, Two Hundred and Twenty-first, Sixth* Bavarian, *Twenty-sixth* RESERVE, *Two Hundred and Thirty-fourth* and *Thirty-sixth, Twelfth*, and the *Hundred and Eighty-fifth* south of the Scarpe between Pelves and Monchy.

"The weight and momentum of his [the enemy's] assault," says Haig, "and the courage of his infantry, who sought to cut their way through our wire by hand under the fire of our machine-guns, sufficed to carry the enemy through the gaps which his bombardment had made in our outpost line. Thereafter, raked by the fire of our outposts, whose garrisons turned their machine-guns and shot at the enemy's advancing lines from flank and rear, and met by an accurate and intense fire from all arms, his troops were everywhere stopped and thrown back with the heaviest loss before our battle positions." †

Below's southern onset, after all-day fighting, was defeated by the Guards DIVISION and the *Thirty-first;* by the *Forty-second*, which drove off two thrusts from the direction of Ablainzevelle, and by the *Sixty-second*, aided by a brigade of the *Fourth* Australians, whose combined efforts beat off some bitter onsets against Bucquoy by the *Fifth* Bavarians, aided by the *Third* Prussian Guards.

In the Arras neighbourhoods, along the Scarpe's north bank, where Below's object was to gain the general line, Vimy-Bailleul-St. Laurent-Blangy, our *Fourth* and *Fifty-sixth* had a hard struggle in which two fresh German divisions were engaged supported by two divisions of line troops; while immediately south of the Scarpe were four German

---

* Byng's left rested a little south of Gavrelle, so Gavrelle itself was in Horne's area.
† Vol. ii., p. 212.

divisions, two of which had been ordered to capture Arras and the heights overlooking the town. In this sector noble work was done by the *Third* and *Fifteenth* BRITISH DIVISIONS. Eight British divisions and a brigade of the *Fourth* Australians divide the honour of this big combat.

No combat of the war is a better illustration of capital defence with enough men on a front very well gunned and prepared. The attack's failure was a bitter set-back to Ludendorff's aims, and we can never be too grateful to the officers and men who fought under Byng and with the FIRST ARMY'S most southern troops. For all that, it was not the power behind the attack which made this combat so important. The FIFTH ARMY faced and baffled hugely greater odds. But the German aim at Arras was a big one, and in attempting to make it real, Ludendorff wasted a great many men, who would have been invaluable to him in the Lys valley and at Armentières and Kemmel. In other words, his blow against Arras was a military mistake; it was easy to foresee and it came so late in the battle that it could not possibly be a surprise. Its effect was to complete the ravages in Below's Army, with the result that Ludendorff had no storm divisions for the Lys battle.

PART III

THE BATTLE IN SOME CHOSEN INCIDENTS AND EPISODES

CHAPTER I

A FEW SCATTERED IMPRESSIONS

§ I

A FIFTH ARMY Londoner is said to have described the retreat as " a bit of 'ell different all d'y long, and me an' many right bang in it. Mostly I 'ad a rat in me belly, 'ard bitin', for I was amost done in most minutes, though some'ow on me pins till a pepperbox of shot from a blarsted M.G. got a bit on me in plices."

One of Nature's gentlemen! As a nation we turn to him when we get into scrapes by acting as valetudinarians in foreign affairs! Perhaps he may not rise to N.C.O. rank; but is he not a symbol of all that is best in British battles? He is like an old English archer named John Pearson, a Coventry man, whose story is related by Leland, and who had one of his legs shattered by a cannon ball at the battle of Dixmund. Such was the fine temper of this archer that he continued to use his bow either kneeling or sitting; and when the French took to flight, he turned to a comrade and said, " Have these three arrows which remain, and continue thou the chase, for I may not." What if this curt and cold bravery should pass away from the British people?

A writer in *Blackwood's Magazine*, " Quex," who fought against Hutier in our *Eighteenth* DIVISION, speaks of the second Somme battle as " perhaps the mightiest, most overpowering assault in military history "; and certainly his words are not ill-chosen. Imagine a Trafalgar which went on and on for a thundering, explosive week, and then, in another set of detonating days, died out. What a commotion this naval Hades would create all over the world! Yet its appeal to the household heart and conscience could not well be more searching than that of the wholesale sacrifice through which our FIFTH ARMY bled and trudged and fought on until enough reinforcements could take over a vanishing front unbeaten. An officer writes :—

"Not even on this twenty-second of March did we realize fully the vast conception and the extent of the German swoop, and that our brigade was as jetsam and as flotsam carried along on the mightiest part of the storm flood."

It follows that a battle so exceptional has a standard of its own when we try to measure the moods of men in battle; moods so curiously varied that a true poet may remember nothing much about the flame and torment and parched bravery, while an ordinary man, by fighting through the same tragedy, may seem to have been discharged from himself and lifted for a while into a poet's intellect.

A certain aloofness from the horror on stricken fields appears to be necessary to inspire leadership; and none can study this battle through and through without being amazed and humbled by the coolness and competence shown from hour to hour by Gough and his principal officers.

There was an absurd legend that Gough had lost touch with his Corps Commanders, and it was believed in some quarters where the sanity of self-control ought to have been present. Far too many symptoms of "nerves" were active *outside* the battle, either in foolish words or in flurried actions. Gough's devoted Staff was riddled with criticism, for example, though the Chief of it afterwards was to be appointed to a very important post in the northern part of Haig's front. A nation that begins to raise large armies after a long-threatened war breaks out cannot expect to improvise genius for every big job while turning her experienced officers into casualties. What she ought certainly to expect is something very different: that her pre-war self-neglect will be hated for ever by historians because of its incessant and horrible results. The wonder is that our wartime improvisations, while claiming the sacrifice of young lives by the hundred thousand, left us guarded by so many capable officers, both staff and trench-stricken. Myself, I like to remember that the French were greatly impressed by the composure and the prompt energy shown by our Staff officers, and that some British war correspondents on the spot received as eye-witnesses equally favourable impressions.

One of them writes:—

"The rapidity of the advance, due to the weight of the attack, caused constant changes in the situation. These were dealt with coolly and capably by the FIFTH ARMY Staff. I was frequently at their headquarters during the retirement, and can add personal testimony to the calm and business-like atmosphere which prevailed there. Every one was working very hard. Bed was out of the question. Meals were snatched as opportunity allowed. Many officers did not take their clothes off during the whole of the battle. But there was no panic or excitement. I saw no signs of indecision. Orders in detail were sent out to each Corps at frequent intervals, showing the next positions to be taken up and the connections to be made. . . . Fresh units were formed to reinforce those parts of the line which were dangerously thin. . . . By such measures our line was kept intact and our powers of resistance were maintained. Never for an instant did the FIFTH ARMY Staff lose grip of the situation." *

§ II

When Quex in *Blackwood's Magazine* described the second battle of the Somme as "perhaps the mightiest, most overpowering assault in military history," he remembered how he himself was "carried along on the mightiest part of the storm flood." There is an incident that he describes about a sergeant who comes to the Colonel with bad news about B Battery :—

"5.30 p.m. A sergeant came hurrying in. '*They've captured the battery, sir,*' he said bluntly, '*and Major Harville is killed. I came to report, sir. I was the only one to get away.*'

"I think sometimes of famous cases of tragedy and passion I have heard unfolded at the Old Bailey and the Law Courts, and the intense, almost theatrical atmosphere surrounding them, and compare it to the simple setting of this story, told in matter-of-fact tones by a sergeant standing at attention. 'We finished all our ammunition, sir,' he began, addressing the Colonel, 'and took our rifles. Major Harville was shot by a machine-gun while he was detailing us to defend the two gun-pits farthest from the place where the enemy had got past our wire. He fell into my gun-pit, sir, shot in the head. Mr. Dawes, who took command, said we would keep on with rifles, and Bombardier Clidstone was doing fine work with his Lewis gun. The Huns didn't seem inclined to come close, and after a conference in my gun-pit with Mr. Bliss, Mr. Dawes asked for a volunteer to try and find the nearest infantry, and to tell them we'd hold on if they could engage the enemy and prevent him rushing us. I said I would try, and crawled on my belly, sir, through the grass to an empty

* Hamilton Fyfe, *Contemporary Review*, January, 1919.

trench. The battery fired several fine volleys; I heard them for a long time. It was slow work crawling away without being seen, and when I had got 600 yards and was trying to get my bearing—I don't know what time it was. Then I noticed that no fire came from the battery. There was no sound at all for over ten minutes. Then about a hundred Germans rushed forward and started bombing the gun-pits, and some of our men came up. I saw about a dozen of them marched off as prisoners.'... 'You are quite sure Major Harville was killed?' asked the Colonel quietly. 'Yes, sir; he fell right in my gun-pit....'

"We all stood silent, looking on the ground. Poor Harville!... A gallant, upright soul. The very best type of the civilian soldier who is fighting this war for England. ... Before the war a professional man who had given no thought to fighting; when he became a soldier it was because he understood thoroughly, and believed in completely, all that for which he was ready to give his life. A clean-living, truly religious man, too, who loathed loose talk and swearing, and lived up to his ideals even amid the slime and filth of war. And his bravery was that of the honest man who fears and yet faces danger, not the bull-headed heroism of the 'man who knows no fear.' Poor Harville!

"The sergeant spoke again. 'Before I came back here, sir, after the enemy had marched off our men, A Battery turned their guns on the Germans in B Battery's position.' 'Did they?' said the Colonel, his face lighting up. 'Splendid!' ... 'Yes, sir; they fired well, a hundred rounds, I should think. They scattered all the Germans, sir; they ran like mad.'"

And this cool, factful sergeant, who maps out what we may call the topography of the spiritual life active in bloodshed, belongs to our hectic days of newspaper headlines and splash pages! He tells the truth, coldly and calmly and courteously, at a time when the art of trade selling, like the virtue of war propaganda, resembles that Western American concerning whom a comrade said in a tombstone epitaph, "As a truth-crusher he was unrivalled." Could anything prove more clearly that drill and discipline are great sedatives and tonics?

Not without exceptions though, as another story told by Quex bears witness. The Colonel speaks, March 22 :—

"Extraordinary attitude of mind some of the men out here nowadays have. Last night they brought in one of the ——'s, who was captured by the Boche in the morning, but escaped and got back to the battalion. He said that their enemy set prisoners bringing ammunition up to the front line. When he was asked how he escaped, he said that a shell killed the *man-in-charge* of the party and he got away. *The man-in-charge*," repeated the Colonel with scorn. "He spoke as if the Boche N.C.O. were a sort of foreman, and as if bringing up ammunition which was to be shot at your own countrymen was the most ordinary thing in the world—Bah!"

And yet, frankly, which in pre-war times did we as a nation try to deserve—the cool, factful sergeant, placid and lucid throughout a tragedy, or this shadow of a man whose surname should be Bah? Recall the tides of sentimentality which flowed and ebbed in our country through sixty years or so; and think of recent days when the Union Jack did not fly above our Board Schools lest it offend idealists. If any great people ever strove to turn themselves into cranks and invalids, it was the British people between the Crimea and 1914; and even to-day an amazing "logic of dreams" tries to undo the restorative traditions which our fighting men have added to our national legacies and heirlooms. In March, 1919, at a public meeting, I was told by several speakers that Conscientious Objectors were the war's real saints, and that Conscription was a very evil thing. A soldier protested and several young men left the hall; but flabby sentimentalities were cheered by most of the persons present. No speaker thought it worth while to explain how we should have fared as a nation if thirty or forty per cent. of our young man-power had been afflicted by Conscientious Objection, or if Conscription, too long delayed, had not been introduced at last.

To pit improvised armies against the German war machine was like pitting improvised fleets against our British Navy; and yet, despite the lack of military training through half a century and more, our impromptu divisions and corps not only managed to carry on real war in a way that every director of the German machine respected; they contrived also to make shift under conditions which our old long-service veterans would have found most damnable. A FIFTH ARMY officer writes:—

"Save for the Colonel and two or three of the signallers and a couple of servants, none of us were experienced soldiers; all our previous experience had been in attack; it was something new this feeling that a powerful, energetic, determined foe was beating down our opposition and getting nearer and nearer. Yet, whatever they may have felt, not one of our little band showed signs of depression or nervous excitement. The signalling-sergeant was cursing the sanitary orderly for not having cleared up a particular litter of tins and empty cigarette packets; the officer's cook was peeling potatoes for dinner, and I heard the old wheeler singing softly to himself some stupid, old-time, music-hall ditty."

The substance of this quotation applies to the whole FIFTH ARMY. The percentage of experienced soldiers was a small one in the ranks and N.C.O.'s; and not even one division had had enough rest and special training after the terrible year, 1917. Thus a Corps Commander wrote: " I know scores of instances in the recent fighting where one or two trained companies could have stopped the whole local retirement!" From the purgatory of fixed warfare in trenches to the hell of mobile warfare in a retreat hard pressed, with false rumours for ever in the air, and the knowledge that on a front so wide splendid success along one sector was always at the mercy of an overpowering flank movement against another; all this and a great deal more made a transformation from trench fighting to open warfare nothing less than abominable to troops who were not instructed enough to be experienced soldiers. Yet from the first morning the thoroughly trained attackers learnt that they dared not take liberties and that their time-table was far behind Ludendorff's plans and needs.

And the cause—the spiritual cause? Fighting temperament. Though cant enables us to astound other nations by chattering always about our gentle pacifism, yet the size of the British Empire proves to all the world that our tiny British Isles have produced the most instinctively aggressive breed of men the world has ever seen. In our mixed blood, happily, there is no unenterprising strain from a timid and craven race. Iberian, Roman, Anglo-Saxon, Celt, Norman, and sea-going Viking have left in the nation's veins mingled drops of their blood; and certainly we provoke suspicion among our allies abroad whenever we permit the old Puritan humbug in our sub-consciousness to prattle about our native meekness and our hatred of aggression. We hate aggression as a good boxer hates to receive a blow on the point. There remains more fighting temperament in the British breed of men than in any other breed, thanks to inherited qualities and sports. Even our Pacifists are never happy unless they are attacking human nature both as a whole and in detail;

A FEW SCATTERED IMPRESSIONS 207

and the separated charities of our three or four hundred modified Christian creeds mark the same native belligerency. But for this inborn and hereditary spirit, a combative individualism, an aggressive tenacity as natural as the heart's automatic beat, our FIFTH ARMY, despite the sound generalship that governed its big movements, would certainly have been worn out and swept away by Ludendorff's legions.

No attack could have been better trained, and more divisions could not have been used by Ludendorff without overpacking his front with targets and jumbling up the brigades. German message dogs, seen on Watts's lines, seem to have done their work unhindered by fog; and it was between Watts's flank and those of Congreve and Maxse that the enemy got early opportunities to forge ahead, as at Ronssoy and Maissemy. Yet he was slow, finding the defence so gripping, as at Epéhy, where the Second Munsters stuck it out nobly, under Colonel Ireland, fatally wounded, and Ireland's officers, Chandler (killed), Whelan, Kidd (severely wounded), Waldegrave, Strachan, King, Cahill (killed), and two or three others.

The German official news chronicled the defence (March 23) : " Heights of Epéhy captured after a hard struggle in which the British were surrounded." Lieutenant Whelan held out in Epéhy till noon of the second day. Enemy aircraft gave the Second Munsters a bad time. C Company brought one down with Lewis-gun fire, and a rifleman with a single shot ended another by shooting the German pilot. Lieutenant Kidd's defence of Malassise Farm, outflanked early on the first day and rushed, was so fine that some German Staff Officers spoke of it afterwards with many compliments ; and what could have been higher in temper than Lieutenant Whelan's yard-by-yard grapple in Ridge Reserve and Tetard Wood ? He had only C Company and a few of B. Every bay of Whelan's trench was a battlefield, men rallying over and over again; though cut down to half handfuls. When the German assault troops had pressed Whelan back into the last two or three bays in Tetard Wood, 4.30 p.m., March 21, he side-stepped into the trench at the head of Catelet Valley, and thence under orders he fell back fighting to the ruins of Epéhy, where survivors of B Company were fighting as bravely as his own men. The German losses were widespread and very large. On the first day, as soon as the fog lifted, German infantry were disclosed packed along Catelet Valley, and were raked by rapid fire. Rifles and machine-guns, again, aimed from Ridge Reserve, searched the Malassise Road to such good effect that the foe's artillery could not move up until the Ridge was carried in reverse from Malassise Farm. The enemy tried to move his guns, but horses and drivers were shot down; so it is no wonder that the Second Munsters made a name for themselves in Ludendorff's bulletin. And this episode is all the more notable because the South Irish suffered greatly; too many of them were not of a piece with the Second Munsters, whose pluck wore shamrock with five leaves, not to be touched by change and decay.

Defence of this tenacity—and it was in vogue on our FIFTH ARMY'S front—needs cool minds and strong wills and swift decisions: fighting temperament, in two words. To know when one is beaten is to know also that one's fighting temperament is out of joint, not what it ought to be; and again and again during the second battle of the Somme bodies of German infantry proved that their thorough training had not endowed them with the grit which true combativeness has naturally. Many of them, happily, sought overmuch after the line of least resistance. Thus an English Colonel of the *Sixty-sixth* noted that the whole advance against his front was methodical until punished; then it seemed for a time to collapse; especially if casualties were increasing; and an attempt was made to find a weak spot elsewhere.

Of his own men this Colonel said that they were content to hold on as long as they were asked to remain; that their courage and individual cheeriness was indisputable, and that in most trying circumstances of gas and fog it was a treat to see their grip and their discipline.

He praised highly the selected and specialist troops in the German attack, noting as lessons two points:—

1. That light machine-guns were pushed forward regardless of opposition.

2. That weak spots on the flanks of our strong posts were found, chiefly by contact airplanes; flares from the ground were sent up frequently, and our positions were then made known to German gunners, who got on the target with immediate accuracy.

Another British officer, a Brigade-Major, belonging to the *Sixty-first* DIVISION, saw at close quarters how the German machine worked. Let us see what his experiences were.

A Boche attack had broken a Colonel's right flank, and this Brigade-Major went to find reinforcements. He returned to Beauvois and found it deserted except by gas; so he set off down the Germaine road. A party of some fifty British stragglers were met and sent up to reinforce. Then he went farther along and saw another party, which he hailed, but got no reply, except a signal to keep quiet. Then all at once, before he knew what had happened, he was rushed by about twenty Boches.

"The first one fired at me at point-blank range," says the Brigade-Major, "and though he missed me, the flash knocked me straight over, and before I could do anything the whole party was around me.

"I must say the officers treated me very well, though my escorts were very rough. I had an intensely interesting and unhappy four hours with them, as they got ready for a further attack. For all my hatred I could not help admiring them intensely, for their deployment, discipline and preparation were an eye-opener.

"They extended into battle order without hardly a sound, and they lay down preparatory for the next assault, bringing up mules dragging light trench mortars, machine-guns and ammunition.

"After a little they handed me over to two ruffians with revolvers which they kept wagging at me and marched me back. The shame of being taken unharmed and the prospect of the indignities ahead decided me to make a bolt for it when I could. I waited my chance till the attention of the escort was distracted by a shell, and then I fell on the nearest man, hurling him as hard as I could at the other and rolling them both into the ditch. They sprang up at once and fired several shots at me, but I was away."

The same officer said that he thought the greatest lesson to be learnt from German methods was the value of personal initiative. Propaganda used to tell us in a routine that German soldiers had no initiative, when, as a matter of plain fact, a great many of them were first-rate in this great quality. Ludendorff set the greatest store by it, and fostered it by every possible means. Also, in his book, he never fails to note when and where it is absent. Note, then, what the British Brigade-Major says :—

"German patrols went forward on their own with limitless objectives and led by N.C.O.'s or even privates. I can testify to the skill of their movement and their thrusting policy, for I had not a look in with the patrol that got me. They were a good mile through our broken line within a very short time of breaking it and still going strong. How

P

they kept connection was a mystery to me, and I could not help wondering how many of our men were trained to such a pitch. Their policy seemed to be to cease fire with the artillery when it had done its work, and give free play to these patrols in the hope that our line between their penetrations would give way, as often it did."

In our officers, when they look back on the days of St. Quentin, it is always a joy to note a brief, chatty, searching candour, instructive, and sound all through, like the same quality in the modest genius of Darwin; and unless civilian Britain shows the same candour towards the merits in German warfare, no general understanding of our FIFTH ARMY'S valour and endurance is at all possible. Man by man, division by division, corps by corps, the Germans were much better trained, and certainly threefold more numerous, and something more than threefold; they were professional soldiers, while our own were amateur; and yet a superior inborn pugnacity carried our men through—a point to be noted by all who are nympholepts of perpetual peace.

Here is a series of pictures drawn by an officer of the Fifth Durham Light Infantry, which belonged to Martin's Brigade of the *Fiftieth* DIVISION. The time is the morning of the fifth day, and the position is behind Péronne in the Biaches neighbourhood. A lull in the fighting was foretelling another German attack :—

"We were quietly resting when word came in that the Germans had established another bridgehead, this time at Eterpigny. We were ordered to counter-attack, and at once set off, A Company leading in a sort of 'artillery formation.' We had to get through a lot of old wire which was rather awkward. As we advanced we were suddenly attacked by five or six hostile airplanes flying low and firing at us with their machine-guns. It was rather alarming, but I did not see a single man hit. When we got into the open country between Barleux and the Canal, I saw that the troops in front were coming back in crowds, and as things looked very black I decided to seize and hold the high ground immediately in front. So we took up a position commanding the shallow valley leading from the Somme to Barleux, and at the same time we rallied the men retiring past us and tried to form a line across the low-lying ground.

"For some hours nothing more happened, but during the afternoon the Germans crossed the Somme in hordes and pushed back the thin British line. Our two advanced companies withdrew with the *Sixty-sixth* DIVISION men, after inflicting heavy casualties on the enemy, and rejoined us. We took up a suitable position on the high ground and rallied as many men as we could. A platoon of the Seventh D.L.I. were on our right, and some men of this battalion were on our left. We got excellent signalling communication with lamps and a post that the battalion signalling sergeant had established near Brigade H.Q.

"It was extraordinarily interesting to watch the Germans working up to and around our flanks. They seemed to come down the hill at the far, or east, side of the Somme, at first in twos and threes, followed by larger bodies such as platoons. Then, after crossing the Somme Canal, they worked their way in small groups till they had accumulated the required number of men at a certain point. They fired white flares to show where they had got to, and gradually made their way to within two hundred yards of us. Further to the south, on the far side of the valley, we could see them working their way along the high ground near Villers Carbonnel. It was rather alarming, as we could see that they were round our right flank and had got at least a mile past us.

"I signalled back to the Brigadier to inform him how dangerous our position was, but his reply was a definite order not to withdraw, but to stay and fight it out. We therefore settled down, realizing that in the morning, we should be surrounded and overwhelmed with no possible chance of escape. Just before dusk the Germans had massed some two hundred yards in front of us, so I signalled back to the Brigadier, and he put some 18-pounders on to them in fine style. Our gunners had the range to a nicety, and dispelled any idea the enemy had of attacking us.

"Later in the evening I thought again that he would attack, so I tried to get our artillery on again, but this time there was no reply from Brigade H.Q., and we understood that they had gone and that we were now on our own. The Seventh D.L.I. had received orders to withdraw, but in spite of this the Seventh D.L.I. officer on our right offered to stay with his platoon and fight it out with us. A singularly brave thing to do as it simply meant that he would share our fate.

"The day had ended, and it was a fine moonlit night. At about 8 p.m. I had reason to think that some mistake had occurred, and Rowe and I, like drowning men clutching at straws, got on to the road towards where Brigade H.Q. had been, just to see if we could get any information. As we got out of the trench on to the road we heard the click of a rifle bolt, and thought the enemy was on us. Like a flash we were across the road and into the ditch with our revolvers out. A false alarm: it was a party of Seventh D.L.I. withdrawing. I explained the position to the officer in charge, and he agreed to stay and watch our flank till we got back from Brigade H.Q.

"When we had gone three or four hundred yards down the road, we found a platoon of Northumberland Fusiliers of our own division; they told us that they had been told off to cover the withdrawal of the Fifth and Seventh D.L.I., and had wondered what had happened to us, as practically all the other troops had gone. It was clear from this that orders to withdraw had been sent us, but had gone astray. It was not long before we were moving in single file, as quickly as possible, down the sunken road skirting Barleux.

"An awesome business. There was a bright moon, so the Germans had a good chance both of discovering that our line was being withdrawn, and also of closing up and cutting off our retreat. It is extraordinary what a noise three or four hundred men make on a still night, however hard they are trying to move quietly.

"Near Barleux a Boche patrol, or what we thought was a Boche patrol, glided in front of us. They did not molest us, but we went on still more on the *qui vive* than ever, with our revolvers and rifles ready for instant action.

"The next excitement was that our guide took the wrong turn, and we found ourselves almost in Barleux, which we believed was held by the enemy! Quickly we halted the men, and the N.F. officer and myself went back whispering, 'About turn' to each man as we passed him, till we got to the road junction where the guide had gone astray. Then we got hold of the halves of the battalion, as it were, and pulled them after us along the right road. Nothing more happened. We got away without a shot having been fired at us; and eventually reached the new line established through Estrées and Assevillers. Here we took up a position that was waiting for us. . . ."

In these sketches, so frank and unpretentious, we find the temper of our Territorials. But in truthful pictures of war we must remember also some other phases of the defence, natural phases, but unpleasant.

Amid such a whirlpool of infantry attack, and such a whirlwind of shot and shell, some dregs did appear both among Gough's men and among Byng's. The wine of bravery has lees, and there were moments when a body of our troops, long overstrained, got out of hand. Occasional local panics led to stampedes; but this epidemic fear soon halted, and took breath, and turned to bay once more. Stragglers were sometimes too numerous, but as soon as they were collected, they fought at once with renewed grit and pride; and as to the small number that failed, and failed badly, harmfully, they have in their aftermath of shame far more pain than they deserve, for a battle of this unusual power and horror needs qualities of brain and body which the weak do not possess.

I dislike very much several pictures of the Great Retreat which General Monash has ventured to publish, though they display neither soldierly judgment nor sympathetic apprehension. They are daily journalism awaiting headlines. Here is a sketch of Byng's troops (pp. 24–25, "Australian Victories in France in 1918"):—

"Basseux rests on the main road from Doullens to Arras, which lies roughly parallel to the line along which, as subsequently transpired, the vanguard of the enemy was endeavouring to advance at that part of the front. That main road I found packed, for the whole of the length which I had to traverse, with a steadily retreating collection of heterogeneous units, service vehicles, and guns of all imaginable types and sizes, intermingled with hundreds of civilian refugees, and farm waggons, carts, trollies and barrows packed high with pathetic loads of household effects. The retrograde movement was orderly and methodical enough, and there was nothing in the nature of a rout, but it was nevertheless a determined movement to the rear which evidenced nothing but a desire to keep moving."

As the THIRD ARMY men in retreat had been in the battle six days and five nights, and as Monash and his troops had not yet fought even an hour, the underlying criticism in this quotation has an unpleasant tone. A schoolboy would describe it "as altogether too cocky."

§ III

There would have been less wear and tear if horsemen had been more common on the FIFTH ARMY'S extending front. Haig notes that—

"their appearance in the battle gave great encouragement to the infantry"; and that "on the southern battle-front, and particularly in the fighting about Noyon, cavalry were once more employed with great effect, and proved their extreme value in warfare of a more open nature. On more than one occasion they were able by rapid and successful action to restore a doubtful situation."

In Butler's Corps cavalry were invaluable from the first day onwards.

"So urgent was the demand for more mounted men," says Haig, "that arrangements were made during the progress of the battle to provide with horses several regiments of Yeomanry who had but recently been dismounted for employment with other arms. In common with the rest of the cavalry, these Yeomanry did excellent service. Without the assistance of mounted troops, skilfully handled and gallantly led, the enemy could scarcely have been prevented from breaking through the long and thinly-held front of broken and wooded ground before the French reinforcements had had time to arrive."

But let us try to view these matters closely, passing into essential details. G.H.Q.'s attitude to cavalry may be divided into a first period of over-confidence, and a second period of under-valuation. In the first period cavalry came up in state to complete a foretold break-through; and as a break-through was never achieved, the arrival of cavalry became a bitter joke to infantry officers and men. "Oh, damn! the cavalry have come up, so our advance must have stopped!" In the reactionary period, two cavalry divisions were given up; and is there reason to believe that the others were used often enough as mounted troops? To bring up cavalrymen in lorries, for example, is not at all likely to keep men and horses together; and as three cavalry divisions equal the man-power of only one infantry division, a division of cavalry is nothing more than a brigade of infantry when it is employed dismounted and at a long distance from its horses. If the cavalry divisions on Gough's front could have been split up into divisional mounted men for the infantry brigades, would their value have been increased? And would this arrangement have made it necessary for G.H.Q. to find, by hook or by crook, more rifle strength and guns for Gough's far-stretching defence? Even in our 3rd Corps, where cavalry formed the British supports, divisional mounted troops were needed, as by the *Eighteenth.*

General Gough believes that we should have got far more value out of the cavalry if they had been organized in smaller

A FEW SCATTERED IMPRESSIONS

units and then attached to the infantry; but G.H.Q. had other views in March, 1918. From these points let us pass on to some very interesting personal experiences written by a distinguished officer of the *Third* CAVALRY :—

"On arrival in the 3rd Corps area, this division was ordered to form a dismounted division and to go forward to occupy certain points of the defensive line. In the subsequent retirements which took place, difficulty was experienced in carrying equipment, rations, ammunition, warm British coats, etc., owing to the unsuitability of the kit of the cavalry soldier for acting for prolonged periods dismounted; hence some equipment had to be abandoned. The horses on this occasion were sent back some miles under orders of the Corps, and were not seen again by the units for three or four days. It has been brought out time after time during the operations that the horses must be kept within reasonable reach of the dismounted men, otherwise the latter lose a great deal of their mobility. Mounted men must always be attached to a dismounted brigade for use as orderlies, patrols, etc., and a mounted reserve kept in hand for counter-attack, or moving quickly to a threatened point, even when the remainder of the units are acting dismounted.

"Pack horses for Hotchkiss, machine-guns, and tools and ammunition, led by men on foot, should always accompany the dismounted brigade or regiment, if it is found that the remainder of the horses for tactical reasons must be sent some distance away. Otherwise, men are used up in carrying the above equipment.

"It was found that when cavalry was sent forward to take up a position to check the enemy, or to fill up a gap which had occurred in the line, the situation was very obscure, and it was very necessary to send officers' patrols forward at once to see the situation.

"In retiring from one position to another it was found advisable to retire by a flank to avoid hostile artillery fire. . . .

"If a retirement of cavalry is to take place when holding part of a line, it should not be carried out mounted. Led horses should first of all be got away, and then the dismounted men should retire on foot. An instance of this occurred with Harman's Force on the 26th March, in the vicinity of Dives. The French gave way on the left about Candor, and Lieut.-Colonel Cook's detachment of the *Second* CAVALRY DIVISION, had to withdraw. The withdrawal was carried out mounted with the result that confusion occurred, and difficulty was experienced in taking up the appointed line in rear. Also, the fact of mounted men moving back has a demoralizing effect on other troops, especially infantry, in the vicinity, and is apt to cause premature withdrawals elsewhere. On the same day the withdrawal of a detachment of the *Third* CAVALRY DIVISION from Bois des Essarts was carried out by sending the horses away beforehand, with satisfactory results. . . .

"The work of patrols throughout the operations was excellent. In the case of Harman's Force, the 3rd Corps were quite in the dark as regards the situation until reconnaissances by officer's patrols were carried out. It was the practice from March 23 to 26 to keep four officer's patrols —strength one officer and ten other ranks—at General Harman's Headquarters, for employment as required. These patrols started out before dawn each day and were drawn in after dark. They worked in certain sectors of the front and supplied reliable information, not only of the position of the enemy's advancing troops, but also of our own infantry or of the French troops. Reports were submitted every two hours, on an average, by mounted dispatch riders. These patrol leaders were able to visit advanced Company, Regimental and Brigade Headquarters, British and French, sending a continuous stream of information of the situation on a front of five or seven miles, which proved invaluable to the Higher Command. No casualties to patrols were reported, although they worked often in front of our infantry in close touch with the enemy. The utmost self-reliance and bravery were shown. . . .

"It is the general opinion that liaison with French troops was bad. The average French interpreter has no military knowledge or vocabulary, and is quite useless for liaison purposes. In the case of Harman's Force, liaison was carried out by means of French-speaking British officers; this was also done in the case of General Seely's Force, and General Seymour's, and it worked well. . . ."

At first the *First* CAVALRY DIVISION was with Watts, but one deed has been assigned in print to its Commander that belongs to the 9th CAVALRY BRIGADE and the H.Q. of the *Sixty-sixth* DIVISION; the recapture of ground east of Hervilly in a dual attack by tank and horse. Imagine the Roisel-Montigny road running from north-west towards the south. Here in the south is Montigny. Over there, east of the road, is Hervilly. West by south of the road, some 3000 yards off, is Nobescourt Farm. From this point the tank attack set out, going east, while from Montigny the 9th CAVALRY BRIGADE advanced, moving in an easterly curve northward; and by good fortune the difficult co-operation was perfect. This counter-attack took place on the second day, at about eleven o'clock in the morning; and although it failed to retake the whole of Hervilly Wood, yet it hurt the foe badly at the very moment when he was trying not only to develop a success of the first day at Templeux-le-Guérard, but to reach and take the Green Line hard by Nobescourt Farm, an important part of the Péronne bridgehead.

The *First* CAVALRY did a lot of digging, once through a whole night, but, as we have seen, its most noteworthy experience was this—that it had to be sent from Watts, whose Corps became increasingly weak, to ease border troubles on and near THIRD ARMY land, where dangers were even more threatening. Afterwards, on the morning of March 25, it was among the FIFTH ARMY troops that reinforced Byng. Then, two days later, it crossed the Somme and rejoined the FIFTH ARMY.

From March 21 to April 11 the *First* CAVALRY lost 1277 in casualties: officers killed 14, wounded 64, missing 9; other ranks killed 166, wounded 801, missing 223.

All the cavalry units did wonderfully well, whether mounted or dismounted, but, as a rule, I believe, the mounted were the more serviceable. Monographs for students of war are certain to be written about Harman's Force, Portal's Force, and other excellent bodies, such as Seely's, Seymour's, Burt's, Paterson's, Legard's, and others.

It is interesting to note that while our infantry, as a rule, lost more in missing than in recovered wounded, the cavalry lost more in recovered wounded than in missing. Let us take an example, choosing the *Second* CAVALRY and the *Eighteenth* INFANTRY.

The *Eighteenth* had 32 officers killed, 64 wounded, and 110 missing; and among the other ranks, 299 men were killed, 1309 were wounded, and the missing numbered 2649.

The *Second* CAVALRY, between March 21 and 26 inclusive, suffered as follows: Officers killed, 10; wounded, 38; missing, 3. Other ranks killed, 121; wounded, 622; missing, 145. Between March 27 and April 1, the losses were: Officers killed, 10; wounded, 48; missing, 2. Other ranks killed, 145; wounded, 781; missing, 93.

Considered as a whole, contrastive figures of this kind are not difficult to explain. No cavalry manned the forward zone, the zone of forlorn hope, from which few men returned because they fought on till they were killed or captured. Further, infantry as a rule formed the rearguards, and in delaying actions by rearguards a great many men are surrounded, or cut off, and taken prisoners. It is their duty to sacrifice themselves for the sake of the general defence. These points are self-evident, but a noteworthy question arises: "Are infantrymen under modern conditions handicapped so much during a retreat that in future wars they will be displaced partly by mounted machine-gunners, and partly by tanks? Have they had their day? Will they disappear as archers and crossbowmen and pikemen disappeared?"

Perhaps the fiercest cavalry fight was the capture of the Bois de Moreuil, March 30, by the CANADIAN CAVALRY BRIGADE. The Germans had captured Mézières and were advancing rapidly towards Amiens. So the brigade was ordered to cross the Noye and Avre Rivers at once and to engage and delay the enemy. It crossed at Castel and marched due east to the northern part of the Bois de Moreuil. At this point machine-guns from the wood's northern face fired upon the Brigade, and as Germans within the wood had a full clear view of the whole valley leading up to Amiens, a swift and successful attack by the Canadians was imperative. The story of what occurred reads like a brilliant page by Alexander Dumas. Both sides fought with extraordinary courage. The wood was taken little by little after complicated movements and the bitterest of bitter fighting, in which squadrons commanded by Nordheimer, Newcomen, Timmis, and Flowerdew suffered heavily and won a fame not to be forgotten. Consider a passage from the Brigade report :—

"Lord Strathcona's Horse (R.C.) were then ordered to send one squadron under Lieutenant Flowerdew to pass round the north-east corner of the wood at a gallop in support of Captain Nordheimer, while the remaining two squadrons of the regiment advanced to the attack dismounted on the northwestern face. Nordheimer's squadron got into the wood and engaged the enemy in hand-to-hand combat. Many of the enemy were killed, all refusing to surrender; but a large party, estimated about 300, retired from the wood south-east of the point where Nordheimer's squadron had entered it. This party was charged by Lieutenant Flowerdew, and many Germans were killed with the sword as they ran to meet the

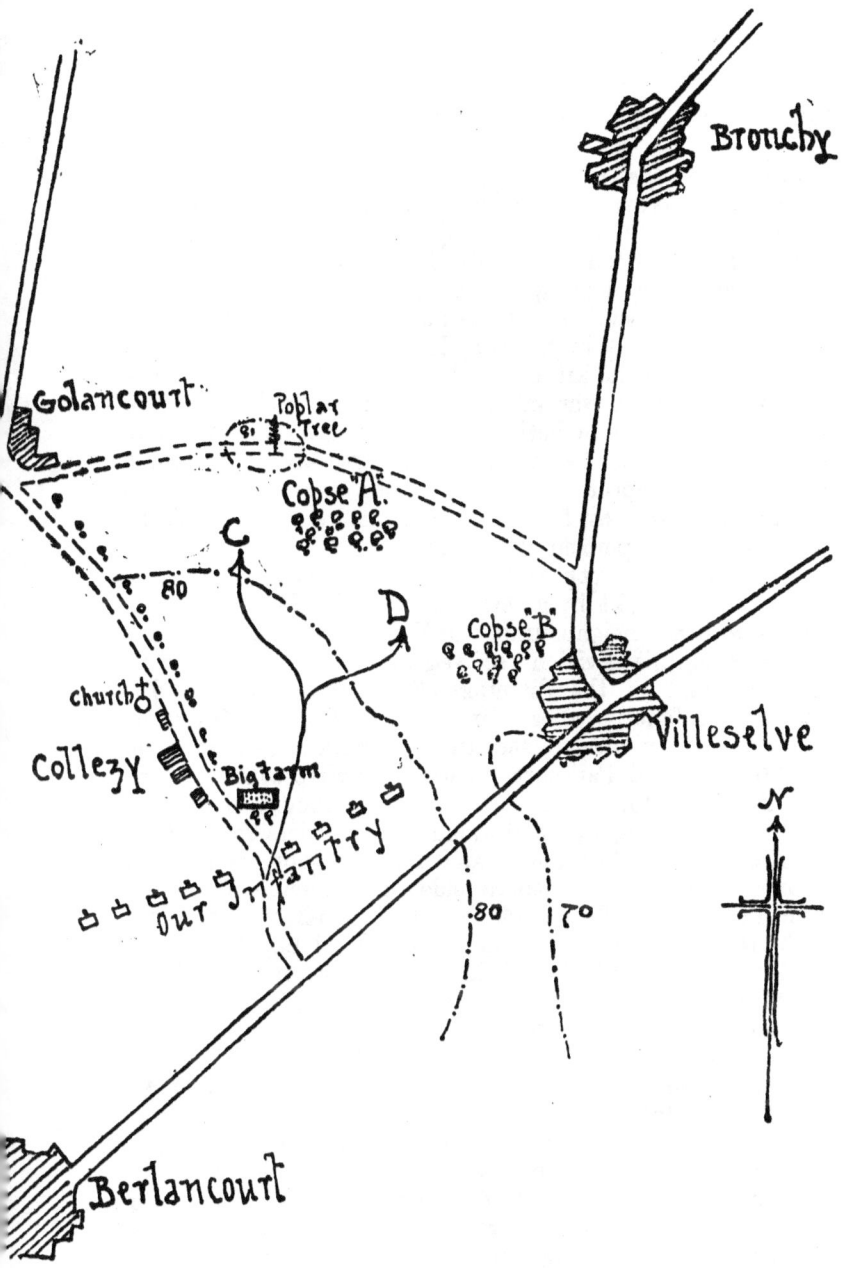

cavalry with the bayonet, showing no signs of surrender. Flowerdew, having passed through them, wheeled about and charged again. He then galloped into the wood at the centre of the eastern face, established himself, and was joined by the dismounted party of his regiment. Fierce hand-to-hand fighting ensued in all the north-east part of the wood, resulting ultimately in the complete capture of this portion of the wood and the killing of all the German garrison. The enemy's resistance was most stubborn; one badly wounded German, shot through both legs and the stomach, refused to allow the stretcher-bearers to move him, saying he would sooner die uncaptured . . . Our losses were severe, most regiments having lost from half to one-third of their officers, and a similar proportion of their men. . . ."

I give a sketch-map to illustrate another action of importance; it was fought by a detachment of the *Third* CAVALRY DIVISION in the neighbourhood of Villeselve. On March 24, at 8.30 a.m., this division received orders at Berlancourt to move forward in the direction of Cugny to support disorganized infantry, whose line had broken at Villeselve. Soon our cavalry re-established the front from Beaumont to the neighbourhood of Eaucourt. Then they were withdrawn to help the *Ninth* FRENCH DIVISION, but this movement caused the line to break again, so Harman issued orders for another restoration. The 7th and CANADIAN BRIGADES were sent mounted round the southern side of Villeselve, and they formed a line from Beaumont, the left of the French position, to the road-junction half a mile north-west of Beaulieu. The 6th BRIGADE, under Major Williams, was sent through Collezy in order that they might charge through the German line, and then swing right-handed in a north-east direction along the foe's front, using the sword only.

The detachment [150 men in all] moved along the main road to Villeselve, taking the sunken track that goes north into Collezy. It came under machine-gun fire from the neighbourhood of Golancourt, but put itself under cover of a big farm at the south-east exit of Collezy. It was formed into three troops by regiments; our Third Dragoon Guards under Lieutenant Vincent forming the first wave, our Tenth Hussars under Major Williams the second wave, and the Royals under Captain Turner the third wave.

The attack was made in infantry attack formation; the first two waves in line extended, and the third in sections, but covering the flanks of the two leading waves. The

A FEW SCATTERED IMPRESSIONS

Third Dragoon Guards rode towards Copse A, meeting some German infantry, who were either killed or captured. Several Germans ran into the copse, but they were followed on foot, and shot in the back at point-blank range. As for the Tenth Hussars and Royals, Williams led them on the west side of Copse A, and here the greater part of the enemy's force was posted. For about a thousand yards our men were under machine-gun fire, and the last two hundred yards was ploughed land. But the attack was in high spirits and cheered lustily, and when it reached the ploughed land the foe began to surrender. The Hussars rode straight through, and the Royals followed, mopping up small parties who had run together after the Tenth had passed through them.

After this mêlée the "Rally" was sounded; prisoners were collected, 106 in all, and the wounded were picked up. Then the squadron returned to the main Berlancourt-Villeselve road. Our own losses were high, about seventy-three, but the counter-attack had a good influence on the infantry, who with renewed confidence pushed forward to a line running from the outskirts of Golancourt almost to Eaucourt, including Hill 81. This result enabled two Ulster battalions, who were cut off in the neighbourhood of Cugny, to retire on Villeselve, where they were reassembled and sent back into the line.

In brief, we owe to all arms an inexpressible debt of gratitude.

CHAPTER II

Dawson's Five Hundred

HOW THE SOUTH AFRICANS WERE OVERWHELMED: SUNDAY, MARCH 24, 1918

AT 9.45 on Saturday evening Dawson's South African troops, now reduced to about five hundred in all, picked their way towards their posts in the *Ninth's* chosen line. By three o'clock on Sunday morning they took up their ground north-west of Marrières Wood, and north of a road running between Le Forêt and Rancourt. Their right had gained touch with Campbell's left, a touch frail and uncertain, as German patrols had entered Cléry-sur-Somme, about two thousand four hundred yards from the southern outskirts of Bois Marrières. Dawson's left had linked itself to a company of K.O.S. Borderers, but did it find the rest of this Lowland battalion, which was in reserve south of Rancourt, some two thousand yards from Bois Marrières' north end? Three patrols tried to find it, but early morning fog made their search ineffectual.

Dawson was on a ridge, with two remnant battalions looking south and one facing east, whence front attack would come. One good trench and two or three bad ones, with a good many shell-holes, were his earthworks. He took up his headquarters in a support trench about three hundred yards behind the front line. Ground went eastward downhill to a small valley, then sloped up and made a somewhat higher ridge, where our foes, while spying on the South African actions, chose damnable fine places for machine-guns. About one thousand yards parted the front line from this German vantage ground.

While fog was passing away Dawson visited his men, improved their stations, and braced them up with a few right words of crisp pre-battle talk. They had two hundred rounds of ammunition apiece, besides a fair supply of Lewis drums. But a section of machine-gunners was down in luck; it had only three belts! What was to be done? Three

THE SOUTH AFRICANS OVERWHELMED 223

machine-guns and their men were sent away—formidable and yet useless. And another trouble was present. In the tiny S.A. force were too many good officers, some being newcomers, and it seemed a crime to waste them. One battalion, with a strength dwindled to a hundred and ten all ranks,

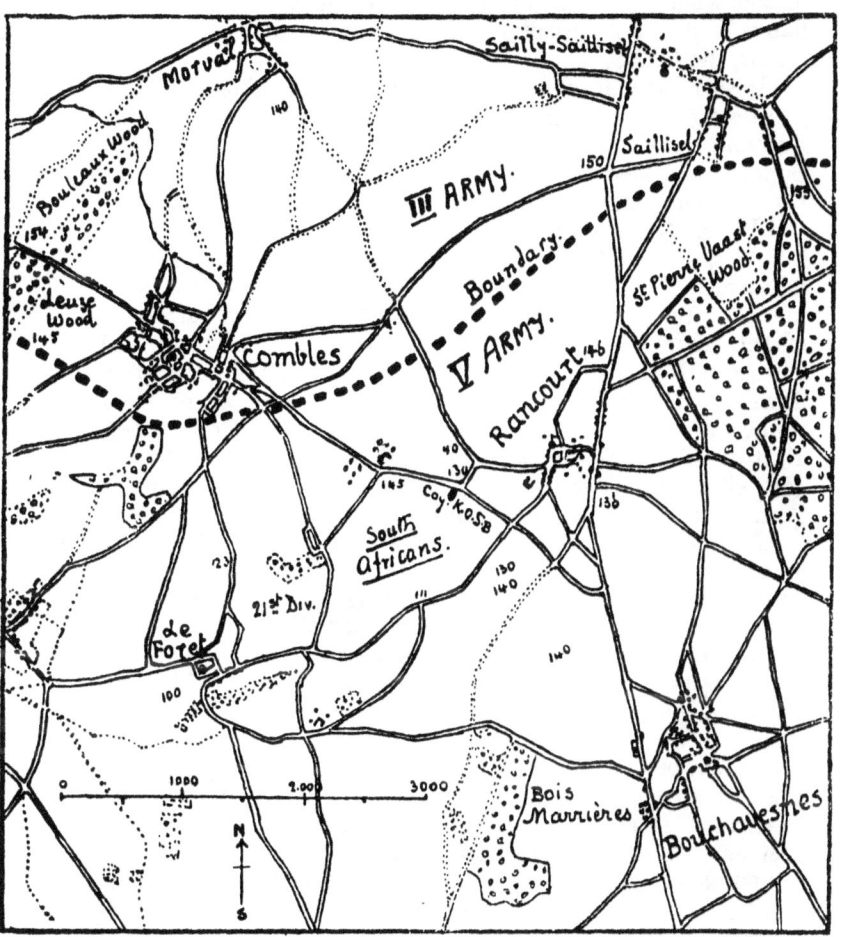

had fourteen officers, for instance. Since March 20 no man had had any hot food or any hot tea. All their rations had been cold. And three cold nights without sleep, and long days in which fighting, sweat, and thirst had collected fog, dust, gas, and shell fumes, had exhausted most bodies but yet in heart all were fit for their forlorn hope. Dawson spoke to his Lieutenant-Colonels, Heal and Christian, telling them that their field of battle was to be held against all odds in a thorough fight to a finish. No man was to retire without orders; every one must do his best to the very last, no matter what might be done by neighbouring troops on the flanks. And a report of this decision was sent by runner to Tudor, the G.O.C.

It was fortunate indeed that Congreve had chosen at this point a fight to a finish; fortunate, too, that both Tudor and Dawson were fighters born, for Marwitz, on this tragical Sunday, had made up his mind to gain an operative breakthrough both north and south of the boundary uniting Gough and Byng. North of the boundary he got through along the line Combles, Morval, Lesbœufs, but south of the boundary he was foiled mainly by the splendid bravery of the South Africans, but importantly also by the fine way in which two battalions of the *Thirty-fifth* DIVISION, the Fifteenth Cheshires and Fifteenth Notts and Derbies, hurried into action soon after dawn, though fagged by a severe forced march, seized Hem Spur, and stopped the German flanking advance from Cléry. Further, if the *Ninth* DIVISION's Highlanders had not been compelled by events in the THIRD ARMY to fight on Byng's ground, the South Africans might have been rescued.

At about nine a.m., as Dawson himself has related, the enemy deployed for attack, and got his machine-guns into action in some old trenches on the ridge one thousand yards east of our front line. His artillery opened fire at the same time. Half an hour later a British airplane passed over, and a feeling of intense gladness heartened the South Africans, for the airplane seemed to be a link with the British troops behind. Dawson waved to the pilot, and the pilot waved back; but perhaps the movement of his hand was not friendly. Perhaps, indeed, the pilot mistook the South Africans for Germans. In any case, at ten a.m. British field artillery, by accident—from the direction evidently of the *Twenty-first* DIVISION—opened a very accurate fire on Dawson's position, one battery being laid on the trench in which Brigade Headquarters was situated. One mounted and two dismounted messengers were sent back, but the fire continued till eleven a.m., when the batteries apparently retired; and afterwards, apart from some heavy gun-firing on Bouchavesnes, no more British guns were heard. Though a number of British shells fell in Dawson's trenches, they are believed not to have caused any

THE SOUTH AFRICANS OVERWHELMED

casualties. But it was found necessary to remove Brigade Headquarters to a shell-hole in the vicinity.

When Marwitz's troops, who were grey, blurred moving spots on their ridge-crest, came west downhill, they were swift and prudent, advancing in all about two hundred and fifty yards. A rush across the narrow valley was not in their orders. To climb a ridge afterwards would need more nerve and vigour than were natural after three days of continuous overstrain. So the front attack was easy to hold; and another from due south, more difficult perhaps, was shot to a standstill. An hour or so went by; and then from north-east came a very clever, even a picturesque onrush. The Boche set fire to dried grass, used wind-blown smoke as a screen, and, combining his movements with gunfire skilfully directed, picked his way slowly forward till he got almost within charging distance of S.A. front line. Between one hundred and two hundred yards were all that he had to rush. Through some hours he strove to get nearer, but always in vain, so accurate was the S.A. shooting. Dawson, knowing that his ammunition could not be replenished, had ordered his men never to shoot at random, but to use their rifles with slow, prudent care, waiting till field-grey targets drew near enough to be pot-shots. Firing at longer ranges than four hundred yards was to be done by Lewis guns, as a rule.

Early in his attack the Boche tried to use a field-gun only a thousand yards off. Such cool cheek angered the defenders at first; it seemed too insolent, too arrogant. Then it amused them, and by reaction eased their stress and strain. They were in a theatre out of doors, and that field-gun, now being wheeled forward by hand in sudden, violent efforts, was the play. Major Ormiston, of the 1st S.A. Infantry, gave orders to a Lewis gunner, while his riflemen held their breath and kept their eyes on the German field-piece. Putt-putt-puttr! The Lewis gun was in action . . . and well on its target, for the Boche gunners, almost ready to open fire, were all knocked out. "Ah!" our men exclaimed in a sort of drawling, husky sigh; and then a rattle of cheers, hoarse and stern, rang from the British defence.

The Boche did not accept his failure tamely. He bore malice; and with his usual detailed thoroughness began to plot and plan, as if his day's fight were a siege and not a hold-up to be finished quickly. Later, with renewed pluck, he made another attempt, in a movement far and away more dramatic. This time his field-gun had its team of horses, and came at a gallop into the arena. Wasted energy! The same Lewis gunner—I wish I knew his name!—had the same cool mind and the same steady hand and effectual eye. He fired: and the team got out of hand, overturned its field-piece, men and horses going down together—a great huddle that plunged and struggled. No wonder the defence shouted with joy. And another cheering thing came before noon. A messenger arrived from Tudor, bringing with him the news that troops from our *Thirty-fifth* were coming up, an invaluable reinforcement, and had been ordered to form line behind the South Africans, half a mile away. Dawson passed on the news to his men, and sent word back to Tudor by runner that the frontal attack had been held, and that his line at 11.40 was still intact, despite dangerous movements in the north and south. No other message came to Tudor from his S.A. Brigade.

In the afternoon, at about two o'clock, British troops on Dawson's right and left retired. This incident caused one of his own officers on his left, with some thirty men, to believe that a general retirement had been ordered. Believing this, they began to fall back past the shell-hole in which Dawson had his Headquarters. Major Cochran and Captain Beverley went to stop them, accompanied by a sergeant-major named Keith. At once German machine-guns became exceedingly busy, concentrating fire on the movements in Dawson's arena. It was easy to stop the retreating men and to place them in a position facing north, perhaps a hundred yards north of Dawson's hole; but, unfortunately, brave Cochran was killed, hit in the neck by a machine-gun bullet, and Ormiston was dangerously wounded by an advance German scout, at a range of about sixty yards, and was left out there in the open. Wounded men, if possible, went or were taken to an old trench that led to the Headquarters shell-hole; and those who were too much hurt to use a rifle were allowed at first to leave the battlefield. Others were sent back to their firing-line, and always they went willingly. But a magnificent fighting temper needs ammunition, and by two p.m. ammunition became short, and Dawson was completely surrounded. Every round was collected from casualties, and men who were not in the front line, or who had no need to use their rifles, passed on their rounds to comrades in front.

On our west side German snipers were alert and troublesome; from north, within two hundred yards of Dawson's H.Q., came another irritating fire; so Lieutenant Cooper, with some twenty men of the Second Regiment, was sent a hundred yards northwards in order to hold some shell-holes from which a very useful counter-sniping could be done by cool, firm pluck. Cooper and his garrison cannot be praised too much. They suffered such heavy losses that they needed frequent reinforcements. Cooper himself was hit, and about an hour later a fragment of shell killed him. But his influence remained; his few men went on firing till their ammunition had gone.

Between two and three o'clock a thrill of excited hopefulness passed all at once through the defenders, as signs of agitation appeared among the besiegers. Then a wounded man from Cooper's handful came to Headquarters and said: "Our men are coming up, and some Germans are bolting for all they are worth!" In fact, north of Dawson's H.Q. the foe fell back, a good target in retreat, and soon German artillery put down a rapid stiff barrage westward, behind Dawson's battlefield. Why? Then some one cried: "We can see the Germans surrendering!" This cry was repeated. Had troops from our *Thirty-fifth* begun to arrive? Hope said "Yes" in every British mind; so our men were heartened—heartened in vain, unfortunately. No battalion of the *Thirty-fifth* had yet had time to come so far. The battlefield being small and quite surrounded, German fire from the west may have hit Germans in the north and east, causing their leaders to believe that British reinforcements were arriving.

"About this time," says Buchan, "Lieutenant-Colonel Heal, commanding the First Regiment, was killed. He had already been twice wounded in the action, but insisted on remaining with his men. He had in the highest degree every quality which makes a fine soldier. I quote from a letter of one of his officers. 'By this time it was evident to all that we were bound to go under, but even then Colonel Heal refused to be depressed. God knows how he kept so cheery all through that hell; but right up to when I last saw him, about five minutes before he was killed, he had a smile on his face and a pleasant word for us all.'"*

At four p.m. a bad outlook cast a chill over every one. Dawson's men could not hold out much longer. They were sick with the nausea called overstrain; ammunition was all but gone; machine-guns and Lewis guns were silent. Since nine a.m. artillery fire had poured on the S.A. front, causing so much dust and falling earth that rifles had to be cleaned frequently. It came from batteries of 7·7 cm., 10·5 cm., and

* "South African Forces in France," p. 186.

15 cm., unseen batteries for the most part. Light trench mortars also were in action, ravaging the north-east part of the S.A. front. Casualties everywhere had been very high, and at four o'clock Dawson had only a few isolated groups of men. Still, though control was now impossible, and though hope of relief had gone, an effort would be made to hold on till dark, when survivors could try to open a path westward.

At 4.20 Dawson had a very great shock. He saw a white flag! Through field-glasses he watched it carefully, and soon, to his intense relief, he could see that it was a German artillery flag. But some harm had been done, several South Africans having accepted the flag as an official surrender. A quarter of an hour later, the last glimmer of hope went out like a lighted candle in the wind.

Beyond H.Q., in the east-north-east, a new attack came into full view; it proved to be one of three fresh battalions. At this moment the S.A. defence had about one hundred effectives, almost without ammunition, and scattered over too much ground. A few shots brought our rounds to an end; the attack came on in waves, cheering and screaming, and all was over.

"Dawson, with Christian and Beverley, walked out in front of a group [of Germans] which had gathered round them, and was greeted with shouts of 'Why have you killed so many of us?' and 'Why did you not surrender sooner?' One man said, 'Now we shall soon have peace,' at which Dawson shook his head. Before he went eastward into captivity he was allowed to find Cochran's body, and rescue his papers." *

For over seven hours handfuls of South Africans, heroic and indomitable, had held up the German infantry and all the guns and transport which were to advance by the Bouchavesnes-Combles road. After the fight this road was seen to be blocked for miles and miles. No wonder German leaders were amazed by such a magnificent stand.

Though the S.A. Brigade had ended its last fight, it did not disappear entirely, I rejoice to say. Two thin companies had lost their way on a dark night, and another small party had become detached from the brigade. These troops, along with some details and the transport of the brigade, about four hundred and fifty rifles, were collected near Maricourt, and formed into a composite battalion under Lieutenant-Colonel

* Buchan, p. 188.

THE SOUTH AFRICANS OVERWHELMED

Young, who had been in charge of the S.A. details. So Dawson's fine spirit did not vanish altogether from the battle. For the rest, I learn from Colonel Buchan that Dawson during the fight had moments of questioning doubt. He wondered whether his final stand would be justified by its results. In his diary Dawson wrote :—

"I cannot see that under the circumstances I had any option but to remain till the end. Far better to go down fighting against heavy odds than that it should be said we failed to carry out our orders. To retire would be against all the traditions of the service."

No combat in the whole battle was more useful and necessary, and even more so to Byng than to Gough. If the V.C. were granted to the superior heroism of units, and not to the superior heroism of occasional men one by one, the South African Brigade would certainly have won and received this honour by its unlimited valour not only on Sunday, March 24, but also on the 21st and 22nd. As General Tudor has said, "None but the best could have got through on the 22nd from the Yellow Line with Heudecourt in the hands of the enemy."

Yet for some reason G.H.Q. glides over the South African defence and its exceedingly great value. It says only that the foe's advance at the junction of the FIFTH and THIRD ARMIES—

"succeeded in isolating a part of the South African Brigade, *Ninth* DIVISION, near Marrières Wood, north of Cléry. These troops maintained a most gallant resistance until 4.30 p.m., when they had fired off all their ammunition and only about 100 men remained unwounded. Early in the afternoon German infantry entered Combles" [in Byng's area], "and having gained the high ground at Morval were advancing towards Lesbœufs. Their continued progress threatened to sever the connection between the FIFTH and THIRD ARMIES and the situation was serious."

What a scrappy and patchy account of the most terrible hours in Marwitz's advance! There is no recognition of the fact that the South African five hundred, by holding firmly through a long morning, and by continuing their intrepid stand till half-past four in the afternoon, were certainly as invaluable to Byng as they were to Gough. Indeed, Byng's southern troops, as the dispatch recognizes, were at Rocquigny and Barastre, and thus far off from a firm liaison with Gough's left. Note the result. With its Highlanders the *Ninth* endeavoured to do work which ought to have been done by the south brigade of Byng's right flank division, the *Forty-seventh*, while Dawson, just south of the boundary, prevented a break-through.

If Dawson's troops had been wiped out in the morning, disaster could not have been evaded. The connection between Byng and Gough would have been completely severed. By continuing to hold on after the fall of Combles and Morval, Dawson confirmed the value of the work done by troops of the *Thirty-fifth* west of Cléry, and by the *Ninth's* Highlanders in Byng's own area. But for him and his five hundred, a rescuing line could not have been formed and held from the Somme at Hem to Trônes Wood and Longueval.

Dawson writes as follows of his men :—

"It is impossible for me to do justice to the magnificent courage displayed by all ranks under my command during this action. For the two years I have been in France I have seen nothing better. Until the end they appeared to me quite perfect. The men were cool and alert, taking advantage of every opportunity, and, when required, moving forward over the open under the hottest machine-gun fire and within 100 yards of the enemy. They seemed not to know fear, and in my opinion they put forth the greatest effort of which human nature is capable. I myself witnessed several cases of great gallantry, but do not know the names of the men. *The majority, of course, will never be known.* It must be borne in mind that the Brigade was in an exhausted state before the action, and in the fighting of the three previous days it was reduced in numbers from a trench strength of over 1800 to 500."

I am glad that Dawson does not know the names of those men because I wish to honour the South African bravery in its Brigade form. "The majority, of course, will never be known" in acts of courage; and hence there will always be much unfairness in the distribution of medals.

Medals are all very well, but corporate spirit in great deeds will endure longer in history and be more useful to the next generations.

For all that, just a few examples of bravery may be given here.

Two hours after Major Ormiston was wounded, a man went out over the open and wanted to bring him to our trench. Ormiston refused to go. "I am dying," he said, "and shall be dead in an hour or so. It would be quite a waste of time to get me in." But the man insisted on

THE SOUTH AFRICANS OVERWHELMED

rescuing the officer. He talked with Ormiston, and prevailed on him to come; and when Ormiston tried to move he found that he was regaining the loss of his legs, which had been paralysed. They crept from shell-hole to shell-hole till they reached the trench. This adventure would have been impossible if the defence had not had the superiority of fire. Our fellows could show their heads while the Germans dared not show theirs. "It was an exceedingly brave action," says Dawson, "but by right the man should have been court-martialled. For it was not his business to go looking for wounded; his job was to fight. All the same, he was a brave fellow."

"Lieutenant Cooper, of the Second Regiment, about two in the afternoon, came in looking as white as a sheet, and saying that he had been hit in the chest. It was found that the bullet had hit his box respirator and given him a heavy blow in the chest, but had not gone through. Cooper sat down till the colour returned to his face, when he said, 'Now I'm going back.' Out he went over the open and rejoined his men. About ten minutes later a man came in and said : 'Lieutenant Cooper is killed. A piece of the last big shell hit him.'"

"At one time in this front trench, where the artillery fire was exceedingly heavy, only two men were left alive, one being Father Hill, and the other a private of the First Regiment, and a linen draper by trade. Among all the brave men on this day he was conspicuous for his courage. Two shells burst on the parapet, and it seemed as if the next would be in the trench. The man said : 'I have been praying hard for the last four hours.' 'Then you have beaten me at it,' Father Hill answered. . . . They both survived, I rejoice to say."

"Another man, with both legs shattered, sat in the trench and refused to let any one bind up his wounds; and with a smile on his face he handed up his ammunition, packet by packet, to the men who were firing. . . ."

CHAPTER III

A FEW LETTERS WRITTEN BY OFFICERS OF THE *SIXTY-FIRST* DIVISION

§ I

FROM a wounded Major to his wounded Brigadier:—
"The battalion had breakfast at Languevoisin [about a mile and a quarter south-east of Nesle] and then marched back [*i.e.* westward] to Billancourt where Brigade H.Q. was. We were just going to have a rest (having put posts out on all the roads), when we received a report that the Germans had broken through Nesle. So we all stood to and lined the Billancourt-Herly road. However, it was a false alarm and was said to have been started by a person in the uniform of a R.A.M.C. captain whom the police were trying to catch, but I do not think they were successful. Heaps of troops received this rumour and had altered their plans accordingly.*

"At 6 p.m. on the 23rd we had orders to go to Languevoisin again and billet ourselves, which we did. Brigade remained at Billancourt. Then we actually had more or less of a night's rest.

"On the morning of the 24th, Brigade telephoned to say we were to go to ———. The wire went 'Dis' in the middle of the message, so I started off with the battalion, and the C.O. went to Brigade to find out the rest of the message. As we went through Breuil I reported to General Evans, who told me that the situation was changed, and that we must not cross the canal. However, at this moment the C.O. came along to say that the Brigade had changed the orders and we

---

* Germans in Allied uniform behind our lines were active—spreading rumours. On March 29, one of our brigadiers, while giving important orders in the field, was interrupted by a man in medical uniform, who came up and said with great excitement that Germans were in the woods a hundred yards off. The brigadier told him to go to that place which is assumed to be much hotter than the Red Sea. His orders given, he called for the excited doctor, only to find that the fellow had ridden away east on a motor-cycle.

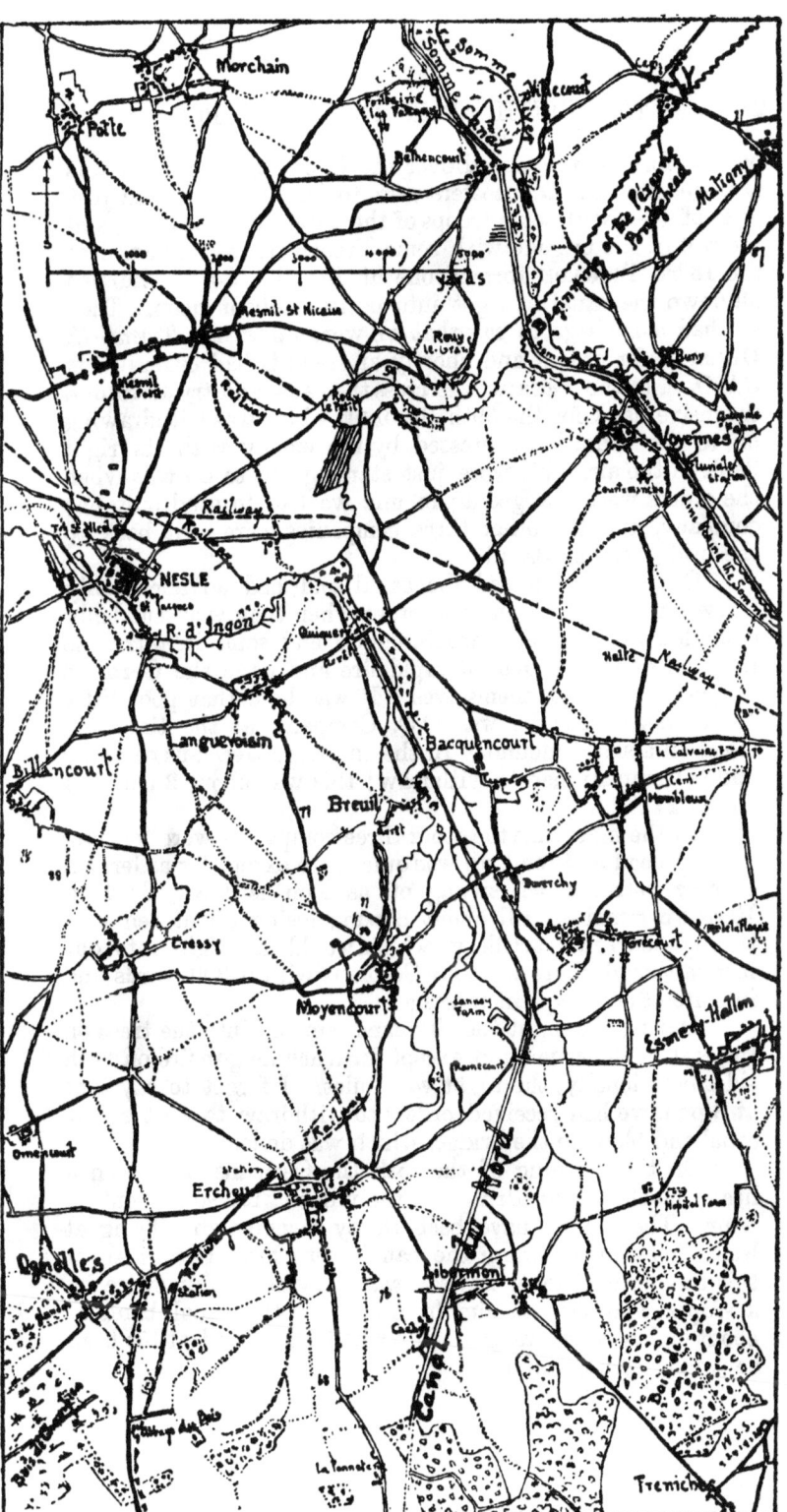

were to form a bridgehead over the Canal [du Nord]; it was
arranged that the Gloucesters were to form a bridgehead just
west of —— with some troops of the *Twentieth* DIVISION, and
the rest of his brigade with some French troops and some of
the 183rd BRIGADE formed one at Breuil. So we hurried
off down the canal and got into position about noon. Then
we had a message to say that we were under the *Twentieth*
DIVISION for orders, and shortly afterwards had orders from
G.S.O. ii. of the *Twentieth* to cross the canal and try to form a
defensive flank for the 59th BRIGADE, which was withdrawing
on to the canal hard pressed by the enemy with its right
flank in the air. We were just starting out to do this when
the orders were changed again, and we had to send only one
company, and the other three companies were sent back to
the bridgehead at Breuil.

"C Company crossed the canal and had advanced only
a few hundred yards in open order when they were suddenly
enfiladed by a German machine-gun and some infantry; so
they got down and opened rapid fire and gave the Germans
as good as they got themselves. It was here that poor little
Lake was killed; he was O.C. Company at the time and
stood on a slight mound. In the end more Germans came up
and C Company had to withdraw; this was about 2 p.m. [on
March 24].

"In the meantime the other three companies were forming
a bridgehead at Breuil, all was quiet here except for a German
cavalry patrol which swung off as soon as it was fired at.
Here we remained till about 8 p.m., losing about ten men
through our own artillery, which would fire right into our
men, although there were no Germans within 800 yards and
in spite of our frequent messages. . . .

"During the night the Germans came up into the trees on
the east of the canal, and, except for machine-gun fire on both
sides occasionally, the night was quiet. I forgot to say that
at 8 p.m. we had received orders to withdraw to west of the
canal and blow up the bridge, which was done.

"On the morning of the 25th the Germans put down a
heavy machine-gun barrage on the village; it lasted about an
hour. There must have been thirty machine-guns firing at
least; a few men lining the canal were hit. It was about
this time that Colonel Lawson was very nearly hit twice by
a sniper who shot at him from close to the canal bank at
about eighty yards range. If he had not aimed at his head
he would have got him.

"We hung on in and in front of Breuil all day. It was noticed that the Huns had established a H.Q. in a large house about 700 yards north-west of the village; mounted orderlies and others were continually visiting it. So we put a section behind a wall in the village, and they made loopholes in the wall and fired at every one who went near the house. They got several, too, and the Huns did not like it.

"Throughout the day the village was very heavily shelled by the Huns, but a few R.A.M.C. men from the *Twentieth* DIVISION did very good work. When Colonel Wetherall was hit, the C.O. went to command the Brigade and I took over the battalion. Howitt came up to see us from Brigade H.Q., which was just west of Languevoisin. He did damned well throughout the show; he was always walking about and visiting people, and worked like a black day and night.

"At 5 p.m. we suddenly saw all the English troops on our right leave the canal and go back in streams; then the Germans crossed the canal on our right, under heavy fire from the Gloucesters, and began to get round our right flank which was now hopelessly in the air. The Germans also tried to cross opposite us, but we held them. Things began to look nasty, but we knew our left was all right as Moore was there with his battalion.

"We were scrapping hard with the Germans getting stronger on our right; so I formed a defensive flank with B Company, who were in support, and they did excellent work and kept the Huns back.

"At this stage I received a written order direct from the *Twentieth* DIVISION, not *viâ* Brigade, to say that owing to the failure of the *Thirtieth* DIVISION to hold the line on our flank we were to withdraw to Cressy; so I sent a message to Moore and ordered the withdrawal of the Gloucesters. No doubt the people on our right had received the same message; that is why they went back.

"The withdrawal was carried out very well with covering fire, in fact we were the only troops that I saw that used covering fire.

"Some of the older officers did awfully well, . . . and the Company Sergeant-Majors of A and B Companies did splendidly. We took a few prisoners and Dudbridge was largely responsible for the capture of an officer. We killed a lot of Huns and did not suffer so very heavily ourselves, though poor Fothergill was killed and C.S.M. Phillips was wounded. One platoon of B Company under C.S.M. Parsons and Corporal Vincent did a bit of a charge and scattered the Huns like blazes, and took a prisoner. . . .

"We reached Cressy just after dark to find a line of posts held by a mixture of French and British troops, so sent out a couple of patrols and thickened the line where necessary.

"At 12 midnight, 25–26, we had orders to march to Roye; so we called in the patrols and started off. We got to Roye about 3 a.m. and had a meal and a little rest, and then started to march again at 6 a.m. The whole British Army seemed to be on the road. We finally reached Mézières at about 1 p.m., having done 21 miles since midnight. Here we had something to eat and then dug in, and were glad to see a French cavalry regiment go through us along the main Amiens–Roye road. By this time the C.O. had come back to us, as Colonel Bilton, Worcesters, had taken over the Brigade. . . .

"Rosières had fallen * and the Germans were expected to attack Caix at dawn. . . . Gloucesters were to dig in between Le Quesnel and Hangest, with the Berks and Oxfords on our left astride the main Amiens road with the 182nd and 183rd BRIGADES on our left. We moved up, got into position, and started to dig in. No one knew who held Hangest, so we sent a patrol there and found a French cavalry brigade in the village. This would be about 1 a.m. on the 27th inst.

"Also we sent patrols to Folies and Arvillers, which were held by British troops. At this time there were two lines in front of us, both held by British, one through Arvillers and Folies, the other through Bouchoir, Rouvroy, and Warvillers. As soon as it was light the C.O. sent me forward to find out the situation. I discovered that Warvillers and Rouvroy had fallen and that Folies, Bouchoir, and Arvillers were held by troops of the 59th, 89th, and 90th INFANTRY BRIGADES. The old Bucks, now an entrenching battalion, were attached to the 59th BRIGADE.

"I had rather an interesting time in Bouchoir. Just before I arrived a Colonel shot a Hun in the main street, at about ten yards range; he seems to have wandered in by mistake. Then I met a subaltern with his platoon, who told me the Germans were massing on the south of the road; so I had a look at them. Never have I seen so many Germans in all my life; a huge black mass about a mile away. With

---

* A false rumour. Rosières had not fallen, as we know, since it played an all-important part in the great combat of the 27th.

glasses one could see howitzers, machine-guns, trench mortars, and field-guns, as well as infantry. It was a wonderful sight. They seemed to be coming down the Roye road and then moving off to the south, and some seemed to stop in a mass about a mile from where we were. And we had plenty of batteries and not a gun was firing.

"So I looked at my map; the place was 31 Central, I remember; and then I went off to the nearest battery and told them to shoot at 31 Central, and they had not got a map between them, so I made them shoot off my map. Finally, I got three more batteries on it, including a battery of French 75's.

"The Germans did not attack Bouchoir, but a force moved south of it and attacked and captured Arvillers. So Bouchoir was evacuated and the 83rd BRIGADE was moved over to our left near Hangest, as the Germans had not attacked Caix as heavily as was expected.

"At 12.30 a.m. of the 28th we were relieved by the French and told that we were going into rest.

"We got into motor buses between Le Quesnel and Mézières, but then they found that the Huns had broken through farther north near Wiencourt and Guillaucourt.* So we rushed up to Marcelcave, got there about 3 p.m., had three hours' rest, and went out and took up a fine position behind a bit of wire with a fine field of fire west of the village just before dawn.

"Then about 10 a.m. they pulled us out and we handed the line over to a mixture of troops—*Sixty-sixth* DIVISION machine-gunners, a R.E. Field Company from some division, and also a Tunnelling Company that had never used rifles before."

Then came the attacks on Lamotte and Marcelcave already described.

"The end of it was that we were ordered to withdraw and dig in, in the dark and a steady rain which was now falling, 600 yards west of the village.†

---

* There was no break-through on this front; but the letter shows twice how divisions during a retreat hear false news about one another. When our *Sixty-sixth* DIVISION reached the line Wiencourt-Guillaucourt, 9.30 a.m., March 28, the foe was far too tired after his experiences at Harbonnières, on the previous day, to give trouble. But our own troops also were "done" and disorganized; there was no such thing as a platoon or a company; and it was deemed necessary to fall back slowly to the line Ignaucourt-Marcelcave, and then to reform the skeleton units.

† Marcelcave.

"The 29th was rather quiet, the Huns did not attack, and there was not much shelling, but a little sniping and machine-gun fire. . . . At about 8.50 a.m. on the 30th, we noticed that all the English troops in the south in the direction of Hangard were retiring in streams; at the same time the Germans started to shell us a lot and opened heavy machine-gun fire.

"So I went down to the line to see if every one was all right; it was a curious line, within half a mile of us were Gloucesters, Royal Berks, Oxfords, Warwicks, and two squadrons of yeomanry, and the servants and staff of the FIFTH ARMY Infantry School.

"I saw some of the Berks and they were very cheery. I asked who was then in command of them and they told me the Intelligence Officer. I went over to speak to him, and as we were talking a shrapnel shell burst near us and hit us both. We were at the railway between the two villages about 600 yards west of Marcelcave. He was rather badly hit, poor fellow. I cannot remember his name; they used to call him John in the mess. . . .

"I am so pleased Colonel Lawson has got the D.S.O. He was splendid all the time and as cool as possible. . . ."

What could be better than this letter? As simple as Bunyan, and generous as a fine May day.

"I fear my writing is very bad, but my arm is not strong again yet."

No, the letter was written in hospital. Not a word of gloom appears in this quiet and chatty epitome of big events. How Carlyle would have rejoiced to add such a letter to a book of his! But yet it is only one letter from a great many, all written in the same serene tone of conversational friendliness. Duty well done fits these officers naturally; their courage needs nothing else as a symbol of V.C. and D.S.O.

Our "nervy" newspapers make much more ado over a lawn tennis match than our officers and men made over the most searching battle of the whole war. What will the British people be after two hundred years of headlined journalism?

§ II

A rearguard officer of the 2/Fifth Gloucesters writes from hospital to the same Brigadier.

"With regard to myself, I was wounded in three places

slightly on the 28th March in the counter-attack on Warfusée, but I was so tired that I took no notice, not even knowing that they [the wounds] were there. On the 29th I got pretty badly buried, which gave me contusion of the spine and I had to go down. When they undressed me at Rouen, much to my surprise, there were the slight wounds. . . .

"I will try to give you a description of what happened to our battalion after you left. . . . At about 5.30 p.m. on March 22 our battalion was distributed in depth, A and B in front, C behind, and my Company in rear. Rickerby and I were in the front line; the Boche rushed us, and we all fell back on my Company line, which was on the railway. He broke through the battalion on our right, leaving our flank in the air. At about 10.30 p.m. that night the Royal Berks, who were on our left, told us that they had had orders to go to Voyennes at once with the 183rd BRIGADE, to whom they were attached. They went, also all the 183rd BRIGADE. I told Colonel Lawson [Eleventh Hussars], who was the only other officer practically there; he had just come. He said we should have to stay, as we had no orders to go there owing to the Brigade-Major being captured; so we extended our line and kept up fire. At this time S.A.A. was getting very short, and the dump at Beauvois was burning very strongly. We stayed in this line, with no one on our right, and no one on our left, till about 3.30 a.m. on the 23rd, when the Colonel thought we ought to go, as it would soon be light, and the enemy would see that he was being held up by only about 150 men on 2000 yards of front.* All night he tried to rush and bomb us, but we kept on firing at any movement. We got out by sneaking around Beauvois and marching to Voyennes, then to Languevoisin, where we had breakfast. We then moved to a place near Herly, but marched back to Languevoisin, and slept the night of 23–24. At 10 a.m. on the 24th we were rushed to Breuil, to hold the bridgehead, and to cover the retirement of the *Twentieth* DIVISION from the canal. The 24th was without much incident. We got into cellars at Breuil the night of 24–25. Early in the morning the Boche attacked the bridgehead we were holding, but we drove him off. He shelled us very badly all day, but we inflicted a lot of casualties on him. At about 4.30 p.m. on

---

* These 150 brave men came into action at 4 or 5 a.m. on March 21. At 3 a.m. on the 23rd they were only two miles back from their original position; and in the meantime their division, Colin Mackenzie's, had been attacked for eight-and-forty hours by three German divisions.

the 25th the people on the bridgehead on our right retired, leaving us in the air, and the Boche got across it. We had to retire to Cressy as hard as we could, after letting Colonel Moore's battalion—Twelfth K.R.R.C. on our left—know.

"We had a few French mixed up with us, and through them I had some lunch. I was fighting a rearguard action with about twenty men and a L.G. when I saw some what I thought to be French, but they seemed to be going the wrong way. I ran to tell them, and captured a Hun captain, sergeant, and batman, with some important maps. It was getting dark by this time, so we got to Cressy, where we stayed till 12 a.m.,* then marched to Roye on the 26th; † and after stopping there a little time we went on to Mézières. We arrived there very tired indeed, but dug a line and had food. About 9 at night we moved up to Le Quesnel, where we dug in again without much incident. . . . At 9 p.m. on the 27th we had orders to embuss and go to Villers-Bretonneux. When we got there we went on to Marcelcave. We counter-attacked Warfusée at 11 a.m., and retired back through Marcelcave at about 6 p.m. on the 28th. . . . Willink was wounded in this counter-attack at Warfusée, but I did not know that he was killed till I saw it in the *Times*. . . . Colonel Lawson was simply grand. . . ." ‡

§ III

The late Colonel A. B. Lawson, 2/Fifth Gloucesters, writing on May 9, 1918, said:—

"We got a Military Cross for Gray who did very well, bar for Dudbridge, and about a dozen M.M.'s. . . . Also they gave me a D.S.O.; don't quite know why except for escaping with a whole skin when so many others had the bad luck not to. . . . Things for the present are fairly quiet, but probably the Boche will develop another effort somewhere again before long; after all his promises to his people he must continue, but I

---

* Getting away from Cressy was difficult. Another officer writes: "I found the Berks and got things fixed up, only to find to my horror when I got back to Cressy that a general withdrawal had been ordered, and we spent a frantic evening trying to separate the sheep from the goats to hold the various villages. It was in this withdrawal that poor old Moore was taken prisoner. . . . You are quite right. General Pagan is a topper, and has already won all hearts. I wish, however, he was not quite so indifferent to shell-fire—he makes me ashamed to duck."

† Covered by a welcome rearguard of armoured cars.

‡ Unhappily killed on June 19, 1918.

trust he will get a knock and wear himself out and then perhaps we shall get a bit of our own back."

"If he has many divisions like the one we met the other day we shall not have a great deal of trouble with him, and I think it is a very favourable sign that there are any to be found who will chuck it as some of them did, when they are supposed to be having a successful offensive and should have their tails right up. I saw one of them jump up and run into our line and shake hands with a man in one of our posts as he went past."

A note of discipline from Colonel Lawson :—

"As soon as we had got ammunition up and companies in position east of Beauvois, the Boches started to come on. X.Y.Z. was in command, in front line. I saw that they had apparently got forward on our right, and then our front line came back. I was rather angry about it because I had given no orders, but X.Y.Z. told me he had told them to as his right was in the air; so I put them all in the third line. It would have had to happen sooner or later, but I should have liked it to have been done more gradually, with more shooting at the advancing Boches, while the retirement was going on, because they gave a very good target."

Another Colonel, acting as Brigadier, describes some events on March 25 :—

"As Languevoisin was sure to be heavily shelled when daylight came, I ordered at 5 p.m. all men out of the village and moved Brigade Headquarters back to a sunken road 600 yards west of the village. Things began to get noisy at 7.30 a.m. when Bennett reported that about two companies of the enemy had tried to get across the canal at Quiquery, but got it badly. They were supported by some field artillery which, judging by the report, seemed to be firing at very close range. I heard about this time that the *Twenty-second* FRENCH DIVISION was coming up to counter-attack from Nesle in the direction of Rouy. Things on our left flank were getting very uncomfortable, as apparently a very heavy engagement was going on, and I began to see about 10 a.m. large bodies of our troops retiring. Soon after this platoons of French infantry passed us and were cheered by our men. They looked very fine men and very much for it.

"At 12.15 p.m. while standing over the telephone waiting for the operator to ring up the division, a piece of shell hit me in the neck and cut a small artery. The Brigade-Major, Captain Howitt, with great presence of mind, got me on my back, and being a very strong man, managed by half strangling me to stop the bleeding after about half an hour, when we got hold of the doctor of the Royal Berks, who tied me very tightly up. While this was going on, I heard that the Germans had taken Nesle; so I ordered up a company of Gloucesters to the threatened flank and, not wishing to be captured for a second time, I got two men to put me on a bicycle and to push me towards Cressy, where the Field Ambulance was. . . . From Cressy I went down to the C.C.S. at Roye and was evacuated to Rouen that night, thus for the third time joining the ranks of the wounded."

PART IV
AFTERMATH
INCLUDING CONTROVERSIES, SIDE ISSUES, AND POLITICAL EFFECTS

CHAPTER I

ON THE LOSS OF PÉRONNE AND BAPAUME

§ I

THE dispatch says:—
"Behind the forward defences of the FIFTH ARMY, and in view of the smaller resources which could be placed at the disposal of that Army arrangements had been made for the construction of a strong and carefully-sited bridgehead position covering Péronne and the crossings of the River Somme south of that town. Considerable progress had been made in the laying out of this position, though at the outbreak of the enemy's offensive its defences were incomplete." *

Incomplete ? An indefinite word ! It never brings before any one's mind a clear picture. Through a fortnight or so about 10,000 Italians toiled on the rear defences, and made them good enough for rearguard actions—if enough troops reached them. Trenches varied in depth from a foot to thirty-six inches. Wire was not continuous anywhere. Isolated platoon posts along the northern sectors were wired, as a rule, while in the south there was less wire, because a great deal more work had to be done there at express speed, partly owing, as we have seen, to the effect of dry weather on rivers and marshes. Briefly, the rear defences were too elastically ambitious for the time and labour which G.H.Q. could put into them; also the foe's airmen must have noted and mapped their course. And who could foresee how many troops would be lost in the forward and battle zones, or how many would reach the rear lines?

On February 9, 1918, Gough received from G.H.Q. a document answering a letter which he had sent there on February 1. Some quotations from it are useful and necessary.†

---

* "Haig's Dispatches," vol. ii., p. 184.
† The italics are mine.—W. S. S.

"The Field-Marshal Commanding-in-Chief considers that in the event of a serious attack being made on your Army on a wide front, your policy should be *to secure and protect at all costs the important centre of Péronne and the River Somme to the south of that place,* while strong counter-attacks should be made both from the direction of Péronne and from the south possibly assisted by the French THIRD ARMY."

What meaning are we to get from the routine phrase "secure and protect at all costs"? In other points the directions belong to elementary generalship. What subaltern could have failed to see the military value of Péronne and the Somme? Our stores, depôts, and hospitals were west of the Somme, as every one knew; so a German invasion west of the Somme—between Péronne and Ham, for instance—would be vastly harmful. Yet this matter was not, and is not, the main one. The main one is the fact that adequate defence of the Somme line depended on the British Government, who alone could supply Haig with enough men and guns. If enough reinforcements were not sent in time from England to France, retribution would fall as usual on our young soldiers, while Ministers might save themselves by using their eloquence as a democratic lifebelt.

Remembering these things, let us consider the phrase "to protect at all costs." It has two meanings: to retire from a thorough grapple against odds before the odds can gobble up the defence, or to perish rather than give ground, as Wellington at Waterloo was prepared to perish. Which of these meanings was the FIFTH ARMY to illustrate by its conduct? We are not told. When poison enters into a doctor's prescription, is it not well to give the dose?

The directions imply, though written six weeks before the battle, that there will be good rear lines and enough men "to secure and protect at all costs" the positions named; for it could not be a reasonable defence for a delaying number of troops to regard their lives as less valuable than land, since defence overwhelmed does not stop the foe's advance. And if strong counter-attacks were to be made from the direction of Péronne and also from the south, possibly helped by the THIRD FRENCH ARMY, surely sufficient reserves should be on the spot and fully equipped. If they arrived without artillery or without other necessary equipments, how could they be effectual?

In the second paragraph G.H.Q. is contradictory:

THE LOSS OF PÉRONNE AND BAPAUME

"While the Forward and Battle Zones in the FIFTH ARMY area should be fought generally in accordance with the principles laid down in G.H.Q., No. O.A.D. 29 1/29, dated 14th December, 1917, the provisions of paragraph 6 regarding the reinforcement of the Battle Zone and its re-establishment by counter-attack require some modification. *Neither is the ground which these Zones immediately protect so important, nor are the communications leading to them so good as to warrant reinforcements being thrown into the fight, counter-attacks on a large scale being launched, or the battle being fought out in the Battle Zone,* unless the general situation at the time makes such a course advisable. *It may well be desirable to fall back to the rearward defences of Péronne and the Somme while linking up with the Third [British] Army on the north, and preparing for counter-attack.*"

If G.H.Q. had put these orders in the first paragraph, its instructions would have been less perplexing. At present we are face to face with impossible things. Since "it may well be desirable to fall back to *the rearward* defences of Péronne and the Somme," what was the use of saying in the first paragraph that Péronne itself must be secured and protected at all costs? If our troops must allow themselves to be scuppered rather than retreat behind the Somme, surely the command should be given plainly, and surely there should be no talk about rearward defences. The rearward defences of Péronne were *behind* the Somme; the forward defences of Péronne were the bridgeheads, major and minor.

Again :—

"In order that there may be no dangerous gap between your defensive systems and those of the THIRD ARMY, *should a withdrawal to the Péronne bridgehead or to the line of the Rivers Somme and Tortille take place,* the necessary switches will be constructed under mutual arrangements to be made by the THIRD and FIFTH ARMIES."

"In order that the above works may be completed with the least possible delay, arrangements are being made for the provision of the necessary labour and transportation personnel for the construction of defences and the necessary development of the existing road and light railway facilities."

As regards the organization and preparation of the rearward defences, the main considerations in their relative order of importance will be as follows :—

(a) "The protection of the river crossings at Péronne will be secured by a bridgehead. The defences of this bridgehead must be sited with a view to securing our road and rail communications through Brie and Péronne.

"The organization and preparations for the defence of the Péronne bridgehead will be completed in detail as soon as possible, including the provision of adequate communications, *i.e.* road and light railways, also additional bridges over the Somme."

(b) "*The retention of the line of the River Somme will be secured by the construction of an emergency defensive Zone as a strong retrenchment along the left bank of that river as far north as Péronne and thence northwards by the Tortille River.* In connection with this defensive Zone small bridgeheads will be constructed as required to secure the immediate crossings over the river.

"The organization of this emergency defensive Zone and the construction of the defences will be carried out concurrently with the work on the Péronne bridgehead with such labour as may be available after the requirements of the latter have been fully provided for."

§ II

And now let us think impartially of those events which caused Gough's withdrawal from the sketchy lines guarding the Somme from a point east of Rouy-le-Grand, north-eastward to Monchy-Lagache and Hancourt; thence north, as a portion of Péronne's bridgehead. This line was the main Green Line; it crossed Hutier's northern boundary (*i.e.* the Vermand-Amiens road) about a thousand yards south of Vraignes and three thousand yards west of the minor Green Line, an offshoot, a trifle east of Pœuilly; so it was affected equally by the attacks directed by Hutier and Marwitz. On both sides of the road wide pressure was exceedingly strong, the southern side feeling the concentrated force of Hutier's right, and the northern side the massed power of Marwitz's left. Early in the battle this circumstance was ill-omened for five reasons :—

1. Only about 6000 yards of straight road separated Vermand from the main Green Line; and at midday, March 22, Vermand was lost, and the foe pressed westwards towards the Green Line offshoot at Pœuilly, outflanking Maxse and Watts.

Daly,* who began the battle weak in numbers, was in

* The *Twenty-fourth* DIVISION.

THE LOSS OF PÉRONNE AND BAPAUME 249

line, with many men gassed, and the rest gripped by that fatigue which fills the mouth with a saliva like phlegm, trickles in cold sweat down the body, and confuses the mind, while seeming to give to every limb and joint a rebellious wit of its own. Marathon runners are tortured by a similar fatigue, when the last three or four miles of open country have to be covered somehow, anyhow. Dazed men had straggled to the rear, where they were met and called together by Brigadier Riddell of the *Fiftieth*, whose Northumberland Fusiliers had reached the Green Line offshoot, between eight and nine of the morning, March 22.

3. Another division of Watts's Corps, Neill Malcolm's,* also weak in numbers when the battle began, was losing too many men in a noble fight against Marwitz; and Hutier's right pressed dangerously on Colin Mackenzie's left,† owing to the breach at Maissemy.

4. The *Fiftieth* (NORTH ENGLISH) DIVISION, after a tiring ourney by night, reached the battle without its artillery and machine-guns, which were coming by road.

5. It had only two brigades along the Green Line offshoot between Bernes and a point near Villévéque—a twisting line difficult to measure, but certainly more than 8000 yards; and both brigades were so overstretched that their power of counter-attack was greatly weakened. Riddell's brigade had to guard five thousand yards of line with three battalions about 1800 men, and a reserve of 800 stragglers from Daly's front, whom he had brought together during the day, and a part of whom he fed in the evening.

Haig relates how, on March 22, as the day wore on, the great concentration of German troops attacking west of St. Quentin, accompanied by untoward events north in the battle against Marwitz, had produced a very bad crisis. During the early afternoon our men east of Holnon Wood were forced to withdraw from their battle-zone trenches; while the *Fiftieth*, after repulsing heavy attacks throughout the morning, were attacked again during the afternoon and evening and compelled to give ground. Troops from the battle zone, fighting fiercely and continuously, fell back through the *Twentieth* and *Fiftieth* holding the third defensive zone between Happencourt, Villévéque, and Boucly, in the hope of reorganizing behind them. . . . By 5.30 p.m. the enemy had reached the third zone at different points, and was attacking the *Fiftieth* heavily between Villévéque and Boucly. This

* The *Sixty-sixth.* † The *Sixty-first* DIVISION.

was a huge span of front for a single division to hold, Boucly being a crow's-flight of 5000 yards from Bernes, and the trench had many bends and curves. G.H.Q. estimates the *Fiftieth's* front as some 10,500 yards, but even a straight line across country between Boucly and Villévêque measures 11,000, and the trench line was certainly 3000 yards more in its bends and curves. Hence the *Fiftieth* was greatly handicapped.

The dispatch says:—

"Though holding an extended front of some 10,500 yards, the division succeeded in checking the enemy's advance, and by a successful counter-attack drove him temporarily from the village of Caulaincourt. At the close of the engagement, however, the troops of the *Fiftieth* about Pœuilly had been forced back, and by continued pressure along the south bank of the Omignon River the enemy had opened a gap between their right flank and the troops of the *Sixty-first* . . . . and of the *Twentieth* farther south. At this gap, during the late afternoon and evening, strong bodies of German troops broke through the third defensive zone about Vaux and Beauvois." *

In this quotation there is some misunderstanding. As a matter of fact, Pœuilly was not lost by Riddell's Northumberland Fusiliers; it was held till the order to retire came; but the Green Line offshoot east of Caulaincourt was badly breached. Though their right was driven in west of this line, the Northumbrians at nightfall were commanding Caulaincourt from a strong position well dug in. Here they remained until four a.m. on March 23, when they were ordered to retire in conjunction with the forces north and south.

Indeed, three divisions—the *Fiftieth, Twentieth,* and *Thirty-ninth*—covered the withdrawal of those troops who were most exhausted by fighting and fatigue. Two or three divisions had little fight left in them, so spent were they, so parched by thirst,† and dazed with want of sleep. The foe pressed the withdrawal, and Gough had thrown into the fight all his reserves. As yet no further support was within reach of the fighting, apart from a gunless French division and some French cavalry in the south, just arrived.

* Vol. ii., p. 194.
† The country in the great bend of the Somme is very waterless, and our troops suffered grievously from thirst. Later the small spring in Barleux Wood was a great refreshment to Malcolm's men, and to other divisions, the *Eighth* and *Thirty-ninth*.

THE LOSS OF PÉRONNE AND BAPAUME 251

And it is worth noting that this gunless French division, the *Hundred and Twenty-fifth*, after marching far and very fast, failed, despite a very brave grapple, to achieve success in a counter-attack, because it became short of rifle ammunition. The counter-attack began at six in the morning of the third day; its aim was to regain the Crozat Canal between Vouel and Tergnier; and troops of our *Eighteenth* took part in it also. There was a mist, and the French soldiers did not know the ground. In these very trying circumstances, a British officer, Colonel Bushill, displayed fine leadership. Taking charge of the French left as well as of his own two companies, he led the attack on, into an intense machine-gun fire, and, though severely wounded in the head, rallied his troops again and again.* Little progress could be made, but Bushell kept the line firm till noon, when he and others learnt from events that the counter-attack was futile. French troops in large numbers came streaming back from Vouel. They had been heavily attacked, and their ammunition had become too scarce. On the third day, then, effective help from our Allies could not possibly be expected, above all east of the Somme.

What was to be done? A false move now would give both Hutier and Marwitz a decisive opportunity. They had numbers enough to annihilate if the overstrained British would stand to fight it out at all costs, instead of withdrawing at the right moment, as Jimmy Wilde would withdraw if he were attacked by Carpentier.

Would a stand be made at all costs along the bridgehead positions? The temptation must have been very great, and for many reasons. After much fatigue from long delaying actions, there comes to most men a burning desire to reach a decision one way or other. "Let's kill and win, or be killed and beaten! To hell with this retreating!" Here is the final rally of a true fighting temper. In a Waterloo its gratification is pretty well miraculous; in the Second Somme battle would it not have been as fatal as suicide, and as foolish?

Haig's answer is memorable :—

"Reports that the enemy had forced the line of the Crozat Canal, combined with the loss of the Vaux-Pœuilly positions, and information obtained by the Air Service that the German front as far back as Mont d'Origny was packed with

* After forming a steady front Bushell went to the rear to make a report and to have his head bandaged; then he went back to the firing line.

advancing troops, led the FIFTH ARMY Commander to reconsider his decision to offer battle afresh east of the Somme. Considering that if involved in a general engagement his tired troops might be exposed to a decisive defeat before help could arrive, and that the situation might then be exploited by the enemy to a disastrous extent, he decided to continue the withdrawal at once to the west bank of the Somme.

"On the morning of the 23rd March, therefore, confirming instructions previously given by telephone, orders were issued by the FIFTH ARMY to the 19th Corps to carry out a gradual withdrawal to the line of the Somme. The 7th Corps was directed to conform to this movement, and to take up a position on the general line Doingt-Nurlu.

"This order involved the abandonment of the main Péronne bridgehead position. It greatly shortened the time available for clearing our troops and removable material from the east bank of the river, for completing the necessary final preparations for the destruction of the river and canal bridges, for re-forming west of the river the divisions which had suffered most in the previous fighting, and generally for securing the adequate defence of the river line."

These consequences of a withdrawal were quite clear to Gough and his officers; but, of course, material consequences have to be viewed in war side by side with the physical state of battle-worn troops. Earlier we have seen (p. 36) Haig's remark that "the forces at the disposal of the FIFTH ARMY were inadequate to meet and hold an attack in such strength as that actually delivered by the enemy on its front." This being true when the battle began, it was more tragically true three days later, after very severe losses and along a wider front. Yet the dispatch speaks of some divisions being rested and refitted west of the Somme, while other divisions, almost as fagged out by overstrain, do the work of both east of the river. How much more could be expected from an army urgently in need of large reinforcements from the first hours of attack?

There are critics who declare that Gough's men were in a less bad state to fight than to retreat. In one sense this criticism is true, because the duty of retreating at the right time is hateful, unless it is regarded with pride as a duty. Many of Wellington's veterans behaved badly in retreats, and so did Moore's army on its way to Corunna, till it was called upon to fight, when it proved that the exhilaration of battle was a strong tonic after the weariness of forced

THE LOSS OF PÉRONNE AND BAPAUME 253

marches. As a rule, it is easier to fight than to retreat under pressure. But let us suppose that Gough had kept his tired men too long at close quarters against superior numbers. Can any sane person suppose that our FIFTH ARMY could have borne without breaking heavier losses than those that tore its ranks from day to day?

That Gough was right when he declined to take decisive risks east of the Somme is proved by a single fact, namely, that when an increasing number of French troops joined our defence *west of the Somme*, they were driven back to Noyon and Montdidier. So vast was the German pressure, that even large additions of strength in the defence could not give stability to the fighting front. If Gough, without reinforcements, had continued to face this pressure with his back to the Somme, would he not have enabled Hutier and Marwitz to achieve their aims?

Few men understand, said Napoleon, the strength of will required by a Commander-in-Chief when he risks the existence of his army and of his nation in a battle which, in the nature of things, is always uncertain. True, no doubt; but an equal strength of will—if not a greater strength—is needed when a commander, in the heat and stress of a vast battle, makes a right decision plainly so unattractive that it is bound to be misunderstood and hated by those who are far off from the atmosphere and pathology of the fighting front.

Many persons talk as though Gough's few divisions should have been composed—not of flesh and blood in a high fever of overstrained battle-passion, but—of bullet-proof steel; should have been as inanimate as tanks, and able to bear through days and nights, without rest, unlimited fatigue.

Then there is the truth that official accounts do not reach logic and history because they suppress facts which officers in the field are obliged to weigh and measure before they make decisions. To suppress certain facts may seem to be patriotic, but in major battles, as in written tragedies, cause and effect are so rapid and so cumulative in action and reaction, that the omission of governing facts must always be wrong and unfair. As well delete the handkerchief from *Othello!* If you omit a fact in order to save the feelings of A and B and C, you are certain to be unjust to D and E and F.

Everything that a commander in the field must weigh and measure ought to be stated plainly in an account of his decisions. When facts are omitted in a published verdict controversy is invited, a painful thing when a war is one of life or death.

In a war of life or death, moreover, when hundreds of thousands perish, a single life or a single name has no more worth than that which truth gives to it; so truth alone has public or historical value.

Gough and his Commanders were obliged to consider other losses besides killed, wounded, and missing. Handfuls of their men here and there, finding the ordeal too relentless for their physical and moral stamina, gave in; but their behaviour was much better that that of many among Wellington's troops in the almost mild retreat to Torres Vedras. Still, those who broke, and straggled far out of the grapple, are to be placed among the losses. And we must remember the sick. In one Corps, for example, between March 21 and April 1, 47 officers and 1250 men were put out of action by sickness. In the first four days 14 officers and 348 men were out of action from illness; and by March 25 most of the forty battalions in this Corps were reduced by losses to an average of only 200 men in each, for the pioneer battalions had fought and had suffered casualties with their comrades. I am speaking of the 18th Corps. On the night of the third day its casualties were estimated as about 392 officers and about 11,681 other ranks, or thereabouts.

Sixty-first DIVISION, 121 officers, 3232 other ranks.
Thirtieth, 132 officers, 4300 other ranks.
Thirty-sixth, 87 officers, 2515 other ranks.
Twentieth, 52 officers, 1634 other ranks.

How can official accounts of a battle be truthful when facts of this sort are left out?

Civilians have a hazy notion about the normal strength of a division; and when, in official dispatches, a division is mentioned from day to day, without any reference to its daily losses, a false impression is made on civilian minds, who forget that divisions do not disappear with their men, but keep their full rank as divisions, however wasted they may be by losses. Yet the dispatch in even its republished form has no footnotes on the casualties. German losses are referred to again and again, even in a new footnote (p. 199), while the British, though the most important to us all, are passed over in silence. So readers are kept in the dark concerning a factor which rules through a retreat over defensive generalship. Could anything be more at variance with the needs of history?

THE LOSS OF PÉRONNE AND BAPAUME 255

Consider the men who were spent and who straggled through sheer numb fatigue. Every corps had sufferers of this sort, hundreds of them, in fact; so an increasing responsibility weighed on those men who were physically tougher and stronger. The survival of the fittest to bear overstrain is never more active than in long fights against long odds.

We have seen, too, in Haig's words, not only that "the strenuous efforts made by the British forces during 1917 had left the Army at a low ebb in regard both to training and to numbers," but also that lack of men had prevented enough training—except with pick and spade and wire. Now in a retreat, after a long winter spell of trench warfare, all defects of training show themselves inevitably, above all when exhaustion drugs the mind with poisoned blood, and when a great many experienced junior officers and non-coms. have been either killed or wounded or captured. Only an army that is war-wise in open warfare chooses unerringly the best positions from which to fight in delaying actions, and displays in full tactical measure the value of its courage and tenacity. When troops are young and jaded, and raw in open warfare, are they not certain to miss many opportunities, and in modern battles more than in the old fights, owing to the great width of battle-front and to the disordering effects of gaps and set-backs on other sectors?

Plainly, then, readers must learn to see war under the form of visual conception : in pictures clear to the mind. Gough had to see facts truly and fully, and to act at given moments in a way which, in his firm belief, was the safest defence—not for an ideal conception of his army, but—for his army as it was in plain truth day after day. The pith and marrow of his forces—die-hards and the great body of men who were soldiers of firm duty rather than soldiers born—were wasting through heavy casualties; and many of them, as the battle went on and on, hobbled like sleep-walkers, whose legs were stiffened very much by rheumatism.

§ III

But, after all, criticisms published on the fall of Péronne have had one very useful effect; inviting students here and there to review the whole drama as thoroughly as they can, and to use their own minds without excessive fear of authority. In so doing, they cannot help wondering why there should have been so much talk about the fall of Péronne and none at all about the loss of Bapaume—a strategical centre not only as important to Byng as Péronne was to Gough, but also, probably, of more importance to the general defence, because its position was to the north-*west* of Péronne and not only nearer to the coast, but also convenient for a rapid flanking advance on Albert.

Even Haig has been inadvertent, passing over the fall of Bapaume so swiftly and vaguely that many readers do not notice what the phrasing means:—

"Before midnight (March 24) the troops of the 4th Corps, who had carried out their withdrawal by stages in the face of constant attacks, were established on the line assigned to them west of Bapaume, between La Barque and Ervillers." *

Not a word more!

When Bapaume fell, " touch between the several divisions of the 5th Corps, and between the 5th and 4th Corps, was not properly established." Now both these Corps belonged to the THIRD ARMY, and the quotation means that the THIRD ARMY'S centre was broken, and that other gaps had formed between the divisions of 5th Corps. These mishaps were not ameliorated for about eight and forty hours. Yet there is no criticism in G.H.Q.'s dispatch, though a paragraph is given to the loss of Péronne. I am very puzzled. Are we to suppose that the précis-writers at G.H.Q. were more genial to Byng than to Gough? Why criticize the under-manned army while leaving the far stronger one free from criticism? Surely students have a patriotic right to complain when they are put in a false position towards two British armies?

Turn to the map, and draw two horizontal lines, one from Bapaume to the far end of Flesquières salient, and one from Péronne to the east of Le Verguier. The first line is about 23,500 yards and the second about 21,500. Now, on the evening of the fourth day, Byng's troops were struggling hard on the eastern outskirts of Bapaume, and by midnight they were obliged to fall back behind the town. On the same evening Gough's troops were still behind the Somme along the Péronne sector. Next day, between dawn and nightfall, Byng's men west of Bapaume retired to Miraumont, about 7500 yards, while Gough's troops behind Péronne fell back in the evening to Herbécourt sector, only about 5500 yards.

What do these matters prove? Surely this: that a retreat is in the nature of war when a superior force strikes an inferior one at the right places and upsets the balance of its defence.

* Vol. ii., p. 200.

THE LOSS OF PÉRONNE AND BAPAUME 257

So I rejoice that Watts's Corps, just in time, got some restorative rest behind the canalized Somme, and that other troops also gained their long second breath with this river before them. In war minutes should be deemed as valuable as hours, and hours as days, and days as months, and months as years; and thus the gain of time behind the shallow Somme was an inestimable boon to the Allied Cause, whose reinforcements had nearly always far to come, and arrived too often without artillery and other necessaries, and sometimes in battalions of different brigades, like our *Thirty-fifth* DIVISION.

CHAPTER II

THE TRANSFER OF FIFTH ARMY TROOPS TO THE THIRD ARMY

§ I

ON Monday, March 25, all FIFTH ARMY troops north of the Somme passed from Gough to Byng. Why? What was the motive power behind this act of swopping horses in midstream?

No explanation of any sort is given by the official dispatch, which, indeed, glides over it swiftly, and even indirectly:—

"It became clear that the THIRD ARMY, which on this day had assumed command of all troops north of the Somme, would have to continue the withdrawal of its centre to the line of the River Ancre, already crossed by certain of our troops near Beaucourt" (about six miles north of Albert).*

Not a word more. Students are left in the dark as to which divisions were taken from Gough and given to Byng; and as for the differing effects of this policy on both armies, they are passed over in silence, though policy in war is tested always by its results, not by good intentions nor by later explanations.

Sir F. Maurice says:—

"It was clear that the main object of the Germans was to reach Amiens and that the weight of their attack was falling upon the FIFTH ARMY. So, in order to allow Gough to devote his whole attention to the enemy advancing south of the river, Sir Douglas Haig placed that portion of the FIFTH ARMY which was north of the Somme under Byng, and it then became a part of the THIRD ARMY."

This explanation is genial, but, for a convincing reason, it cannot be accepted as correct. On the same day, south of the Somme, an event occurred which thrust so many drawbacks on Gough and his officers that they could not possibly devote their whole attention *unhindered* to the German odds. Though French reinforcements were still weak in numbers

* Vol. ii., p. 203.

and so ill-armed that they could not do justice to their fine qualities, yet they were ordered, as we learn from Haig, "to assume responsibility for the whole battle front south of the Somme, with general control of the British troops operating in that sector." Strange, indeed; for Haig tells us also that "*some days had yet to pass before the French could bring up sufficient strength to arrest the enemy's progress.*" As a matter of fact, in the huge central battle, north and south of the highway to Amiens, the whole defence remained in British hands; and southward, where the French were active, with six ill-equipped divisions, by about nightfall of the fifth day, British troops formed the main defence, except in a few sectors. Indeed, the attack had added to its odds as many reinforcements as the French had brought into the battle; so British guns of every sort, like British rifles and British generalship and tenacity, were as essential on the fifth day as they were on the first. Remember, Hutier alone had ten, if not twelve, divisions in his reinforcements; and it was Hutier who assailed our 18th and 3rd Corps, to whose relief French troops were hurried.

Yet, somehow, anyhow, on this fifth day, Gough was thrust officially under French orders south of the Somme, though Foch had not yet been appointed to Supreme Command; and north of the Somme he was deprived of all authority. He and his officers and men were slighted and shackled, though they had still to go on proving that bad statesmanship in the Allied Councils could not ruin the Allied Cause. In a later chapter these matters will be considered fully. At present the main point is that Sir F. Maurice has not explained the transfer of Congreve, with the bulk of 7th Corps, from Gough to Byng. Political interference, French and British, was busy, doing harm through fear; but as G.H.Q. made no protest at present known to us, we cannot at present free our Commander-in-Chief from all responsibility. Some laymen of influence believe—and in a democracy all circulating opinions count till they are refuted—that Lord Milner failed entirely to see the nobility of the work achieved by the FIFTH ARMY, and was not its friend either during or after its ordeal. In March, 1918, and afterwards, he was certainly a great influence, representing the British Government at the Doullens Conference on the 26th of March, for example; but, after all, wrong political actions in a time of war should be attributed, not to any one man, but to the whole War Cabinet.

Some military experts affirm that—

"Congreve went under Byng for the good and sufficient reason that his line of retreat took him north of the Somme, and it was desirable to have the river as a flank guard of the force operating there."

This affirmation is unconvincing because Congreve's retreat did *not* take him entirely north of the Somme. We have seen, indeed, that already the remains of two of his divisions, the *Sixteenth* and *Thirty-ninth*, had crossed the river to the south bank (p. 115); and others would have crossed at Bray-sur-Somme if Byng had been able with his own troops to follow the army boundary from Montauban down to Bray— a steep run south-west by which a narrow one-division front was formed immediately east of Bray and in Gough's land. Congreve could have held this riverside front with Hunt's Force and a reserve, while the rest of his troops—the *First* CAVALRY, the *Thirty-fifth*, and remnants of the *Ninth* and *Twenty-first*, would have followed the *Sixteenth* and *Thirty-ninth* into the great centre battle. Bray, then, was the place at which Byng could have taken command of all land north of the Somme without harming the FIFTH ARMY's fighting strength.

Again, what sort of flank guard would the river be if the defence on one side fell back more rapidly than that on the other, uncovering the other's flank and rear? In this matter the troops on both riverside fronts had to guard each other's rear, knowing that the Somme could be turned by the foe into a passage way; and no impartial mind after studying this battle can settle down in the belief that land north of the Somme would be safer under Byng than under Gough. If Gough's decisions had not been right, Ludendorff's aims would certainly have been made real during the first four days, so excellent were the German plans, and so well trained were the odds—more than three to one—which tried to annihilate a thin defence increasingly overstretched. Further, if Gough's orders had not been translated into effectual action by his officers and troops, all along a forty-two miles front which became wider and wider, complete disaster would have been inevitable. Results are facts in essence, and therefore too strong for a great many persons. In this battle results depended on three things: swift and sufficient achievement by the attack, swift and sufficient reinforcement by the defence, and such generalship and tenacity in the FIFTH ARMY as would ravage

FROM FIFTH ARMY TO THIRD ARMY

and baffle the attack till enough reserves had come into line. We have seen how slowly the reserves came up; and Haig assures us (vol. ii., p. 205) that on the fifth day "the whole of the troops holding the British line south of the Somme were now greatly exhausted, and the absence of reserves behind them gave ground for considerable anxiety." And now we must recall to memory another fact, namely, that Gough would have had thirty divisions if his front had possessed the same man-power per mile as Byng's. Why, then, was Byng reinforced with FIFTH ARMY troops?

Only a few hours after this event happened—by 1.45 on March 25—Gough's H.Q. Staff was warned by the THIRD ARMY that Byng's centre would fall back by night behind the Ancre, and that Congreve's troops would hold from Albert to Bray inclusive. In this fact we draw close to the best military reason that could govern the transfer from the THIRD ARMY's standpoint. It is a fact with two meanings:—

1. The THIRD ARMY, owing to its broken centre, between 4th and 5th Corps, and to gaps between the divisions of 5th Corps, intended to use troops from the FIFTH ARMY to form its right wing on its own soil.

2. The night retreat would uncover about six miles behind Gough's left, as we have seen in an earlier chapter (p. 118).

At this point several questions arise: "Was G.H.Q. aware of these two meanings when it either sanctioned or initiated the transfer of Gough's troops to Byng? Did it know that these troops in a few hours would be a reinforcement on the THIRD ARMY's own ground? And did it wonder by what means Gough and Watts could guard about six uncovered miles of riverside? If so, why are these important affairs omitted from the dispatch?"

Reinforcing the THIRD ARMY was among the great deeds done by the FIFTH, and a very unfair thing is plainly implied when it is passed over in silence by official print and speech. This unfair thing is that Gough's judgment was distrusted justly by G.H.Q. as by other powers when his northern Corps (less two remnant divisions, but just strengthened by the *Thirty-fifth*), was suddenly taken from him and placed under the THIRD ARMY.

The dispatch is dated July 20, 1918, and for three months the Government feared to publish its criticisms. Consider all the slander that poured over the FIFTH ARMY between March 21 and October 21, and all the official injustice that accompanied the defaming rumours which were noised abroad by the common crowd. In these circumstances, then, should we not believe that complete candour from all officials, both lay and military, would have been good for the whole nation—both good and necessary?

There was no need to hide the presence of FIFTH ARMY troops along about 8000 or 9000 yards of Byng's right wing; no need, that I can see, for the dispatch shows plainly what was happening in 4th and 5th Corps, and as soon as the foe reached the Hébuterne sector, and occupied Hébuterne cemetery with machine-guns, the Ancre line was badly outflanked from the north-west, and the presence of this great menace justified the use of any essential reinforcements which would ease the danger.

Congreve's troops were very conveniently placed; and to set them to hold from 8000 to 9000 yards of the 5th Corps' front was to free this Corps for other necessary work. It would fill the gaps between its divisions by closing up to the north, and would collect nearly all its tired strength north of Albert. If these reasons directed the transfer, no doubt the use of FIFTH ARMY troops on the THIRD's own land was justified in so far as it concerns the northern battle; but when we look south of the Somme, and recall to memory the centre fighting north and south of Vermand-Amiens road, how can we fail to see that Gough's left south of the river was injured and imperilled? It needed those troops from Congreve's Corps who would have crossed the Somme at Bray if 5th Corps, THIRD ARMY, had been able to keep to its southern boundary.

G.H.Q. had no troops to send there (apart from Heneker's division, which was south of Amiens road); and if on the fifth day enough reinforcements had mended the THIRD ARMY's broken centre, and had strengthened the 5th Corps' left, then 5th Corps could have closed down south towards the Army boundary—and also, I assume, towards a base, chosen to serve its southern brigades. For the boundary between Gough and Byng was not altered a month before the battle merely in order to keep map-makers busy. It entered at once into the administration of both armies.

One point more. All students of war know that an important river or valley forms *tactically* one of the most dangerous boundaries between allied armies. Yet the Somme was chosen as a convenient dividing line, up to which the French responsibility was to come after the whole FIFTH ARMY had been relieved " according to plan." On March 25, the French were by no means fit to undertake this responsibility. British troops in a number far too small had to baffle the foe in the great central conflict; and hence the sudden transfer of Gough's troops to Byng cannot be explained or excused by saying: "It helped the French to take over the central fighting."

I should like to be able to believe that Authority had no other idea than the swift reinforcement of the northern defence when it put Congreve under the THIRD ARMY, for no other motive seems at all reasonable. But we must remember some other things. One of them is the terrific strain which pressed by day and night on G.H.Q., as on all officers governing the defence; and, again, we must never forget that Supreme Authority collected wrong notions from the imperfect reports mingled with thronging rumours which came unceasingly from so many miles of moving front. Among these wrong notions was the belief—or let us say the assumption—that grave mishaps in Byng's right were caused by Gough's left. Or, to use the everyday phrase, that "the Byng boys had been let down by Gough's men." Soon after the battle, in a scurried speech before the House of Commons, the Prime Minister showed that he did not understand the battle because his military advisers had put wrong notions into his mind.

General Sir John Monash has shown very clearly, in his book on "Australian Victories in France in 1918," how prevalent these wrong notions were, his own conception of the battle being completely out of focus and perspective. Consider this amazing passage on the position of affairs at about one a.m. on March 27. The italics are mine: "I gleaned further that the 7th Corps was now the south flank Corps of the THIRD ARMY, *and that as the* FIFTH ARMY, *south of the Somme, had practically melted away,* while the French were retiring south-westerly *and leaving an hourly increasing gap between their north flank and the Somme,* General Byng had resolved *to make every effort not only to maintain the flank of his* THIRD ARMY *on the Somme, but also to prevent it being turned from the south,* while the Commander-in-Chief was taking other measures to attempt next day to fill the gap above alluded to." *

It would have been easy for General Monash to study the battle as a whole before he wrote the opening pages of his book. There was no need for him to repeat in a book, long afterwards, the absurdly inaccurate views which he formed

* "Australian Victories in France in 1918," p. 27.

while his reserve troops were being ordered here and there, as
though Authority wavered a great deal in its attitude towards
the use of its reinforcements. As General Monash knew that
"the 7th Corps was now the south flank Corps of the THIRD
ARMY," he ought also to have known that Gough's left had
just reinforced Byng's right; and he could have learnt without difficulty that on two successive days—March 25 and
26—THIRD ARMY orders had uncovered Gough's rear south of
the Somme. This was the only gap in the central battle, and
General Monash would have been interested to see how good
fighting and sound generalship saved a very bad situation.
How very ingenuous is the statement that "General Byng
had resolved to make every effort not only to maintain the
flank of his THIRD ARMY on the Somme, but also to prevent
it being turned from the south?" Would that General Byng
had been able with his own troops to keep to his southern
boundary! Then the battle would have been very different.
Still, General Monash's misconceptions enable us to guess why
Mr. Hamilton Fyfe tried in vain to publish refutations of
wild rumours, which had been accepted as true by too many
persons in high stations.

Though these and other misconceptions are absurd, yet, as
elements of a battle's history, they are things to be looked at
quietly. During a very perilous retreat it may have been
quite natural to think that the much weaker army on
the much broader front would make more mistakes or be
more unlucky than the THIRD ARMY, which G.H.Q. had
strengthened with the greatest care as it expected the main
German blow to fall between Sensée River and the north
base-angle of Flesquières salient. As a rule, too, those who
are onlookers are apt to feel perilous events more nervously
than those who are inside the perils and thus too occupied for
brooding fear and speculation.

We may assume, then, without any great extravagance
that Authority, certainly overstrained, and certainly eager to
improve a huge crisis, may have hoped to strengthen the
defence partly by giving Byng a wider front, partly by giving
Gough less to do. But misunderstandings, which may be
natural when immense battles are being fought along a vast
and continuous line, should be corrected at the earliest
possible date and in the plainest words. The official dispatch
is often vague when it should be definite, and by ill-fortune
these vague passages do not help the people to understand the
loyal aid given by the FIFTH ARMY to the THIRD. On the

contrary, a cynic might suggest, giving reasons, that facts are being hidden officially because they throw too much light on the THIRD ARMY'S troubles. To lay stress on the fall of Péronne, for instance, while gliding swiftly over the fall of Bapaume, was, as we have seen, a blunder by which students would be provoked into search and research.*

* General Monash points out that his division on March 22 received orders " to move east, that is, back into Flanders, and not south to the Somme valley, as all had hoped. The prescribed move duly started, but by March 24, had been arrested, for orders had come to cancel the move and await fresh orders. . . . Later came detailed instructions that the division was to be transferred from the Australian Corps to the 10th Corps, which latter was to be G.H.Q. Reserve, and that the whole division was to be moved the next night to the Doullens area, the dismounted troops by rail, and the artillery and other mounted units by route-march." Now Doullens was the best place from which Byng could be reinforced either at Albert or at Arras. And note, too, how time was wasted in the handling of these invaluable Australian reserves—wasted by the Higher Command, though from midday on the 21st the position was critical along several spans of a battle-front perilously in need of men.

CHAPTER III

ORIGIN OF THE CÉRISY EPISODE

THIS dramatic episode belongs to the transfer of Gough's 7th Corps to Byng's right wing, and its origin is a very delicate thing to write about. It occurred at a time when the crisis in the THIRD ARMY north of the Somme was nearing its culminating point with fortune strongly on the German side.

In crises of this tenseness telephoned or spoken orders cannot always be put afterwards in a written or typed form, in accordance with routine, because the pressure of work is determined by the foe's movements; and a military order coming from a mind abnormally active may have only a slight effect on that mind's memory. There can be no doubt that Wellington's memory was not clear on several points in the battle of Waterloo; and some failure of memory occurred, I believe, in several minds, during and after the origin of the Cérisy episode. Here is an example from the official dispatch:—

"Farther south, the Bray-sur-Somme-Albert line had been taken up successfully on the night of March 25–26 [*by troops moved into* THIRD ARMY *land from Gough's left*], and fighting of a minor character occurred during the morning, particularly at Méaulte, where troops of the *Ninth* DIVISION [*removed from Gough's left flank*] beat off a strong attack [*about four miles inside Byng's right wing*]. Owing, however, to a misunderstanding, the Bray-sur-Somme-Albert line was regarded by the local commander as being merely a stage in a further retirement to the line of the Ancre, south of Albert. Accordingly, on the afternoon and evening of the 26th March, the withdrawal was continued, and when the higher command became aware of the situation the movement had already proceeded too far for our former positions to be re-established." *

As a matter of fact, there was NO misunderstanding. The Bray-Albert line *was* "merely a stage in a further

* Vol. ii., pp. 207-208.

ORIGIN OF THE CÉRISY EPISODE

retirement to the line of the Ancre, south of Albert." As such it is stated to be in THIRD ARMY instructions, and better instructions could not have been given at the time when they were issued. Much later they were changed, and changed because the perilous position north and north-west of Albert had improved; but when the altered orders arrived, troops at Bray and north-west of this town had begun under orders to obey the earlier instructions, as they had a much greater distance to march before they reached the Ancre and its very difficult crossings over long bridges. Let us then consider a brief and true time-table side by side with the military events by which the first instructions were made necessary:

1. By 1.45 p.m. on Monday, March 25, Gough received a message through his Staff from the THIRD ARMY that Byng's troops were falling back by night behind the Ancre, and that Congreve with his Corps would hold from Albert to Bray inclusive.
2. On the same day, at about seven p.m., the units of Congreve's troops received a Corps warning by telephone that another withdrawal would occupy the night; and at 8.45 p.m. orders were received to fall back to the line of the Bray-Albert road, rearguards to remain in position till two a.m. These were THIRD ARMY orders transmitted through Congreve and his Staff. Take their effect on the *Ninth* DIVISION. Highlanders were ordered to Dernancourt-sur-Ancre, and the thin South African battalion to Ribemont-sur-Ancre, while the Lowlanders were to hold from east of Méaulte to Albert exclusively. This information shows that the *Ninth's* fighting front was for rearguard purposes.
3. At 2.15 a.m. on March 26, the Corps confirmed this order and issued full guidance to its divisional commanders, the chief point being that they were to fight on the Albert-Bray line to delay the foe as long as possible, but without becoming so "involved" that they would be unable to break off and retire. Further, not only was the Bray-Albert line chosen for rearguard defence, but the Ancre itself, south-west of Albert, was to be regarded also as the provisional main defence; provisional, for until Byng and G.H.Q. had learnt from events what would happen in the night, and on March 26, to the

THIRD ARMY'S broken centre and very distressed 5th Corps, what line of defence south and south-west of Albert could be anything but provisional ?

Prospects were somewhat brighter after dusk on the 25th; the foe was becoming tired, considerable reinforcements had reached Byng, and others were coming up rapidly, as the G.H.Q. dispatch narrates. But yet, unluckily, the crisis had not passed away, because there was a " dangerous gap about Serre," in the Hébuterne sector, and only twenty-two and three-quarter miles north-east from the centre of Amiens. As long as this gap existed, then, no line of defence below Albert could be chosen by a soldier's mind as one fit for a last stand north of the Somme; and on March 26, during the morning, " the situation was not yet clear between Hamel and PUISIEUX,"* in the Serre-Hébuterne neighbourhood. " A gap still existed in this area between 5th and 4th Corps through which bodies of German infantry worked their way forward and occupied Colincamps with machine-guns." Now Colincamps is two and a half miles south-west of Hébuterne and it outflanks the northern Ancre at Hamel badly, Hamel being about three and a half miles to the south-east. At Colincamps, then, the attack was culminating.

What happened afterwards? First of all the *Second* DIVISION sent forward "a section of field artillery, which gallantly galloped into action and engaged them [the German machine-guns] over open sights," and so silenced them.† Next, "early in the afternoon troops of the New Zealand Division, under Sir A. H. Russell, retook Colincamps, while a brigade of the *Fourth* AUSTRALIAN DIVISION, E. G. Sinclair-Maclagan commanding the Division, filled the gap between Hébuterne and Bucquoy. In the fighting in this area our light tanks came into action for the first time and did valuable service." Moreover, " with the arrival of fresh troops, our line on this part of the front became stable, and all attempts made by the enemy during the [rest of the day] to drive in our positions about Bucquoy and to the north were repulsed with great loss." ‡

Clearly, then, it was not till "early in the afternoon of March 26" that any change could be made in the policy that

* " Haig's Dispatches." I have drawn a sketch map to show the influence of these events both on the Bray-Albert rearguard line and also on the river Ancre south-west of Albert.
† " Haig's Dispatches," vol. ii., p. 207.
‡ Vol. ii., p. 207.

March 26:
The Crisis N.W. of The Ancre
Boiry
St. Leger
Ecoust
Battle Zone
Ayette
Courcelles
Ervillers
Ablainzeville
Mory
Vaux
Hébuterne
Bucquoy
Achiet
Sapignies
Rear
Beugny
Sailly
Puisieux
Grevillers
Bapaume
Colincamps
Serre
Irles
Zone
Beaumont-Hamel
Beaucourt
Pys
Beaucourt
Ancre
Mailly
Le Sars
Le Transloy
Rocquigny
Hamel-sur-Ancre
Thiepval
Flers
Ancre R.
Pozière
Lesboeufs
Bazentin
Morval
Senlis
Ginchy
N
S
Montauban
Albert
Combles
Rancourt
Lavieville
Mametz
de Forêt
Carnoy
Maurepas
Bouch-Javesnes
Dernancourt
Méaulte
Maricourt
Buire
Ribemont
Curlu
Ancre R.
Hem
Buzanne
Tortille R.
Maricourt
Morlancourt
Bray
Péronne
Vaux
Sailly-le-Sec
Somme R.
Cappy
Vaire
Sailly
Chipilly
Dompierre
Biaches
La Hamel
Cerisy
Barleux
Proyart
Brie
Warfusée-Abancourt
Amiens Road
Foucaucourt
Miles 1 2 3 4 5 6 7 8 9 10 11 12 13 14
W.S.S. 28.3.20

governed the defence between Albert and the Somme, because a German break-through south-west from the Serre-Colincamps sector would have been disastrous to the whole Ancre line south-west of Albert. So we return to the detailed instructions issued at 2.15 a.m. on the 26th.

I note that when retirement from the rearguard Bray-Albert line became necessary, Congreve's troops were to cross the river Ancre and hold its northern bank as a rearguard position. After the crossing all bridges were to be blown up, and artillery would cover the crossing from the northern bank, heavy guns coming into position north of the Amiens-Albert road on a line named in the orders. Similarly, the span of riverside front to be held by each unit, as by Hadow's Force, was carefully noted in the orders. Thus the *Thirty-fifth*, the mainstay, whose G.O.C. had been placed in command of the Bray-Albert line, was told that its right must rest on Buire in touch with the *Twenty-first's* left, and its left on Dernancourt in touch with the *Ninth's* right. The *Twenty-first's* right was to rest on Ribemont, supported and covered by 2000 men under Hadow. As for the *Ninth's* left, it was to form liaison at the outskirts of Albert with Byng's 5th Corps, which, but for its ill-fortune, would have needed none of these FIFTH ARMY troops, nor the Australians and New Zealanders at the other end of its front.

Every detail helps to prove that at 2.15 a.m. on March 26 a retreat to and across the Ancre was the governing policy between Albert and the Somme. Hence rearguard actions must not prevent its fulfilment by becoming too "involved," as soldiers say. But a change of policy took place, and in many quarters it is attributed to a decision made by Foch at Doullens on March 26. In these quarters it is believed that Foch asked why the Bray-Albert line was to be held temporarily; that in his view it should be held with the utmost firmness. If this belief is accurate—and surely a Generalissimo has criticisms to offer—I assume that Foch expressed his judgment early in the afternoon, after much better news had come from Colincamps, Hébuterne, and Bucquoy; and certain it is that, shortly after three p.m., another policy was announced by telephone from Congreve's H.Q.

"Army orders that every effort must be made to check the enemy's advance by disputing ground. It is to be distinctly understood that no retirement is to take place unless the tactical situation imperatively demands it."

In the meantime many things had happened. Transport

ORIGIN OF THE CÉRISY EPISODE

had been moved to and across the Ancre, and big guns also; this movement had progressed very well. But the right of our line was in danger of being exposed, for troops in this part, under Brigadier Headlam, had about seven miles to march in retiring from Bray to Ribemont-sur-Ancre, while north of them the line ran westward till it was close to the river, with the result that the *Ninth* DIVISION'S small reserve was already behind the Ancre.

The southern troops at Bray were a composite brigade of the *Twenty-first,* and very overtired. On their left, across the plateau, were two brigades of the *Thirty-fifth,* and well behind them was the third brigade guarding Morlancourt. North-westward, covering Méaulte and Albert's southern flank, were troops of the *Ninth* DIVISION. Field artillery guarded the whole front, and well ahead of the line were outposts disposed in depth.*

If the northern part of this line went back too fast the southern would be left far in the south-east and exposed; so a retirement in echelon would begin from the Bray end, and the G.O.C. of the *Thirty-fifth* decided that it should begin at three p.m., if no attack developed, because a retreat after dark, with the business of crossing the river by long bridges, might get the right flank into very grave difficulties. The reserve brigade at Morlancourt would hold its position to cover the withdrawal, and then cross the river at Buire.

At three p.m., then, the retirement began from the right with the men disposed in depth, those nearest to Etinehem and Morlancourt being the first to move. It included the *Twenty-first* at Bray and the *Thirty-fifth* north-west of it. At the same time the G.O.C. received the new Army order—that the Bray-Albert line was to be held. Haig says: "By the time the withdrawal had been stopped, the right of the THIRD

* I have drawn a map to show these positions. The *First* CAVALRY was warned at seven p.m. of the 25th that, owing to events farther north, Congreve's Corps would fall back by night to the line Bray-Albert, and that the dismounted party of the *First* CAVALRY was to hold from Bécourt to Albert. So I placed them there in my map; but now I am doubtful whether any men of the *First* CAVALRY were able to reach the Bécourt sector. At 1.15 a.m. of the 26th, the Dismounted Brigade concentrated at Carnoy, covered by a rearguard, and at six a.m. it borrowed 40 G.S. waggons from the *Ninth* D.'s C.R.A. and went to Buire-sur-Somme. On arriving there at about seven o'clock they were ordered to return to Bussy-les-Daours. Later, at 10.15 a.m., the *First* CAVALRY was made responsible for the crossings over the Ancre south of Ribemont. In the south of the line they did excellent work, as by General Beale-Browne's Column, supported by the 1st and 2nd Cavalry Brigades, which till seven p.m. helped to hold the foe's advance on a line north and south through Morlancourt.

Army rested on the Somme about Sailly-le-Sec, while the FIFTH ARMY still held the south bank of the Somme north of Proyart, about five miles farther east." Therefore it was dangerously uncovered—and uncovered, too, in the irony of ill-fortune, by FIFTH ARMY troops who were reinforcing Byng's right.

Still, there was no "misunderstanding." Till three p.m. the THIRD ARMY'S policy as known to its right wing was a withdrawal to and behind the Ancre, with the Bray-Albert line for rearguard action. One obvious point in this policy was to place valuable equipment behind the river; another, to prevent the crossings from being blocked; and a third, not to be caught napping below Albert if the foe managed to go ahead through the gap in the THIRD ARMY'S centre. Why, then, should any one be blamed? For one reason only. When the uncertainty of war, combined with a change of order that arrives too late, produces a dangerous position, victims are demanded by irritable nerves near the spot and by nervous minds at a distance. In this case blame has fallen partly on the G.O.C. of the *Thirty-fifth*, who employed his judgment most carefully in obeying a THIRD ARMY order, and partly on his Corps Commander, who would have stopped the withdrawal had it been possible.

For the rest, civilians wonder (*a*) why the withdrawal could not be stopped and turned back, and (*b*) whether the *Thirty-fifth* DIVISION, having passed all right through the morning and its fighting, should have turned back to re-occupy the Albert-Bray line.

Troops of the *Thirty-fifth*, who had been continuously in very strenuous fighting since the 24th March, were now actually in motion in a movement of retreat based upon preceding orders received by their Commander. Does any reader, not acquainted with the conditions of war, conceive what it means in battle, to convey orders from a Division Commander through Brigade and Battalion Headquarters, down to companies and platoons in the firing line? It is a matter of hours, and many hours, before the order, which left Division Headquarters by motor cyclist, has filtered through till it reaches the Company Commander by a runner, who has possibly crawled for the last half mile under machine-gun fire. In some cases, it may never reach him at all.

Imagine the chaos which would be created by such a counter order upon troops in movement in a rearguard action along a front of four or five miles! Some units would

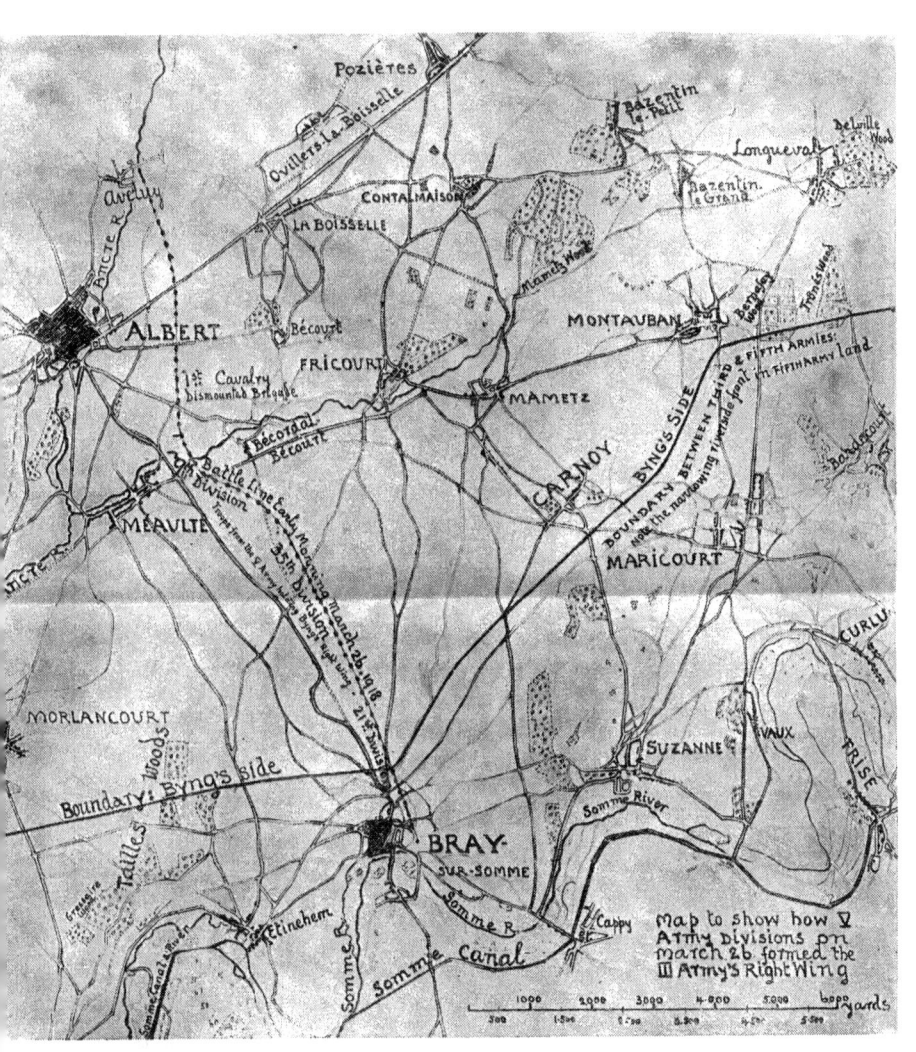

SHOWING HOW TROOPS FROM THE FIFTH ARMY ON MARCH 26 FORMED THE THIRD ARMY'S RIGHT WING ON BYNG'S TERRITORY

ORIGIN OF THE CÉRISY EPISODE

receive the order, perhaps, hours after others: Some would never receive it at all, because the runners had been shot: Some would be moving forward, others back; confusion and dismay would result in the most critical of all movements in war—a retirement in face of the enemy.

Such an order could not be circulated and acted upon, without disaster to the force engaged, till a stable line had been reached. Between the line Albert-Bray and the line to be held on the Ancre, no possibility existed of communicating this order to the troops in such a manner that it could be put into effect. It should, at least, have reached the Commander of the *Thirty-fifth* before 10 a.m., whereas, it reached him— and then only by telephone—shortly after 3 p.m. The counter-order was issued at least five hours too late, more probably even *seven hours too late*, for effective action. It was issued when the Commander, following his previous orders, could not act upon it without risking disaster to his division and the whole line. A break in the line at this point would have meant the loss of Amiens. After visiting the front, seeing the situation, and consulting his brigadiers, he decided that the counter order could not be acted upon without disastrous consequences. And his decision was justified next morning when the German attack was met and repulsed by a stable line, though he was no longer in command of it.

Moreover, the peril at Albert had not yet passed away.

Haig says, indeed: " During the night of March 26–27, the enemy had gained possession of Albert after some fighting with our rearguards in the town, and obtained a footing in Aveluy Wood." It is a fact, too, that alarming night rumours received by some men of the intrepid *Ninth* caused a slight panic in the neighbourhood of the Albert-Amiens road, which was allayed by Captain Darling of the Eleventh Royal Scots. Also a machine-gun which the foe had manœuvred into a position between the *Ninth's* posts did too much harm before it was put out of action by a local counter-attack.

And now apply these night facts to the retreat from Bray. As the foe had troops enough to take Albert after dark, the position at Bray would have been very dangerous if no withdrawal had taken place. Though the retirement from Bray was a very great peril to Gough's left south of the Somme, yet I cannot help believing that the peril might have been much greater if the withdrawal had begun from Bray after Albert fell. It would have been a pressed withdrawal, and

T

after midnight, probably, with our men depressed and the foe heartened. Even on March 27 the position at Albert and north of Albert was not altogether reassuring. Otto von Below captured Ayette and Ablainzevelle, north of Bucquoy, and Marwitz tried hard to debouch from Albert, happily without success. A brigade of the *Fourth* Australians was lent to our *Ninth* DIVISION, which needed support. As usual, the foe pushed forward snipers and light machine-guns, and as usual much worry was caused by those manœuvres.

As for the taproot causes of all the trouble, they were the 5th Corps' ill-luck and the breach in our THIRD ARMY'S centre, which remained open and very menacing from an hour unstated on March 24 till early in the afternoon of March 26. Historians will wish to know why it was not mended earlier with reinforcements. Australians are naturally proud that it was mended by one of their brigades at a time when further delay would have been far and away too hazardous.

CHAPTER IV

HOW OUR MEN WERE RELIEVED IN THEIR GRAPPLE AGAINST HUTIER

§ I

"FROM the time when the indications of an offensive on my front first became definite," says Haig, "I had been in close touch with the Commander-in-Chief of the French Armies. On different occasions, as the battle developed, I discussed with him the situation and the policy to be followed by the Allied Armies. As a result of a meeting held in the afternoon of March 23, arrangements were made for the French to take over as rapidly as possible the front held by the FIFTH ARMY, south of Péronne, and for the concentration of a strong force of French divisions on the southern portion of the battle front. . . ." *

When speaking of the fourth day, Haig says :—

"Though French troops were coming rapidly to the assistance of the 3rd Corps, which on this day passed under the command of the THIRD FRENCH ARMY, the Allied Forces were not yet in sufficient strength to hold up the enemy's advance." †

In these quotations the history is too official; and since the French are famed both for clarity of statement and for their firm grasp on matters essential to discussion and history, they are not at all likely to believe that cardinal matters should be deleted from British accounts of St. Quentin's Week. Better to pass an Act of Parliament to forbid all writing on the war than to be squeamish towards operative facts.

Our 3rd Corps—Butler's Corps—had 30,000 yards of land to guard, only 16,000 less than that which the whole of Byng's Army had to protect; and in comparison with the urgency of its needs from the first hour of battle, relief did

* Vol. ii., p. 198.   † Vol. ii., p. 202.

not, and could not in the circumstances, arrive rapidly. It came with all possible speed, but French divisions arrived here, and on the right of Maxse's front, without their equipment, both military and administrative. French Generals came with their keenness, but their troops had no guns and no more rifle cartridges than they carried; and for several days both they and the Allied defence were weakened by these grave hindrances. How then could the French do justice to their fine qualities? And I regret to add that one of the most reasonable of old military rules was broken by the manner in which, under orders, the French reinforcements gradually relieved our troops.

This old military rule concerns the use of reinforcements during a battle. First we have to see whether the French reinforcements were able to arrive quickly enough to do something more than balance our heavy casualties. By the end of March a French cavalry division and ten divisions of French infantry appeared in the fighting front, never at first as complete units, since it takes a longish time for the battalions of a division to be brought into action. These are all that I am able to find, and their value as reinforcements was very much lessened by the reinforcements which Hutier and Marwitz had added to their odds. In Hutier's reinforcements there were ten divisions. The French were enough to give the front sufficient stability for local fighting but not to justify counter-blows on an effective scale.* Here are the days during which they are mapped for the first time:—

Third Day—*First* FRENCH CAVALRY, and *Ninth, Hundred and Twenty-fifth* FRENCH INFANTRY. The last was in the battlefield at dawn; the others appear in the evening map.

Fourth Day—*Tenth, Sixty-second,* and elements of *Twenty-second.*

Fifth Day—*Hundred and Thirty-third.*

Sixth Day—*Thirty-fifth.*

Seventh Day—*Fifty-sixth, Hundred and Sixty-second,* and *Hundred and Sixty-sixth.*

As Hutier's advance stretched a widening flank south towards the Allied power, there is reason greatly to regret that the Allied reinforcements could not be powerful enough to strike such counter-blows as would have prevented Ludendorff from attacking at Armentières and the Lys. In these

* Haig says (vol. ii., p. 234) that, by the end of March, some ten German divisions were active against the French. Other French divisions arrived during the first week of April.

reinforcements, before April 9, were twelve British divisions, who were replaced in the north by divisions which had been reduced to skeletons by recent fighting, then hurriedly repaired with drafts brought over from England. Next, suddenly and urgently, disaster on the Lys made claims upon Foch and Haig, who hurried reserves north to the new battle. Could any set of circumstances have been more opposed to an effective use of reinforcements?

Yet I do not understand all the mingled uncertainty, scamper and improvisation that I meet with in the reinforcing. "It was evident," says General Monash, "that the plans of the Higher Command were the subject of rapid changes, in sympathy, probably, with fluctuations in the situation, which were not ascertainable by me." Yet no fluctuations ran counter to the plain lessons taught by the first day's fighting. Reinforcements all along the line both north and south of the Somme was the main lesson, for Byng had been obliged to employ, and therefore to tire, three of his reserve divisions. It seems very strange, then, that G.H.Q.'s reserves could not be handled at once with method and composure. Though Monash was warned on March 21 to prepare his division for a move, and to stand by in readiness to start at a few hours' notice, he was kept till the 25th in a state of uncertainty; and at last, at break of day on the 26th, after seeing that every one was correctly on the move, he started out by motor-car to the country behind Byng's area, in order to find the 10th Corps H.Q. They had moved from Hautcloque and also from Frevent, so in despair he went to Doullens, where he "tumbled into a scene of indescribable confusion. The population were preparing to evacuate the town *en masse*, and an exhausted and hungry soldiery was pouring into the town from the east and south-east, with excited tales that the German cavalry was on their heels. . . ." How was it that Monash and his troops, eager to be in battle since the 21st, were compelled to squander their energies through nearly six whole days? Why were they not sent at once to the Péronne bridgehead? And Maclagan's Division of Australians had a similar experience. On the 26th, says Monash, it "had already been on the move, by bus and route march, for three days without rest." On the move for three days—and not once in the battle!

Could it have been helped? No doubt the root causes were Haig's impoverished rifle strength, and the horrible losses which the French had suffered since 1914. What care in the making of pre-battle plans could prevent the act of reinforcing from becoming too much like feverish improvisation?

We have seen (p. 48) that one pre-battle plan arranged between Haig and Pétain was this: that if a dangerous attack fell on Gough's wide front the chief reserves would come from the French. But Pétain, having Reims, Champagne, and Paris very much in his mind, kept his reserves far back, and he could not or would not reinforce Gough's right till he was certain that Ludendorff's attack on Gough and Byng was the main German offensive.

Hence that slow arrival of Allied reserves which Ludendorff notices, and which causes him to believe that his preparations for attack were little known to the Allied Command. Ludendorff argues that if his foes had been aware of the vast concentration of German troops behind his lines, and had observed the hugely increased railway transport which had been going on, "the Entente's defensive measures would have been more effective, and its reserves would have arrived more quickly."

Further, when we consider the arrangements made between Haig and Pétain, two matters more enter this debate:

1. Was it a good thing in March, 1918, that nearly all the French reinforcements were sent to Gough's front south of the Somme, while nearly all the British went north of the Somme to Byng?

2. How should reinforcements be used on a stricken field? Is it their business to do no more than reinforce till they are well enough equipped to take over the fighting front? Or should authority *outside* the battle place them in a position of command over the officers and men who have been in battle from the start and whose local and general knowledge must needs be fuller and better?

These are test questions; and now that the tremendous events of March, 1918, are passing from phrases into facts, from propaganda into truth, no harm can be done if we study them with temperate frankness.

Let us look for the correct answer to the first question: "Was it a good thing that nearly all the French reinforcements were sent to Gough's front south of the Somme, while nearly all of the British went north of the Somme to Byng?"

§ II

If we put this question in another form we shall draw closer to its main issues. Was it wise to mingle too many

French troops on one front with our own men when the swirl and fever of a retreat were gathering to a very hazardous climax? If not wise, was it inevitable? The answer to this question is the answer to another—namely, for what reasons, and by whose advice, were far too many troops detained in the British Isles?

Sir F. Maurice says, in his monograph on "The Last Four Months," page 54: "Had the Government taken in time the measures which it had been urged to take, the reduction of two cavalry divisions and of more than one hundred infantry battalions might have been avoided, and both Gough and Byng might have had sufficient men to have enabled them to hold their battle positions against all attacks, while Haig's reserve might have been increased by at least two divisions."

When Mr. Lloyd George spoke at Leeds, on December 7, 1918, he said, among other memorable things, "I need not tell you about March 21, how, when the great crisis came, men were hurried across the Channel." Need not tell us, indeed! Are we to forget Hamlet and King Lear when we think of their tragedies? Haig's want of enough men for his front of 125 miles was the taproot cause of all our tragic troubles. According to official figures published in the *Times* (on January 2, 1920), our combatant strength in France on March 11, 1918, was 1,293,000, including a rifle strength of 616,000; and on April 1, it was only 1,131,124, including a rifle strength of 528,617. Between these dates, then, we lost 161,876 in combatant strength, including 87,383 infantry.

These official figures do not say whether the losses include men on leave as well as battle casualties; but Ludendorff in his book states that his armies in March took "some 90,000 unwounded prisoners," including the French. Further, are we to believe that the official figures, as published in the *Times*, were checked and approved by G.H.Q.? In days of propaganda, and of Government offices with publicity departments, we cannot be too cautious. Is it a fact, then, that on March 11, 1918, Haig's 58 divisions had a rifle-strength of 616,000 men? Certainly not! The figures mean that every one of the 58 divisions had a few more than 10,600 riflemen. Mere camouflage! Even the *Ninth* DIVISION, comparatively a well-manned unit, had no more than 8834 riflemen, including pioneers and details. But the official figures, though propagandist, throw some light both on Haig's weak numbers and also on his losses.

Yet the Prime Minister, when speaking more than five

months after the battle, did not think it worth while to say why abundant reinforcements were kept in the British Isles till a terrific attack, long foreseen, had caused a great crisis, with a lamentable appeal for succour to President Wilson (see p. 309). If Haig had been given resources enough for his known responsibilities, there would have been no reason to strike that bargain with Pétain which caused a sudden mingling of French and British troops, with sudden changes of command and much confusion. And is it not common knowledge that differing fighting temperaments among nations, with their different methods, customs, traditions, do not mingle together on a battle front? They come from distinguishing traits in racial character—great and enduring qualities which are changed only by slow and gradual evolution. Even when they are trained together by the same drill and firm discipline, the heat and stress of battle are likely to separate them; and when they have *not* been trained together, how can we reasonably expect them to coalesce merely because they are suddenly thrown together during a perilous retreat?

As every one knows, a British brigade and a French one, so unlike temperamentally and in fighting method, never wish to fight alongside each other, mixed up. Indeed, each believes that it is let down by the other; both are certain that they support each other best when they have spheres of their own in the battle front.

It is to be regretted, then, that the FIFTH ARMY owed most of its relief to the French, whose reserves could not come up swiftly enough to act as a genuine relieving force, strong enough on the fourth or fifth day to take command without "swopping horses in midstream."

§ III

When President Lincoln refused to swop horses while crossing a stream, he employed in a great war the virtue of humorous good sense; not by any means an easy gift to display when the fever of battle circulates from brain to brain, magnifying both good and bad so much that few persons see any event, as a whole, in focus and perspective. Lincoln's maxim is good sense in all dangerous times, but above all, when the stream is a river in spate, and both horses are off their feet and trying to swim as corks do. Yet Gough and his officers and men were set to swop horses, several times, in a river boiling towards rapids, when contrary currents were pressing in full flood against the horses.

French troops without their artillery and other essential things, though operating on ground for which British commanders had every reason to feel responsible, were not placed under British orders; it was our troops who were placed under French orders and in a disjointed manner to be studied as a warning by every one of us. Owing to these frequent changes of command, unity of control was impossible. Sometimes the French issued orders direct to British subordinate units, without informing their British Commanders.

Can any one believe that either Marlborough or Wellington, in the middle of an enormous battle, would have sanctioned these changes of command, which seemed to imply bluntly that British national pride did not exist, that British officers and troops were inferior to the French, and that the French would have been humiliated if their reinforcements had obeyed British orders until they took over the fighting front?

There are those who say that most Frenchmen outside the battle looked upon Gough as a beaten General, under whom their troops could not serve until his men were relieved and withdrawn. If this opinion did come into vogue *outside* the battle—and many wild opinions were circulated—it would have been corrected by a frank official statement giving the perilous number of Gough's infantry when the battle began; and certainly no French soldier *inside* the battle could have been blind to our FIFTH ARMY's greatness, since its remnant divisions—as battle-maps proved every day—never retreated more rapidly than their French Allies. Both French and British were assailed by a force which compelled them to choose between bending and breaking; and why should any one have supposed that a confusion in command would be useful? Surely a sudden change of treatment during a great battle, as in a critical illness, however right in principle, becomes dangerous in practice when it is applied inaptly at an unfitting time? Consider also the part played in battle by national feelings and qualities. Let us take an illustration.

If Blücher had arrived at three o'clock in the afternoon of Waterloo, he and his men would have come under Wellington, not Wellington under Blücher; and this would have been essential, quite aside from any question of military preeminence. For mankind's gifts of the spirit are abnormally sensitive to all influences, good and bad, during the heat and stress of a great battle. Every British soldier on the field of Waterloo was so proud of being under Wellington that his whole nature was Wellingtonized; and this general feeling of proud loyalty to the Chief was accompanied by regimental attachment of men to their officers, Picton's men to Picton, for example, and Colborne's to Colborne. Imagine, then, what the shock would have been to officers and men alike if Blücher had arrived at three in the afternoon and had taken command of the British infantry and of Wellington also.

And now apply this war psychology—that is, this knowledge of the human mind and spirit in soldiers, one by one, and in divisions united into an army—to Gough and his officers and men. If any depleted divisions ever had reason to be proud of their leaders, they were those who baffled Hutier and Marwitz when Marwitz and Hutier were at their strongest. They fought with intense British pride against Germans; they knew that the undermanning was no fault of their Army's H.Q.; and from day to day their fraying frayed line stretched more and more, as when Maxse on the fourth day aided Watts along about three thousand yards of front. And then all at once, and bit by bit, they were taken from their own officers and placed under the control of French reinforcements, whose artillery and other needs were on the road, far off. Was this fair to their natural desire to fight on under British control till they were withdrawn from their ordeal? Would French troops in the Verdun campaign have been willing to pass all at once from their own Generals to be controlled by British reinforcements? I hope not, for the most valuable thing in war is national pride among good soldiers.

One of the most distinguished of Gough's officers has written as follows:—

"Although the British formations were placed under various French general officers for the purpose of fighting the enemy, these French generals (through no fault of their own) were at first unable to exercise command in the field, either over their own or over our troops. They had been sent up in a great hurry . . . without their staffs, without telephones and dispatch riders, without artillery and without any small arm ammunition beyond the eighty rounds carried on the men. They were short of transport and short of machine-guns; and this state of things lasted during several days.

"These difficulties were valiantly contended with, but

were a hindrance to handling troops effectively in contact with a vigilant enemy. Good comradeship got over the difficulty of language and the difficulty of understanding foreign methods, but could not overcome the difficulty of obeying the contradictory French orders which reached our units in quick succession.

"It thus transpired that our subordinate formations were compelled to look to their own Corps for tactical instructions as well as for administrative services, and the Corps Staff thus became engaged in reconciling French orders and French wishes with what was practicable at the moment. This was done as tactfully as possible, but with a firm intention of not permitting the enemy to penetrate any gap inside the FIFTH BRITISH ARMY.

"The French retired south-westward from Roye at the start. Our line of retreat lay due west. If we had implicitly obeyed the French orders we received there would have been a gap of at least ten miles between Montdidier and Beaucourt. The French Generals on the spot at the time recognized this situation, and there was never any friction between us; but it should be placed on record that a ten-mile gap was avoided only by the firmness of purpose displayed by General Sir Hubert Gough, commanding the FIFTH ARMY. In fact, we held the gap in defiance of orders from superior French Generals who were unacquainted with the local situation. . . ."

Let these matters be viewed frankly and temperately, side by side with a sound military rule which says that reinforcements ought to do no more than reinforce till they are properly equipped to take over the fighting front. Till then, they should be governed by the army whose strength they restore.

Now and then sound principles in war have an application governed by differing circumstances, and there are critics who believe that the transfer of our 3rd Corps on the fourth day to the THIRD FRENCH ARMY may have been useful, partly because the most southern division—the *Fifty-eighth*—had become detached in French territory,* and partly because Butler's line of retreat was towards the Noyon region, which the

* This division, the *Fifty-eighth*, passed under French control earlier in the battle, and thus before the fourth day. On the evening of March 22, at ten o'clock, our *Eighteenth* DIVISION received information that the *Fifty-eighth* had passed under command of the French, whose *Hundred and Twenty-fifth* DIVISION was moving up to regain the Crozat Canal line about Vouel and Tergnier. The *Eighteenth* was asked to co-operate. This evidence seems to show that as soon as a gunless French division was hurried breathlessly into action, it was put in command over a British division, whose right at Barisis had not been attacked, and whose left had fought magnificently.

French were particularly eager to guard. On the other hand, not all units of our 3rd Corps had come naturally into touch with a French command. Both cavalry and infantry were doing all that was possible under their own officers; and how is any one to believe that these British officers did not know more about current events and needs, both local and general, than the French officers who arrived in great haste?

As for the 18th Corps, in its case there should be no doubt at all. It bore with success the brunt of Hutier's attack. Why, then, was it not permitted to fight entirely under its own Army's control till its units were withdrawn? Why impose on British troops a subordination to French reinforcements which may be regarded by them as a political panic coming from outside the fighting or as censure passed publicly on themselves and their officers? In these matters I feel as an Englishman who has always been greatly moved by British battles, and who is certain that a great nation's just pride of self-respect is a natural element of greatness which should be treasured.

§ IV

At first the French troops associated with our 18th Corps took line along the Libermont Canal from Quiquery to Libermont. Four companies of French infantry reinforced the right of the *Twentieth;* then this British unit—to which, after the crossing of the Somme, remains of the *Sixty-first* were attached—passed for a time under the French commander, whose men belonged to the 2nd French Cavalry Corps, General Robilot.

In the evening of March 24, Gough and Robilot discussed a combined attack on the foe north-west of Nesle, to drive him back over the Somme along the Bethencourt sector. An extensive plan was debated and arranged. By night the French *Twenty-second* was to man the line Rouy le Grand-Mesnil St. Nicaise, in order to attack in a north-eastern direction, while the *Eighth* British, under Heneker, was to co-operate by thrusting south-east. And the British *Twenty-fourth*, brought forward from its position in reserve, was to advance due east, assailing with all its might; and these combined movements were to be set in action at 8 a.m. on the morning of the fifth day. A barrage table was timed, and our officers and men made all necessary preparations.

When dawn came the French were not in position; they

asked for a postponement of three hours. Three hours went by; no change in the situation occurred; and then it became known that General Robilot had issued no definite orders because he regarded the whole scheme as a "project" only, a fight in an isle of dreams. It is quite easy for men to view a piece of business differently when they speak different languages, and when reinforcements do not belong to an Army Commander's direction.

But misunderstandings have results, not often welcome. A German thrust advanced through Nesle, and the French *Twenty-second* was driven back south-west a considerable distance towards Roye. By noon, moreover, some three or four miles north of Nesle, heavy German columns of attack debouched from Morchain and pushed the right of Watts's Corps through Licourt and Pertain. By evening Watts was being attacked on the railway line from Omiécourt north-east to the Somme, but his troops held their own, retaining also the bridges of St. Christ and Brie. Then two pieces of bad news had to be weighed and measured. In the south German pressure was closing upon Noyon, and in the north Byng's right was to retire by night to the Bray-Albert line, uncovering about six miles of Gough's flank and rear. So Gough ordered Watts to withdraw to a new line in order to ease as much as he could the northern menace, while Maxse remained face to face with awkward matters, his troops and the *Twenty-second* French holding a line approximately as follows—Beaulieu, Liancourt, Fouches.

Next day, March 26, the official policy which, on March 25, placed the French in general control south of the Somme, made matters worse. The British *Thirty-sixth* was relieved for a spell of rest by the French *Sixty-second*, and passed under French orders. Williams also * was placed

* Williams = our *Thirtieth* DIVISION. It would be difficult to speak too highly of this unit, which began the battle with about 5600 rifles. A brief summary of its doings runs thus: On March 21 Williams's men lost their forward zone, after a very tough resistance from the Sixteenth Manchesters and the Second Wiltshires. In the evening of the second day they were forced out of their battle zone: they in this case being the Second Yorks, the Seventeenth Manchesters, Second Bedfords, and Second Royal Scots Fusiliers. One brigade was in Corps Reserve. They withdrew to Ham. Here on the morning of March 24 they were pressed back, but slowly, and only as far as Libermont Canal, five or six miles west of Ham; and this line they held till the evening of the 25th, when they were relieved by French troops. Libermont Canal was the farthest point to which they were driven back. On the 26th, in the morning, they took up another line, Bouchoir-Rouvroy, and held it firmly until French troops relieved them at 1.30 p.m. on the 28th. Then they got a night's rest—the first one since the battle began at dawn on March 21.

under the French *Sixty-second*, and the only troops now remaining technically under Maxse, their Corps Commander, were the *Twentieth* (now returned to him from a French Commander) and the remains of Colin Mackenzie's Division. Then at five in the afternoon Maxse was placed under General Humbert, THIRD FRENCH ARMY; and a few hours later our troops knew that the FIFTH ARMY as a whole had passed under French control, though the confusion caused by the local subordination of our own troops to French reinforcements had not yet been resolved into order.

Indeed, it was early on the sixth day that two French divisions, the *Twenty-second* and *Sixty-second*, when withdrawing south-west towards the valley of the Avre, took with them Nugent's Ulstermen, the *Thirty-sixth*, and nearly all of the 18th Corps artillery, both field-guns and heavies; and through the rest of this day and the greater part of March 27, our troops had to hold up the foe's advance unaided by artillery support—not an easy thing to do, for although the attack on these days was weak in gunfire, it had enterprise in several places.

Gough personally asked the French Commander, General Humbert, to return the field-guns, if circumstances at present detained the heavies; and this was promised for the next day. Meanwhile orders were given to defend to the last all roads and bridges, and to check the advance while more French troops were being detrained at Montdidier and elsewhere.

At four in the afternoon our 18th Corps received a French order sent through Gough's H.Q. In this order Maxse and Watts were told that they must maintain at all costs the line Guerbigny-Erches - Bouchoir - Rouvroy-Rosières - Proyart—to the Somme. French troops were in movement to relieve them along this line.

But in a wide stretching retreat it is an easy matter at a distance with a good map before you to fix on a strong line and to issue firm orders, while generals on the spot are striving here and there to learn precisely where the foe is and where their own men are. On the morning of March 27, for example, a few local situations were so obscure that some small hitches occurred both to ourselves and to the Germans. In the neighbourhood of Bouchoir some German transport

---

Next day the French withdrew, and many persons said—and have continued to say—that Williams and his men retired. The habit of blaming our FIFTH ARMY has invented many myths.

HOW OUR MEN WERE RELIEVED

rambled inadvertently through our lines and was captured. It belonged to the 55th German Foot Artillery, and had in it two loaded ammunition waggons, a watercart with two machine-guns, a cooker full of soup, good or bad, and six men fit to be prisoners. Again, early in the morning the G.S.O.1. of our *Thirty-sixth*, wishing to clear up the situation on his front, started in a car, ran into a party of Germans, and was captured. Later the car was found by one of our ambulance motors and brought in.

For the rest, during the morning of this seventh day it became known that the *Fifty-sixth* French would relieve Nugent's Ulstermen at once; that in the evening the *Hundred and Thirty-third* French would replace Williams, and that General Mesple, of the French Army, would take command over Maxse's front. Of course, these British divisions, and the others, were remnants only, glorious shreds and patches; but yet, after their seven days and six nights of incessant overstrain, somehow their stamina was fit for other adventures, as there was work elsewhere for them to do. What rest could there be? What but violence can be done to the bravest of the brave when an army enters battle very short of men, through no fault of its own? Early on the 28th, when Maxse handed over the command to Mesple's 4th French Corps, the *Twentieth* was still holding Hutier astride the Roye-Amiens road near Le Quesnel; the *Thirtieth* and *Thirty-Sixth*, after being relieved, were to remain with the French as long as they were required; while Mackenzie's men had gone north to help Watts at Villers Bretonneux.

Colin Mackenzie's troops had twelve days of continuous fighting, with a night shift in 'buses from one Corps to another. Their ranks became tragically thin, of course, and so tired that really they seemed to be stricken with locomotor ataxy; but not a sign of defeat was to be seen in any face. Continuously, since August 27, 1917, they had been in line, apart from a few short periods in trains or on the roads, when moving from one part of the line to another.

As a nation we are very fond of talking about high thoughts and right feelings; sometimes our virtue is confident enough almost to imply that our British shoulder-blades are adorned with angels' wings brisk for flight; but do we really cheat ourselves into the belief that we have a moral right not only to keep a division in line for seven whole months, but also to let it fight afterwards through twelve days and eleven nights ? Here is one lesson to be learnt from the immense battle against Hutier. It teaches us to know the difference between reasonable warfare and cruelty to our own soldiers, who represent our country's manhood at its very best.

CHAPTER V

UNITY OF COMMAND

"ON this day, the 26th March," says the official dispatch, "the Governments of France and Great Britain decided to place the supreme control of the operations of the French and British forces in France and Belgium in the hands of General Foch, who accordingly assumed control."

I wish this quotation said a great deal more. Why should it keep Democracy in the dark concerning many things? At the very moment when Mr. Lloyd George was appealing to President Wilson for succour, to be brought over in ships withdrawn from our essential industries (p. 309), General Foch received his new honour, yet American troops were not placed under his control! Why announce a swift change of policy before it was fit to be true Unity of Command? And who would not be glad to know also for what reason British politicians approved this policy in the middle of an enormous battle, when two British armies were retreating on French soil? Why were they so poor in spirit? With much self-congratulation they told the world that British arms needed at once a French head. Not a moment more must be lost! So our politicians talked to Dora, and Dora inspired the Press by means of confidential fervour enclosed within two envelopes, and soon a great flinging-up of caps was a journalistic exercise all day long.

Our descendants will prefer that high story of Nelson, who as a young man was in the Mediterranean with a squadron too small for big dangers, which at any moment might appear along the offing in French white sails. Its sailors were uneasy, so they cheered with relief when a Neapolitan battleship sailed up under full canvas to reinforce the British weakness. Nelson was hurt and angry, because he knew that his country had no right to sink into debt from the duty of being self-dependent. The greater the nation the less she can afford to owe overmuch to her partners—above all, to new co-belligerents. What would Nelson have said to a Prime Minister who, while British soldiers were retreating, and when the world hummed with false accusations brought against a British army, chose a Generalissimo from one Ally and begged for armed succour from another?

Mr. Lloyd George has had a reputation as bright as bubbles are, and it is bursting like bubbles. A thousand pities; for he had fine instinctive ideas as well as matchless energy; but the most recent plausible talk from his trusted associates deflected his right intuitions as a compass is deflected by a magnet. He desired unity of command, only to find that racial susceptibilities were as active in Allied warfare as they were and are in any other emulation. Different schools of opinion, both in our own country and in France, viewed unity of command variously and opposingly. What Mr. Asquith says to-day about unity of command is not of a piece with two or three other British beliefs or convictions; and if you tried to sum up briefly what was said on this great matter by the rival followers of Foch and Pétain, and Nivelle, you would find that your epitome would be discordant. Yes, and German autocracy discovered also that unity of command was an ideal almost as elusive as a mirage. German backbones did not offend Bulgaria and Austria-Hungary, but German orders all along the line were hated as a policy of pinpricks. Ludendorff had to mind his P's and Q's.

All good and necessary things are unpeaceful, they divide us into rival sects, into squabbling schools; but the main point to be considered here is not the selection of a Generalissimo, it is the policy of taking this action suddenly, hurriedly, feverishly, while the whole world talked about two British armies in retreat across French soil, talked without knowledge of governing facts, and seldom in a tone at all good for Britain's fame abroad and dignity at home. Also, while this talk continued, the War Office and the War Cabinet made no effort at all to contradict it; their silence was a foe to our troops, and also an injustice which historians will never condone.

But officialism says: "The appointment of a Generalissimo was made imperative by the immediate danger of the separation of the French and British Armies." But this danger was not a new thing; it existed as a darkening menace before the battle began. Further, the main thing to be considered is not the appointment itself, but the act of announcing

UNITY OF COMMAND

it at a most inopportune time and without correcting the vile slanders on British troops.

As a rule the manner of doing big things is as important as are the things to be done; and to do a right thing at a wrong time is often neither less foolish nor less harmful than to neglect doing a right thing at the right moment. The appointment of Foch, abrupt and untimely, was hated by those who had not been camouflaged out of their British dignity and self-respect. A London artisan, with three sons at the front, put this natural feeling in picturesque words. "Let's us down sharp, doesn't it?" he said to me. "And what a smack in the eye for Haig, and a knock-out for Gough and Byng! Yes. Yet the noospapers are all a-bubble with their old eye-wash!" ... "All a-bubble with their old eye-wash!" I like this mocking, scornful phrasing. Isn't it good enough to be spoken by a Shakespearean character?

Slighted patriotism speaks plainly; but statesmen are so drugged by atmospheres unlike those of the world outside diplomacy that they are overapt to be foes to inborn sensitiveness. Too often Allied Councils were a tiresome orchestra in which France held the conductor's baton, while the British Empire played second fiddle, as if she were not the Allies' composer and financier.

And was it fair to Foch himself thus to give him control —hurriedly, feverishly, in the midst of a British retreat— over all British forces in France and Belgium, while journalists with stock phrases tried to lift their readers into high expectations?

Was it supposed that he could gather all at once into his hands, as by a miracle, the many strings of military government, British, Belgian, French, which were necessary to the free successful use of his great gifts? If this impossible achievement were not expected, what useful purpose could be served at once by advertising a decision which seemed to a great many persons nothing less than a plain act of censure passed on our own Generals and troops during a British retreat on French soil?

What if the Governments of France and Great Britain *did* expect Foch all at once to improvize victory? If so, they ran the grave risk of undermining from the start what their Generalissimo needed most of all—Allied confidence. For it happened in the ironical mischances of war that Foch began his reign with three defeats—defeats bad enough to have caused among the French a desire to displace Foch by Pétain. One defeat was at Armentières, Kemmel Hill, and in the Lys Valley; * another, far bigger and more humiliating, was the swift German onrush over the Chemin des Dames and thence to the Marne, with leverage pressure west and south-west of Soissons; while the third is described by Ludendorff as the battle of Noyon, which began on June 9, and strengthened the long German flank between Montdidier and Noyon.

When these matters are weighed and measured, I am certain that it would have been much fairer to Foch, and much fairer also, of course, to our national pedigree and just pride, if the act of appointing a French Generalissimo had been deferred till the retreat had ended, and till Mr. Lloyd George had explained frankly that Gough, through no fault of his own, began the battle perilously short of men; had received reinforcements with a slowness which could not be avoided; and yet had baffled the immense efforts of Hutier and Marwitz, winning time both for the arrival of piecemeal relief and for the incoming of U.S.A. troops.

To my mind this unhurried and truthful policy would have been not only the better one, but also the very best. There would have been in it no symptoms of nerves far *outside* the battle, nerves among statesmen, and its truth would have contradicted false rumours and debasing calumnies, very painful and unjust to the stricken army which had done so much against "a world of odds," to use Shakespeare's phrase correctly.

But although this policy appeals to me as evidently the best, I am not unmindful of the jostling circumstances which ran counter to it, in political circles mainly, but not entirely, as British Generalship had rival creeds and sects.

* Between Foch's appointment as Generalissimo and the opening of the Lys battle there were fourteen days. Hence it has been unfair to put all the blame on Haig, who had no real reserves—no spare troops to meet the dangers of a vast emergency.

CHAPTER VI

THE TROUBLES OF MINISTERS

§ I

NO stroke of national misfortune could have been worse than the fact that the greatest danger to our armies in France had grown under Lloyd George's coalition, not under that of Asquith and Bonar Law. In 1916, just before Asquith fell, Germany's condition became desperate, as Ludendorff has confessed. Yet she made a swift recovery, and then brought us to the very brink of ruin.

He who had spoken most eloquently against Too Late had to reap a dire crop of evils from the same old peril. What was to be done? Would Ministers admit their errors of judgment, or would they pass into scapegoat hunting, the last resort of unnerved statesmanship? Would they employ the hoaxing rhetoric called either camouflage or propaganda, while unloading their mistakes on good soldiers? Political human nature is not improved by crisis, and so critical was the situation that clear reasoning and right action must have been extremely difficult. Though Ministers had failed tragically their fall from office would have caused harmful political disorder; and yet their fall might have been brought about by the people if the true causes of the retreat had been admitted. Action and reaction being equal and opposite, we must remember that Ministers had allowed the newspaper Press—the *Morning Post* was an exception—to encourage over-confidence while Ludendorff was preparing his offensive.

So much was published about our airmen's ascendancy over their opponents that a great many persons regarded a German attack as a folly to be smashed up by our airplanes; and a fortnight before the foe struck Mr. Bonar Law affirmed that "there would be no dangerous superiority on the Western front from the point of view of guns any more than from the point of view of men." Yes, and he was "still a little sceptical" about the foe's threatened offensive!

There is a wide difference between Ration Strength and Combatant Strength, and Mr. Bonar Law may have meant that the total Allied ration strength on the Western front was larger than the combatant strength which Ludendorff would employ. In any case we have learnt from Haig that Ludendorff on the first day employed "at least sixty-four German divisions . . . a number considerably exceeding the total forces composing the entire British Army in France." As Ludendorff assailed fifty-four miles of our front, which in all was one hundred and twenty-five miles wide, the words put into circulation by Mr. Bonar Law were very indiscreet, being not at all fit to brace his countrymen for an uncertain ordeal or to aid his Government if our troops were obliged to bend much in order to avoid breaking.

What military adviser gave this excessive confidence to Mr. Bonar Law? The C.I.G.S.? Or did Mr. Bonar Law collect his over-confidence at first hand from his own hopes? In France, too, the same wild excess of hope was active. Many a simple person prayed that Ludendorff would strike—to receive at once a fitting punishment of defeat.

Then, of course, as soon as the crisis came, feeling in France—a natural feeling of mordant anxiety mingled with irritation and swift unreasoning criticism—made the position of statesmen, both French and British, as delicate as it was perilous. Even details of the retreat, and notably the destruction of French bridges and railways, represented an immense loss, both present and future; and as a gun from seventy-five miles dropped shells on Paris, much civilian panic was added to political distress and fear. Many will recall to memory a touching speech on this crisis made by M. Clemenceau at Amiens, in July, 1919. The worst moments in the Second Battle of the Somme were recalled:—

"If the Germans took Amiens, what would be the consequences? This question was discussed at Abbeville, and we asked whether it was better to try to hold up the advance on Paris or to prevent the Germans from reaching the sea. Two points of view were urged by men of equal weight and authority. When I recall these hours I experience again one of the greatest emotions a man can feel. We were playing a hand on which hung the fate of the Fatherland."

But although it is easy to keep heartily in touch with all French anxieties, the crisis in France was much more than a

French one; it was an Allied crisis which pressed as heavily on British prospects as on French freedom. Surely, then, neither words nor acts should have been made of some consolation to the French unless they were at the same time amply fair both to our national dignity and to our officers and men.

§ II

Unluckily, this cardinal aspect of the crisis was passed over almost without attention. Defaming rumours were permitted to circulate; shortly after the battle a deplorable speech was made by Mr. Lloyd George to the House of Commons, a speech which he has not yet corrected, though its errors were notable from the very moment they were uttered; and while the Prime Minister was proving again that his *forte* runs counter to an exact use of facts in a sequence, a strange experience came to one of our war correspondents, Mr. Hamilton Fyfe, who desired to tell the truth, only to find that Authority at the front would not let him, though vile slanders were passing from random gossip into printed innuendoes.

Already I have given a part of Mr. Fyfe's experiences (p. 5), and now let us see what he says concerning the causes which made the people so easy to mislead. The public acceptance of a false view is to be attributed, he believes:—

"1. To the refusal of the public to believe anything written by war correspondents, a refusal for which I do not blame the public, considering how often they had been deceived before they realized the conditions under which war correspondents worked.

"2. To the loose and exaggerated accounts of the retreat given by wounded men of the units which went to the relief of the FIFTH ARMY.

"3. To the statement made in the House of Commons by the Prime Minister, with incomplete knowledge and misunderstanding of important facts.

"4. To the treatment of General Gough . . . who was deprived of his command without court-martial or inquiry. . . ."

Note, too, what was being said in France:—

"About the retreat, and especially the FIFTH ARMY part in it, many absurd stories were afloat. What was particularly unfortunate was that American soldiers arriving in France were apt to be told that British troops became a disorderly rabble, that officers lost their heads, that men wandered like sheep without a shepherd, and that their unworthy conduct caused a grave set-back to the Allied Cause. Such stories were, I dare say, set agoing, many of them, by spies and traitors, very likely by paid German agents. They were repeated by habitual grumblers, by those who like to 'seem to know,' and even by many who passed on this kind of talk merely because they had nothing better to say. One story which was widely told represented General Gough as having dined in London * on the night of March 21!"

In the large aspects of truth there was nothing obscure. As Mr. Fyfe says:—

"The Germans had so many divisions that they could take them out of the line as soon as they were tired and let them recover. Our men had no intervals. They were on their feet day and night. When they were not fighting, they were falling back or hastily improving old defensive positions. They grew so heavy-headed from want of sleep that officers had to go round shaking them to keep them awake. Numbers of them fell by the roadside and slept from exhaustion. This largely swelled the numbers of prisoners taken by the enemy. Yet throughout the six [eight] days of battle there was nothing approaching a rout or a panic, there was no disorder on the roads. I have seen other retreats with these features. In this retreat there was hardly so much as disorganization on any large scale . . . From hunger few suffered, thanks to the devotion and steadiness of the Army Service Corps, and to the regularity of the regimental arrangements for distributing rations. But what they suffered from weariness no one can imagine. Yet they kept their faces towards the foe. They never let him get through. Thus they spoiled his plan . . ." †

And let us note also how the Germans in some of their newspapers admitted that their strategic plan had miscarried. On March 26, for instance, the *Frankfort Gazette* said bluntly:

---

* Didn't gossip say Paris also, and on the same evening? Two magical dinners eaten on the same evening in places far apart!

† Hamilton Fyfe, *Contemporary Review*, January, 1919. Mr. Fyfe might have added with truth that much nonsense was circulated by the natural vanity of reserves who arrived suddenly, and who knew nothing of what the men in line had suffered since March 21. Even General Monash was moved by this vanity, and magnified very much the work done by the Australians, who did not enter the battle till the Germans were nearing the end of their physical strength.

"A real advance has been checked by the foe's obstinate defence. As long as our enemy is able to occupy chosen positions and to mend breaches in his dam with reserves, operative movements are impossible."

Ludendorff himself gave warnings to German correspondents. The British fought tenaciously, he said, and concealed their machine-guns with great skill; it had been necessary to begin the battle with many German divisions who were still fatigued by their night marches to the battlefield; and forward movements were arduous. "Railways are torn up," he said, "and our horses are jaded, but every effort will be made to keep up the speed now active at the front." According to Herr Scheuermann, of the Berlin *Tageszeitung*, Ludendorff made another remark: "A great battle has been fought, a victory gained: but nobody can tell what the result of it will be." If these words were given correctly by Scheuermann, Ludendorff at once described the battle accurately. His words admit that he has been baffled in the big strategic aspects of his plans.

But other things must be kept before our minds, and among them is the shifty self-help which clings around party politics. Beaconsfield described politics as "a stinking profession"; but after all, this candour is too blunt, it provokes reprisals; and my aim is to be fair, and to make due allowance for the terrible fix into which Ministers and their advisers drifted.

A few days after the battle ended Colonel Repington summed up the case in the *Morning Post*. His first paragraph said:—

"I notice that the Government Press is doing its best to unload the responsibilities of its masters upon the soldiers, and especially to blame our Command in France and our FIFTH ARMY for the success of the German attack on March 21 and subsequent days. The War Office permit these insinuations and innuendoes to be published broadcast without reply, and therefore I am entitled to defend my old campaigning comrades and to establish the facts."

Of course, this behaviour of the Government Press was odious; and much later—on October 21, 1918, when at last Haig's dispatch was published *—journalists on the Government side were a great deal too reticent, as though an awful battle's horrible effects on young lives were of less importance

* It is dated July 20.

than was the act of trying to hide the big mistakes made by our Ministers and their advisers.

In several passages the dispatch appeals to me as perhaps the most notable indictment of British Ministers ever written by a British Commander-in-Chief. Some parts of it were deleted by the Government; but that Haig himself still regards the omitted parts as useful, if not necessary, to his argument, is proved by the fact that they are marked by stars (* * * *) in the republished dispatch, as you will see by turning to pages 177, 178, and 179. These cuts are all in that portion of the dispatch which Mr. Lloyd George regarded as a reflection on himself and his Cabinet.

Here are a few quotations collected from the dispatch as published :—

"The broad facts of the change which took place in the general war situation at the close of 1917, and the causes which led to it, have long been well known and need be referred to but shortly.

"The disappearance of Russia as a belligerent country on the side of the Entente Powers had set free the great bulk of the German and Austrian divisions on the Eastern Front. Already at the beginning of November, 1917, the transfer of German divisions from the Russian to the Western front had begun. It became certain [by the middle of February, 1918] that the movement would be continued steadily until numerical superiority lay with the enemy. . . ." *

"In three and a half months twenty-eight infantry divisions had been transferred from the Eastern theatre and six infantry divisions from the Italian theatre. There were reports that further reinforcements were on their way to the West, and it was also known that the enemy had greatly increased his heavy artillery in the Western theatre during the same period. These reinforcements were more than were necessary for defence, and, as they were moved at a time when the distribution of food and fuel to the civil population in Germany was rendered extremely difficult through lack of rolling stock, I concluded that the enemy intended to attack at an early date. . . .

"By the 21st March the number of German infantry divisions in the Western theatre had risen to 192, an increase of 46 since November 1, 1917. . . ." †

"Although the growing Army of the United States of America might be expected eventually to restore the balance

* Vol. ii., p. 177. † Vol. ii., p. 182.

THE TROUBLES OF MINISTERS

in our favour, a considerable period of time would be required to enable that Army to develop its full strength. While it would be possible for Germany to complete her new dispositions early in the new year, the forces which America could send to France before the season would permit active operations to be recommenced would not be large. . . ."*

"The strenuous efforts made by the British forces during 1917 had left the Army at a low ebb in regard both to training and to numbers. It was therefore of the first importance, in view of the expected German offensive, to fill up the ranks as rapidly as possible and provide ample facilities for training. . . ." †

But as the ranks were not filled up, "a defensive policy was adopted"; and "the extent of our front made it impossible, with the forces under my command, to have adequate reserves at all points threatened. It was therefore necessary to ensure the safety of certain sectors which were vital, and to accept risks at others. . . ." ‡

What have Ministers to say? And upon whose military advice did they act?

Mr. Lloyd George has related how Sir Henry Wilson foretold the aim and place of Ludendorff's assault. Yet Haig was left in great need of more men. Why?

Meantime, there's another side that invites questioning comment. Did G.H.Q.'s anxiety linger too long north of Bapaume-Cambrai road? Its dispatch fails to note that a vital whole is no stronger than its most vulnerable part; hence Ludendorff struck hardest against the St. Quentin sectors.

Further, as Gough's front was one-third of Haig's whole line, and as it spanned the very heart of France, I am unable to see why all of the risks were crowded along its areas. Hutier's attack alone is known in France as the battle of Picardy! And there is also the technical question of bearing strength. A girder showing uniform wear and tear to a degree not immediately unsafe is a much better thing to trust under jolting pressure than a girder perilously weak along a third part of its length. This applies also to stretching elastic. I suggest, then, after making allowance for the uncertainties of war, that when a G.H.Q. is compelled to take great risks in defence, it might well spread them uniformly from end to end of the line rather than crowd them

---

* Vol. ii., p. 177. † Vol. ii., p. 178.
‡ Vol. ii., p. 216.

all along a third of the whole front. Even when this one-third has good luck against odds, and is only driven in badly, reinforcements must be sent to it at high-pressure speed and in greater numbers than an even distribution of risks would need, probably; and if the foe, after causing this displacement of reserve strength, strikes elsewhere at a place skilfully chosen, as Ludendorff struck against Armentières and on the Lys, the use of defensive reserves becomes flurried and feverish again. Is it too much to say, then, that risks are likely to be multiplied when they are congested along one wide area of a vast battle line, just as they are multiplied by concentration when a gambler stakes his all on a single throw?

§ III

Though it is necessary to examine a case from all fair and reasonable standpoints, the main point of all, no doubt, is the great need of rifle strength imposed on G.H.Q. between the Ypres salient campaign and March 21, 1918. What defence has been offered by the Government's followers?

Many persons say: " G.H.Q. should have stopped all leave. Why on March 21 were about 70,000 of its men on leave?" The answer is plain, because every G.H.Q. has to keep overworked troops in a temper fit for battles. Pétain also was obliged to grant leave to his trenchworn men. After the immense losses suffered in 1916 and 1917, it would have been an act of wild folly to add to the stress and strain by forbidding the usual routine that enabled brave soldiers to visit their homes for a few days.

Other persons say: "It was a very bad mistake to extend the British front. Lloyd George had no right to give way in this matter."

The French began to press for this relief in September, 1917. Much discussion followed, and went on till January, 1918. Then the French lines were taken over by Gough in two instalments, between January 10 and 12, and January 26 and February 3. Obviously, to increase the French reserves by taking over a two-corps French front was to impoverish the British resources at a bad time. But yet the French, from their own standpoint, had right on their side. Since 1914 they had held a very much wider frontage, while British statesmen and pressmen talked about the increasing millions recruited by the British Empire. This part of our national propaganda made no reference at all to combatant strength; the ration strength alone was given, and it included troops in the British Isles, in India, Egypt, and elsewhere galore. So Frenchmen, like hosts of British persons, said among themselves, "Where are all these millions of British troops? How is it that a cry for more men comes incessantly from British Generals in France and Flanders?"

After the Armistice, official propaganda announced that our Empire had employed 8,654,467 troops, while admitting at the same time that, in 1918, our strength on the Western Front was as follows:—

	Ration strength.	Combatant strength.	Rifle strength.
March 11	1,828,098	1,293,000	616,000
April 1	1,667,701	1,131,124	528,617
September 23	1,752,829	1,200,181	493,306
November 11	1,731,578	1,164,790	461,748

We have seen already that these figures are propagandist, and as a consequence untrustworthy, but yet they admit officially that rifle strength dwindled constantly, though it was too weak on March 11; while ration strength, after a big loss, between March 11 and April 1, made a recovery between April 1 and September 23. The falling off in combatant strength between March 11 and November 11 was 128,210, and in rifle strength, 154,252. Suppose the U.S.A. had not entered the war, would Foch's finale have then been at all feasible? Moreover, as ration strength figures, even if correct in themselves, were deceptive as regards rifle strength and combatant numbers, the French people became more and more urgent in their desire to see the British front grow wider.

The weight of this deception was borne by Haig and his Generals. Consider, then, once more, Haig's most difficult problems:—

"The strenuous efforts made by the British forces during 1917 had left the Army at a low ebb in regard both to training and to numbers. *It was therefore of the first importance, in view of the expected German offensive, to fill up the ranks as rapidly as possible and provide ample facilities for training.**

"So far as the second of these requirements was concerned, two factors materially affected the situation. Firstly, training had hitherto been primarily devoted to preparation for

* The italics are mine.—W. S. S.

offensive operations. Secondly, the necessity for maintaining the front-line systems of defence and the construction of new lines on ground recently captured from the enemy had precluded the development of rear-line systems to any great degree.

"Under the new conditions the early construction of these latter systems, involving the employment of every available man on the work, became a matter of vital importance. In consequence, it was difficult to carry out any elaborate course of training in defensive tactics. On the other hand, in the course of the strenuous fighting in 1916 and 1917 great developments had taken place in the methods of conducting a defensive battle. It was essential that the lessons learned therein should be assimilated rapidly and thoroughly by all ranks." *

Compare this position with another:—

"Meanwhile, in marked contrast to our own position," says Haig, "the large reserves in the Western theatre which the enemy was able to create for himself by the transfer of numerous divisions from the East, enabled him to carry out extensive training with units completed to establishment. . . . In all, at least sixty-four German divisions took part in the operations of the first day of the battle, a number considerably exceeding the total forces composing the entire British Army in France. The majority of these divisions had spent many weeks, and even months, in concentrated training for offensive operations, and had reached a high pitch of technical excellence in the attack."

Our own men had to snatch a bit of training, so tied were they by holding the lines and by hard toil with spade, pick and barbed wire. A lucky division that obtained two or three weeks of training, like the *Ninth*, was helped greatly in the battle. The *Thirtieth* also, which took over its line on February 23, finding the forward zone almost finished, and the battle zone well wired, was able to combine training with manual toil, attacking sometimes, and sometimes defending, trenches in the battle zone dug by its own troops. Counter-attacks by brigades, battalions, companies, platoons, were worked out as "Tactical Exercises without Troops," in many cases down to Section Commanders; and by the troops themselves in the cases of companies and platoons. On March 21 and 22 one battalion carried out no fewer than eight counter-attacks over the actual ground on which they had previously

* Vol. ii., pp. 178-179.

been rehearsed. In six of these attacks they took prisoners and recovered lost lines.

And the artillery of the *Thirtieth* was fortunate also. In January and February it was out of the line for nearly six weeks, and weather and countryside being very good for exercise, field training was constantly practised, with excellent results. Indeed, after their division had been pushed from its forward zone, its R.A. did not lose a gun in profuse rearguard fighting, though it kept close to the infantry, often limbering up after the infantry had passed through.

What a blessing it would have been if every British division could have been trained as thoroughly as the German units were! With us manual toil was the first essential.

"All available men of the fighting units, with the exception of a very small proportion undergoing training, and all labour units, were employed on these [preparation] tasks. *Though the time and labour available were in no way adequate, if, as was suspected, the enemy intended to commence his offensive operations in the early spring, a large portion of the work was in fact completed before the enemy launched his great attack.* That so much was accomplished is due to the untiring energy of all ranks of the fighting units, the Transportation Service, and the Labour Corps." *

What have Ministers to say in their defence? And their military advisers in London? What excuses or explanations have they to offer?

It is a national duty to press these questions, since war devours the most virile young men while leaving middle-aged politicians in safety.

* Vol. ii., pp. 179-180.

CHAPTER VII

SOME SIDE ISSUES AND POLITICAL EFFECTS

§ I

UNDER contemporary war conditions the usual weaknesses of statesmanship are likely to increase, because it is almost impossible to tell the people frankly about any need or danger by which the reputations of leading statesmen are compromised. In the autumn of 1917, Press correspondents at the front knew that our combatant strength had shrunk far too much, but they did not know how this vital fact could be printed and published. George A. B. Dewar says, for instance :— *

"I came to the conclusion, before the first week of the battle was ended (*i.e.* the battle of Cambrai, which began on November 20, 1917), that we wanted many more men for our work in France; but, though I tried hard to state this in print, I was not allowed to do so. Authority would not allow me. But I was able—as an indifferent second best—to get into print before the battle was quite over, a statement that . . . 'The British force, with the material at its disposal, has done great things by the well-prepared and suddenly administered stroke of the THIRD ARMY . . .' This was absolutely true.

"*More men*—this was our aching want at Cambrai, before Cambrai, after Cambrai. (The munitions were all right. Thanks to the working classes at home, these goods were delivered.) Coming over on the boat from France on one occasion, I travelled with a member of the War Cabinet, and ventured to say this to him. He mused, as if thinking aloud: 'The man-power question is becoming pressing'; but added, 'unfortunately, when we do find more men they are lost.' Passchendaele and the later Flanders fights were in his mind. The casualties were heavy there. But that is war.

"When I returned to England I tried hard to ventilate

---

* "A Younger Son." By George A. B. Dewar. Grant Richards, London, 1920, page 187.

this question; for I dreaded what might happen in 1918 in case of a great German offensive—and what actually did happen on March 21, 1918. But I was unsuccessful. Then how I wished I had a paper of my own to press the matter home week after week, even day after day! I found the terrible delusion prevalent that we had any amount of men but no generalship, no light and leading. One gentleman to whom I mentioned our urgent need replied that he could not give me leave to agitate the question. If at any time we really were in want of more men in France, all Haig needed to do was to turn his cavalry into infantry. Fancy! one little Cavalry Corps."

In war every one pays lip-service to Truth while showing all day long that Truth is a peril to be evaded for the nation's good! How easy it is to say that veracity will encourage the foe, or dishearten our own civilians, or depress our troops in the field, or offend our allies, or be mistaken for a want of patriotism, or do harm to a statesman whom we like, or make mischief in some other way. After the Armistice a wounded Tommy said, "They tell me we've pulled through at last all right 'cause our propergander told better lies than the German. So I say to myself, 'If tellin' lies is so —— good in war, why should tellin' truth be —— good in peace?'"

Ludendorff speaks enviously of our propaganda, so it must have been effective; but yet in many ways it recoiled as a boomerang and hit our best interests badly, as it did by inviting the world to mistake our ration strength figures for combatant power. Another mistake was to talk so much about the German Scrap of Paper when neutral nations remembered our treatment of Denmark in 1864, and knew how unprepared we were in 1914 to fulfil with success our obligation to Belgium, whose invasion had been foreseen by General Joffre as well as by Lord Roberts. In the midst of all this camouflage talk, how could statesmen ask in good time for an extension of compulsory service? After an invited tragedy had passed through its first act, they were obliged to extend the age limit, and to-day the result is evident. The people's hatred of conscription is far greater than it ever was in pre-war days. After the Ypres salient campaign, with its vast losses, Ministers had reason to say, partly in self-defence, "When we did find more men they were lost." But they should have added that when a nation declines to prepare herself for a long-threatened war, and starts to improvise huge armies after war has been declared, glorious young lives by the tens of thousands must be thrown away before enough experience and training can be collected from battles and campaigns. The youth of our Empire had to serve an apprenticeship under fire of three horrible years—1915, 1916, 1917. Did any gain on the Western Front offset the blood cost of this awful apprenticeship? And do many politicians consider this question side by side with the pre-war follies? *

Nothing is better worth consideration while an austere cenotaph to the Dead is being built, for this monument should mark national remorse as well as national gratitude, since the Dead have among them a vast number of lads who in pre-war days were too boyish to care for any party game played with votes as counters.

Sorrow for slain boys may have been among the reasons that detained some 200,000 troops in the British Isles while Ludendorff was prepared for his immense blow. Many persons have said: " The reserves at home were mainly lads. How could Ministers send them into battle unless a bad crisis demanded a wholesale sacrifice of boyish lives?"

Yes, these boys were not among the voters who paid no heed to German warnings: and if Ministers remembered this fact, and were guided by its abiding pathos, they have one good reason to offer for Haig's riskful difficulties.

On the seventh day of the battle, March 27, Colonel Repington said in the *Morning Post:*—

"I do not wish to refer now to the terrible responsibilities which our War Cabinet have incurred by their past blunders and neglect. The moment of returning to this subject has not yet come. Nothing that they can do now can retrieve for many months to come the faults of omission and commission which lie at their door. But I hope, in their natural anxiety to appear to be doing something and to be busy, they will not commit fresh follies. *I should consider it a folly to throw into this boiling cauldron of a great battle the youths between eighteen and nineteen now in training at home."* †

Many thousands of these boy troops were sent at once to France; very soon the age limit was extended: and propagandists told us with pride how losses at the front were being promptly balanced by reserves!

How amazing is the drama of British politics. Generation

---

* Ludendorff notes what a great many persons have noted—that Allied losses show a heavier percentage than the German, usually much heavier in dead. In war thorough training is a sort of half-effectual lifebelt.

† My italics.—W. S. S.

after generation a similar sort of eloquent statesmanship carries the political milk cans with a similar carelessness; and as soon as inevitable bad waste occurs, most people say in defence of it, "Accidents will happen, of course, so let us not weep or swear over spilt milk!" As though the words "spilt milk" in matters of life and death were not a synonym for "causes," which, like bad wounds healed into scars, have at their best effects of an enduring sort.

Every nation condones her own wrong acts and tragic blunders, perhaps more readily than she remembers those committed by her foes; and every political party in a State magnifies its rival's mistakes and sins while practising forgiveness towards its own. And have you ever asked yourself, and answered frankly, the terrible question: "If there had been no German crimes gradually to drive neutral after neutral into the Allied cause, by what human means could the original Entente Powers, Russia excepted, have been rescued from their own mistakes?" No question in our history is more searching than this one. In the years to come historians will dwell on it when they study the awful events of March, 1918, and many another battle. The tragedy of being Too Late, of being unprepared for a long-threatened war, had evil consequences which only future generations will know completely. . . .

Progress remains a halt-footed adventurer that revisits old tragedies; and those who pay in blood for this routine, periodically and by instalments, are soldiers and sailors, young enough to bear immense dangers under conditions which would kill middle-aged politicians.

It is necessary thus to unite the second Somme battle and the FIFTH ARMY to those ample permanent issues which should always be present in written histories of a great war. The origin of St. Quentin's Week goes back to the year 1864, when our country, by declining to fulfil her obligations to Denmark, helped to start Prussia along a wide, smooth road of purposeful aggression.

§ II

Is it possible that the great need of large reinforcements on the Western Front was misunderstood by Ministers, as in Mr. Bonar Law's speech? If so, why and how did the misunderstanding arise? Was the Prime Minister's mind fixed so confidently on Palestine, and Mesopotamia, and Salonika, that it could not see in focus the Western problems and peril? In his speech at Leeds, December 7, 1918, the Prime Minister spoke with a zest akin to schoolboyish levity about "side-shows," as though unmindful of his Cabinet's association with the awful events of March. "If we had dropped the side-shows," he said, "the war would not have been over to-day. Turkey fell, Bulgaria fell, then Austria fell; and Germany said, 'Here, they are all gone; it is time we stopped'—and they are marching back as hard as they can." Joyous actor! As Ludendorff's offensive very nearly won the war, light-hearted prattle about side-shows should come from young journalists, and not from Ministers who left Haig disastrously short of men.

And consider another point. If Ministers awaited the arrival of American troops rather than ask the people to accept an extension of compulsory service, did they fail to perceive that the risk they were running was not only very vast, but also vast in a way not to be weighed and measured by forethought?

To make ample allowance for the needs of our war industries and for the restlessness of Labour is as easy as it is necessary. When Ludendorff struck on March 21, a menacing unrest was astir among our coal miners, and the Prime Minister went to placate them with another speech, and with comments on the huge battle. As a nation we were paying penalty for that worship of volunteering which employed such endless deceptive talk after real volunteering had been displaced by white feathers and newspaper press gangs, humiliating posters, and many other phases of vulgar and noisy pressure. Labour was very eager to say that British volunteers had beaten the German conscripts; and many others besides manual workers had precisely the same wish. They ventured even to insult their own Allies by declaring that a British volunteer was equal in fighting value to at least four foreign pressed men.

As compulsory service increased this mood, this illusion about a voluntary service which in a few months ceased to be either voluntary or dignified, the Government, between Passchendaele and March, 1918, was unluckily situated. If its members feared to ask for an extension of conscription, then I, for one, would not be surprised; for this fear, if it existed, was backed by peremptory needs in our shipyards and in many other essential industries.

For all that, war obligations of a rival sort should be

SOME SIDE ISSUES AND POLITICAL EFFECTS

weighed and measured fearlessly, without any bias, because the decisive test of a war policy is the result it produces. It is bad if the results are bad, right if its results are good. And this being the sane and just rule in war, above all when war claims millions of young lives and means the life or the death of nations, Ministers and their advisers must needs be held responsible for the March retreat and its effects. They alone could supply Haig with enough combatant strength.

Among the huger effects which historians cannot fail to note is the fact that the Entente Powers, after March, 1918, became dependent on American troops, who were hurried across 3000 miles of sea in the manner described by Mr. Lloyd George:— *

"I need not tell you about March 21, how, when the great crisis came, men were hurried across the Channel.† I shall never forget that morning when I sent a cable to President Wilson, telling him what the facts were, and how it was essential that we should get American help at the speediest possible rate: inviting him to send 120,000 infantry and machine-gunners per month to Europe. If he did that, we would do our best to help to carry them. I sent that telegram, and the following day came a reply from President Wilson. 'Send your ships across, and we will send 120,000 men.' Then I invited Sir Joseph Maclay, the Shipping Controller, to 10, Downing Street, and said: '*Send every ship you can.*' They were all engaged in essential trades, because we were cut down right to the bone. We said: 'This is the time for taking risks.' We ran risks with our food, we ran risks with essential raw materials. We said: 'The thing to do is to get these men across at all hazard.' America sent 1,900,000 men across, and out of that number, 1,100,000 were carried by the British Mercantile Marine."

This vivid story is dramatic, but far from pleasant, and far also from completeness, as it makes no reference to Gough and Byng, whose armies, as Haig has said :—

"held up the German attack at all points for the greater part of two days, thereby rendering a service to their country and to the Allied cause, the value of which cannot be overestimated. Thereafter, through many days of heavy and continuous rearguard fighting, they succeeded in presenting a barrier to the enemy's advance until such time as the arrival

---

* In a speech at Leeds, December 7, 1918.
† Could Voltaire have written a more cynical sentence than this?

of British and French reinforcements enabled his progress to be checked." *

It is all very well for Mr. Lloyd George to relate how he acted while the FIFTH ARMY was grappling against a world of odds, but a cable to President Wilson could not have been effectual if Gough and his few divisions had permitted themselves to be overwhelmed. Besides, Belgium was still enslaved, and we set out to rescue her without any thought of help from the U.S.A.

President Wilson, too, has given his own account of the wonderful way in which American troops were poured into Europe :—

"A year ago [1917] we had sent 145,918 men overseas. Since then we have sent 1,950,513, an average of 162,542 each month, the number, in fact, rising in May last (1918) to 245,951, in June to 278,760, in July to 307,182, and continuing to reach similar figures in August and September —in August 289,570, and in September 257,438.

" No such movement of troops ever took place before across 3000 miles of sea, followed by adequate equipment and supplies, and carried safely through extraordinary dangers which were alike strange and infinitely difficult to guard against. In all this movement only 758 men were lost by enemy attack, 630 of whom were upon a single English transport, which was sunk near the Orkney Islands.

" I need not tell you what lay at the back of this great movement of men and material. It is not invidious to say that at the back of it lay a supporting organization of the industries of the country and of all of its productive activities more complete, more thorough in the method and effective in result, more spirited and unanimous in purpose and effort than any other great belligerent had been able to effect."

These speeches by President Wilson and Mr. Lloyd George have been hidden as much as possible by propagandists. After prolonged war it is never difficult to hide deep unpleasant matters from a single generation, for ordinary

* Vol. ii., p. 235. Haig impairs the historic value of this testimony by putting the FIFTH and THIRD ARMIES on the same level towards the gratitude of the Entente Powers. He begins by saying : " On the 21st March the troops of the FIFTH and THIRD ARMIES had the glory of sustaining the first and heaviest blow of the German offensive. Though assailed by a concentration of hostile forces which the enemy might well have considered overwhelming, etc., etc." This implies that great odds were active against the THIRD ARMY, whereas the plain truth is that Byng's battle was a very prolonged Waterloo in which Byng was well-manned for a defensive grapple with contemporary weapons. The FIFTH ARMY'S ordeal was vastly heavier and more terrible.

persons have very little grasp on causes and effects, even from the natural temper of their minds. They do not look at things as part of a whole, and often will sacrifice the most important and precious parts of a great historic lesson, or admonition, from mere simplicity and want of apprehension.

To them a battle is no more than a military study of fighting; they pass over its many side issues and its aftermath, whose ultimate consequences are often more important than the battle's ups and downs.

CHAPTER VIII

WIDESPREAD INJUSTICE AND THE PEOPLE'S EQUITY

§ I

WHAT is the worst result of political or official injustice? This phase of injustice forms widespread myths as tenacious as quitch grass; breeds in its defence a party temper which, like fanaticism, seems unable to tell the truth; and its partisans try to keep a whole nation in a false position overswept by cross-currents of unrest. These are shabby, low-bred evils, but yet we do not find among them the very worst.

Why is it that political injustice, after it has been accepted as equity by a great many simple persons, is extremely hard to reach by those who attack it with facts? There are two reasons, and when they are united they compose the very worst evil bred by political unfairness. Mr. Lloyd George found it easy to be fluent about the cries for help that he sent across 3000 miles of sea to President Wilson, and could speak calmly of the reserves which were sent to Haig *after* a great crisis, long foreseen, had come; but how many words of gratitude did he offer in the same speech to the young troops under Gough and Byng who enabled Ludendorff to mourn over the miscarriage of great strategical aims? No such word appeared in Press reports of his eloquence. Is this to be the perennial mood of mind bred and fostered by politics?

No person can run counter to it without seeming to be an advocate, for every statesman belongs to a party, and advocacy is distrusted by those—and they are very numerous—who hate and shun the work of "making up their minds." Instead of deciding when to say Yes or No to a difficult question, they compromise weakly and say: "Well, there's no smoke without fire, you know. In this case, perhaps, a good lot might be said for and against both sides. Who knows—

INJUSTICE AND THE PEOPLE'S EQUITY 313

and who cares? It's two years old and more. Good Lord! Why bother?"

No matter how impartial fact-giving opponents to political injustice may be, their attack is certain to have warmth in it, since injustice *should* be hated; and this warmth is noted at once by the astute devotees of injustice, who say, in speech and in print, "Here's the advocacy of over-zealous friends!"

Then there's another troublesome hindrance. A great many persons who have accepted an injustice as a truthful thing do not read published facts by which it is shown up; so they continue innocently to support the injustice. A full year after the second Somme battle a man told me that the THIRD ARMY would never have lost a yard had it not been "let down" by Gough and his troops. I asked this man, whose voice was educated, to read Haig's dispatch and to grip the battle on correct maps through a few honest days. He shrugged his shoulders, smiled at me with irony, and said: "D'you remember Lloyd George's speech in Parliament? When did he go away from its plain statements?"

What national justice needs is a court of inquiry which would be evenly fair and thorough towards Byng, Gough, G.H.Q., and the Government.

§ II

A French artist and scout, Paul M. Maze, wrote as follows some weeks after the battle:—

"General Gough's name alone was sufficient to rally men falling asleep after eight days' fighting. . . . Some remnants of some of his divisions still remain mixed up with the French. They have been told to go back and retire 100 yards behind the front line. As soon as they hear the rattle of the machine-guns, they come up again and line up with the French. I could tell you heaps of wonderful tales about these men, and trust one day to have the opportunity of doing so. . . . What trash has been uttered . . . and what useless words in front of the work which remains to be done."

Another soldier, writing to a Divisional Commander, says:—

"I shall never forget the morning he [General Gough] went away. I met and saw him and had quite a long chat with him alone. Then we all said good-bye to him, and gave him a send-off with a guard of 200 signallers with the Artillery School Band playing 'Auld Lang Syne.' I tell you it was an effort to keep back one's tears that day; for one felt how one was losing not only a great friend, but also a Commander who knew how to command, and whom one could have followed just anywhere."

It was at about 4.30 p.m. on Thursday, March 28, that Gough handed his command to Rawlinson. Haig says:—

"The nature of the fighting on the southern portion of the battle-front, where our troops had been engaged for a full week with an almost overwhelming superiority of hostile forces, had thrown an exceptional strain upon the FIFTH ARMY Commander and his Staff. In order to avoid the loss of efficiency which a continuance of such a strain might have entailed, I decided to avail myself of the services of the Staff of the FOURTH ARMY, which was at this time in reserve. General Sir H. S. Rawlinson, Bt., who had but recently given up the command on appointment to Versailles, accordingly returned to his old army, and at 4.30 p.m. on this day assumed command of the British forces south of the Somme. At the same time the construction of new defence lines made necessary by the enemy's advance called for the appointment of an able and experienced Commander and Staff to direct this work and extemporize garrisons for their defence. I accordingly ordered General Gough to undertake this important task."

This explanation comes from the chivalry of a noble-minded soldier; but chivalric explanation cannot dismiss from public knowledge and talk several familiar facts; as, for example, that Sir Hubert Gough was not employed again in the war, because he was suspended by the political party spirit.

Let us be glad that battle-maps, when true, are blunt, impartial historians to be trusted entirely. The terrific power of the German attack in March, 1918, is revealed by comparing the ground lost by two British armies; one on a forty-two miles front and perilously short of enough troops; and the other on a twenty-seven miles front, with only one division less in line and a much larger reserve. Any frank, impartial mind, after studying correct maps of the retreat made by these armies, will be brought by the logic of cause and effect to a simple argument.

"Both armies belong to the same Empire and contain divisions of the same mettle, but the Guards are with Byng, and most of the British Empire reinforcements go to him during the most critical days of the fighting. Both armies fight with equal valour; and since the much stronger army

INJUSTICE AND THE PEOPLE'S EQUITY

on the much narrower front is compelled by the foe's power to retreat in five days from Flesquières salient almost to Hamel-sur-Ancre and Thiepval, about 22 miles, how comes it that the much weaker army on the much wider front is not swallowed up in these five days by the same German power?

"In these five days, again, the deepest loss of ground on the weaker army's front is about 25 miles, from the south-east of Urvillers west to the east of Hattencourt. Is the German attack more numerous and more strenuous in its onslaught on Byng's troops? No, it is at its strongest against the weaker British forces. What, then, saves these weaker forces from being overwhelmed? It is right and timely and much superior generalship? What else can it be?"

Nothing else is visible. Nothing else is probable. For in a long battle against great odds right generalship is an incessant reinforcement by which the larger aspects and results are determined; right generalship in brigades, divisions, corps and army orders. To this conclusion every impartial and truthful mind must arrive after studying all evidence now known; the best part of this evidence being that which makes correct battle-maps, not debatable opinions and beliefs. It needs neither excuses nor apologies; in curt and plain facts it passes judgment while acting as a cold witness.

Ludendorff and his very able Generals won a great many acres from Gough, but what large strategic aims did they make real? None! They failed to make an operative breakthrough at every place where annihilation of Gough's defence was essential to their plan of campaign. Ludendorff says: "While in the defence the [German] forces in a given sector were more evenly distributed, in the attack *the problem was to discover some decisive point and arrange the dispositions accordingly*" (vol. ii., p. 573). Well, he chose Gough's front—the centre battle, as he calls it—because "the weakest part was on both sides of St. Quentin," and he "was influenced by the time factor and by tactical considerations, first among them being the weakness of the enemy" (vol. ii., p. 590). But yet, after choosing his decisive point for a vast offensive, and after finding that this known weak point in the British defence had become weaker through the parching effects of dry weather on the Oise and its marshes, as on the Somme, Ludendorff discovered that his Carpentier attacks could be baffled by the Jimmy Wilde defence of the FIFTH ARMY. No fact in British battles is more notable than this one, and I dare to doubt whether there is one so notable, an attack of more than three against one along forty-two miles of front being unique, particularly when we remember that the front widened as the salient's arc grew ampler.

Only at one place did the foe's enormous efforts lead on in swift sequence to another advance; and this one place was very much nearer to Byng's front than to Gough's—at Armentières and in the Lys Valley, and thus in one of those northern sectors which on March 21 were most strongly defended because of their nearness to the coast.

Surely we have a right to know why Sir Hubert Gough, with several of his Generals, was withdrawn from further active service in the War? Was it because a loss of ground accompanied his invaluable work? No. Byng also lost ground, considerably more in depth per brigade of man-power than Gough; and his services were retained on the Western front—justly retained, unless British Generals are to be suspended whenever they are obliged to bend in order to avoid breaking.

It is easy for impartial students to see that the FIFTH ARMY possessed a Commander who knew what his men should be expected to achieve; when and where they should be able to stand, and where and when they must fall back to evade annihilation. Only a man endowed with imaginative sympathy, as well as with rare self-control, could have *seen and felt* from day to day, swiftly and correctly, a convulsed and threatened line always too wide and far too thinly defended along all sectors. Every sector of his front was a patient in a high fever; the Commander had to be to it as a physician; and if he had ordered things unfit for its remaining strength, a few miles of suffering would have broken for ever, and a column of German troops would have been free to pass through.

Would an inferior General have seen with his imagination the whole widening battle-front, with its remnant brigades and divisions? I cannot believe so. He would have prescribed for patients whom his mind did *not* see, whose physical and moral state he could not apprehend; would have asked always for too much, arguing to himself that G.H.Q. and all folk at home would certainly expect what he did demand from his men; and thus, by failing to be in full sympathy with his troops in their limitless ordeal by battle, he would have lost all by striving to get impossible results.

And there is another point of very great value. In

INJUSTICE AND THE PEOPLE'S EQUITY 317

modern war an Army Commander sits and thinks and gives orders, but the execution of his ideas passes at once from his hands. On the battlefield he has interpreters, and if they fail his ideas are lost, no matter how great they may be.

Now G.H.Q. could do but little for the FIFTH ARMY after supplying it with a burden of risks. Even two of the three reserve infantry divisions were not on the FIFTH ARMY'S front when the battle began, so anxious was Haig about fronts nearer the coast. So Gough and his Generals and their few divisions had to win through the worst days with their own united promptness and apt endurance. Army orders would have been futile if they had been misapplied in the field. Gough and his Army were one, then, and should be one in our gratitude.

Marlborough was ruined by the indecisive campaign of 1711, and in 1809 Wellington was all but ruined by the retreat from Talavera; for the British people, despite their fighting temperament, have little military intuition or judgment, and are apt to attach too much value to deceptive phrases coined by political leaders. But in the long run they are loyal to their men of action, and make ample amends for past unfairness and ingratitude.

Finally, the wrong done to the FIFTH ARMY and its Commander came wholly from politicians and their misadvisers. Haig, of course, had nothing to do with the misdeed that closed a famous general's career in the War, while withholding from him the right of appealing to a court-martial. I note, too, that our Commander-in-Chief in his final dispatch, when reviewing what he owes to his most notable officers, dwells with pride on the varied and great services of Sir Hubert Gough:—

"I desire to associate with them [*i.e.* the five Army Commanders at the close of the War] the names of General Sir Charles Monro, who left the command of the FIRST ARMY to assume the Chief Command in India; of General Sir Edmund Allenby, who, after conducting the operations of the THIRD ARMY in the battle of Arras, 1917, has since led our arms to victory in Palestine; and General Sir Hubert Gough, who, after distinguished service as a Brigade, Divisional and Corps Commander, commanded the FIFTH ARMY (first known as the RESERVE ARMY) during the battles of the Somme and Ancre in 1916, east of Ypres in 1917, and finally in the great and gallant fight of March, 1918, the story of which is fresh in the minds of all."

INDEX

ABBEVILLE, 51, 294
Ablainzevelle, 191, 197, 274
Acheville, 197
Airmen, British, 20-23, 74, 293
Airmen, German, 21, 23, 74, 104, 119, 163, 207, 210
Airplane contact patrols, 21, 208
Aizecourt, 174, 182
"Alberich Movement," 11
Albert, 104, 187, 188, 191, 193
Albert-Bray line, 266 et seq.
Allenby, General Sir Edmund, 36, 317
Allies dependent on American reinforcements, 301, 309, 310
Allied losses heavier than the German, 306
America. See United States
American aid, Mr. Lloyd George cries out for, 289, 290, 309
American engineers, 98
American troops, 308, 309, 310
Amiens, 74, 93, 94, 112, 115, 116, 121, 122, 131, 134, 135, 187, 189, 196, 294
Ancre River, 116, 187, 190, 191, 193
Ancre line in peril north-west of Albert, 187, 191, 193, 267-271
Anstey, Colonel, 121
Armentières, 196, 292, 316
Army Commanders no longer eye-witnesses, 8
Army Service Corps, 296
Arras, 143, 146, 195 et seq., 198, 213
Art of retreating, 19, 20, 84, 89, 90, 139, 140
Artillery, 78, 95, 106, 108, 109, 112, 117, 124, 131, 144, 153, 163, 174, 175, 188, 192, 196, 208, 211, 228, 286
Artillery procedure, New German, 66, 67
Arvillers, 236
Asquith, Mr. H. H., 290, 293
Assevillers, 112, 113, 116, 117, 120, 212

"At all costs," 172, 178, 224, 246
Athies, 109
Attack on Arras, 195 et seq.
Attilly, 72
Aubercourt, 133, 134
Aubigny, 84
Aubin, Captain J. F. G., 111
Australian defences, 13
Australian troops, 35, 101, 133, 141, 187, 265
Austria-Hungary, 43
Austrian artillery, 46
Auxiliary troops, German, 66, 120
Aveluy Wood, 273
Avesnes, 95
Avre bridgehead, 93, 95
Avre River, 134, 218, 286
Ayette, 274

B BATTERY, the story of, 203, 204
Bainbridge, Sir E. G. T., 159
Bancroft, Lieut., 153
Bapaume-Arras, battle of, 136
Bapaume, 52, 53, 136, 138, 142, 161, 182, 183
Bapaume-Cambrai road, 150, 158, 160
Barastre, 230
Barisis, 35, 50, 95, 283
Barleux, 113, 115, 116, 117, 118, 210, 212
Bassett, Lieut., 69
Basseux, 187, 213
Battle of Picardy, French name for Hutier's attack, 80
Battle zone, the, 11, 12, 145, 173
Battles, modern, their four parts or periods, 3, 4
Battles, modern, between fairly equal forces, 195, 310
Bayonvillers, 131
Bazentin, 183, 185, 192
Beale-Browne's column, 271
Beaconsfield on politics, 297
Beaucourt-sur-Ancre, 190
Beaucourt, near Mezières, 283

INDEX

Beaufort, 94
Beaulieu, 220, 265
Beaumetz, 148, 150, 159, 160, 179
Beaumont-Hamel, 191
Beauvois, 23, 250
Bécourt, 271
Beet-sugar factories, 124, 165, 178
Belgium's captivity, 310
Bell, Captain, 127
Bellingham, Brigadier, 195
Below, Otto von, Commander of the SEVENTEENTH GERMAN ARMY, 6, 40, 136, 142, 143, 146, 187, 195, 196, 198, 274
Below and Marwitz, their joint attacks, 146-158, 159-167, 168-198
Benay, 74, 78, 96
Bennett, Major Herbert, 2/Fourth Oxford and Buck's Light Infantry, 241
Bernafay Wood, 183, 191, 192
Bernes, 88, 161, 170
Bethencourt, 111, 284
Beverley, Captain, 162, 226, 228
Beviss, Lieut., 153
Biaches, 101, 112, 113, 210
Bihucourt, 190
Bilton, Colonel, 236
Birdwood, General Sir W. R., 195
Black Watch, 144, 184
Blücher, 281, 282
Boehn, General von, SEVENTH GERMAN ARMY, 40, 48, 54, 92, 95, 97
Bois des Essarts, 216
Bois Favière, 191, 192
Bois de Mareuil, 218
Bois St. Pierre Vaast, 138, 178, 181
Bois des Vaux, 138
Bolshevism in German Army, 42
Bombardment, a terrible, opens the battle on March 21, 1918...64-68
Bonar Law, 293, 294, 307
Boraston, Lieut.-Colonel J. H., Haig's private secretary, 136
Borderlands north and south of Byng's Army, 136-145, 146-158, 159-167, 175-193
Borderlands north and south of Vermand-Amiens road, 100-120, 121-135
Borrett, Brigadier, 117, 133
Bosanquet, Captain, 112
Bouchavesnes, 138, 176, 178, 180
Bouchoir, 236, 237, 285, 286
Boucly, 102, 107, 161
Boundary uniting Gough and Byng, 136, 137, 138, 140, 141, 142, 143, 162, 175, 178, 179, 180, 182, 184, 185, 193

Bouvrey, 197
Boyd, B.G.G.S. of 5th Corps, 179
Boyelles, 191
Bray-Albert line, 266 et seq.
Bray-sur-Somme, 114, 118, 136, 137, 138, 184, 191, 260
Breach of Byng's centre, 186, 187, 188, 189, 190, 193
Breach of Green Line, Nobescourt Farm, 164, 168, 170
Breaking an old military rule, 276, 278, 283
Breuil, 234, 239
Bridgeheads, 84
Bridges, destruction of, 17, 18, 84, 89, 109, 110, 171, 285, 294
Brie, 84, 100, 102, 109, 112, 116, 248
Brigade-Major's adventure, 209, 210
Brigade of *Second* DIVISION transferred for a while to the *Ninth*, 166, 167 ; it retreats without orders, 178, 179, 180
Brigade Staff at Harbonnières, episode of, 127-129
Brigades, British, deprived of one battalion apiece, 75
Briqueterie, 192
Britain's pre-war self-neglect, its horrible results, 202, 205
British Army in France, March 21, its total strength, 33, 34, 279, 301
British boundaries, Corps and Divisional, their unfortunate slope south-west, 169
British combativeness, 206, 207
British Corps, those in the FIFTH ARMY. *See* the Order of Battle
British Mercantile Marine, 309
British feeling against retreats, 89, 90
BRITISH FIRST ARMY, 35, 196
British Government, its attitude to Haig's dispatch, 5
British guns fire on British troops, 113, 224, 234
British losses omitted from official reports and dispatches, 159, 254
British officers, their chatty candour, 210
Brouchy, 84
Brown, Lieut., 127
Brown Line Defence System, 145, 150, 152, 162, 164, 165
Bruchmüller, Colonel, famous artillery expert, 54
Buchan, John, Lieut.-Colonel, 146, 162, 182, 227
Bucquoy, 187, 190, 191, 268, 270, 274
Buire, 102, 270, 271
Bulgaria harasses Ludendorff, 42

INDEX 321

Bunce, Captain, 154
Burt's Force, 217
Bushell, Colonel, 251
Bussu, 174
Butler, Lieut.-General Sir R. H. K., Commander of 3rd Corps, that held 30,000 yards of vital front on Gough's right, 5, 12, 50, 74, 76, 80, 81, 91, 118, 214, 275, 283
Byng, the strength of his Army, 5, 6, 34, 35, 103, 104; his retreat to the Ancre, 116, 118; receives troops from the FIFTH ARMY, 35, 122, 137, 258-265; suppression of facts in Byng's battle, 5, 136, 137, 266-274; his right wing's drama, 137, 138, 139, 140, 141, 144, 165, 166, 174, 175, 177, 182, 184, 185, 186, 193; employs 8½ divisions on the first day, 147; his battle zone invaded, 147, 148; Haig's account of Byng's first day, 148, 149; his second day, 159-161; misled by a conjecture, 166, 167; cannot be grateful enough to the South African Brigade, 182; centre of his Army broken, 183, 187, 190, 191, 193; his 5th Corps reinforced by Gough's northern troops, 186, 193, 258-265; his ordeal a prolonged Waterloo, 195; his great defence of Arras, 195 *et seq.*; his troubles, 258-265

CÆSAR, Julius, 120
Cahill of the Second Munsters, 207
Caix, 115, 129, 130, 132, 236, 237
Cambrai, 91, 139
Campbell, Major-General D. G. M., commanding the *Twenty-first* D., 143, 152, 154, 157, 161, 185
Canadian batteries, 98
Canadian cavalry, 218
Canadian railway engineers, 112
Canal du Nord, 138, 147, 174, 175, 180
Candor, 205
Canny-sur-Matz, 91
Carey's Force, so called, 112, 123, 185
Carnoy, 271
Carpeza Copse, 101, 157, 161
Carter - Campbell, Major - General G. T. C., commanding the *Fifty-first* D., THIRD ARMY, 148
Cartigny, 108
Castel, 218

Casualties, British and German, 81, 83, 85, 86, 88, 91, 96, 101, 102, 108, 150, 154, 159, 172, 173, 175, 189, 194, 202, 207, 211, 220, 228, 254, 255, 276, 304
Catelet Valley, 207
Cator, Major-General A. B. E., Commander of the *Fifty-eighth* D., on Gough's extreme right, 85
Caulaincourt, 88, 96, 102, 104, 105, 106, 108, 109, 170
Cavalry, British, 122, 213, 214-221, 305
Cavalry, Canadian, 218
Cavalry casualties, 217, 218
Cavalry, German, 40, 234
Cavalry in modern war, value of, 213, 214-221
Cayeux, 130
Centre fighting, the, 100-120, 121-135
Cérisy crisis, 116, 121, 122, 126, 130, 266-274
Champagne, 65, 92
Chandler of the Second Munsters, 207
Channel ports, 36, 37, 196
Chapel Hill, 145, 149, 152, 154, 157
Chaulnes, 92, 115
Chauny, 50, 85, 93, 97
Chemin des Dames, Foch's defeat, 292
Chevalier du Teil, 18
Chipilly, 89, 122
Christian, Colonel, of the South African Brigade, 164, 224
Clarence River, 139
Clastres, 76
Clemenceau, 9, 294
Cléry-sur-Somme, 180, 184, 185, 230
Cochran, Major, 226, 228
Colborne at Waterloo, 282
Colincamps, 187, 193, 268, 270
Collezy, cavalry at, 220, 221
Colliers, their unrest in March, 1918... 308
Cologne River, 100, 101, 136, 143, 150, 152, 154, 161, 170
Coolness and competence shown by Gough's Staff, 202, 203
Cooper, Lieut., 226, 231
Combativeness, British, 206, 207
Combe, Captain E. P., M.C., at Le Quesnoy, 94
Combles, 142, 180, 181, 182, 184, 230
Compiègne, 50, 88, 93, 97
Conference at Catelet, Gough's, 25-28
Conference at Doullens, on March 26, 18..259, 265, 270, 277

Y

322 INDEX

Conference at Homburg, Ludendorff's, 44, 45
Confusion caused by the misuse of French reinforcements, 99, 275-288
Congreve, Sir W. N., V.C., etc., Commander of the 7th Corps, 6, 100, 114, 118, 122, 133, 137, 138, 145, 150, 152, 161, 164, 165, 166, 170, 184, 189, 190, 191, 193, 194, 195, 224, 260
Conscientious Objectors, 205
Conscription, 205, 305, 308
Conta, General von, 51
Contact airplanes, German, 21, 208
Contescourt, 65, 79, 149
Contests of mind, 33-39, 40-45
Cook, Lieut.-Colonel, 215
Corbie, 122, 123, 194
Coucy la Ville, 97
Couper, Major-General Sir Victor Couper, Commander of the *Fourteenth* D., 76. See also under *Fourteenth* DIVISION
Courcelette, 190
Courcelles, 102
Cressy, 235, 236, 240, 242
Croft, Brigadier-General, of the *Ninth* D., 144
Croisilles, 53, 148, 160
Croix Moligneux, 171
Crossley, Sergeant, his bravery, 89
Crozat Canal, 76, 81, 83, 84, 85, 96, 97, 173
Cugny, 220, 221
Cummings, Brigadier-General, 188
Cunningham, Lieut., at Enghien, 72, 73
Curlu, 191

DALY, Major-General A. C., Commander of the *Twenty-fourth* D., 19th Corps, 100, 102, 104, 122, 131, 156, 161, 171
Darling, Captain, 273
Dawson, F. S., Brigadier-General, Commander of the South African Brigade in our *Ninth* DIVISION, 23, 144, 153, 161, 162, 163, 176, 177, 180, 181, 222-231
Dawson's Five Hundred, 222-231
Deceptive official figures, 279, 301
Decisive test of a war policy, 309
Defence in depth, its defects, 13, 14, 16
Defences of the FIFTH ARMY, chap. ii., Part I., 10-24
Demicourt, 52, 148
Demuin, 98, 112, 133, 134

Denmark, 305, 306
Dernancourt, 267, 270
Dessart Wood, 139, 158
"Details," 176, 177, 178
Details, excessive, 3, 82
Deverell, C. J., Major-General, 148
Devonshires of the *Eighth* DIVISION, 128
Dewar, George A. B., 304, 305
Difference between ration strength and combatant strength, 300, 301
Different fighting temperaments and methods, 280
Difficulties of an army in retreat, 19, 20, 89, 90
Difficulties in writing on modernized war, 3-7
Dimmer, Colonel, V.C., dies in action, 74, 129
Dispatch rider, 162
Disunity in 5th Corps, Byng's Army, 183, 184, 189, 190
Dives, 215
Divisional cavalry, 130, 214
Doignies, 148, 150
Doingt, 102, 174
Domart, 133
Douglas Smith, Major-General of the *Twentieth* DIVISION, 114, 131, 134
Doullens, 213, 259, 265, 270, 277
Doullens, a momentous conference at, March 26, 1918...259, 265, 270, 277
Drama of British politics, 306, 307
Drama of Byng's right wing, 137, 138, 139, 140, 141, 144, 165, 166, 174, 175, 177, 182, 184, 185, 186, 189, 191, 192, 193
Dregs in the defence, 212, 213, 254
Drummond, Captain, 112
Dry weather, its bad effects, 11, 25, 26, 36, 245, 315
Dublin Redoubt, 78
Dudbridge of the *Sixty-first* D., 235, 240
Dugan's Brigade, 156
Dunkirk, 65
Durham Light Infantry, 102, 106, 107, 108, 110, 113

EAUCOURT L'ABBAYE, 183, 220, 221
Economy of Force, 14
Ecoust St. Mein, 148, 150
Eighth Black Watch, 144, 184
Eighth DIVISION, under Heneker, 89, 111, 114, 116, 124, 128, 129, 168, 187, 284
Eighth Durham Light Infantry, 108, 126

INDEX 323

Eighth King's Royal Rifle Corps, 76
Eighth Rifle Brigade, 76
Eighth Royal West Surreys, 156
Eighteenth Corps. *See* under Maxse, and the FIFTH ARMY's Order of Battle
Eighteenth DIVISION, 13, 40, 76, 78, 131, 214, 251, 283
Eleventh Royal Scots, 144, 157, 163, 273
Elstob, Lieut.-Colonel, dies gloriously, 73, 129
Ellis Redoubt, 70
Ennemain, 109
Enghien Redoubt, defence of, 69, 70
Epéhy, 145, 150, 154, 157, 161, 195, 207
Epénancourt, 114, 115
Epine de Dallon Redoubt, 73
Epine de Malassise, 176
Epinette Wood, 162, 167, 175
Eppeville, 87
Equancourt, 139, 162, 166, 174, 179
Erches, 286
Ervillers, 142, 183
Essigny, 59, 74, 76, 96, 149, 150, 160
Estrées, 112, 117, 119, 212
Eterpigny, 210
Etinehem, 271
Etricourt, 164, 175, 178
Evans, General, 232
Evolution of weapons, 120
Exchange of troops between Hutier and Marwitz, 94
Experiences of a Cavalry Commander, 215 *et seq.*
Exuette River, 158

FALVY, 84, 89, 110
Fampoux village, 160
Fanshawe, Lieut.-General Sir E. A., Commander of 5th Corps, the southern Corps of Byng's Army, 165, 166, 176, 193
Fargniers, 76, 79, 96
Favière Wood, 191, 192
Fay, 119
Fayet, 63, 69
Feetham, Major-General E., 101, 113, 115, 121, 123, 152, 161
Fifteenth DIVISION, 148, 198
Fifteenth Cheshires, 184, 224
Fifteenth Notts and Derbies, 184, 224
Fiftieth DIVISION, 36, 75, 96, 100, 102, 103, 106, 107, 108, 121, 128, 134, 170, 210, 249
FIFTH ARMY. *See* under Gough
Fifth Camerons, 144, 164, 182

Fifth Corps, Byng's Army, 137-141, 154, 165, 167, 174, 175, 179, 180, 183, 186, 189, 190
Fifth Borderers, 123
Fifth Durham Light Infantry, 102, 106, 107, 108, 113, 124, 170, 210
Fifth Gloucesters, 234, 235, 236
Fifth Gordons, 70
Fifth Northumberland Fusiliers, 104, 106, 109, 110, 111, 116, 117, 120, 126, 129
Fifty-eighth DIVISION, 85, 283
Fifty-first DIVISION, 146, 148, 159
Fifty-ninth DIVISION, 146, 148
Fifty-sixth DIVISION, 197
Fighting temperament, 206, 207, 208, 222-231
Final dispatch, Haig's, 317
Final rally of a true fighting temper, 251
Fins, 138, 164, 167, 175, 178
First Battle of the Marne, over-confidence produced by it, 44
First CAVALRY DIVISION, 115, 130, 131, 150, 183, 185, 186, 190, 192, 216, 217, 271
First Royal Inniskilling Fusiliers, 73
Flame projectors, 45
Flavy-le-Martel, 78
Flesquières salient, 34, 51, 52, 53, 136, 139, 140, 142, 146, 147, 148, 150, 157, 158, 159, 161, 166, 174, 179
Flowerdew's Squadron, 218, 219
Foch, Field-Marshal, reinforces the Noyon-Montdidier line, 97; at Doullens, 270; appointed to the Supreme Command, 289; unfair to him, 291; begins his reign with defeats, 292
Fog and the battle, 56-60, 83, 95, 101, 104, 111, 123, 147, 152, 156, 157, 159, 181, 195, 207, 222
Folies Village, 236
Fontaine-les-Clercs Redoubt, 73, 80
Fontaine-les-Croisilles, 148
Foresight in war, 25, 26, 27
Fortieth DIVISION, Byng's Army, 146, 148
Forty-first DIVISION, Byng's Army, 104, 148
Forty-second DIVISION, Byng's Army, 35, 197
Forty-seventh DIVISION, Byng's Army, 146, 147, 148, 165, 166, 167, 174, 175, 176, 179, 180, 230
Forward zone, the, 11, 13, 145, 173
Fothergill, of the *Sixty-first* D., 235
Foucaucourt, 104, 112, 119, 120

INDEX

Fouches, 285
Fourmies-Chimay, 95
Fourteenth DIVISION, 76, 131, 134
Four Winds Farm, 175
Fourth Australians, 35, 187, 197, 268, 274
Fourth Corps, THIRD ARMY, 183, 186, 189, 190
Fourth DIVISION, 197
Fourth North Staffords, 191
Fourth Northumberland Fusiliers, 104, 109, 117, 121, 128, 129
Fourth Yorks, 106, 107
Framerville, 120, 121, 122, 128
Framerville Church, incident at, 121
Franks, Major-General G. McK., commanding the *Thirty-fifth* D., 169, 184, 189, 191, 192, 270, 271, 272
French attempt to recover a span of Crozat Canal, 251
French Divisions, 276, 284, 285, 286
French reinforcements, 80, 98, 99, 114, 135, 168, 187, 258
French study of Hutier's attack, 88, 95
French THIRD ARMY, 246
Fresnoy Redoubt, 70, 93, 197
Frévillers, 104
Frevent, 277
Fricourt, 192
Frise, 118
Frontages, safe and unsafe, 103
Fyfe, Hamilton, war correspondent, 5, 16, 246, 295, 296

G.H.Q., attitude towards youthfulness, 14; towards defences, 11–17, 173; towards the foe's airmen, 23; towards the Oise front, 25, 26; invites criticism by a series of arguments, 37–39, 252; perplexing in its views on risks, 37, 38, 39, 299, 300, 309; and on the German intentions, 52; moves divisions from corps to corps, 25; keeps support divisions too far from the battle front, 100, 103; nebulous in all that concerns the boundary troubles between Byng and Gough, 137, 138; accepts faulty information concerning Byng's right and Gough's left, 141, 166, 177; the drama of Flesquières salient, 34, 51, 52, 53, 136, 139, 140, 142, 146, 147, 148, 150, 157, 158, 159, 161, 166, 174, 179; passes over British losses, impairing its accounts of battles, 159, 253, 254; some G.H.Q.
instructions, 171, 245; seems to undervalue the South African bravery, 182, 229; attitude towards mounted troops, 185, 214, 215; passes over the loss of Bapaume, 256; reinforcing Byng with Gough's northern troops, 258-265; the official use of reinforcements, 38, 39, 48, 263, 264, 265, 276; the retreat to and from the Bray-Albert line, 266; training problems, 301, 302
Gallwitz, General von, 47, 50
Garnet Green, Captain, 152, 153, 164
Gas attacks, 63, 101, 158
Gauche Wood, 145, 152, 153
Gavrelle, 196, 197
Gayl, General von, 49, 50, 76, 85, 87, 92, 97, 143
Gell, Lieut.-Colonel E. A., 124, 128, 195
Genin Well Copse, 154
German artillery, Ludendorff's remarks on, 45, 46
German barrage, Ludendorff speaks of it, 68
German cavalry, 40, 234
German crimes and Allied blunders, 307
German divisions, 49, 51, 78, 87, 92, 94, 197. *See* also the large map of the approximate Order of Battle, British and German
German gas attack, 67
German initiative, 209
German message dogs, 207
German newspapers on the battle 296, 297
German patrols, enterprise of, 209, 210
German reinforcements from Russia, etc., 34; on Gough's front, 40
German shells and British redoubts, 63–81
German tanks, 79
German training, its main characteristics, 45, 46, 58
Germans in Allied uniforms behind our lines, 232
Germany's wonderful resistance, 43
Ginchy, 184
Givenchy, 139
Glorious young lives thrown away, 305, 306
G.O.C. of the *Ninth* D. makes an urgent visit of warning to 5th Corps, THIRD ARMY, 175, 176
Golancourt, 220, 221
Gorringe, Major-General Sir G. F.,

INDEX

commanding the *Forty-seventh* D., THIRD ARMY, 143, 146, 156, 165 Gough, General Sir Hubert de la Poer, his need of men, 4, 33, 38, 51; some causes of this need, 36, 37; new front, 10, 11; his defensive systems, 11 *et seq.*; how he allotted his troops, 13; foretells the aim of Ludendorff's attack, 25, 27; his manifestoes, 29–32; his frontage and divisions, 35; his remarks on the fog, 59–60; his action at the close of first day, 79–80, 82; his withdrawal from the Péronne bridgehead, 91, 171, 172, 245–257; his generalship succeeds, 93, 95, 96, 97, 98, 99, 158, 168, 169, 185, 253, 260, 292, 315; an appeal to G.H.Q., 100; his centre in peril, 102; he bears all the risks, 104, 299, 300; raises Carey's Force, so called, 112; loses Congreve's troops transferred to Byng, 114, 115, 258–265; his left uncovered, 118; the Cérisy episode, 116, 121, 122, 126, 130, 266–274; eager to give a counter blow, 131; falsely accused of "letting down" Byng's right, 141; his left sends urgent warnings to Byng's right, 141, 175, 176; pressure against his northern corps, 152 *et seq.*, 165, 166; hears of the breach of Green Line in Watts's defence, 164; accused of nursing his Army too much, 172; was his retreat too slow rather than too fast? 172–173; his Staff, 202, 203; some men behaved badly, 212, 213, 254; on cavalry, 214, 215; what he had to weigh and measure, 254, 255; political interference puts Gough and his troops under the orders of French officers, whose divisions are gunless, 259; suffers from the official hesitancy in the use of reinforcements, 276, 277, 278; stops a gap which French orders would have opened, 283; an arrangement with Général Robilot, 284, 285; incident of the guns, 286; the FIFTH ARMY gains time for the importation of American troops, 310; Gough suspended, and Rawlinson assumes command south of the Somme, 313, 314; unity of splendid effort in the FIFTH ARMY, 316, 317; Haig's recognition and grateful thanks in his final dispatch, 317

Gouzeaucourt, 34, 52, 137, 138, 145, 157, 162
Government's propagandist figures of Haig's fighting strength, 279, 301
Government Press, 297
Governments of France and Britain put Foch in supreme control, 289–292
Grant, Major-General P. G., 112
Gray of the 2/Fifth Gloucesters, 240
Greenland Hill, 196
Green Line System of Defence, 76, 88, 96, 102, 103, 106, 107, 161, 162, 164, 165, 166, 170, 174, 175, 179
Grévillers, 183, 190
GUARDS DIVISION, 144, 148, 197
Guerbigny, 286
Guillaucourt, 129, 130, 132, 133, 236
Guillemont, 137
Gunless French troops, 168, 276
Guyencourt, 162

HADLOW, Lieut., 153
Haig, very short of men, 4, 33 *et seq.*, 38; on German airplanes, 74; on reducing the fighting strength of brigades, 75; his character in battle, 96; on the position south of the Somme, 114; his Dispatch fails to give the complete boundary uniting Gough and Byng, 136, 137; on Byng's first day, 148, 149; on Byng's second day, 159; remarks on the South African defence, 182; on the loss of Combles, Morval, and Lesbœufs, 183; on Franks's fine defence, March 25, 189; on the breach of Byng's centre, and the gaps in Byng's southern corps, 187, 190, 191, 193, 268, 270, 274; on the many reinforcements sent to Byng, 193; on the menace to the Ancre line, 193; on the attack against Arras, 196, 197; on cavalry, 213–214; implies that he would not have retired from the Péronne bridgehead, 251, 252; on lack of training, 255; passes over the loss of Bapaume, 256; the official use of reinforcements, 38, 39, 48, 263, 264, 265, 276; too vague in matters affecting FIFTH ARMY movements, 264, 265; on fall of Albert, 273; arrangements with Pétain, 48, 275, 278; on his difficulties, 298, 299, 301, 302; the apportionment of risks, 37, 38, 39, 299, 300; on

326 INDEX

Gough's suspension, 314; his praise of Sir Hubert Gough, 317
Hadow's force, 184, 186, 270
Ham, 84, 87, 111
Hamel, 95, 122, 315
Hancourt, 91, 103, 170
Hangard, 95, 101, 115, 133, 134, 238
Hangest, 236
Harbonnières, 101, 112, 123, 126, 127–129, 130
Hardecourt, 185, 192
Hargicourt, 101, 123, 172, 173
Harm done by magnifying the British Empire forces, 279, 301
Harman, Major-General, A. E. W., commanding *Third* CAVALRY D., 215, 216, 220
Harper, Lieut.-General, Sir G. M., commanding 4th Corps, THIRD ARMY, 193
Harvey, Colonel, 112
Hattencourt, 118, 315
Hautcloque, 277
Have infantry had their day? 218
Havrincourt, 140, 147, 157, 158
Havrincourt Wood, 161
Haybittel, Captain, his valour, 78
Hazebrouck, 139
Headlam, Brigadier, 271
Heal, Lieut.-Colonel, 224, 227
Herbécourt, 113, 117, 256
Hébuterne, 187, 268, 270
Hem, 184, 189, 191
Hem Spur, 180, 191, 224
Heneker, Major-General W. G. G., *Eighth* DIVISION, 112, 114, 116, 121, 124
Henin, 160
Herly, 239
Hermies, 147, 157, 159, 161, 179
Heroic linen-draper, 231
Hervilly, 101, 161, 170
Hervilly Wood, 216, 217
Hessler, Captain J. K. M., 107
Heudecourt, 162, 163
Highland Ridge, 51, 139, 157, 165
Highland Brigade, *Ninth* D., 142, 144, 153, 162, 164, 166, 175, 176, 178, 181, 182, 184, 224
High Wood, 183
Hill, Father, of the S.A. Brigade, 231
Hill 109...120
Hill Redoubt, 74
Hinacourt, 76
Hindenberg Line, 51, 139, 157, 166
Holnon, 69, 70, 72, 149, 170
Holnon Wood, 74, 249
Horne, General Sir H. S., commanding the FIRST ARMY, from Gavrelle northward, 35, 196
Hours of Marwitz's most deadly thrust, 181, 182, 184, 187, 193, 221–231
How cavalry should withdraw, 216
How the German machine worked, 209, 210
Howitt, Captain, 235, 241
Hull, Major-General Sir C. P. A., 143, 150, 154, 161
Humbert, Général, 286
Hunter's Brigade, *Sixty-sixth* D., 127, 133
Hunt's Force, 185, 186
Hurlbatt, Lieut.-Colonel, dies gloriously, 124, 129
Hutier, Oskar von, commanding EIGHTEENTH GERMAN ARMY, 6, 27, 28, 40, 48, 49, 51, 54, 94, 97, 134, 169, 282, 284, 287, 288
Hutier's attack, 63–81, 82–99; also 275–288

IGNAUCOURT, 130
Indian labour, 17
Indian troops, 36
Injustice to the FIFTH ARMY, 4, 5, 136, 150, 166, 254, 258–265, 295, 296, 310, 312–317
Injustice, Political, and the People's Equity, 312–317
Interchanges of help between undermanned units, 142
Ireland, Colonel, of the Second Munsters, 207
Irles, 190

JACKSON, Major-General H. C., *Fiftieth* D., 112, 113, 121, 124, 132
Jeffreys, Major-General G. D., of the *Nineteenth* D., 148
Joffre, 305
Joint attacks by Marwitz and Below, 146–158, 159–167, 168–173, 174–198
Jussy, 76, 85, 87, 92

KAISER on the British *Ninth* D., 182
Keith, Sergeant-Major, 226
Kemmel Hill, 198, 292
Kennedy, Brigadier, of the *Ninth* D., 144, 153
Kidd, Lieut., of the Second Munsters, 207
King, of the Second Munsters, 207
Kingham's scratch battalion at Harbonnières, 123, 124, 126, 128
Knox, Second Lieut., his bravery, 89

INDEX

La Bassée Canal, 80
La Chapellette, 164, 174
Labour Corps on the FIFTH ARMY'S front, 17
Lacey Thompson, Captain, 111, 129
Lack of training, 301, 302. *See also* under Training
La Damery, 93
La Fère, 35, 66, 97
Lagnicourt, 148
Lake, of the *Sixty-first* D., 234
La Maisonette, 117
Lambay Wood, 78
Lamire Farm, 117
Lamotte, 112, 122, 123, 130, 131, 194, 237
Lancashire Trench, 153
Lancashire troops, 117, 123, 124, 126, 143
Languevoisin, 232, 235, 239
Lassigny, 91, 92
Last days of Northern fighting, 186–198
Last stand of Dawson's Five Hundred, 181, 182
Lawson, Colonel A. B., 234, 238, 240, 241
Lawson, Colonel, Eleventh Hussars, 239
Laurie, Major-General C. E., 190
Laymen and the War, 7, 8
Leapfrogging by German divisions, 93, 146, 147
Le Barque, 183
Le Cateau, 157, 182, 194, 195
Leeds, Lloyd George's speech at, 279, 280, 308, 309, 313
Le Forêt, 181, 222
Legard, Brigadier-General D'A., 192, 217
Le Mesnil-en-Arrouaise, 110, 178, 179
Le Quesnel, 236, 240, 287
Le Quesnoy, 93, 94
Lesbœufs, 182, 183
Le Sars, 183
Le Transloy, 180
Letters from British officers, 210, 232–242
Lever, Charles, and Wellington, 7, 8
Le Verguier, 149, 156, 161
Lewis guns, 153, 184, 207, 222, 225, 226, 227
Liaison between Gough's left and Byng's right, 165, 166, 167, 175, 178, 179, 180, 182, 183, 184, 185, 186, 189, 192
Liancourt, 285

Libermont Canal, 114, 284, 285
Licourt, 115, 116, 245
Liéramont, 163
Liez, 85
Ligny-Thilloy, 183
Lihons, 120, 127
Lincoln, Abraham, 29, 280
Lincoln troops, 157
Little, Colonel, of the Fifth Borderers, *Sixty-sixth* D., 123, 133, 134
Little's scratch battalion, 123, 124, 125, 126, 128, 129, 133
Lizerolles, 76
Lloyd, Colonel, 101
Lloyd George, on the British defences, 15; pre-battle failure of his Coalition, 34, 38; and Carey's force, 112; his speech at Leeds, 279, 280, 308, 309, 313; his present reputation, 290; failure of his Coalition between the fall of Asquith and March, 1918...293; his deplorable speech in the House of Commons, 295; his Easternism, 307, 308; his cry for help to President Wilson, 289, 309, 310
London artisan and Foch's appointment, 291
London Gazette, 5
London Territorials, 146
Longatte, 148
Longavesnes, 152
Longueval, 184
Lorraine, 92
Loss of guns, 59, 163, 164, 194, 303
Loss of Bapaume, 256; passed over in the official dispatch, 256
Loss of Peronne, 172, 245–257
Louvaval, 148
Lowland Brigade, *Ninth* D., 144, 175, 176, 178, 181
Lowland support, 154
Luce River, 115
Ludendorff, his main problem, 8; fears the forward zone, 14; on aircraft, 21; his knowledge of Haig's need of men, 34, 37, 38; was aided by the British battle front, 39; his central aim, 41; his fear of the U.S.A., 41–42; hampered by his partners, 42, 43; on his immense task, 44, 45; on his artillery, 45, 46; on feints, 47; how he increased the Franco-British anxiety, 47, 48; eager to cut off the troops in Flesquières salient, 52, 139, 140; decides to help Hutier personally, 54; on gas, 54; on the fog, 58; on

the German barrage, 67, 68; on losses during a retreat, 81; on storm troops, 84; on food-searching by his troops, 86; his candour, 87, 135, 147; his orders to first-line troops, 88, 92, 146, 147; on his unfavourable strategical position, 93, 135; mistakes Gough for Haig, 96; his aim in Hutier's attack misunderstood, 99; on machine-guns *versus* infantry, 120; aims of the northern fighting, 142; new tactics, 147; on Below's losses, 147; misses an opportunity, 157, 158; anxious to break through north of Albert, 186; on Below's exhausted troops, 190; his mistake in attacking Arras, 198; his encouragement of initiative, 209; surprised by the slow arrival of Allied reinforcements, 278; on his capture of men, 279; Ludendorff and unity of command, 290; German newspapers and Ludendorff, 297; British propaganda, 305; on attack and defence, 315

Lüttwitz, General von, 51, 87, 92

Ly-Fontaine, 76

Lys battle, 83, 86, 138, 196, 198, 292, 316

MACHINE-GUNS, 79, 83, 95, 104, 105, 109, 110, 116, 117, 118, 119, 120, 121, 124, 128, 131, 132, 133, 144, 148, 152, 153, 154, 183, 184, 196, 197, 210, 217, 218, 220, 221, 226, 227, 230, 234, 238, 251, 273, 274

Mackenzie, Colin, Major-General, *Sixty-first* D., 102, 104, 131, 170, 239, 249, 286, 287, 288

Maissemy, 59, 79, 96, 149, 156, 157, 160, 170

Malcolm, Major-General Neill, *Sixty-sixth* D., 91, 100, 101, 102, 112, 113, 116, 117, 121, 123, 124, 133, 143, 150, 156, 157, 249,

Malassise Farm, 145, 207, 208

Manancourt, 139, 164, 166, 175, 179

"Man Battle Stations," 24, 64

Manchester Redoubt, 73

Manchester troops, 157

Manicamp, 50, 85

Mangin, Général, 81

Map-drawing, 8

Maps and map-making, 314, 315

Marcelcave, 91, 112, 123, 130, 131, 133, 237, 240

Marchélépot, 115

Maricourt, 138, 184, 185, 189, 190, 191, 192

Marindin, Brig.-General A. H., 191

Marlborough, 281, 282, 317

Marne, 292

Marrières Wood, 181, 182, 222

Marteville, 74

Martin's Brigade, 102, 103, 106, 107, 210

Marwitz, General von der, 40, 51, 53, 101, 136, 142, 143, 147, 169, 282

Marwitz and Hutier in the centre fighting, 100-120, 121-135, 193, 194

Maurepas, 138, 185

Maurice, Sir F., on the need of men in March, 1918, 4, 144; on the FIFTH ARMY'S courage, 9; on the THIRD ARMY'S strength, 35; on Allenby's excessive number of white troops, 36; on German over-confidence, 44; an oversight, 189; on the transfer of Gough's northern troops to Byng's right wing, 258; on the Government's neglect, 279

Maxse, Sir Ivor, commanding the 18th Corps, FIFTH ARMY, 6; his corps, 12, 14

Maxse's Corps, 65, 69, 74, 76, 79, 82, 89, 91, 98, 100, 115, 130, 170, 276, 286

Maze, Paul M., 313

Méaulte, 137, 266, 267, 271

Men who behaved badly, 212, 213, 254

Mericourt, 122, 184

Méry, 97

Mesnil-en-Arrouaise, 110, 175, 179

Mesple, Général, 130, 287

Metz-en-Couture, 161, 175, 179, 180

Mezières, 131, 218, 236, 240

Military huts set on fire, 119

Military writing and laymen, 7, 8

Milner, Lord, was he unfriendly to the FIFTH ARMY? 259

Miraumont, 190, 256

Misery, 104, 111

Misuse of reinforcements, 276 *et seq.*

Mixing together French and British troops, 280 *et seq.*

Modern battles, their division into four parts or periods, 3, 4; great difficulties in writing about them, 6-8

Modern war has a certain kinship with architecture, 8

Moislains, 138, 163, 164, 174, 176

Monash, Sir J., 187, 188, 213, 263, 265, 277, 296

Monchy-Lagache, 91, 108

Monro, General Sir Charles, 36, 317

INDEX

Mons-en-Chaussée, 108, 109
Montauban, 137, 183, 185, 189, 190, 191, 192, 260
Montdidier, 51, 91, 93, 94, 95, 97, 283, 286, 292
Montigny, 216
Mont St. Quentin, 138
Moods of men in battle, 201, 202
Moore, Lieut.-Colonel Godfrey, of the Twelfth K.R.R.C., 235, 240
Moral influences in war, 29
Morchain, 114, 285
Moreuil, 94, 95, 112
Morlancourt, 271
Morning Post, 293, 297, 306
Morval, 142, 180, 182, 183, 184, 230
Mory, 148, 150, 160
Most important thing in war, 97, 98

NAMES in the War's battles are too numerous, 6, 7
Napoleon, 14, 253
" Nasty jobs " in war, 10
Natal troops, 154
National feelings and politics, 281, 282
Natural gaps formed by retreating, 19, 20
Nelson, 65, 289, 290
Nerves outside the battle, 99, 202, 292
Nesle, 54, 169, 242, 284, 285
Newcomen's Squadron, 218, 219
New Zealand troops, 187, 268
Nicholson, Major-General C. L., 148
Ninth Cavalry Brigade, 216, 217
Ninth DIVISION, 53, 115, 137, 141, 143, 144, 145, 150, 152, 153, 154, 155, 156, 157, 160, 161, 162, 163, 165, 166, 167, 174, 175, 176, 179, 180, 181, 182, 184, 185, 186, 190, 191, 193, 194, 222, 224, 230, 266, 267, 271, 273, 279, 302
Ninth Manchesters, 101
Ninth Seaforths, 144
Nineteenth Corps, 107, 108, 150. See also under Watts
Nineteenth DIVISION, 146, 148, 190
Nineteenth Liverpools, 79
Nineteenth Northumberland Fusiliers, 191
Nivelle, General, 290
Nivelle and Verdun, 58
Nobescourt Farm, 96, 101, 102, 106, 107, 164, 168, 169, 170, 173, 217
Nordheimer's Squadron at the Bois de Moreuil, 218, 219
Noreuil, 148

Northern attacks, the, 136-145, 146-167, 168-198
Northumberland Fusiliers, 103, 104, 105, 106, 108, 109, 110, 111, 118, 119, 120, 121, 124, 126, 127, 128, 129, 134
Noye River, 218
Noyon, 50, 85, 86, 88, 91, 93, 94, 97, 118, 283, 292
Nugent, Major-General O. S. W., and his Ulster troops, 93, 286, 287. *See* also *Thirty-Sixth* DIVISION
Nun of Harbonnières, the, 127, 129
Nurlu, 138, 167, 174

OETINGER, General von, 51, 87
Officers' patrols, 215, 216
Official accounts of battles omit too many facts, 253-255
Official history, 253 *et seq*., 275
Oise front, 25, 97, 118
Old military rule broken, 276, 278, 283
Ollezy, 84
Omiécourt, 285
Omignon River, 10, 95, 101, 103, 104, 105, 109
Oppy, 197
Ordinary manhood in war, 85, 86, 87
Ormiston, Major, 225, 230
Outflanking the Ancre line, 187, 193, 262, 268, 270
Outflanking the *Ninth* DIVISION, 152, 153, 154, 157, 158, 161, 162, 163, 166, 167, 176, 181
Outpost system of defence. *See* Forward zone
Over-confidence, British, 4, 44, 293, 294
Orvillers, 94
Oxford and Bucks Light Infantry, 68, 70

PACIFISTS, 206
Pagan, Lieut.-Colonel, of the Gloucesters, who acted as Brigadier of 184th Brigade after the Hon. Robert White was wounded, 240
Palestine, 36
Panic, 111, 213
Pargny, 114
Paris, 294
Parsons, Sergeant-Major, 235
Passchendaele, 10, 90, 96, 304
Paterson's Force, 217
Patience in troop trains, 100
Pearson, John, an Old English Archer, 201
Peirson, Captain G., 194

Peiziére, 145, 154, 157, 161
Pelves, 197
Péronne, 53, 101, 113, 116, 142, 150, 172, 210, 245-257
Péronne bridgehead, 91, 96, 101, 102, 108, 138, 161, 164, 169, 172, 174, 245-257
Pertain, 285
Pétain, Général, 39, 48, 275, 290, 292 300
Phillips, Sergeant-Major, 235
Picton at Waterloo, 282
Pierrepont, 51
Pithon, 84, 89
Plessis de Roye, 94
Pœuilly, 88, 106, 108, 170
Points and Cross-Questions, 168-173
Political injustice and its effects, 312, 313
Pollard's Brigade, 172
Pontoise, 49, 50, 85
Portal, Brigadier, 50, 217
Potte, 111
"Prepare for Battle," 24, 64
"Prepare to Man Battle Stations," 24
Prideaux-Brune, Lieut.-Colonel, 76
Proctor, Captain, 110
Propaganda, 279, 301, 304, 305
Providence and British statesmen, 9
Proyart, 116, 121, 122, 123, 124, 286
Puisieux-au-Mont, 190, 193, 196
Pys, 190

Quast, General von, 197
Quentin Redoubt, 152, 153
Quessy, 76, 79, 85, 149
"Quex," in *Blackwood's Magazine*, 201, 203, 204, 205, 206
Quiquery, 241, 284

Racial susceptibilities, 290
Railton, 154
Raimes, Major A. L., 102, 107, 210
Rancourt, 181, 222
Ration strength *versus* combatant strength, 294, 301
Rawlinson, General Sir H. S., 314
Rear zone, 12, 173, 245
Red Line Defence System, 145, 154
Rees's Brigade, *Fiftieth* Division, 103, 106, 107, 108, 112
Reinforcements, wrong notions formed by, 187
Reims, 47, 48, 50, 65, 80
Repington Colonel, 297, 306
Retreat from the Bray-Albert line, 266-273

Retreating from a narrow salient, 139, 160
Retreating often more difficult than hard fighting, 252, 253
Revelon Farm, 154, 157
Ribemont-sur-Ancre, 267, 270, 271
Richards, Lieut., 73
Rickerby of the 2/Fifth Gloucesters, 239
Riddell's Brigade, *Fiftieth* Division, 103, 104, 105, 106, 108, 110, 111, 112, 113, 117, 119, 121, 124, 126, 127, 129, 131, 132, 134, 247
Ridge Reserve, 207, 208
"Rifle carriers," 120
Risks of war, 37, 38, 297, 300, 309
Roberts, Lord, 305
Robb, Colonel, 105
Robilot, Général, 284
Robinson, Colonel, 106
Rocquigny, 175, 178, 180, 230
Rœux, 196
Roisel, 102, 161, 170
Ronssoy, 59, 100, 145, 149, 150, 152, 157
Rosières, 92, 100, 115, 119, 121, 122, 123, 124, 128, 129, 236, 286
Roupy, 79
Rouvroy, 236, 285, 286
Rouy-le-Grand, 91
Rowbotham, Captain, 70
Rowe of the Fifth D.L.I., 211
Royal Fusiliers, 156
Royal Irish Rifles, 73
Royals, 220, 221
Roye, 95, 236, 240, 285
Russell, Major-General Sir A. H., 268
Russia's defeat, 298

Saillisel, 178, 179
Sailly-le-Sec, 116, 184
St. Christ, 84, 92, 109, 110, 114, 116
St. Émilie, 150, 152, 161
St. Gobain, 35, 49
St. Leger, 146, 148, 150, 159, 160
St. Pierre Vaast Wood, 138, 178, 181
St. Quentin, 3, 50, 54, 249
St. Quentin Ridge, 145
St. Simon, 76, 87
Sacrifice of young lives caused by political bungling, 202 *et seq.*
Sapper, story of a, 119
Saulcourt, 152, 170
Savy, 79, 149
Sayer, John William, Lance-Corporal, how he died in winning the V.C., 156
Scapegoat, Fifth Army a political, 5, 297

INDEX

Scarpe River, 52, 66, 148, 160, 196, 197
Scattered impressions, 202-221
Scott, Lieut., 107
Scrap and scraps of paper, 305
"Scratch" forces, 185
Second Battle of the Somme, 3, 4
Second Bedfords, 79
Second CAVALRY DIVISION, 85, 215, 217
Second INFANTRY DIVISION, 139, 148, 166, 167, 175, 180, 268
Second Munsters, 150, 207, 208
Second Royal Scots, 285
Second Wiltshires, 65, 73, 285
Second Yorks, 79, 285
Seely's force, 216, 217
Sensée River, 52, 53, 104, 146, 148
Serre, 190, 193, 268
Seventeenth DIVISION, 146, 147, 148, 159, 192
Seventeenth Manchesters, 79, 285
Seventeenth Royal Scots, 191
Seventh Corps, Gough's northern Corps, commanded by Congreve, 137, 165, 186, 189, 191, 259
Seventh Buffs, 78
Seventh Dragoon Guards, 161
Seventh Durham Light Infantry, 211, 212
Seventh Rifle Brigade, 76
Seventh Seaforths, 164
Seymour's Force, 216, 217,
Side Issues and Political Effects, 304-317
Side-shows and Lloyd George, 308
Sinclair-Maclagan, Major - General E. G., 268, 274, 277
Sixteenth DIVISION, South Irish, under Sir Amyatt Hull, was a unit of 7th Corps, 150, 152, 154, 157, 194, 260
Sixteenth Manchesters, 65, 73, 285
Sixth Durham Light Infantry, 104, 105, 106, 109, 110
Sixth DIVISION, 146, 148
Sixth King's Own Scottish Borderers. 144, 163, 175, 181
Sixth Northumberland Fusiliers, 116, 117, 127, 128, 129
Sixty-first DIVISION, a unit of 18th Corps, fought under Colin Mackenzie, 23, 64, 69, 84, 102, 130, 131, 208, 250, 284
Sixty-second DIVISION, 35, 197
Sixty-sixth DIVISION, Lancashire troops, under Neill Malcolm, was a unit of 19th Corps, 101, 102, 106, 107, 115, 116, 117, 118, 120, 124, 127, 133, 134, 170, 208, 211, 216, 237
Sixty-third DIVISION, 146, 148, 166, 183, 190
Skinner, Brigadier P. C. B., 76
Slighting the FIFTH ARMY during the battle, 259
"Slits," 13
Smoke screen, 152
Soissons, 97, 292
Somme Alley Trench, 153
Somme line, 88, 91, 93, 95, 100, 110, 111, 113, 115, 116, 122, 126, 171, 172, 174, 183, 189, 192, 210, 211, 245-247, 270.
Sorel-le-grand, 163
South African Brigade, *Ninth D.*, 144, 152, 153, 154, 157, 160, 161, 162-164, 176, 177, 180, 181, 222-231, 267
"South African Forces in France," by Buchan, 146, 182
South African Scottish, 154
South Irish, 115, 122, 124, 126, 150, 152, 154, 161, 164, 208
Specialist German troops, 208
Staff officer from the *Ninth* warns the *Forty-seventh*, 165
Statesmen, British, their customary mistakes, 9, 306, 307
Stockley, Brigadier-General A. F. U., 7
Storm troops, 83, 162
Straggling, 86, 123, 127, 213
Strachan of the Second Munsters, 207
Strathcona's Horse, 218
Strong and weak forces in line together, a rule of war concerning, 140-141
Submarines, German, 41, 42
Suzanne, 185
Switches, 11
Swopping horses in midstream, 280 *et seq.*

"TACTICAL exercises without troops," 302
Tanks in action, 149, 160, 170, 181, 183
Tanks and horse at Hervilly, 216, 217
Templeux-le-Guérard, 100, 150, 152, 156, 217
Tennyson, Captain the Hon. A., 76
Tenth Corps, 277
Tenth Hussars, 220, 221
Tergnier, 85, 251, 283
Tertry, 104, 109

Tetard Wood, 207
Thiepval, 315
Third Australians, 35, 95
THIRD ARMY. *See* under Byng
Third DIVISION, 146, 148, 160, 198
Third CAVALRY DIVISION, 215, 216, 220. *See* also under Harman
Third Corps. *See* under Butler
Third Dragoon Guards, 220, 221
Thirst, sufferings from, 250
Thirteenth Corps, 196
Thirtieth DIVISION, 65, 79, 235, 285, 302. *See* also under Williams, W. de L.
Thirty-first DIVISION, 104, 148, 197
Thirty-fifth DIVISION, 115, 169, 181, 184, 186, 187, 189, 190, 191, 192, 194, 224, 226, 227, 230, 270, 271, 272, 273. *See* also under Franks
Thirty-fourth DIVISION, 146, 148, 160
Thirty-ninth DIVISION, 101, 115, 121, 122, 123, 129, 133, 152, 162, 194, 250, 260. *See* also under Feetham
Thirty-sixth DIVISION, 73, 84, 285, 286, 287. *See* also under Nugent
Timmis' Squadron, 218, 219
Tincourt, 152
Too Late, the Creed of, 123, 293, 307
Tortille River, 138, 172, 174, 177
Training, 16, 19, 21, 22, 67, 70, 152, 205, 206, 208, 301, 302
Transfer of Gough's northern troops to Byng's right wing, 186, 193, 258–265
Transfer of land from THIRD FRENCH ARMY to Gough, 10, 11, 25, 300
Travecy, 78
Trefcon, 170
Trench mortars, 45, 153
Trônes Wood, 185, 189
Troubles of Ministers, 293–303
Truth uncommon in war, 4, 5, 305
Tudor, Major-General H. H., *Ninth* D., 143, 150, 151, 152, 154, 156, 157, 162, 165, 175, 176, 179, 180, 224, 226
Tugny, 89
Turkey, 42
Turner, Captain, of the Royals, 220
Twelfth DIVISION, 35
Twelfth Highland Light Infantry, 184, 185, 191
Twelfth King's Royal Rifle Corps, 240
Twelfth Royal Scots, 144
Twentieth DIVISION, 36, 84, 90, 98, 100, 114, 131, 134, 234, 235, 239,
250, 284, 286, 287. *See* also under Douglas Smith
Twenty-fifth DIVISION, 146, 148, 159
Twenty-first DIVISION, 152, 154, 157, 162, 174, 176, 177, 180, 181, 186, 191, 194, 224, 270, 271. *See* also under Campbell
Twenty-fourth DIVISION, 103, 106, 108, 122, 131, 284. *See* also under Daly
Twenty-second Entrenching Battalion, 111, 126, 127, 132
2/Fifth Gloucesters, 234, 235, 236
2/Fourth Royal Berkshires, 74
2/Eighth Worcesters, 70

U-BOAT campaign, 41
Ulster troops, 73, 84, 285, 286, 287
United States of America, 41, 42, 44, 112, 309, 310.
U.S.A. bridgebuilders, 112
Unity of command, 289–292
Urvillers, 76, 315

Vaire Wood, 95
Varesnes, 85
Vaucellette Farm, 145
Vaulx Vraucourt, 159, 179
Vauvillers, 119, 120, 121, 128, 129
Vaux, 250
Vaux Wood, 138
Vendeuil, 76
Verdun, 33, 47, 50, 65
Verlaines, 84
Vermand-Amiens road, 84, 170
Vermand, 88, 96, 102, 103, 150, 170
Véry lights, 118
Victoria Cross, an episode, 73 another episode, 156
Villecholles, 79, 170
Villequier-Aumont, 85
Villeret, 172
Villers Bretonneux, 131, 240
Villers Carbonnel, 115, 116, 117, 211
Villers Faucon, 161
Villers-lès-Roye, 93
Villers Plouich, 139, 140, 158, 160, 166, 174, 175
Villeselve, 220
Villévéque, 103, 107, 170
Vincent, Corporal, 236
Vincent, Lieut., 220
" Vital" portions of a front, 27, 80
Von Boehn, General. *See* under Boehn
Von Below, Otto. *See* under Below
Von Hutier, Oskar. *See* under Hutier

INDEX

Von der Marwitz, General. *See* under Marwitz
Vouel, 85, 251, 283
Voyennes, 92, 111, 114, 239
Vraignes, 170
Vraucourt, 159, 179

WALDEGRAVE, of the Second Munsters, 207
War Cabinet, British, its grave mistakes, 4, 5, 290, 304, 306
War correspondents, 295
Warfusée-Abancourt, 122, 239
Warnings sent by Gough's left to Byng's right, 165, 166, 167, 179
War Office, 290, 297
War propaganda, 104, 105, 204, 305
Warvillers, 122, 236
Waterloo, 195, 281, 282
Watts, Sir H. E., Commander of the 19th Corps, 6, 12, 74, 91, 92, 110, 111, 117, 118, 130, 131, 133, 150, 156, 164, 169, 170, 171, 173, 174, 216, 217, 285, 286
Webern, General von, 51, 87
Wellington and "Charles O'Malley," 7, 8
Wellington, 14, 65, 111, 281, 282, 317
Wetherall, Colonel, 72, 235
Whelan, Lieut., of the Second Munsters, 207

White, the Hon. Robert, Brigadier-General, 23, 73, 238; letters written to him, 232-242
Whitehead, Lieut.-Colonel H. F., 124
Widening Haig's front, 10, 25, 300
Wiencourt, 129, 130, 236
Williams, Major-General W. de L., 285. *See* also under *Thirtieth* DIVISION
Williams, Major, at Collezy, 220
Willink, of the 2/Fourth Royal Berks, 240
Wilson, Sir Henry, 299
Wilson, President, 289, 309, 310
Wine of bravery has lees, 213, 254
Wire entanglements, 12, 70, 105, 124, 177, 197, 210, 302
Woodcock, Lieut.-Colonel W. J., 124
Worship of volunteering, 308
Wright, Colonel, 129
Wrong notions circulated during the battle, 5, 16, 246, 263, 264, 295, 296

YELLOW Line Defence System, 145, 154, 164
Yeomanry, 214
Young, Lieut.-Colonel, 229
Ypres salient, 10, 96, 200
Ytres, 160, 175, 179, 180

www.ingramcontent.com/pod-product-compliance
Lightning Source LLC
Chambersburg PA
CBHW050121170426
43197CB00011B/1673